Time-Constrained Memory

A Reader-Based Approach to Text Comprehension

Time-Constrained Memory

A Reader-Based Approach to Text Comprehension

Jean-Pierre Corriveau

Ψ Psychology Press
Taylor & Francis Group
NEW YORK AND LONDON

First published 1995 by Lawrence Erlbaum Associates, Inc.

Published 2014 by Psychology Press
711 Third Avenue, New York, NY 10017

and by Psychology Press
27 Church Road, Hove, East Sussex, BN3 2FA

*Psychology Press is an imprint of the Taylor & Francis Group,
an informa business*

Library of Congress Cataloging-in-Publication Data

Corriveau, Jean-Pierre.
  Time-constrained memory : a reader-based approach to text
comprehension / Jean-Pierre Corriveau.
    p. cm.
  Includes bibliographical references and indexes.
  1. Discourse analysis--Data processing. 2. Discourse analysis-
-Psychological aspects. 3. Memory--Data processing. 4. Knowledge
representation (Information theory) 5. Reading comprehension--Data
processing. 6. Connectionism. I. Title.
  P302.3.C67 1995
                                        95-19949
                                        CIP

ISBN 13: 978-0-805-81711-9 (hbk)
ISBN 13: 978-0-805-81712-6 (pbk)

Publisher's Note
The publisher has gone to great lengths to ensure the quality of this reprint
but points out that some imperfections in the original may be apparent.

À mes parents à qui je dois tout
À Valérie, mon amour, qui est tout pour moi
Aux quatre petits anges qu'elle m'a donnés

CONTENTS

Foreword

Every once in a great while I have encountered a new set of ideas that cause me to have an "aha" reaction, a feeling that what was once murky has suddenly become much clearer. Jean-Pierre Corriveau's thesis evoked this feeling in me when I read it in 1991. I was convinced at that time that this was a seminal piece of work that will (or at least should) have a major impact on the field of natural language processing, causing some lines of research to be terminated, and launching other new ones. This book recapitulates and extends the thesis, and I am again very much impressed.

Let me list some of the reasons: Using only scrupulously simple mechanisms, Corriveau takes on the full sweep of natural language phenomena, from lexical disambiguation and reference resolution to judgements of text coherence and topic. Corriveau takes time and memory to be the key starting points for language understanding. He concentrates singlemindedly on foundations, and avoids fads (though he uses connectionism and spreading activation judiciously). I believe he is the first person to build a system fully in keeping with the spirit of Minsky's society of mind ideas, insisting on using only the simplest, clearly mechanistic operations in his system, and avoiding any question-begging importation of conceptual structures. Corriveau conceives natural language processing as reader-centered, and allows for (and accounts for) different interpretations by different readers or by the same reader at different times. Despite the simplicity of his basic mechanisms, he makes an excellent case and demonstration for the soundness of his ideas. In retrospect, Corriveau's choices and means of using them seem obvious, though everyone else seems to have missed them!

In particular, Corriveau's conception of the pervasiveness of time-based processing is a brilliant insight. It has allowed him to provide solutions to questions that had barely been recognized -- let alone solved -- in natural language processing: How does a system know that it's done with a sentence? What traces are kept after processing? How long? How can we account for the identification, representation, and effects of context?

The book is scholarly, summarizing an immense bibliography of relevant historical and current work (there are more than 600 references!). But it is also wise: Corriveau has a grand unifying conception, and uses it incisively to review this vast literature, endorsing or demolishing ideas according to their fit with his vision. Finally, scholarly does not mean dry. The fact that English is Corriveau's second language makes the quality of the writing even more remarkable. This book, like Corriveau's thesis, is a delight to read both for its style and its content.

David Waltz
Princeton, NJ
April 1995

Preface

Marvin Minsky (1986, p.18) wrote at the beginning of *The Society of Mind* that "to explain the mind, we have to show how minds are built from mindless stuff, from parts that are much smaller and simpler than anything we'd consider smart". Does this assertion constitute an implicit endorsement of the subsymbolic paradigm? Not quite, for the thesis of his famous *Perceptrons* (Minsky, & Papert, 1988) is that such systems do not scale up to the complexities of cognition.

In the domain of natural language processing (NLP), the current debate between symbolic and subsymbolic approaches is not restricted to artificial intelligence (AI), but also encompasses other disciplines relevant to cognitive science such as philosophy, psycholinguistics, and neurosciences. Researchers from both the symbolic and subsymbolic schools of thought have proposed a multitude of models for the different facets of linguistic comprehension (e.g., syntax, lexical disambiguation, inference, reference, etc.). Yet few have offered an integrated view for the comprehension problem in its entirety, and in particular, few have addressed the interpretation of an unrestricted written text.

On the one hand, the symbolic approach rests on the quest for universal (read *innate*) rules of comprehension. Such a strategy has resulted in a plethora of more or less general rules and algorithms for the different facets of linguistic comprehension. However, the integration of these rules has seldom been considered, and their "grounding" in Minsky's "mindless stuff" remains highly problematic. Indeed, such rules often appear to be arbitrarily complex, if not completely ad hoc! On the other hand, connectionist research proceeds from the grounding of cognition in networks of highly idealized "neurons", which correspond to simple numeric processing nodes exchanging simple numeric signals. Within this school, two significantly different approaches compete: The "structured" (or "local") connectionists represent knowledge over a set of named nodes, whereas the distributed connectionists represent knowledge at the subsymbolic level, that is, as patterns of activation across unnamed nodes. The distinction is important. Structured connectionism ultimately reduces to a symbolic technique that uses a standardized processing model:

- All nodes implement the same simple threshold function and exchange the same kind of simple numeric signals.

- There is typically an explicit correspondence between some of the nodes of the network and the postulated rules of comprehension and cognition.

Moreover, as with other symbolic systems, structured connectionism typically does not address learning. Conversely, the parallel distributed processing (PDP) approach heavily depends on a learning algorithm and seems to capture a number of cognitive abilities (e.g., learning by examples, context sensitivity, robustness to new input, etc.) exhibited by humans and yet quite difficult to model with symbolic architectures. However, despite a standardized strategy for processing and for knowledge representation, there is still an overabundance of PDP models, each researcher varying the number of layers in the network, the learning algorithm itself, or its parameters (e.g., the learning rate) for the specific task at hand. PDP models have been proposed for several facets of linguistic comprehension. But very few PDP text interpretation systems have been presented, for they require developing an architecture that coordinates several PDP networks, each assigned with a specific task. The difficulty with such an approach is that it depends on the "prespecified, structured representations [of the] input and output layers [of these networks.]" (Miikkulainen, 1993b, p. 99). In other words, the tasks of these networks, as well as their interactions, are not learned nor grounded in "neurons", but arbitrarily established by the designer. PDP does not scale up to the whole cognitive architecture: Its relevance seems limited to individual networks. More specifically, as with symbolic systems, existing PDP models for text understanding ultimately rely on prespecified patterns of interpretation called *schemas* (or *macrostructures*), which are not grounded in "mindless stuff"!

The question then is two-fold: What can we "ground", and what is this "mindless stuff"? In this book, I attempt to answer both of these questions for the problem of the interpretation of an unrestricted written text.

The key postulate leading to an answer to the first of these two questions is quite radical: The quest for any sort of *universal* rules of cognition, and in particular, for a set of macrostructures for the interpretation of a text, is pointless from a multitude of viewpoints. I defend this position by summarizing the arguments presented by the French linguist François Rastier in his seminal book "Sémantique et recherches cognitives" (1991). The abandonment of such universals implies that knowledge cannot be grounded per se. More precisely, knowledge is taken to significantly differ from one individual to the next, leaving only the expression and processing of knowledge to be "grounded". This is the starting point of my work: I do not search for rules of interpretation, but rather investigate how such "rules" may be expressed in an architecture that is purely mechanistic, that is, grounded in "mindless stuff".

This leads us to the second question: In what shall we "ground" this architecture? Several conceptions of cognition have been proposed throughout history (see Sternberg, 1990). We have already seen that neurons constitute an inadequate solution to this interrogation. In fact, any grounding of cognition in the brain suffers from our current lack of understanding of this extremely complex organ, despite our numerous observations on the functionality of some of its specific areas. In other words, we still do not have an answer to the "mind–body" problem, which studies the relationship between the complex mental operations apparently needed for cognition and linguistic comprehension, as suggested by psycholinguistics, and the anatomy and physiology of the brain. Consequently, we can only "ground" our architecture in some sort of metaphor that abstracts away from the details of what we do know and what we do not.

In order to avoid the mind–body problem, I adopt a methodological reductionism to the metaphor of human memory. "Memory" indeed constitutes, at this point in time, a metaphor: We do not know how many different memory systems we possess, nor where they may be located, nor how they operate. In essence, we simply conceptualize memory as a mechanism for the assembling and storing of knowledge and experience. However, this mechanistic viewpoint is precisely what we are looking for to achieve "grounding"! In other words, we will have respected Minsky's demands if we can show how the complex mental operations hypothesized for linguistic comprehension can be reduced to purely mechanistic memory operations.

There are several other reasons motivating the choice of "memory" as my basic metaphor. In particular, the notion of memory allows us to model a *diachronic* system, that is, a system that changes with time. This is essential, as the rejection of universals proceeds from acknowledging the diachronic nature of language, and by extension, of interpretation. In other words, in my opinion, there is no such thing as the *correct* interpretation of a text, but rather an interpretation at a certain point of time with respect to a given individual in a particular state of mind. Such a hermeneutic standpoint constitutes a *reader-*

based approach to comprehension: Interpretations will vary across individuals, and for a single individual, with respect to one's memory-processing parameters (such as short-term memory capacity, decay rate, learning rate, etc.). In other words, even for a single reader, we should be able to model the possibility of obtaining different interpretations corresponding to different sets of processing parameters. This requirement constitutes the main goal of this work. More precisely, in this book, I want to:

    1. Provide a description of a purely mechanistic computational model of memory. This model addresses the processing of knowledge in a "grounded" architecture.

    2. Explain how a user of this model can input the knowledge assumed necessary for text interpretation, specify a set of processing parameters, and launch an interpretation. This explanation therefore addresses the *expression* of the knowledge to be used by the proposed grounded architecture.

I want to immediately emphasize that it is not my intent to develop here a model of text interpretation per se, but rather to detail how one goes about specifying such a model "on top of" the proposed grounded cognitive architecture. In other words, I deliberately attempt to avoid as many epistemological and hermeneutic commitments as possible with respect to the construction of this grounded architecture. Obviously, if this were not the case, this architecture would not be grounded, for it would embed "mental" considerations. Consequently, the following assumptions that I make pertain to the organization and processing in "memory":

    1. Memory is organized in terms of temporal partitions;

    2. Processes in memory can be concurrent;

    3. Processes in memory have a short amount of time to execute; they are *time-constrained*.

This last assumption is the most original and pervasive of my work. It proceeds from acknowledging the real-time processing constraints of human cognition. More specifically, because it can only involve a limited number of computational steps, linguistic comprehension (and by extension, text interpretation) is taken to be a *time-constrained process* —a *race*. I suggest that such hypothesis not only partially explains the non-determinism implied by a reader-based approach to text understanding, but also leads to a computational model that is tractable both in time and in space complexity.

    The ideas of this book proceed from those originally presented in my doc-

toral dissertation and implemented in a prototype named **IDIoT** (for Idiosyncratically-Directed Interpretation of Text). I would like to thank first my
advisor, Graeme Hirst, who initiated and nurtured my interest in computational linguistics and cognitive science. His patience and guidance throughout
my Ph.D. were invaluable. I am also grateful to my external examiners, David
Waltz and James Hendler, who both contributed by their comments to the
improvement of the original dissertation. I especially appreciated David writing an evaluation report that helped silence the opposition I received from
those researchers that believe only in the relevance of logic and/or of a universal grammar for cognition. In particular, I thank Hector Levesque for his systematic criticism of my work.

Two factors significantly contributed to the improvement of the ideas of
the original dissertation: my exploration of Minsky's fascinating *The Society
of Mind* and my "discovery" of Rastier's work. I am indebted to both of these
authors for having invested a few hours in talking to me. The three-hour discussion with Minsky at FLAIRS-94 helped finalize the argumentation of this
book. The day spent with Rastier in 1992 was determinant. Not only did he
reaffirm and convincingly motivate our anti-innatist, anti-universalist stance,
but he also introduced me to his remarkable work on semantics and text interpretation. In doing so, he provided much needed arguments to motivate my
model. Furthermore, he set out a research program for me, as I intend to investigate in coming years the implementation of his "differential semantics" on
top of **IDIoT**.

I am indebted (the word is not strong enough) to Edwin Plantinga for the
countless discussions that helped me conceive, simplify, and criticize my
ideas. I would also like to thank Adriana Lopes Diaz, Tania Kaszpak and
Sharon Liska for their investigation and implementation of **IDIoT** in various
concurrent object-oriented programming languages. Many thanks to Raymond Aubin, George Berg, Andy Brook, Michel Corriveau, Judy Dick, Tom
Fairgrieve, Ken Forsythe, Helen Gigley, Diane Horton, Deepak Kumar, Susan
McRoy, Franz Oppacher, Mohsen Rais-Ghasem, Stephen Regoczei, Walid
Saba and Nicola Santoro for their help and comments.

I am grateful to my parents, Roland and Madeleine, for giving me the
opportunity to study. I cannot thank them enough for their constant encourage-
ment, support, and love. I also want to thank Marie-Jeanne, Simon-Pierre,
Charles-Etienne and François-Xavier for their patience with their father, who
often spent more time finishing this book than playing with them in the last
few months.

In the end, this work would never have been completed if it were not for
the loving presence of my wife, Valérie Chaplain, who always believed in me

more than I did. Busy with her own full-time studies in biology, she found the time and energy in the last five years to have and educate our four children and to typeset this book.

Finally, financial support from the Natural Sciences, and Engineering Research Council of Canada in the form of graduate scholarships and more recently, of operating grants, is gratefully acknowledged. I extend my appreciation to Bell-Northern Research for support while I was a Ph.D. student. Finally, to conclude, I would like to thank Carleton University, and in particular Les Copley, as well as its School of Computer Science, especially John Pugh and Frank Fiala, for entrusting me with an academic position as well as providing an excellent environment for this research.

Jean-Pierre Corriveau

Part I
Foundations

Chapter 1

Overview

1.1 THE PROBLEM DOMAIN

Since the early 1970s, significant advances have been realized in the field of natural language processing (NLP). However, research has mainly focused on user interfaces and the parsing of isolated sentences; the processing of larger linguistic units has typically remained a stumbling block (Habel, 1983; Winograd, & Flores, 1986, chapter 9). There exists a multitude of models for the different facets (e.g., syntax, lexical disambiguation, inference, reference, etc.) of linguistic comprehension (or equivalently, "understanding"). In contrast, however, there are currently few computational models that tackle the comprehension of long, unrestricted, *written text* (henceforth, text). I use the term "text" in the broad sense in which Muller (1977, p. 5) defined it as:

> any utterance or any succession of utterances, any use of speech or fragment of speech, with no restriction on its extent, produced by a single speaker or writer and displaying a certain unity.

This "certain unity" of text is taken to be central to comprehension: *Subject matter* (or equivalently, "aboutness") is what gives a text this certain unity. It is generally accepted that if we fail to perceive the subject matter of a text, we find it difficult, if not impossible, to understand that text (Bransford, & Johnson, 1973). In this book, I address the problem of text comprehension, and in particular, the issue of the *perception* of subject matter. I view the *expression*, as opposed to the perception, of subject matter as a distinct problem that has more to do with the tasks of language generation (Jacobs, 1987; Ward, 1988) and memory recall (Baddeley, 1976; Kintsch, & van Dijk, 1978; van der Meer, 1987), which are not addressed here. The acquisition of reading and interpretative skills (Bertelson, 1987; Balota, Flores d'Arcais, & Rayner, 1990) is also ignored.

Of the computational models that have been proposed over the last two decades for text understanding (e.g., Schank, 1972, 1982; Cullingford, 1978;

Dyer, 1983; Wilensky, 1978, 1983b; Norvig, 1987, 1989), most are symbolic conceptual analyzers primarily concerned with the problem of *inference* (Kass, 1986), and more specifically, with recognizing causal (van der Meer, 1987) relationships between the "facts" identified from the input text. *Reference* (see Kleiber, 1981) constitutes the other fundamental problem of linguistic comprehension. In essence, this task consists in retrieving from what has been memorized of the input text, the referent (e.g., a "character", a "fact", an "episode", etc.) of a particular linguistic entity (such as a proper name, a pronoun, a definite noun phrase, a sentence, etc.). Both of these problems will be studied at length later in this book. For now, this intuitive introduction will suffice to understand a first commonly accepted hypothesis with respect to text understanding, namely that comprehension requires the use of knowledge beyond what information may be "in" the input text. For example, knowledge about committing suicide and hanging is required in the following example in order to understand the causal link between "rope" and "kill": John bought a rope *because* he wanted to commit suicide:

Example 1.1.1 *John wanted to kill himself. He went to the store to buy a rope.*

Similarly, the reader must possess linguistic knowledge about pronouns in English (e.g., "her" should refer to a single female human being) in order to decipher this:

Example 1.1.2 *Mary started distributing the course outline to the students. Each one of them got it from her.*

Neither of these "pieces of knowledge" are "in" the text. Instead, they are part of the conceptual material a reader may bring to the act of interpreting a text.

Another fundamental assumption states that text comprehension entails information loss. For example, we do not remember the exact wording of the sentences of a book (see Gernsbacher, 1985; Phillips, 1985, pp. 3–4), and we often forget some of the facts we identify and some of the inferences we make while reading, much to the delight of mystery novelists. It follows that at the end of a reading, we have somehow assembled together a mental entity, which we will call a *trace* of the text, corresponding to what we have remembered of this text. Clearly, this trace is diachronic: It will change over time, during and after reading. Indeed, over the years, the vast majority of a trace may become totally unretrievable, if not completely forgotten.

It is generally acknowledged that the construction (e.g., Meutsch, 1986) of a trace is central to the perception of subject matter as well as to a posteriori tasks such as recall, summarizing, and question answering (see Graesser, & Clark, 1985). This construction process is taken to subsume several facets of linguistic comprehension such as word recognition, syntactic analysis, word sense disambiguation, reference resolution, inference generation and convergence, and perception of subject matter. Each of these tasks in itself constitutes a complex problem that is discussed later. For example, word sense disambiguation depends on a multitude of factors such as context, reader's goals and expectations, prior processing, memory parameters, etc. However, it is not sufficient to address individually the different facets of linguistic comprehension; we must also consider their interactions: An *integrated* approach to interpretation is required, and although most of these facets are relevant at the level of the sentence (called the *sentential* level) or "lower" levels (such as the word or, equivalently, *lexical* level), some (e.g., perception of subject matter) are, however, specific to text understanding. In particular, the *convergence problem* (Corriveau, 1994c) consists in explaining how the multitude of inferences *potentially* generated by a text can be reduced to the small set that ends up in the trace. In other words, because a reader never draws all the possible inferences a text could suggest (for lack of time or lack of usefulness, and because there may be an infinity of such inferences), a model of text understanding must not only explain how inferences are created, but also how they are limited to a manageable number for further usage.

1.2 MOTIVATIONS AND GOALS

Minsky's wrote the following at the beginning of *The Society of Mind* (1986, p.18):

> To explain the mind, we have to show how minds are built from mind-less stuff, from parts that are much smaller and simpler than anything we'd consider smart. Unless we can explain the mind in terms of things that have no thoughts or feelings of their own, we'll only have gone around in a circle. But what could those simpler particles be— the 'agents' that compose our minds? There are many questions to answer. . . These questions all seem difficult, indeed, when we sever each one's connection to the other ones. But once we see the mind as a society of agents, each answer will illuminate the rest.

My interpretation of this paragraph is that cognitive scientists must aim at building *grounded* (as opposed to "semantic" or "intelligent") cognitive architectures, that is, architectures that are purely mechanistic and that do not embed within themselves any sort of knowledge, any type of epistemological commitment. In other words, an architecture that embodies either explicitly (in the form of rules or schemas) or implicitly (in the form of algorithms, procedures, nodes, and/or connections) any kind of knowledge, presents the problem of having this knowledge not reduced to "mindless stuff", and thus, not explained per se, but rather granted an a priori existence.

Minsky's paragraph also emphasizes the importance of an *integrated* approach to cognition, as opposed to a method that focuses on individual problems in isolation. Ideally, because the interactions between the different facets of cognition also need to be grounded, integration should become *uniformization*. In other words, within a grounded system, all knowledge should be processed in the same uniform way, that is, regardless of what kind of knowledge is in question (i.e., whether it is syntactic, lexical, semantic, pragmatic, etc.). Any other approach (e.g., one that presupposes the existence or the format of representation of schemas, one that prespecifies modules with specific cognitive tasks, etc.) suffers from depending on a priori mental entities and processes that are not grounded (by definition).

The present book proceeds essentially from this interpretation of Minsky's challenge. More specifically, within the domain of text comprehension, my primary goal is to motivate and develop such a grounded uniform architecture and illustrate its relevance to the interpretation of written text. This goal is justified by observing that existing models of text understanding are not grounded and often quite incomplete.

On the one hand, the symbolic approach relies on arbitrarily complex data structures, rules, and algorithms that lack any sort of reduction to mindless stuff (Feldman, 1984). Most of these models have concentrated on inference generation and schema recognition and have ignored important problems such as syntax, disambiguation, reference resolution and so forth. Similarly, in local connectionist networks (see Preface) for text comprehension (Bookman, & Alterman, 1991; Bookman, 1992, 1994), a priori rules of interpretation (e.g., for case–role and thematic analysis) are embedded in the nodes and connections of these networks. However, such rules are not grounded, by definition.

On the other hand, the few existing PDP models of text comprehension typically oversimplify the problem by addressing only the learning and recognition of schemas (e.g., St. John, 1990; Golden, & Rumelhart, 1993), often from pre-processed texts. Miikkulainen (1993b, p. 258) remarked that such networks are not text understanders per se because they are too restricted; they do not offer any insight on the interactions between the different tasks of interpretation. Indeed, it appears that only his system constitutes an integrated PDP approach to text comprehension. However, as mentioned in the Preface, this is possible only through the use of prespecified structured representations (for interactions between a priori modules), which are not grounded.

Thus, without going in any further details (which are provided in the next chapter), it seems that there is indeed the need for a grounded uniform cognitive architecture for text interpretation. Bechtel (1994) confirmed this standpoint put forth by Minsky (1986) when he remarked:

> The notion of levels has been widely used in discussion of cognitive science, especially in discussion of the relation of connectionist to symbolic modeling. I argue that many of the notions of levels employed are problematic for this purpose, and [I] develop an alternative notion grounded in the framework of mechanistic explanation. By considering the source of the analogies underlying both symbolic modeling and connectionist modeling, I argue that neither is likely to provide an adequate analysis of processes at the level at which cognitive theories attempt to function: one is drawn from too low a level, the other from too high a level.

The architecture I propose immediately presents the advantage of not depending on any sort of prespecified "levels" nor on any "universal" (i.e., innate) rules of interpretation, a notion that I will reject later.

I now want to submit that the use of a grounded architecture can lead to a standardization, not only in the processing underlying a model of text understanding, but also in the expression of this model. This claim stems from the blatant absence of such standardization in symbolic systems, systems which, I repeat, typically use arbitrarily complex structures and algorithms. Conversely, both structured connectionism and PDP have the virtue of using a standardized processing model (see Feldman, 1985a, 1985b). However, for the latter, there is still significant diversity (see Miikkulainen, 1993b, chapter 2 for details) with respect to architectural characteristics (e.g., number of hidden layers, number of networks and format of interactions between them, recurrent or non-recurrent network, etc.) and learning techniques (e.g., supervised versus unsupervised). For example, Miikkulainen (1993b, p. 9) abandoned the "standard" learning algorithm, namely backpropagation (see McClelland, & Rumelhart, 1986) for his model of memory, because it is not well suited for text comprehension.

Because it avoids epistemological commitments, a grounded architecture standardizes

1. **the processing of knowledge**: The system has no predefined knowledge "types", structures, modules, or interactions. It merely follows what von der Malsburg (1985) calls a *trivial algorithm* that

fixes the general form of operations: All knowledge is treated as data.

2. **the expression of knowledge**: All data, and thus all rules and schemas hypothesized for text interpretation, are expressed in a uniform
fashion. Otherwise, the system would have to embed distinctions
based on the different types of data.

Such a standardization obviously cannot be rigorously proven for all existing
types of knowledge, but merely demonstrated through examples. Such a demonstration constitutes the second goal of my work and occupies a large portion
of this book. The demonstration consists of two parts:

1. The technique of expression of knowledge, what I shall call the
representational scheme, is motivated and described in details.

2. The applicability of this representational scheme to the most
important facets of text understanding is illustrated at length.

As suggested above, a standardization in the processing of knowledge
depends on a trivial algorithm. But this algorithm must be rooted in some
underlying metaphor of cognition. For example, von der Malsburg (1985)
defined the trivial algorithm as the operational foundation of the brain. I have
already stated in the Preface that my architecture is to be rooted in the metaphor of human memory. This choice is discussed further at the end of the next
chapter.

Additional processing standardization can be obtained by having the trivial algorithm controlled by a set of external parameters. In the case of my basic
metaphor, this amounts to having the proposed architecture take the form of a
model of memory whose parameters' values are user-specified. As will be
explained in chapter 4, these parameters may control both the structure (e.g.,
thresholds for temporal partitions, short term memory capacity) and the operations (e.g., decay rate, learning rate) of memory. In other words, structural
and operational characteristics are not necessarily entrenched in the grounded
architecture. Instead, some are controlled through parameters. Such a strategy
presents the advantage of minimizing the static (or fixed) aspects of the system
by avoiding embedding in it specific architectural decisions. In turn, this
allows the system more flexibility in its processing through the use of these
"standard" parameters: Only the parameters are predefined; their values are
specified by the user of the model. As part of my second goal, the relevance of
these parameters to text comprehension is explored as we investigate the
applicability of the proposed representational scheme to text understanding.

In order to identify this set of parameters, I turn to the extensive evidence

found in psycholinguistics with respect to the role of memory during comprehension (see section 4.1). Psycholinguists also presented a considerable number of issues and results for the different facets of reading (see Mitchell, 1982;
Balota, Flores d'Arcais, & Rayner, 1990; Gernsbacher, 1994; Underwood, &
Batt, 1995). A third goal of the present research is to briefly overview this evidence and discuss how the proposed model of memory accommodates some
of it, and although this model does not address the acquisition of reading
skills, as a corollary goal, the problem of learning is quickly investigated.

Finally, computational linguists tend to forget that the implementations of
their models constitute software to the same degree as the implementation of
any other tool or theory. Thus, as with any other software, these models should
be developed according to sound software engineering principles (see Sommerville, 1992). In particular, it is essential that any model be tractable both in
time and in space complexity (Shastri, 1993). A fourth goal of this book is to
demonstrate that the proposed model of memory is indeed tractable both in
time and in space complexity.

1.3 READER-BASED TEXT PROCESSING

The goals put forth in the previous section suggest a new approach to the interpretation of text, which now is overviewed. This approach is based on two fundamental observations made by Rastier (1991, p. 160):

> 1. It is not necessarily the case that an input text must be interpreted
> in one and only one unique way. In fact, a text generally has multiple
> interpretations (or equivalently, *determinations*) and, for some read-
> ers, a text may lack any interpretation. In other words, linguistic com-
> prehension is *non-deterministic*.

> 2. It is not necessarily the case that an interpretation (in the form of a
> trace) be static over time. In other words, an interpretation is *diach-
> ronic*, much like a language itself.

Both of these observations are further discussed in the next chapter. At this
point in the discussion, it is only necessary to understand that these two postulates imply the abandonment of the traditional view of text understanding as
the process used to establish the "correct" interpretation of the input. In other
words, there is no quest in this book for a set of "rules of interpretation", for
some sort of "innate competence to interpret", that would explain how, given
a text, its correct meaning is constructed.

Instead, as I hinted in the Preface, a *reader-based* strategy (see subsection

2.4.1) is adopted. The interpretation of a text depends on both of the following:

1. **The knowledge of a specific reader at a given point in time**: This knowledge may vary from one reader to the next, and evolve over time for a single reader.

2. **The settings of the external parameters controlling the model of memory that subsumes the interpretative process**: Different interpretations may be obtained by varying the values of these parameters.

In other words, it is the reader, as opposed to some static algorithm embedded in the system, that controls the act of interpretation. All epistemological commitments are external to the system: All knowledge is treated as external data residing in some sort of repository, which we shall call the *knowledge base* (KB). The grounded architecture merely consists in a purely mechanistic model of memory implementing a trivial algorithm.

Within this framework, the interpretation of a text follows the steps listed below:

1. The user launches the system, which, you will recall from the Preface, is named **IDIoT** for Idiosyncratically-Directed Interpretation of Text.

2. The user opens the *knowledge base browser* to examine, set, or modify the knowledge to be used for the current interpretation. Each user can keep a library of several distinct KBs, but only one KB is used per interpretation. The knowledge base browser controls the selection of this KB.

3. The user opens the *memory control browser* to set the different external parameters of the model of memory. Default values are built into **IDIoT** for each of these parameters. Therefore, this step is optional. (The memory control browser is a straightforward field-filling window and is not discussed further in this book.)

4. The user selects from the main menu of **IDIoT** the file containing the input text. This input file is **not** *pre-processed* in any sort of way.

5. The system inputs each word of the selected text one-by-one. Each word typically triggers one or more elements of the selected knowledge base (e.g., "features" of the word, parsing rules, inferences, etc.). We shall call *knowledge units* (KUs) the elements of a KB. In essence, each KU tries to become activated either directly from read-

ing a word in the input text or through receiving signals from other KUs. The fundamental operational characteristic of the model is that a KU has a short amount of time to become activated. In other words, activation is a time-constrained process. Upon its activation, each KU may send signals to other KUs and modify the trace existing at that point in time. In other words, the trace is constructed from a series of activations resulting from interactions between KUs.

6. A trace of the interpretation is built as words, sentences, and paragraphs are processed. **IDIoT** uses the current values of the parameters of the model of memory to manage this construction task. For example, the current capacity of short-term memory is determinant for the creation of inferences (e.g., Daneman, 1987): Intuitively, too small a capacity will greatly reduce the number of generated inferences, whereas too large a capacity will possibly lead to "far-fetched" inferences.

7. Once all words of the input text have been processed, **IDIoT** opens up a *trace browser* that presents to the user the contents of the trace and allows the user to "navigate" (in the hypertext sense of this term) in this trace. The "raw" trace constitutes the output of **IDIoT**.

8. The user may choose to open the *integration browser* to select the parts of the trace to be integrated by **IDIoT** in the KB. This simple form of learning follows the proposal of Bookman (1992) and is briefly discussed in chapter 12.

The details of each of these steps are presented in the later parts of this book. It is important, however, to immediately notice that the system does not include any module to further process the trace, for example, for question answering or summarization. The reason for this is simple: Any such module would require epistemological commitments in the form of rules and algorithms for each of these tasks. For example, it is typical for summarization to define an algorithm that identifies the "most relevant" constituents of the trace. Clearly then, because such modules would not be grounded, they would violate the design philosophy of the system.

1.4 APPROACH

Given this reader-based approach to text processing, I propose the following methodological steps to satisfy the goals set out earlier:

1. Motivate the need for a grounded cognitive architecture.

2. Design this architecture and emphasize

   a) its tractability both with respect to time and space complexity.

   b) its uniform processing of any type of knowledge.

3. Overview the interface to this architecture.

4. Briefly discuss the implementation of this architecture.

5. For some of the key facets of text interpretation;

   a) briefly overview existing computational and psycholinguistic work on this facet.

   b) discuss the expression of typical rules of interpretation with the representational scheme of **IDIoT.**

   c) demonstrate the processing of typical examples with **IDIoT.**

6. Discuss the limitations of the system.

7. Conclude with some foreseen enhancements to **IDIoT** and a final evaluation of it.

Within the scope of this book, I focus on the following facets of text interpretation: syntax, reference resolution, lexical disambiguation, structural disambiguation, and inference.

1.5 A GUIDE TO THE READER

The plan for the rest of the book follows the approach outlined in the previous section.

Chapter 2 completes Part I of the book and encompasses the theoretical foundations of the work. It consists of a review of the existing approaches to text understanding with respect to their "grounding". The reader may want to consult an introduction to the philosophy of language (e.g., Devitt, & Sterelny, 1987) before starting this chapter. First, symbolic approaches, which are associated with the currently dominant position in the cognitive sciences, are examined. I argue that the information-processing paradigm rests on a *structuralist* and *objectivist* theory of interpretation in which text is seen as the repository of a single determinate meaning placed in it by the writer; a "competent" reader merely retrieves this meaning. This approach is rejected in that not only is it not grounded, but it also has difficulty accounting for contextual meaning and does not address the reality of a text having several possible interpretations. Second, I investigate local and PDP connectionist models of understanding. The former are found to be essentially symbolic models using a spreading activation process strategy. As with other information-processing models, the local connectionist models typically depend on a priori macro-structures for the interpretation of text. As for the PDP models, though they are grounded in "neurons", we shall see that they require a priori symbolic representations in order to have their different components interact together. The study of these models does reveal, however, several issues that a text comprehender must address. A review of Rastier's (1991) objections to current research and an overview of his interpretative theory will lead us to establish the fundamental postulates from which **IDIoT** proceeds.

In Part II of this book, I design the proposed model of memory. First, in chapter 3, I introduce the notion of diachronic interpretation and derive from it the requirements for the implementation of **IDIoT**. In order to promote reusability and because spreading activation is adopted as the underlying processing model, this implementation shall take the form of a concurrent object-oriented *framework*, that is, of a set of reusable classes (see de Champeaux, Lea, & Faure, 1993). The model of time-constrained memory per se is presented in chapter 4, which starts with a brief survey of issues in research on human memory. The internal structure and behavior of *knowledge units* (KUs) are then explored. In essence, a KU acts as a feature detector and as a cluster builder. A feature is a semantic entity, and its detection consists in satisfying a local threshold constraint of a KU. A cluster merely consists of a group of features, possibly organized hierarchically. The "knowledge" of the model is not in the connections of the network, but rather in the KUs, which are small strictly "mindless" finite state machines (i.e., non-semantic computational automata) implementing forward and backward chaining (i.e., two very simple mechanisms used for inferencing; see subsection 4.6.1). Each KU contains an *expansion procedure*, which is a sequence of primitive cluster operations (i.e., "grounded" operations). Once a KU satisfies a local constraint, its expansion procedure is executed by the *memory manager*, which is responsible for the manipulation and management of clusters. Through the execution of its expansion procedure, a KU can modify the contents of memory, allowing for both the enforcement and application of the rule(s) associated with the detected feature. Chapter 5 proceeds with a discussion of the implementation and user interface of the current prototype of the model and concludes with an annotated example.

In Part III, I address the specification of a text processing system over time-constrained memory. In chapter 6, I first review three prototypical models of text understanding from which the different tasks of linguistic comprehension are identified. Then, in the next five chapters, for each of the tasks of syntactic processing, reference resolution, lexical disambiguation, structural disambiguation, and inferences, I first briefly review existing computational and psycholinguistic work, then argue for the omnipresent importance of time-constrained memory and, finally, demonstrate how a user of **IDIoT** can specify rules that capture simplified solutions to these problems. I must emphasize that the goal at hand is not to specify "correct" rules, but to illustrate how typical rules can be encoded in **IDIoT**. Several of the 89 examples running with the current prototype in Smalltalk (Goldberg, 1984) will be presented in scenarios that consist of sequences of events summarizing the actual sequences of messages exchanged between KUs.

Finally, in Part IV, which consists of chapter 12, I propose some enhancements and future directions for **IDIoT**. In particular, the issue of learning is addressed. This last chapter concludes with an evaluation of an approach to cognitive science rooted in the notion of a "grounded architecture".

1.6 TERMINOLOGY AND CONVENTIONS

For convenience, I list here some of the terms used throughout this work:

1. **Knowledge Unit** (KU): A user-defined element of the knowledge base.

2. **Knowledge Base** (KB): The repository of all knowledge/data defined by the user (in the form of Knowledge Units).

3. **Cluster**: An element of dynamic memory, that is, a constructed cognitive structure, as opposed to the KUs of the knowledge base. A cluster holds a set of *features*, each feature governing a set of clusters.

4. **Feature**: A semantic entity detectable by one or more knowledge units.

5. **Short-term Memory** (STM): Short-term memory in the conventional psychological sense.

A few conventional abbreviations are also employed for syntactic categories:

1. **NP**: noun phrase.

2. **PP**: prepositional phrase.

3. **VP**: verb phrase.

Also, in a grammar rule, a superscript asterisk on an item means that the item may be repeated zero or more times; square brackets denote optionality.

Throughout the book, the name of a feature appears in bold. Names follow the Smalltalk (Goldberg, 1984) convention: They may be arbitrarily long and consist of a single word in which some letters may be capitalized to simplify reading.

Finally, here are some abbreviations for the bibliography:

1. **AAAI**: (Proceedings of the Annual Conference of the) American Association for Artificial Intelligence.

2. **ACL**: (Proceedings of the Annual Meeting of the) Association for Computational Linguistics.

3. **CSCSI**: (Proceedings of the Conference of the) Canadian Society on Computer Science and Information.

4. **FLAIRS**: Florida Artificial Intelligence Research Symposium.

5. **HICSS**: Hawaiian International Conference on Systems and Software.

6. **ICCI**: (Proceedings of the Annual) International Conference on Computers and Information.

7. **IJCAI**: (Proceedings of the) International Joint Conference on Artificial Intelligence.

8. **PACLING**: (Proceedings of the) First Conference of the Pacific Association for Computational Linguistics.

Chapter 2

Models of Understanding

2.1 THE CONDUIT METAPHOR

According to the *Webster's Ninth New Collegiate Dictionary* (1981, p. 641.), "*language* is a systematic means of communicating ideas or feelings by the use of conventionalized signs, sounds, gestures, or marks". Phillips (1985, p. 3) observed:

> There is one ultimate fact about text. This is that it consists of elements of linguistic substance juxtaposed in linear sequence. In the case of written text, the. . . reader somehow internalizes from the encounter with graphic substance. . . the meaning of the text.

For written text, the marks (or graphemes) recorded on a certain medium (e.g., paper) are physical (graphical) instantiations of linguistic elements. These linguistic elements do not have physical substance per se: They belong to the reader's *mind*, that is, the entity or set of entities that controls abilities such as understanding, feeling, perceiving, thinking, willing, and reasoning. For example, the letter *t* does not exist in a three-dimensional blot of ink on a piece of paper, but rather in the mind of a cognitive agent. By looking at the blot of ink, the cognitive agent may *perceive* (or equivalently, *apprehend*) a *t*, or may fail to do so.

The linguistic elements that form a text have a symbolic nature: They *symbolize* other *mental* (or equivalently, *cognitive*) entities typically called *ideas* or *meanings*. It is generally accepted that the perception of the subject matter of a text involves the perception of the meaning of the constituents of the text. In other words, it is typically assumed that the perception of the subject matter of a text requires the ability to perceive the meaning of the smaller linguistic elements that form the text. For simplicity, let us appeal momentarily to the intuitive notions of *word*, *phrase*, and *sentence* to refer to these smaller linguistic elements.

Many researchers have attempted to explain the relation of language to meaning. Reddy (1979) has suggested that a complex metaphor, which he calls the *conduit metaphor*, underlies most current linguistic theories. This metaphor disposes us to think of linguistic communication as follows:

1. Ideas are mental objects.

2. Linguistic expressions are containers.

3. Communication is sending.

To effect communication, a speaker puts ideas *in* words and then sends them to a hearer who takes the ideas *out* of the words. What a linguistic expression *means* depends solely on what the speaker put into the container (Plantinga, 1986).

For written text, the conduit metaphor is writer-based; the reader merely retrieves the *determinate* meaning that the author put into the sentences. Searle (1979, pp. 117–119) has summarized the most common view of meaning that proceeds from this metaphor:

> Sentences have literal meanings. The literal meaning of a sentence is entirely determined by the meaning of its component words (or morphemes) and the syntactical rules according to which these elements are combined. A sentence may have more than one literal meaning (ambiguity), or its literal meaning may be defective or uninterpretable (nonsense). . . . The literal meaning of the sentence is the meaning it has independently of any context whatever; and diachronic changes apart, it keeps that meaning in any context in which it is uttered.

Assuming that each word in language has a few possible meanings that are readily accessible greatly simplifies the task of sentence understanding: The meaning of a sentence is determined by the meaning of the words that form it. Words are taken to *refer* to "reality" and, therefore, the meaning of an utterance can be obtained by evaluating the *correspondence* to reality of the meaning contained in its words. With the "correct" algorithm, "the" meaning of a sentence is obtained. Similarly, it is hoped that with the "correct" algorithm, "the" meaning of a text will be *computable* from the meaning of the words and sentences of the text. To put this another way, the linguistic elements that form the text carry their own meaning; they constitute *information*, and the reader receives meanings contained in words. According to this viewpoint, the reader uses an *information*-processing algorithm: By recognizing the *rules of composition* of meaning used by the author, the reader is able to retrieve the subject matter of the text. Meaning and subject matter are objectified through the words of the text; comprehension is *normalized* with respect to the set of rules of composition used by the writer. As Plantinga (1987) observed, "the individual has been banished from contemporary linguistics. . . Linguistics studies language but not *homo loquens*".

This concern with normalized understanding by a *competent* comprehender, one who possesses and uses the correct set of rules, can be traced back to Ferdinand de Saussure (1916), who was the first of the few modern linguists who achieved fundamental insight into the problem of meaning. The first principle of his *Cours de Linguistique* emphasizes the *arbitrariness* of the linguistic *sign*: the linguistic sign consists of an arbitrary relationship between a *signifiant* (or symbol) and a *signifié* (or referent). In other words, Saussure asserted that there is no necessary correspondence between the systems of language and our experience of phenomena. However, if the relationship is arbitrary, it must also be *conventional*, "for if the relationship between "signifiant" and "signifié" were not conventional, there could be no question of exercising stylistic choice or of creativity of the poetic work which attaches new and unexpected meanings to familiar words" (Phillips, 1985, p. 7).

Phillips (1985) remarked that the crucial consequence of the principle is that signs are not mutually substitutable and that, therefore, a system has to be established to keep them distinct in use. Both extreme homonymy (i.e., multiple referents mapping into identical signs) and extreme synonymy (i.e., a single referent realized by a multitude of signs) would lead not to an *unworkable* system, but to the *absence* of system. Thus, with the acceptance of the fundamental Saussurian tenet, the rest of linguistics can be seen as a specification of the limits to arbitrariness.

The information-processing paradigm, I repeat, focuses on the conventions of linguistic comprehension and ignores the arbitrariness of linguistic communication. The paradigmatic goal is to find *the systems* of language and meaning, that is, sets of rules for understanding. Since the relation of language to meaning is highly complex, several separate classes of systems have been proposed. Let me first review these different classes and discuss their adequacy for text comprehension.

2.2 INFORMATION PROCESSING AND TEXT COMPREHENSION

2.2.1 On Story Grammars and Discourse Analysis

The definition of *language* quoted earlier suggests that a certain systematicity is generally accepted for linguistic communication. Typically, language is viewed as consisting of a number of interrelated systems operating at different levels of analysis. The commonly recognized levels of linguistic analysis are the phonological, the graphological, the morphological, the lexical, the syntactic, the semantic, the pragmatic, and the discourse levels. For the comprehension of written text, it is generally assumed that the phonological level of analysis does not enter into consideration, "nor does the graphological one since typographical features do not operate at a unique level of linguistic analysis, but rather cut across a number of different levels. Moreover, although such features make some contribution to the overall semantics of the text, it is a relatively superficial one. The morphological level of analysis is also inappropriate to the investigation of text[:] word morphology relates to the function of words in syntactic frames; that is, it largely reflects syntactic structuring". (Phillips, 1985, pp. 30–32).

Within the information-processing paradigm, it is generally agreed that the perception of subject matter depends on "global semantic structures of text-as-whole", known in psychology as *macrostructures* (van Dijk, 1980):

> We should distinguish between the (general) *form* of a narrative and its (actual) *content*, which is of course an old insight . . . . We will call a *story* any discourse which has a narrative structure. Hence, we distinguish between a *discourse type* (stories), its *narrative global form* (superstructure[)], its narrative global content (macrostructures; which may be conventionalized[)] and, of course, the actual linguistic expression of these in the form of a sequence of sentences: a discourse.

Phillips (1985, pp. 3–4) explained:

> It seems, then, that appreciation of textual meaning is a large-scale phenomenon which does not depend directly on those structures which are responsible only for the local organization of linguistic expressions. . . . It is widely accepted that... non-linear conceptual structures are elaborated by the reader and are the mechanism which underlies the reader's ability to summarize, paraphrase and generally state what the text is about. This ability raises some interesting problems. It has been pointed out that to be able to state what a book is about depends on the processing of thousands of sentences which cannot normally be memorized individually by the reader. . . . In general, it is the "gist" of a text which is recalled rather than the wording.

In modern theoretical linguistics, syntactic concerns occupy the center of attention in investigations of *grammar* (i.e., the set of rules required to assemble meaningful symbols into a meaningful utterance). In particular, the theory of *generative grammars*, whose most notable proponent is Chomsky (1965, 1980, 1982), introduces powerful notational mechanisms that can be carried over to the textual level. It has therefore been suggested that the meaning of a text can in some sense be accounted for within the framework of grammatical theory.

Story grammars were initially proposed to reformulate Propp's (1968) theory of Russian folktales. Rumelhart (1975) suggested the first more general grammar. This grammar's first rewrite rule was:

Rule 1: *story → setting + episode*

This rule states that a story is composed of an element called a "setting" followed by an element called an "episode". Each of these components is defined by subsequent rules: a setting, as a sequence of stative propositions, and an episode, as an event followed by some reaction of the protagonist of this episode. Each rewrite rule is associated with a semantic constraint. For example, for the preceding rule, the semantic constraint specifies that the setting must "enable" the episode.

Some researchers (e.g., Johnson, & Mandler, 1980) have presented more elaborate grammars in which *transformations* specify the passage from the *surface structure* of a story to its *base* (or *deep*) structure. It is generally assumed among story grammarians (the notable exceptions being Johnson, & Mandler) that the proposed grammars characterize cognitive *schemas* (or schemata) used during comprehension (van Dijk, 1980). The realization of these schemas in language is of no import to these researchers (see comments of Allen in Wilensky, 1983a).

A very critical review of the story grammar paradigm can be found in Wilensky's (1983a) article "Story Grammars versus Story Points" and the comments of his peers that follow the paper. Garnham (1983) also vigorously argued against the approach. The immediate difficulty with a story grammar is that it ultimately relies on the intuitions of the grammarian himself for the definition and recognition of its *terminals* (e.g., "event"). Furthermore, the relevance of the grammatical framework to text comprehension is rather dubious: Perception of subject matter is not an issue of grammaticality, that is, of well-formedness, but of what a text is about.

From my point of view, discourse analysis (see de Beaugrande, 1980, for reviews) is very similar to story grammars in that it focuses on the techniques used by the writer to introduce the topic, rather than on the perception of the subject matter of a text itself. Though these techniques are relevant to understanding, *how* something is presented is not sufficient to account for *what* is presented. Phillips (1985, p. 35) elaborated:

> I am left with the uncomfortable feeling that not only is the proposi-

> tional content of text relevant to [its understanding], but is the central
> issue and one which in discourse analysis is necessarily avoided. . . .
> Moreover, the highest unit of analysis at present generally recognized
> within discourse analysis is the "event".... The unit is, however, not
> very well defined and seems to depend for its recognition on the ana-
> lyst's intuitions in particular circumstances.

In summary, both story grammars and discourse analysis provide *intuitive* insights with regards to the techniques used to *assemble* a text's subject matter. These considerations, however, are not sufficient in order to explain what a text is about, or how it is comprehended. This remark also applies to the recent work of both Riley (1993) on "story structure", and Jacobs and Rau (1993) who proposed an "innovative text interpretation" system that *parses* a hand-coded text without addressing any of the complexities of linguistic comprehension.

2.2.2 Text Linguistics

Story grammars constitute an attempt at characterizing macrostructures in terms of cognitive schemas. These schemas are psychological constructs that orient the reader to the text and guide his interpretation of it, but the use of macrostructures is not systematic, and comprehension cannot be reduced a priori to such a use. For example, Kintsch and van Dijk (1978, p. 373) remarked that

> if a reader's goals are vague, and the text that he or she reads lacks a
> conventional structure, different schemas might be set up by different
> readers, essentially in an unpredictable manner. . . . In many cases, of
> course, people read loosely structured texts with no clear goals in
> mind. The outcome of such comprehension processes, as far as the
> resulting macrostructure is concerned, is indeterminate.

In psychology, several researchers (e.g., Britton, & Black, 1985; Graesser, & Clark, 1985; Haberlandt, 1980; Kintsch, 1980; Kintsch, & van Dijk, 1978; Riley 1993; Rumelhart, 1975; van Dijk, & Kintsch, 1983) have proposed a multitude of different schemas and corresponding comprehenders for textual analysis. These models typically assume that the text–understanding process is controlled by a macrostructure, and rely on complex, purely semantic, mechanisms (e.g., coherence graphs, supervised application of macrorules, etc.) lacking computational principles.

Research on text comprehension in psychology and NLP has been combined under the umbrella term *text linguistics* and generally adopts *schema-based* models. Habel (1983) pointed this:

> Most of the work done . . . involving the investigation of larger textual units, i.e., beyond the level of sentences, has to do with 'stories.' But these 'stories' are different from those texts which literary critics study. . . . Most of the stories are not authentic; i.e., they were produced by the researchers themselves in order to test the system in question. [Also,] they are restricted with respect to several important parameters, among others: the length of the text, the vocabulary used, and the domain of the stories.

The difficulty with schema-based models that use macrostructures to account for a text's structure and subject matter is that ad hoc conceptual constructs (the macrostructures) and algorithms are postulated to fit the text and then used to explain it. In other words, the description of macrostructures is conflated with an explanation of the comprehension process.

For example, let us consider the distinction (Garnham, 1983; Vipond, & Hunt, 1984) between a *story* and a *narrative*. In his work, Wilensky (1982, 1983a, 1983b) introduced the notion of *story points* to try to enforce this dichotomy. Points are schemas that specify those things that a story can be about. They characterize the content that can constitute "reasonable" stories and account for the existence of a story as an item to be communicated. A person tells, or listens to, a story because it has a content of some intrinsic interest. The content that bears this interest value is termed the *point*. A text that does not possess story points is not considered to be a story. Two kinds of points can be distinguished. An *external point* is some goal that a storyteller may have in telling a story (e.g., to entertain). An *internal* or *content point* is some part of the story itself that generates interest. Wilensky's model is limited to content points. Other researchers have focused on external points (e.g., Schank, Collins, Davis, Johnson, Lytinen, & Reiser, 1982). Story points constitute the macrostructures of Wilensky's model of comprehension: They define relevance and, therefore, they implicitly specify what a text may be about (i.e., its subject matter).

BORIS, the program written by Dyer (1983), relies on no less than seventeen different types of conceptual structures. In particular, the same way story points are the macrostructures of Wilensky, Dyer's thematic abstraction units (TAUs) are predefined macrostructures that enumerate the possible gists of a narrative. Winograd and Flores (1986, p. 122) commented:

> If we examine the workings of **BORIS** we find a menagerie of script-like representations that were used in preparing the system for the one specific story it could answer questions about.

All schema-based approaches to text comprehension share common technical problems (see Birnbaum, 1985; Norvig, 1983a, 1983b). In particular, how to decide which schemas are relevant to a particular text remains problematic. Some researchers (e.g., Alba, & Hasher, 1983; Thorndike, & Yekovich, 1980) have also criticized the corresponding theories of human linguistic memory: Do we indeed store schemas or are they merely a methodological artifact?

Text linguistic models of understanding all view a text as consisting of a coherent sequence of sentences. *Coherence* is a *semantic* relation; that is, it applies to meaning; *cohesion* is a *structural* one (i.e., it applies to the symbols). From this viewpoint, schema-based models are primarily semantic approaches to language and meaning. In particular, though exceptions exist (e.g., Lytinen, 1984), schema-based text linguistics models have generally ignored the role of syntax during comprehension (e.g., Dyer, 1983; van Dijk, & Kintsch, 1983).

In a coherent text, each sentence is considered as expressing one or more ideas. Coherence of the text means that these ideas are related one to another and "make sense" together. Often, these relations are conditional: One idea will make another possible, probable (i.e., *expected*) or necessary. *Local coherence* allows the reader to perceive parts of the sequence of sentences as a set of related ideas; *global coherence* emphasizes the notion of a text as a whole, and thus is directly related to subject matter. It is generally agreed that to preserve the local impression of coherence, the reader must constantly use prior knowledge to infer the implicit information that is necessary to "bridge" from one sentence to another. Graesser and Clark, who used the term *bridging inferences* (1985, pp. 28–30), remarked that there is a consensus regarding the existence of such inferences. Consequently, several taxonomies have been proposed in psychology (e.g., Graesser, & Clark, 1985, pp. 17–32; Graesser, & Kreuz, 1993, Table 1; Rickheit, Schnotz, & Strohner, 1985) and in artificial intelligence (e.g., Norvig, 1987, chapter 2) for bridging inferences. A survey of these references will demonstrate the multitude of different models proposed even for a specific type of bridging inference (e.g., temporal and causal ones).

Let me illustrate this notion of bridging inference using one of Wilensky's (1983b) examples:

Example 2.2.2.1 *Willa was hungry. She picked up the Michelin guide.*

Here is a possible sequence of bridging inferences assumed to be necessary to understand these sentences:

1. The word "hungry" represents an instance of the *concept* HUNGER.

2. HUNGER creates the *goal* of EATING.

3. The EATING goal must be satisfied by the EATING *plan*.

4. The EATING plan requires knowing the location of FOOD.

5. FOOD is available at a RESTAURANT.

6. EATING at a RESTAURANT requires finding one.

7. The MICHELIN GUIDE satisfies the goal of finding a RESTAU-RANT's location.

In fact, this sequence could be even more fine-grained, and by no means are bridging inferences limited to this type of inference. The point is that bridging inferences are the rules of composition of schema-based approaches: The meaning of a word is determined by the set of (syntactic and semantic) schemas it refers to, and the meaning of a larger linguistic element is determined by the rules of composition (i.e., the bridging inferences) used to combine the schemas referred to by the words that form this linguistic element.

With respect to bridging inferences, existing computational schema-based models of text comprehension can be partitioned into two principal categories: The first uses models in which bridging inferences are predefined in schemas (e.g., Cullingford, 1978; DeJong, 1982; Dyer, 1983; Lebowitz, 1980, 1988; Schank, 1972, 1982). In this case, understanding is reduced to *matching* the input against an a priori set of schemas, but few schema-matching models have schemas that account for the global coherence and gist of a text. Generally, schema-matching models can process only texts that closely match their schemas, and they fail badly unless there is a close match. For example, Mooney and DeJong (1985), after pointing out that their **GENESIS** system does not handle syntax nor expectations, added:

> Since **GENESIS** does not conduct a complete search for an explanation, it is incapable of 'understanding' narratives which have large gaps and do not suggest known schemas.

Recognizing these flaws, Kass (1986) and Leake and Owens (1986) proposed a system, **SWALE**, that "learns" schemas by modifying old ones in order to understand "anomalous" events in stories. Like all programs in the Schankian tradition (see Schank, 1982), **SWALE** heavily relies on the notion of "anomaly" (e.g., expectation or goal failure) and failure-driven memory. In fact, **SWALE** consists of a schema-matching model in which some schemas are "meta–schemas" used to *tweak* (i.e., modify) simpler ones. (The tweaking schemas cannot modify other tweaking schemas). Leake (1989) used the notion of anomaly to develop **ACCEPTER**, yet another schema-based story understanding program, which uses gradual anomaly detection strategies.

More recently, Ram and Leake (1991) "demonstrate[d] that syntactic approaches are insufficient to capture important differences in [text] explanations, and propose instead that choice of the 'best' explanation should be based on an explanation's utility for the explainer". This concept of utility is rooted in the notion of a reader's *knowledge goals* (Ram, 1990b, 1991; Ram, & Hunter, 1991; Ram, & Leake, 1991), which constitute one of the two types of macrostructures of the **AQUA** system, which also uses *explanation patterns*. As with **SWALE** and **ACCEPTER**, **AQUA** can "learn" schemas (Bhatta, & Ram, 1991; Cox, & Ram, 1991). Thus it departs from other more traditional case-based systems (e.g., Hammond, 1986, 1989; Kolodner, 1988). Ram (1990a) explained:

> Case-based reasoning and learning programs deal with the issue of using past experiences or *cases* to understand, plan for, or learn novel situations. . . . The intent . . . is to avoid the effort involved in re-deriving these lessons, explanations or plans by simply reusing the results from previous cases. However, this process assumes that past cases are well understood and provide 'good' lessons to be used for future situations. This assumption is usually false when one is learning about a novel domain, since cases encountered previously in this domain might not have been understood completely. Instead it would be reasonable to assume that the reasoner would have gaps in the knowledge represented by these cases.
>
> Even if past cases are not well understood, they can still be used to guide processing in new situations. However, in addition to using past cases to understand the new situation, a reasoner can also learn more about the old case itself, and thus improve its understanding of the domain. . . . [We] describe a case-based story understanding system that retrieves past explanations from situations already in memory, and uses them to build explanations to understand novel situations encountered in newspaper stories about terrorism. The system learns in an incremental manner, by filling in the gaps in the retrieved explanation that is being used as a precedent in understanding the new situation.

The approach of **AQUA** epitomizes what Norvig (1989) called "a strong method", introducing complex symbolic representational mechanisms and schema-matching sequential algorithms to recognize specific classes of inferences. The immediate disadvantage of these models is that new algorithms and data structures have to be created every time a knowledge structure is proposed.

Rejecting methods tuned to process a particular set of knowledge structures, the other group of schema-based models builds and evaluates inference chains at reading time (e.g., Alterman, 1985; Charniak, 1983; Granger, Holbrook, & Eiselt, 1983; Martin, 1989; Norvig, 1987; Rieger, 1975; Riesbeck, & Martin, 1985; Wilensky, 1983b). The basic strategy for inference chaining consists of generating chains (or paths) of bridging inferences at reading time and somehow evaluating these paths to decide which provide a "good" explanation. For example, Wilensky's **PAM** program attempts "to match inputs to known goals [and plans] of the actor, and to backward-chain to these goals if they [can't] be matched directly" (Kass, 1986).

Inference chaining is based on *marker-passing* architectures (see Anderson, 1983): Given a semantic representation of the next input, *markers* are passed from each concept of this representation to adjacent nodes, following the links of the semantic network specified by the knowledge base. Markers start out with a given amount of marker activation or energy, and are spread through the network, spawning new markers with less energy, stopping when the energy value reaches a minimum. In other words, a *spreading activation* mechanism (Hendler, 1987, 1989) underlies such architectures. From this perspective, marker-passing systems constitute models of associative semantic memory in which the information (i.e., the markers) exchanged between the elements of memory is either very simple (e.g., Fahlman, 1979; Granger, Eiselt, & Holbrook, 1986), or complex (possibly including control information) (e.g., Charniak, 1983, 1986a, 1986b; Hirst, 1987).

Typically, markers are complex information structures from which the path to the original concept, that is, the concept that initiated the passing, can be requested. When two or more markers are passed to the same node, a marker collision occurs. For each such collision, the associated path consists of one half originating from the initial representation, and one half that leads to the inferred node. Each collision denotes a *possible* inference. Therefore, the path associated with each collision must be *evaluated* according to some fixed a priori criteria that cause the inference to be either made, rejected, or even deferred. For example, Norvig (1987, 1989) presented a model of text comprehension, **FAUSTUS,** based on a marker-passing algorithm that detects six general classes of "valid" inferences. Such systems typically combine a parallel semantic network for spreading activation with an inherently sequential path evaluator for inference creation: Through the propagation of markers, paths corresponding to inferences (Charniak, 1986b) are constructed in the semantic network and submitted to the path evaluator. Some inference-chaining models proceed directly from Wilensky's **PAM** in that they specify the knowledge required for the evaluation of paths in schemas (e.g., the six inference classes of **FAUSTUS**). In other words, the path evaluator is merely a pattern matcher. Others (e.g., Charniak, & Goldman, 1988; Hobbs, Stickel, Martin, & Edwards, 1988; Hobbs, Stickel, Appelt, & Martin, 1993; Pollack, & Pereira, 1988; Stallard, 1987) postulate a path checker module that provides a formal truth-based algorithm for evaluating inference chains. Thus, such inference-chaining systems typically suffer from the computational inefficiency of either having to sequentially consider a large, if not unmanageable, number of inferences suggested by their semantic network, or to depend on an intractable evaluation process (e.g., abduction).

To address this problem, Yu and Simmons (1989) introduced the notion of *constrained* marker passing. In essence, markers carry within themselves patterns defining "legal" paths. Nodes in the network use these complex markers to immediately eliminate potential paths that do not partially match these patterns. In other words, the evaluation process is distributed over the nodes. In the same vein, Berg (1987) proposed an enhanced parallel semantic network with nodes that have the ability to change links and add new nodes to the network. Nodes are activated by the energy spreading through the underlying network eliminating the need for a centralized controller/evaluator. Spreading activation is also the basis for a simple conceptual analyzer, which does not scale up to text understanding.

The representational schemes of these models vary considerably. For example, abandoning the simple semantic network used in **NEXUS** (Alterman, 1985) and **FAUSTUS**, **WIMP3** (Charniak, & Goldman, 1988) uses, instead, frame-like structures mixed with probabilities, whereas **TACITUS** (Hobbs, et al., 1988) relies on Prolog rules combined with costs and weights. In other words, inference chaining still leaves the door open to arbitrarily complex data structures.

Finally, with respect to text comprehension, it is important to notice that inference-chaining models are generally limited to local coherence and do not address the problem of the perception of global coherence and subject matter.

2.2.3 Lexical Statistics

The basic problem with the methodologies reviewed above is that either they are restricted to the local scale, or they arbitrarily specify a set of a priori gists. Some researchers resort instead to a *knowledge-free* statistical approach to subject matter. For example, Skousen (1985) took an anti-rule standpoint in order to motivate an approach to analogy based on *probabilities of use* extracted from an extensive data set derived from actual language data. Such a strategy, however, has the disadvantage of not scaling up to the problems of text comprehension.

Similarly, in computer-assisted literary analysis, the fundamental postulate of *lexical statistics* is that the choice of vocabulary in a text is largely a function of subject matter. More precisely, researchers in lexical statistics assume that the distribution of lexical patterns over large amounts of text directly correlates to subject matter (e.g., Ide, 1986; Muller, 1977; Phillips, 1985).

In the simplest form of lexical statistics, the patterns are individual words, and the statistics are limited to frequency counts. This technique is problematic. For example, a certain word may be repeated ad nauseam in one chapter of a book without having any major impact on the perception of the subject matter of the whole text. In other words, the problem inherent to any straightforward frequency-count approach is that there is not sufficient justification to correlate frequency of occurrence to subject matter. Conversely, a strictly distributional approach, that is, one that measures the distribution of a pattern over a text, is also inadequate, because a certain lexical pattern may appear throughout a text and yet not often enough to affect aboutness. Thus, researchers in lexical statistics typically use a combination of both frequency of occurrence and distribution. This methodology is taken to be more meaningfully reflective of the subject matter of a text than the consideration of either characteristic alone.

In order to *interpret* the results of such statistical analyses, researchers require the absolute probability of use of each pattern. For example, a word with low absolute probability of use need not appear as often as one with high probability to be marked as relevant. The notion of probability of use, however, is problematic. Consider Muller's (1977, p. 46) warning:

> The notion of probability of use should be applied only to a lexis of
> situation, and not to the lexis of the individual, still less to the lexis of
> the collectivity.

In other words, "the notion of an individual word, without regard for its context, as the identifiable signifier for a particular concept or meaning is problematic" (Ide, 1986). (This fundamental observation is not restricted to lexical statistics but, as we shall see in the next section, concerns the whole information-processing paradigm.) Because lexical statistics operates at the lexical level of analysis, the notion of *situation* (or equivalently, *context*) must be defined only in terms of lexical items. Consequently, the concepts of *node*, *span*, and *collocation* are introduced (Phillips, 1985, pp. 43–44):

> The *node* refers to the lexical item in the focus of attention, *span*

> relates to the number of items in the immediate [linear] context of the
> node and *collocation* is the term used to denote a common co-occur-
> rence of items within a given span, that is, the joint occurrence of a
> node and a particular *collocate*.

With regards to the notion of span, Phillips (1985) remarked that "it is crucial
to have a clear idea of how far the "influence" of a word extends into its syn-
tagmatic environment since this determines the limits within which patterns of
association are to be sought. It was found that a span setting of four orthographic words on either side of the node yields optimum results".

The immediate difficulty with lexical statistics is that the determination of
its analytical categories (i.e., the nature and length of the lexical patterns to be
scrutinized) is typically carried out by hand. In other words, the task of identifying patterns that refer to a common concept or theme ultimately depends
on the intuitions of an expert. The interpretation of the statistical results also
rests on an expert, and, most importantly, lexical statistics presents the problem of ignoring subtle (semantic) relations among the words of a text that may
significantly affect the perception of subject matter. For example, neither pronoun comprehension (Hirst, 1981; Stevenson, 1986) nor lexical disambiguation can be tackled without some semantic "knowledge", as we discuss later.

In summary, in dealing only with the *surface text*, that is, with the stream
of characters that constitutes the text, lexical statistics is inherently restricted
to analyses of the frequency and distance between configurations of lexical
items. The point I want to stress is that lexical statistics consists in an a posteriori *knowledge-free analysis* of a text and thus cannot serve as a cognitive
model of text comprehension. For this reason, I do not discuss this methodology any further.

2.2.4 Other Information-Processing Approaches

2.2.4.1 Other Approaches

For completeness, I briefly discuss two other approaches to linguistic comprehension, but I ignore more domain-dependent approaches such as the one of
Appelt, Hobbs, Bear, Israel and Tyson (1993) who claimed that "information
extraction should not be addressed by a general text understanding system".
(Instead, these authors restrict linguistic processing to the use of non-deterministic finite state languages, ignoring altogether the psychology of reading.)

First, concerning *probabilistic interpretation* (see Charniak, 1994), Wu
(1993a) wrote:

> Probabilistic methods for language interpretation have recently come

to the fore, spurred by developments in uncertain reasoning and statistical linguistics. [P]robalistic methods are computationally expensive in domains with complex dependencies like natural language[. Existing] methods fall into two main categories with respect to the type of concession made for computational feasibility. On the one hand are methods that sacrifice the expressiveness of the language in which constraints are represented. On the other hand are methods that restrict precedence ordering of dependencies between constraints. . . Methods of the first category do not permit expressing compositional constraints. Examples are Markov models and stochastic context free grammars. . . It is also possible to view PDP models that have probabilistic interpretations as members of this category. [Members of the second group] (e.g., Goldman, & Charniak, 1990) are based on Bayesian belief networks.

Difficulties that arise with this second category are discussed in Wu (1993b). In essence, a priori knowledge is used to restrict the number of potential inferences.

To address the flaws of existing methods, Wu (1993a) suggested an approach that allows

a fully compositional frame representation, which permits co-indexed syntactic constituents and/or semantic entities filling multiple roles. In addition the knowledge base contains probabilistic information encoded by marginal probabilities on frames. These probabilities are used to specify typicality of real-world scenarios on the one hand, and conventionality of linguistic usage patterns on the other.

The "thematic role system" of this model is developed in yet another paper (Wu, 1993c). A closer look at this work reveals an architecture that relies on complex nested schemas, which have no correlation with the actual input sentence. Indeed, as is too often the case with sophisticated representational schemes, a pre-processor is required.

Beyond this dependence on arbitrarily complex structures, Wu's approach suffers from the same problems of any probabilistic approach to text comprehension, namely,

1. it is not clear that it can address global coherence and subject matter without postulating a priori schemas of interpretation;

2. it relies on probabilities whose determination is question-begging as suggested in our previous discussion of lexical statistics with respect to the usage of linguistic patterns.

In contrast, Delisle (1993) adopted a *semi-automatic* approach to the processing of technical texts. More specifically,

> sentence syntax is the basis for organizing the semantic relations in **TANKA**, a project that aims at acquiring knowledge from technical text. Other hallmarks include: an absence of precoded domain-specific knowledge, significant use of public-domain generic linguistic information sources, involvement of the user as a disambiguating agent, and learning meaning representations during text processing. These elements shape the objective of the project: train a text processing system to propose correct semantic interpretations to the user. A three-level model of sentence semantics, including a comprehensive case system, provides the framework for its representations.

In essence, a complex parser first analyzes the input text. Whenever the input is structurally ambiguous (i.e., it does not match one of the a priori rules of parsing, or it matches several), the user is asked to select the correct interpretation. The system learns this choice and proceeds with the rest of the text.

The semantic interpretation strategy, which is further detailed in Delisle, Copeck, Szpakowicz and Barker (1993) and Barker and Szpakowicz (1994), is similar. It rests on an elaborate case system which extends the work of Fillmore (1968), though case systems have always been controversial (see Somers, 1987, chapters 7 through 9), as we will see later in this chapter. Again, whenever the case module fails, it asks the user for help and "learns" the answer. Therefore, such a system is not fully automated, only semi-automatic.

With respect to text comprehension, the fundamental drawback of this system is that it does not address the problem of inference, and thus, text understanding per se. In fact, it is mainly a large parser whose corresponding semantic module consists of a multitude of ad hoc rules and algorithms. If we momentarily forget its semi-automatic nature, **TANKA** epitomizes the traditional approach to natural language processing (Allen, 1987):

1. It is a mainly a sentential system.

2. The syntax module works first and produces a parse tree.

3. The semantic module first carries out a case analysis based on the parse tree.

4. Some sort of propositional analysis is eventually carried out.

As is often the case with such systems, there is no consideration for ill-formed input, figurative language, lexical disambiguation, and so forth.

2.2.4.2 On the Relevance of Formal Approaches

Lee and Moldovan (1991) claimed that knowledge processing requires inheritance, recognition, classification, unification, probabilistic reasoning, and learning. Several of these processes lend themselves to mathematical methods, but Manaster-Ramer (1992) attacked the relevance of mathematical methods (e.g., Partee, Meulen ter, & Wall, 1990) for natural language processing.

It is too often forgotten that formal logic is a mathematical artifact. Indeed, the reduction of linguistic units to propositions, that is, to expressions in some formal logic-based language, is pervasive to a multitude of models of linguistic comprehension and text understanding (e.g., Palmer, Passonne, & Weir, 1993; Rossi, 1991; van Dijk, & Kintsch, 1983; for text comprehension; Stabler, 1993, for parsing). Moreover, in the field of knowledge representation (see Brachman, & Levesque, 1985), a plethora of logics have been proposed (e.g., "default" logic, Etherington, & Reiter, 1985; Hwang, & Schubert's [1993] "episodic logic"!).

In this section, I summarize the main arguments against such a reduction. Rastier (1991, pp. 91–93) summarized the dominant position in cognitive science (my translation):

> We are faced with the problem of the correspondence between the linguistic level and the conceptual level. The most widely used approach to solve this matter consists in thinking of the conceptual level as a formal language, the language of thought (Fodor, 1975). It is composed of logical propositions linked by inferences and decomposable into concepts (or words of the mental language). The meaning of words and sentences thus resides in their translation into their corresponding concepts and propositions. The optimists, like Kintsch [1980, 1991, 1994)], claim that the words of natural language correspond almost exactly to those of the mental language[.] The more prudent authors, like Sperber and Wilson [(1986)], emphasize that semantic representations constitute incomplete logical forms, that is, at best, fragmentary representations of thoughts.

> Thus, meaning is simply not considered as one of the dimensions of language. A natural language is reduced to a syntax and a phonology. As Jackendoff [(1983, 1987)] suggests, what we call 'rational thought' consists in computations on conceptual structures that exist independently from language.

> [In the end], natural language is reduced to a pure signifiant [(de Saussure, 1916)]. This fits perfectly in the Aristotelian tradition, continued by Augustine and Aquinas [in which] *vox* denotes the linguistic sign,

> merely a phonetic unit, and *conceptus*, the corresponding representa-
> tion, taken as universal and independent of natural languages. This
> explains why logic has always played the role of semantics. . . . Thus,
> orthodox cognitivism reiterates the principal theses of the Western
> idealist tradition.

At the root of such theory, we find a Chomskyan partitioning of linguistic phenomena into the three separate categories of syntax, semantics, and pragmatics. Despite its dominance in linguistics, Chomsky's approach to language
(1965, 1980, 1982, 1984), which rests on the notion of an innate set of rules
implementing a universal grammar, has been rejected by several researchers
(e.g., Gupta, & Touretsky, 1994; Rastier, 1991; Shanks, 1993). Beyond grammatical considerations, it is his whole approach to language that has been criticized. For example, while respecting this partitioning, the so-called
Californian *cognitive* school (*e.g.*, Lakoff, 1987; Langacker, 1987) substitutes
topological rules for logical forms. Functional linguistics (e.g., Fox, 1989;
Chafe, 1990) constitutes another significant departure from the Chomskyan
viewpoint, as best exemplified by Givón's work on grammar (1993a), coherence (1991, 1992, 1993b), and pragmatics (1989). Moreover, as Rastier (1991)
remarked, the whole comparative approach to linguistics (e.g., Hjelmslev,
1971, 1985) has been widely ignored in North America. The relevance of
propositions for linguistic comprehension has also been rejected from a psychological viewpoint (e.g., Braine, 1978; Graesser, & Clark, 1985; Minsky,
1975; Wagener, & Wender, 1985).

Beyond the distinction between syntax, semantics, and pragmatics, it is
the reduction of meaning to concepts that is problematic. More precisely, the
majority of researchers in cognitive science and artificial intelligence still
assume the supervenience of language, that is, the existence of language as an
artifact subsumed by a conceptual level. Over the years, such a position has
been attacked by researchers from philosophy, linguistics, anthropology, and
other disciplines. For example, Nolan (1994, chapter 3) explicitly rejected the
idea of linguistic supervenience. For her, there are several levels of representation between the perceptual and the conceptual, and it is incorrect to postulate a priori of the conceptual level, of its nature, organization, or modus
operandi (as formal approaches do). Instead, the conceptual level must be
explained in terms of the lower levels and of a learning strategy. From this
viewpoint, Nolan's argument was quite similar to Minsky's (1986) requirement that the "mind" be grounded in "mindless stuff".

In the same vein, Rastier (1991) also rejected linguistic supervenience and
offered a scathing review of propositional approaches to language, which are
typically restricted to the literal meaning of sentences (as opposed to texts).

Montague (1974) is credited with addressing context, but Rastier remarked that there is quite a long way between trying to reduce context to indices and determining how to set these indices. However, all truth-conditional semantics (including Barwise and Perry's (1983) work on situations) suffer, in his opinion, from the same fundamental flaw, namely, their dependence on a set of *universal* (i.e., language independent, purely mental) concepts, exemplified by Leibniz's search for a *characteristica universalis*, an alphabet of human thoughts. As we see in subsection 2.4.2, this universalist hypothesis is self-defeating for it escapes any validation and invalidation. Furthermore, universalism unavoidably leads to a normative theory of text interpretation, that is, to the notion of an innate ability to obtain the correct interpretation of a text. Rastier explained (1991, p. 160):

> In AI, as in linguistics, the general strategy adopted consists in eliminating interpretations taken to be incorrect, postulating the univocity of the processed text. This rationalist presupposition dates back to the elatic philosophy. We prefer another approach. For an interpretative semantics, the equivocity is a fundamental given. Generally, we must deal with several interpretations. In the best case, we can establish that one interpretation is preferable to all others. In other words, and though all our hermeneutic tradition goes against this conclusion, the meaning of a text does not belong to the order of truth, but of the plausible. Rather than rejecting the interpretations considered incorrect, one thus must hierarchize them, grading their plausibility with respect to a given strategy.

It precisely this rejection of the possibility of the multiple determinations of a text that, in my opinion, ultimately requires abandoning truth-conditional approaches to meaning, a position Minsky (1986) echoed in this observation:

> Formalization has been a disaster. . . Logic as an attempt to understand thinking is just bad psychology. . . . Logic only explains a fraction of adult thinking. Philosophy hasn't reached Freud or Piaget.

The following observation reminds us of the comment of Pascal in his Pensées (in Dreyfus,1992):

> [A]ccustomed to the exact and plain principles of mathematics, and not reasoning till they have well inspected and arranged their principles, mathematicians are lost in matters of perception where the principles do not allow for such arrangement . . . These principles are so fine and so numerous that [one is not] able to demonstrate them in order as in mathematics, because the principles are not known to us in

the same way, and because it would be an endless matter to undertake it. . . Mathematicians wish to treat matters of perception mathematically, and make themselves ridiculous: . . . the mind. . . does it tacitly, naturally, and without technical rules.

2.2.5 Specific Objections to Information-Processing

2.2.5.1 On the Existence of Macrostructures

I have already stated that, within the information-processing paradigm, all cognitive approaches to the perception of subject matter assume the existence of certain global patterns of textual organization that have been called *macrostructures*. The analytical categories and the postulated macrostructures of these approaches stem from a strictly psychological methodology: The schemas, which capture the rules of a given model, are derived from empirical methods. In other words, statistical analysis directs the design of the rules. This is particularly obvious in Dyer's (1983) and Graesser and Clark's (1985) work. Beyond methodological issues (see Haberlandt, 1994), the problem with this approach is that it is not clear that laboratory experiments do not set up an artificial environment that can affect the results. Spiro (1980), for example, argued that if the experimenter tells the reader what he intends to ask after the reading of a text, then the reader may obtain different results for recall and interpretation (also see Mitchell, 1982, pp.102–103). Spiro's conclusions have important repercussions.

Text linguists assume a priori that there is a unique, small, correct set of macrostructures (e.g., Dyer's thematic abstraction units, Lehnert's (1981) plot units). According to them, the perception of subject matter simply consists in finding out which macrostructure(s) the text corresponds to. From this viewpoint, comprehension is *normalized*. Normalization implies an authoritative *expert* who sets the standard, that is, who decides what is normal and what is not, what constitutes a correct interpretation and what does not. In other words, an expert is needed to interpret the results and specify rules from them. Spiro's claim is that the expert can condition the results (that is, how a reader reports his or her comprehension of a text) through the design and control of the experience itself. From this observation, Dillon (1980) simply rejected the existence of macrostructures. For him, only the expert (as opposed to a "natural unconditioned" reader) seeks macrostructures (i.e., rules of interpretation) in a text.

The point to be grasped is that researchers generate rules that may not *directly* apply to comprehension, but rather to an a posteriori or an artificial *expression* of meaning and subject matter. It is important not to confuse information that is actually stored in memory with reconstruction of information on the basis of inferential reasoning (Wagenaar, 1988). Also, the difficulty with the notion of macrostructure stems from the absence of a validation method to guide the specification of rules encoded in a model. This situation is reflected in the following comment from Graesser and Clark (1985, p.1):

> There is widespread disagreement about *what* inferences are generated, *when* inferences are generated, *how many* inferences are generated, and *what knowledge sources* contribute to the generation of inferences.

The recent debate between minimalist and more elaborate theories of inference (Garnham, 1992; McKoon, & Ratcliff, 1992; Singer, Graesser, & Trabasso, 1994), which will be summarized in chapter 11, indeed exemplifies this situation.

Van der Meer (1987, Figure 6, p. 51) made another important remark in arguing that the types of bridging inferences used during comprehension (especially inferences about time as it pertains to the story line) are *not* the ones that researchers in text linguistics have been studying (e.g., causality, consequence, finality, and superordination).

In summary, the existence of a small, correct set of macrostructures on which existing information-processing models of text comprehension depend is problematic.

2.2.5.2 Beyond Literal Meaning: Tractability and Context

I previously stated that, in the framework of the conduit metaphor, a common view holds that a sentence has a literal meaning. Some researchers reject the assumption that obtaining the literal meaning of an utterance is a necessary step on the path to understanding. Gibbs (1984), for example, wrote that "the literal meaning of a sentence is an inadequate place to start figuring out an utterance's meaning". Searle (1979) argued that literal interpretation can only account for the meaning of some sentences. Consider, this example:

Example 2.2.5.2.1 *John quickly cut through the red tape.*

John may literally be cutting a red tape in order to unwrap his Christmas gift, or John may be particularly efficient in his dealings with bureaucracy.

Graesser and Clark (1985, p. 27), reported:

> There has been some debate in psychology about the time course of interpreting the literal meaning of a request versus the intended (illocutionary) meaning of a request. . . . According to one alternative, the

comprehender first interprets the literal meaning and subsequently infers the illocutionary meaning by integrating the literal meaning with the context of the speech act. A second alternative is that the process of constructing a literal meaning and the process of constructing an illocutionary meaning are executed simultaneously. A third alternative is that the illocutionary meaning is directly interpreted and that the literal meaning may not be interpreted in some contexts.

From the above example, it seems that the issue is not limited to requests but, in fact, extends to any utterance whose meaning *may* depend on context (see Dascal, 1989; Gibbs, 1989).

A most fundamental problem hides behind the immediate methodological puzzle: Meaning comes from rules, and it seems that some rules *must* consider context since the *signifiant* and the literal meaning are not enough in certain cases to obtain the *signifié*. It follows that the "single-sentence" paradigm is oversimplified. Consider the following example:

Example 2.2.5.2.2 *It is certainly getting hot in here.*

This sentence has at least four interpretations:

1. **Literal**: It's hot in here.

2. **Speech act**: It's too hot in here, could you open a window.

3. **Ironical speech act**: It's freezing in here; could you close the door.

4. **Figurative**: This discussion is degenerating into a bitter argument.

The example can be understood literally, but this provides no clue as to which interpretation is adequate. The question then is to know where meaning comes from. The conduit metaphor explicitly claims that the meaning is *in* the words, but apparently this is not the case: Words are not enough; we need context. This remark is not limited to the meaning of sentences, but also applies to the meaning of individual words. For example, consider the word *red* in the following idioms:

- Red carpet, red tape, red light, red light district, red meat, red wine, redhead, red herring.

- To see red.

- To be in the red.

- To catch someone red-handed.

In these examples, the meaning of the idiom does not proceed from the individual meanings of its elements; the idiom must be treated as an indivisible semantic whole. The problem then is to recognize an idiomatic meaning from a literal one. For example, as explained above, *red tape* can be taken literally or idiomatically; only context may allow one to discriminate between the two usages.

I want to emphasize that contextual influence on meaning is not restricted to a small set of idioms, but, on the contrary, it permeates language. Consider, for example, this utterance:

Example 2.2.5.2.3 *Wylbur is a pig.*

A dictionary (e.g., Webster, 1981, p. 862) suggests *some* possible interpretations:

- Wylbur is a young swine not yet sexually mature.

- Wylbur is an immoral woman.

- Wylbur is a policeman.

A dictionary, however, does not exhaustively list all possible uses of the word *pig* and, therefore, typically provides an extremely vague definition, such as "one resembling a pig", to account for idiosyncratic uses. Such an analogical definition is problematic because the perception of the *soundness* or *felicity* of an analogy largely depends on the comprehender. Consider, for example, other possible interpretations of the above utterance:

- Wylbur eats like a pig.

- Wylbur is some sort of sexual maniac.

- Wylbur has poor bathing habits.

- Wylbur simply did something I resent.

The contextual view of meaning is associated, in British linguistics, with the name of Firth (1957). For him, language is essentially a social and conventional phenomenon. Text is viewed as the only immediate component of a context of situation that lends itself to analysis. Context of situation, which Firth regarded as the prime analytical category, is an abstraction of a system of relations from the life of humans in society. Firth argued that the complete meaning of a word is *always* contextual. Phillips (1985, p. 14) observed that this leads Firth to the *apparently* extreme position of considering each use of a word in a new context as an occurrence of a new word. Similarly, Firth (1957) remarked:

> An isolated word which does not function in a context of experience
> has little that can be called meaning.

Contextual meaning is highly problematic within the conduit metaphor in which, typically, meaning is decontextualized, and comprehension is reduced to an invariant algorithm that ignores all *subjective* (or equivalently, *private* or *idiosyncratic*) aspects of the act of interpretation itself. Let me justify this observation. Within the information-processing paradigm, it is generally assumed that the meaning of a sentence can be "reasoned out", that is, obtained by means of rules of inference (that can be content-blind, as in the case of modus ponens, or content-dependent as in "if you are hungry, then you need food"). These rules of inference operate on symbols that are taken a priori to be context-dependent (or equivalently, domain-dependent). The difficulty with such an approach is that the postulated rules only have an a posteriori explicative nature. That is, they do not address the problems, first, of deciding which symbols (words and sentences) *may* have a non-literal meaning, and second, of *discriminating* between the several possible contextual meanings of a symbol. In other words, the context (or domain of discourse) is a given, and the issue of recognizing it is altogether bypassed. Some researchers (e.g., Dyer, 1983; Schank, & Abelson, 1977) tackle the problem of contextual meaning by advocating the use of a *scriptal lexicon*, which tries to specify rules of recognition for all possible contexts. This approach is still problematic (Rastier, 1991, p. 156). For example, Birnbaum (1985) remarked:

> No single explanatory inference rule can be expected to attend to all
> the aspects of a situation which might affect the truth or relevance of
> the explanation it offers.

In other words, it is quite frequently (if not always) possible to present an example that violates a context-recognition rule. Therefore, within the conduit metaphor, the problem of contextual meaning is typically transferred to the individual words of a sentence.

The first difficulty with doing that comes from the lack of availability of an accepted *exhaustive* list of meanings for words. Dictionaries constitute one possible source for the definition of words, but Firth (1957) argued vigorously against the view of meaning as somehow "contained" in words that "express" the meanings enshrined against their written forms in dictionaries. Assuming that words have lexical meanings that anyone can access by consulting a dictionary offers only a very partial solution to the problem of meaning, for people seldom use words in such a rigid way, as the preceding examples demonstrate. Moreover, the organization of a dictionary and, consequently, of the lexicon of a model, is problematic (Miller, 1985). Ultimately, we require an expert to *standardize* meaning, that is, to specify an a priori lexicon. This is a formidable, if not impossible task. "Abstract" words such as *love* and *freedom* generally have vague definitions. Indeed, the definition of *language* that is quoted at the beginning of this chapter uses the term *idea*, whose meaning has been debated by philosophers for centuries (Adler, 1985, chapters 1–3)! (The meanings of the words *meaning* and *understanding* are themselves problematic!) In other words, the *explicit, precise* definition of certain words seems very difficult—and impossible when we acknowledge that, despite the existence of dictionaries, the *actual uses* of a multitude of "concrete" words seem to escape characterization. Consider, for example, the verb *fly* in the following hypothetical dialogue (Regoczei, & Plantinga, personal communication):

How can you tell a bird from another animal? *Birds fly.*

Do birds fly all the time? *No.*

Do little chicks fly? *No.*

Do dogs fly? *No.*

Do dogs on airplanes fly? *Well, yes...*

Do I fly? *No.*

Do I fly when I am flying to Montreal. *Well, yes...*

Do flying squirrels fly? *Yes.*

Do bats and insects fly? *Yes.*

Does the above dialogue merely play on two *clear, distinct* meanings of the word *fly* or two *shades* of a same meaning (Waltz, & Pollack, 1985)? Regardless of the answer, Rastier (1991) argued this cannot be the case in parataxic sentences such as these:

Example 2.2.5.2.4 *A dime is a dime.*

Example 2.2.5.2.5 *Even when punishing his child, a father remains a father.*

In each instance, the words "dime" and "father" has the context determine their meaning:

1. The first occurrence of "dime" emphasizes the small amount of money this word denotes.

2. The second occurrence of "dime" highlights the fact that any amount of money is important.

3. The first occurrence of "father" emphasizes the role of a father as an educator.

4. The second occurrence of "father" highlights the benevolent facets of the word.

Also, against the possibility of an exhaustive list of well-defined concepts, Sowa (1984, p. 346) observed that "even the boundary between [a] tree and [its] environment may be indistinct: the tree may have started as a sprout from the root of another tree and may still share a root system with its parent and siblings". Does a tree growing from another one constitute a different tree? Generally, the semantic distinctions we make are not adequate in "boundary cases". The notion of *death* in its common, medical, and legal uses exemplifies this remark.

The need to avoid an a priori *static* classification of the uses of words is echoed in the following four principles of language taken from Odell's (1984) list of twelve:

• *Open Texture*: Even if we legislate sets of necessary and sufficient conditions to govern what [words] mean, we can't be sure that our legislations preclude the existence of contexts where we will be uncertain what our words mean. that is, we can still *imagine* cases where we wouldn't know whether or not a given word applied.

• *Creativity*: We use language in inventive and innovative ways to amuse, clarify, convince, annoy, insult, and so forth. Punning, poetry, word play, and pre-eminent prose all depend on our ability to use language with a certain impunity.

- *Family Resemblance*: [(Wittgenstein, 1953)]: What most, if not all, general empirical terms *mean* in natural language, as opposed to what we might *mean by* them on specific occasion, cannot be specified formally, that is, in terms of necessary and sufficient conditions.

- *Non-Functionality*: What a given string of words means is not a function of the formal characteristics that string possesses. "Why not?" can be used to make a request, even though its *form* is that of a question.

In summary, it is futile to hope that an exhaustive list of all possible contextual uses of an extended set of linguistic elements may be achievable. As stated by Firth (1957) and reiterated by Rastier (1991), such a utopia denies language one of its fundamental features, namely, the dynamicity of meaning, the diachronic nature of meaning and of interpretation (see section 2.4). In the end, as Plantinga (personal communication) put it: "Meaning is a gerund".

The second problem with having to resort to such an exhaustive lexicon is that it leads to an inescapable trade-off between representational blindness and algorithmic intractability, which I now briefly explain. On the one hand, all possible (literal, idiomatic, and figurative) meanings of a word must be stored in some explicit representations (either in the schemas of the lexicon or in the rules of the understanding algorithm). Even if we restrict ourselves to the definitions given in a dictionary, each word will "point" (or refer) to a large number of meanings. On the other hand, if a word does not point to a small number of meanings, the model will be faced with an intractable number of inferences (i.e., compositions of meanings) at understanding time.

In a computational framework, intractability is totally unacceptable. It follows that the implemented models of linguistic comprehension restrict the number of meanings of each word in one way or another. Schema-matching models simply use small lexicons. Inference-chaining models typically postulate the sort of context-blind interpretation rules (e.g., Wilensky's (1983b) *meta-plans*) that I have criticized above. The difficulty with such solutions to the problem of contextual meaning is that they lead to an *artificial* (i.e., fixed-patterned) language outside of which "comprehension" is impossible. Though in computer science it is usually the case that the human user must resort to an artificial language to communicate with the machine, this is not acceptable in the case of *natural* language processing. Winograd and Flores discussed this issue at length and concluded that models that legislate contextual meaning merely create "a narrowed microworld that reflects the blindness of [their] representation[s]" (1986, p. 123).

The trade-off between intractability (resulting from an exhaustive lexicon) and blindness (of the representations used in models that considerably limit contextual meaning) is best exemplified by a most counterintuitive feature of all schema-based models: The more these models "know", the slower they become. This is in direct contradiction to the commonly accepted assumption that the more familiar an input is, the quicker it should be processed.

Recapitulating, I remark that the consideration of the role of context appears to lead to a tremendous increase in the number of rules or schemas that an information-processing model must specify. In turn, the resulting increase in processing complexity leads to a choice between inherent intractability and representational blindness (i.e., oversimplicity).

2.2.5.3 Vygotsky's Conclusion

Luria, one of the prominent neuroscientists of the twentieth century once wrote (as reported in Cole, John-Steiner, Scribner, & Souberman, 1978):

> Vygotsky was a genius. After more than half a century in science, I am unable to name another person who even approaches his incredible analytic ability and foresight. All my work has been no more than the working out of the psychological theory which he constructed.

It is in this context that the words of Vygotsky (in Cole, et al., 1978) take all their meaning:

> Thought is not expressed in the word, it is realized in it.

2.3 Connectionism and Text Comprehension

2.3.1 On the Existence of Rules: The Connectionist Attack

Even within the information-processing paradigm, the existence of "rules" *appears* to be problematic (Pereira, & Grosz, 1993):

> The debate between rule-based and case-based approaches has been central in AI for at least 20 years. . . . The linguistics and natural language processing communities have been debating between rule-based and principle-based approaches for a similar length of time. This debate. . . . contrasts phrase-structure rule descriptions of natural language syntax in which the rules are typically language specific, with principle-based approaches in which a set of language-independent principles are modulated by certain parameter settings, for

> instance with respect to word order, to characterize particular natural languages. . . . In rule-based systems, generality comes from the choice of descriptive primitives that allow large collections of situations with similar outcomes to be identified and acted upon by rules; in contrast, generality in a case-based system comes from the case retrieval and matching procedures that determine the outcome of a new situation from the outcomes for similar stored cases. . . . While case-based approaches to NLP have drawn much of their inspiration from ideas in cognitive science dealing with the organization of memory and common-sense inference, rule-based approaches have derived mostly from strong traditions in linguistic and formal-language theory.

Within the specific area of text comprehension, this debate is still "raging". For example, one should contrast the rule-based model of Khan, Ahmad, Mahmood and Fatmi (1993) or the abduction strategy of Hobbs, et al., (1993) with the case-based approach advocated by Leake (1993) and Uramoto (1994).

However, in reality, this debate is somewhat artificial, for it merely touches upon the nature and form of the underlying interpretative schemas, not upon their existence per se. All theories of language and meaning that proceed from the conduit metaphor postulate that linguistic comprehension involves *rules of composition* (e.g., grammars, schemas, inference engines, theorem provers) over symbols. From this point of view, these theories consist of a priori symbolic manipulations. Recently, the existence of such *rules of language* and *rules of thought* has been challenged by the connectionist paradigm (see McClelland, & Rumelhart, 1986). However, this is a fundamental debate that symbolic researchers too often quickly dismiss. Consider, for example, the recent special issue of the *Artificial Intelligence* journal on NLP, edited by Pereira and Grosz (1993): It simply ignores connectionist work altogether. Yet, both rule-based (e.g., Rumelhart, 1984) and case-based (e.g., Katz, 1989) accounts of linguistic comprehension have been criticized from a connectionist viewpoint.

The fundamental hypothesis of connectionism (also called "neuronal modeling"), a basic metaphor rooted in the body, is that if we acknowledge that the human brain is involved in the act of comprehension, then the consideration of its anatomy and physiology may provide helpful insights for the design of a computational model of cognition (Feldman, 1984, 1985a, 1985b). All neuronal models proceed from the so-called "biological constraint", which consists of the following observations about the brain:

1. Neurons are orders of magnitude slower than current electronic devices.

2. Neurons exchange "simple" non-symbolic signals.

3. Neurons carry out "simple" computations.

Within this framework, Feldman (1984) summarized the connectionist attack on the information-processing paradigm:

> One consequence of taking [biological] computational constraints seriously is a profound reservation on the ultimate viability of many of the information-processing models currently dominating the field. Any paradigm that depends on central control, data structures or symbol manipulation presents the problem of having no obvious reduction to the underlying computational system. Researchers motivated by biological constraints have tended to work on positive results rather than argue paradigms and have been exploiting insights gained through traditional approaches. But it does seem likely that many problems that appear intractable in conventional information-processing paradigms will be accessible in a more natural formalism[.]

Indeed, several connectionist models (e.g., Waltz, & Pollack, 1985) appear to handle, for example, contextual meaning in a most natural way, which contrasts with the trade-off inherent to schema-based approaches.

Connectionist models have been suggested for a multitude of tasks (see Levine, 1991), including several aspects of cognition: (e.g., Schweickert, Guentert, & Hersberg, 1989, for short-term memory modeling). Several recent collections of papers (e.g., Barnden, & Pollack, 1991; Clark, & Lutz, 1992; Hinton, 1991; Levine, & Aparicio, 1994) illustrate eloquently this variety. In particular, several facets of linguistic comprehension have been tackled, including

1. **parsing**: e.g., Selman, 1985; Miikkulainen, 1993a,

2. **lexical disambiguation**: e.g., Bookman, 1987; Cottrell, 1984, 1989; Kawamoto, 1993; Mayberry, & Miikkulainen, 1994; McClelland, & Kawamoto, 1986; Selman, & Hirst, 1987; Waltz, & Pollack; 1985, and

3. **inferences**: e.g., Eiselt, & Granger, 1987.

Several other models for NLP are presented in Reilly and Sharkey's (1992) recent monograph, though none address text understanding per se. Miikkulainen (1993b, chapter 13) offers an extensive and excellent survey of all connectionist work on linguistic comprehension. Therefore, in the next subsection, I mainly summarize his observations and take a closer look at existing connectionist models for text comprehension.

2.3.2 Connectionist NLP

2.3.2.1 Localist NLP

Recall from the Preface that the "structured" or "local" connectionists represent knowledge over a set of named nodes, whereas the distributed (PDP) connectionists represent knowledge at the subsymbolic level, that is, as patterns of activation across unnamed nodes. Also, structured connectionism typically does not address learning. Localist techniques have been applied to parsers, sentence generation, Chomsky's government and binding theory (1982), and selection of scripts (e.g., Bookman, & Alterman, 1991) (see Miikkulainen (1993b, section 13.3) for more details).

Several researchers argue that localist architectures ultimately reduce to a symbolic technique (Derthick, & Plaut, 1986). Miikkulainen (1993b, section 13.3) wrote:

> They are characterized by spreading activation, a general constraint satisfaction method for retrieval, variable binding, and inferencing. In spreading activation, continuous values are propagated through weighted links between nodes[.] Initial activity is supplied by instantiating some of the nodes, for example corresponding to the words in the input text. The activity spreads automatically through weighted links, and eventually settles into a stable pattern. The set of the most highly activated nodes constitutes the interpretation of the input. The propagation mechanism is simple and general, but also weak because it lacks structure. Numerous spurious paths are created and often result in severe crosstalk problems.

The attentive reader will have recognized in this description, the same mechanism that underlies inference-chaining models. Indeed, some researchers have recently attempted to combine the advantages of spreading activation and marker passing (see 2.3.2.3).

Closer to "pure" spreading activation, Lange (1993) presented **ROBIN**, a non-determinist network similar to the one of Waltz and Pollack (1985). Simple markers called signatures, implemented as real numbers, uniquely identify their source. This allows the system to implement variable bindings and complex inferences, something that simpler spreading activation networks cannot do. There is no need for a path evaluator: The nodes of the best interpretation in a given context become the most highly-activated. Crosstalk is eliminated using "gated" links: Only signatures that match the prototypical fillers may propagate through the gate. This is quite similar in spirit to Yu and Simmons's (1989) approaches (which was previously discussed), and thus suffers from the same fundamental problem: The gates constitute a priori rules of interpretation. **ROBIN** also relies on rules of interpretation prespecified in nodes of the network (e.g., inside-of-opaque, inside-of-dishwasher, etc.).

A very similar system, which uses a phased clock to implement variable bindings, is presented in Ajjanagadde and Shastri (1989, 1991), Anandan, Letovsky, & Mjolsness (1989), and Shastri and Ajjanagadde (1993). This model, however, restricts itself to the problem of inference and does not tackle other facets of text understanding such as word sense disambiguation and reference resolution. Sun (1989, 1993) also described a comparable system.

Bookman (1992, 1994) introduced a two-tier model of semantic memory specifically for text comprehension. A relational tier captures a set of dependency relationships between concepts. The analog semantic feature (ASF) tier represents common or shared knowledge about the concepts in the relational tier, expressed as a set of statistical associations. Much like **ROBIN**, his system, named **LeMICON**, tackles most facets of text comprehension, except syntax. Thus neither model offers a unified approach to syntax and semantics. **LeMICON** has, however, the advantage of tackling both automatic acquisition of knowledge from on-line text corpora and integration of a text's interpretation into the knowledge base, as overviewed later. In fact, **LeMICON** constitutes a very rich NLP model (the richest in my opinion) in that it addresses several problems that are typically ignored by others. For example, it models the loss of information in working memory, the time-course of inferences, as well as their construction process. In other words, **LeMICON** takes into account several psycholinguistics theories. In particular, it subscribes to Haberlandt and Graesser's (1990) "delayed-integration" hypothesis, which will be discussed in Part III.

Bookman (1992, pp. 78–79, 182, 196) provided several tables comparing his system to other text comprehension architectures, including the original prototype of **IDIoT**. Not surprisingly, **LeMICON** ends up with the best "mark", and thus deserves the detailed review that follows.

ASFs (Bookman, & Alterman, 1991) are derived from Waltz and Pollack's (1985) notion of "microfeatures". Yet they are different both in how the features are chosen and how they function. In essence, ASFs are the prespecified conceptual *primitives* of the system. For **LeMICON**, they are based on and organized according to the conceptual categories and classification used by a thesaurus, with some additional ASFs added to account for the specific domain at hand. Bookman (1992, pp. 29–30) also stressed that ASFs differ from both the semantic markers of Katz and Fodor (1963) and the microfeatures of PDP models (see McClelland, & Rumelhart, 1986):

> If concepts are represented in terms of components, one choice is in terms of qualitative components called features. An alternate choice is in terms of quantitative components called dimensions. For example, the concept of *automobiles* could be represented in terms of a few scaling dimensions, such as degree of luxury[.] Alternatively, the automobile concept could be represented by a set of features: e.g., for Yugo these might include vehicle, transportation, and foreign. Features can be classified as structured, i.e., there exists an expressed relationship between the features, or nonstructured, i.e., as a simple list of features describing the concepts. For example, in characterizing *bachelorhood*, Katz and Fodor (1963) describe the *bachelor* concept using a simple list of features: single, male, etc. In contrast, the *arch* concept . . . is an example of a structured object, consisting of the features (lintel and two posts) and the relationships between the features (e.g., the lintel is supported by the two posts). A further characteristic of features is that they can be either analog or binary. An analog property measures the feature's strength in association to the parent concept. In contrast, a binary property determines if the feature is present or absent.

> The ASFs used in this research were chosen based on the category structure of Roget's thesaurus (3rd edition, 1962) [which] can be roughly described by eight classes: abstract relations, space, physics, matter, sensation, intellect, volition and affections, with each class further subdivided into finer classifications. . . The total number of classifications in a thesaurus is extremely large[.] I chose a subset of 458 of these classifications to represent ASFs. . . My purpose is only to demonstrate that ASFs are useful. I hypothesize that people have idiosyncratic but probably redundant sets.

Thus, each concept in **LeMICON** is associated with a background frame consisting in a vector of 458 ASFs (Bookman, 1992, p. 237). Furthermore, each of the 17 stock market stories processed by the system is pre-parsed into ASF clauses. For example (Bookman, 1992, p. 237),

Clause 1: (decline (OBJ stock market) (VALUE 50 points) (TIME yesterday))
corresponds to the sentence:

The stock marker declined 50 points yesterday,
with the proviso that "the actual input consists of this parsed input, but with each concept and its filled case slots replaced by their respective learned ASF encodings" (Bookman, 1992), where an encoding is a vector of dimension 458.

There are three problems with such a preprocessing strategy. First, any non-automated translation process is arbitrary and typically eliminates important facets of comprehension (such as structural ambiguity, see chapter 10). Second, both the structure of the input format and the specific primitives (e.g., *OBJ*, *VALUE* and *TIME*) used in the actual input must be known a priori and thus be embedded in the system. In other words, the processing strategy relies on a fixed prespecified representational scheme that makes specific epistemological commitments. Third, it appears that the model has poor, if not intractable, space complexity with respect to the size of the input (see Shastri, 1993). Put another way, the amount of space required by the architecture to represent the input seems to "explode" with the size of the input, because each concept requires a vector of dimension 458.

Bookman emphasized (1992, p. 32) that the analog values of these vectors are learned: "In order to determine the strength of a relationship between each concept and ASF, the information theoretic measure of mutual information was applied to each sentence from an on-line corpus containing approximately 7 million words". More specifically (1992, pp. 130–132):

1. The concepts that form the relational tier are predetermined: **Le-MICON** uses "approximately 100 concepts [that] were chosen based on how representative they were for the given stock market domain".

2. The "mutual information" (read collocation) of each possible pair of these concepts for each paragraph of the large database (namely, the *Wall Street Journal* corpus) is established: "In essence this process encodes the average of all occurring instances of each concept".

3. The strength of the association between two concepts is determined from this analysis.

4. The relationships between the predetermined concepts are implemented in the relational tier.

5. Each ASF is associated with a dictionary tree of related words: "A dictionary tree encodes a concept (e.g., an ASF) with a set of related words, via the relations of synonymy, is related to, as compared to, in contrast to, and antonymy. . . A dictionary tree represents an extension to the ASF "thesaurus classification'".

6. The mutual information between each concept and each of the 458 ASFs is computed.

7. An *ad hoc* algorithm (Bookman, 1992, Figure 6.3) is then used to encode the background frame for each concept.

8. Each concept of the relational tier consists in a prespecified schema defined by the 13 possible case relations (see Fillmore, 1968) known to the system.

The automatic creation of an initial knowledge base is a very attractive idea. However, it seems to ultimately rely on the problematic notion of collocation (as discussed in 2.2.3), and on a set of prespecified primitives, concepts, and case relations, which are not grounded.

With respect to the integration of an interpretation into the system, Bookman explained that there are two situations in which semantic memory is dynamically changed:

> i) If in the input text a concept occurs that is not known to the system, i.e., it does not appear in its semantic memory, then concept is added to semantic memory by linking it to the 'semantically closest' concept there.

> ii) As a result of its processing of a text, **LeMICON** generates two sources of knowledge: a set of compressed ASF trajectories and an interpretation graph. The compressed set of ASF trajectories is a representation of the ASF knowledge **LeMICON** has accumulated ('learned') in working memory as a result of its processing of the text. From the interpretation graph, the conceptual roots are extracted[.] Since the conceptual roots provide the framework, that is, the basic events, of the constructed representation/understanding, they are incorporated into semantic memory. . . as is the information from the compressed ASF trajectories.

Several points need to be made from this description:

1. The integration process relies on prespecified algorithms and notions (such as "closeness". which is, however, mathematically defined, as opposed to being purely symbolic).

2. Working memory is organized in terms of the 13 case relations known a priori to the system.

3. A complex algorithm is required to run the architecture and produce both an interpretation graph and ASF trajectories. These two outputs can then be used by a summarization algorithm. In particular, the "important" concepts of the interpretation are determined with respect to their respective activation level: the "higher" the activation, the more important the concept.

4. An ASF trajectory represents a history of the active ASFs in work-

ing memory.

Thus, in the end, **LeMICON** uses local connectionist representations, but achieves comprehension only by

1. imposing structure upon these representations: Concepts of the relational tier are frames, a type of schema.

2. pre-specifying algorithms, concepts, and other primitives (such as case relations).

2.3.2.2 Specific Objections to Localist NLP

As previously mentioned, "localist" architectures appear to be a constrained form of symbolic architectures. As such, they generally do not address the biological constraint and typically suffer from the problems of other text linguistics approaches (see section 2.2.2). For example:

1. They may depend on complex pre-specified multi-step algorithms (e.g., **LeMICON**).

2. They may embed rules of interpretation in their nodes and/or links (e.g., **ROBIN**).

3. They may rely on an a priori small set of primitives (e.g., **LeMICON**), in much the same way as Schankian models rely on the theory of Conceptual Dependency and its famous few primitives (e.g., *PTRANS, INGEST*, etc.) (see Dyer, 1983, appendix C).

4. They attempt to partially, if not totally, pre-specify the context of each concept (e.g., the strengths of ASF encodings in **LeMICON**).

The main difference between localist architectures and text linguistics models resides in their processing philosophy. Text linguistic (i.e., schema-matching and inference-chaining) systems generally use arbitrarily complex algorithms and data structures. Conversely, local connectionism avoids symbolic algorithms (e.g., for variable binding, matching) and, instead, tries to operate within the limits set by the spreading activation metaphor. This is best exemplified in the work of Lange (1993) and Shastri and Ajjanagadde (1993). In the case of Bookman's (1992) **LeMICON**, it is important to understand that although complex algorithms are used, each step of these algorithms (e.g., establishing conceptual "closeness") generally corresponds to a mathematical, as opposed to an arbitrarily complex, computation. Indeed, Bookman even presented an analysis of the complexity of his model. Thus, local connectionism provides a "standardized" processing framework, which is absent from text linguistics. However, this standardization of the processing model does not entail a complete standardization of the representational schemes used by these models. For example, **LeMICON** uses ASFs, whereas Shastri and Ajjanagadde used rules, and **ROBIN**, frame-like structures. These distinct types of representations differ considerably in terms of epistemological commitments; they are only similar with respect to the way in which they are processed.

To conclude, with the exception of **LeMICON**, which addresses the problem of convergence (Corriveau, 1994c) through the use of a working memory modeling information loss, it appears that most of these systems reduce to inference-chaining models limited to local coherence. In other words, as Bookman (1992, p. 182) observed, most of these models do not scale up to the perception of subject matter.

2.3.2.3 On Hybrid Models

Hybrid models aim at combining the advantages of the symbolic approach with those of PDP and/or of local connectionism. Most of the existing models have been proposed by students of Dyer (e.g., Dolan, Lange, Lee, Nenov, & Sumida). Miikkulainen (1993b, p. 264), another student of Dyer, explained:

> From an engineering point of view hybrid models clearly make sense, because the strengths of the three approaches complement each other. PDP systems capture the implicit statistical regularities in the data, and they are good at learning, associative retrieval, data fusion, generalization, and robust processing. With localist models, it is easy to perform parallel constraint satisfaction. Symbolic systems, on the other hand, can represent and apply rules, schemas, variable bindings, and sequential control naturally. . . . The result is a hybrid model that demonstrates how the PDP components can support higher cognitive functions.

These models typically employ some elements of connectionism within a spreading activation architecture: for example, link weights, activation values, and thresholds (Chun, & Mimo, 1987; Lange, & Dyer, 1989; Lange, Hodges, Fuenmayor, & Belyaev, 1989; Lee, Flowers, & Dyer, 1989), and distributed microfeatures (Hendler, 1989, 1991; Sumida, 1991; Sumida, & Dyer, 1992). These models may rely on complex symbolic data and processes such as complex markers, symbolic variable binding, and heuristics (e.g., rules of composition for paths).

For example, Lange and Wharton (1993) developed **REMIND**, a system that performs both episodic memory retrieval and language understanding with a single spreading activation mechanism.Thus, there is no need for an explicit schema retrieval strategy unlike that found in:

1. case-based approaches, which rely on schema indexing (e.g., Ram, 1990a).

2. analogical retrieval models, which depend on structural comparison (e.g., Thagard, Holyoak, Nelson, & Gochfeld, 1990; Gentner, & Forbus, 1991).

However, **REMIND** involves a preprocessor for syntax and relies on schemas (in the form of the goals and plans of the characters of the text).

Hybrid models have been proposed for several tasks, such as language acquisition (Nenov, 1991) and parsing (Simmons, & Yu, 1990; Jain, 1991). With respect to linguistic comprehension, we shall briefly review the models of Lee (1991), Dolan (1989), and Sharkey (1990).

DYNASTY (Lee, 1991) consists of several separate neural network modules for developing word and event representations, parsing and generating sentences, recognizing goals and plans, and generating inferences. It does not address word sense disambiguation nor syntax. The PDP networks are structured by a complex symbolic architecture, which includes such things as a plan selector, a goal/plan associator, an encoder for case-roles, an action generator, and so forth. Each module is trained individually. Interactions between modules are prespecified and require symbolic control. The goal/plan tree of the system also needs to be represented symbolically. From this viewpoint, **DYNASTY** resembles Dyer's (1983) **BORIS** system, inasmuch as it introduces several complex modules and processes that ultimately rest on the existence of macrostructures (in this case, goals and plans). The advantage of **DYNASTY**, however, is that individual modules are implemented as PDP networks.

The **CRAM** model (Dolan, 1989) reads thematic (schema-based) stories, learns new themes, generates summaries, and gives planning advice for the main character in the story. It does not address word sense disambiguation nor syntax, and obviously relies on the existence of macrostructures. In **CRAM**, the high-level modules are symbolic, whereas the low-level processes such as role binding, schema instantiation, long-and short-term memory are based on PDP techniques.

Finally, Sharkey's (1990) system for processing script-based narratives is based on combining localist representation and relaxation techniques (see Feldman, 1985b) with PDP learning and mapping mechanisms. The work explicitly draws on Van Dijk and Kintsch's (1983) idea of propositional units called macro-units, so named because of their similarity with this author's macropropositions. Macro-units are compacted representations of the lower level propositional representations. Macrostructures are implemented as a localist "scene" (or sequence) network, in which weights are hand-coded. Inferences per se are not addressed. Miikkulainen (1993b, p. 271) commented:

> Although all units are localist representations of actions and scenes, the mapping between them and the mapping of actions into sequences are represented distributively in the weights, making the system an interesting example of the hybrid localist/distributed approach.

From this brief survey, I conclude that hybrid models for text comprehension focus on processing techniques that mix different processing models, but fundamentally follow text linguistic and localist models in either being restricted to local coherence or relying, more or less explicitly, on macrostructures. This dependence on macrostructures is most evident in the "construction-integration" model proposed by Kintsch (1991, 1994).

2.3.2.4 On PDP NLP

Very few PDP models for natural language understanding have been built so far. Miikkulainen (1993b, p. 254) added that "emphasis has been more on demonstrating specific techniques than on contributing to the understanding task". Moreover, of those models that do address linguistic comprehension, most have focused on specific tasks (e.g., parsing), and in particular, on lexical disambiguation (Kawamoto, 1993; Mayberry, & Miikkulainen, 1994; McClelland, & Kawamoto, 1986).We shall briefly discuss the work of St. John, Golden and Rumelhart, and Miikkulainen.

St. John (1990, 1992) extended his initial sentence-processing model to process script-based stories. The initial model consists of a sequential-input backpropagation network, which reads the constituent of a sentence and builds in a hidden-layer of the network (see McClelland, & Rumelhart, 1986) a "gestalt", that is, a representation of the whole sentence. Another network is trained to answer questions. For script processing, a sequence of propositions is, instead, used as inputs. As previously mentioned (in subsection 2.3.1), depending on propositions is problematic for NLP. Questions that supply a predicate are then used with the other network in order to retrieve the whole script. As such, this model does not constitute a text comprehension system. But it demonstrates a problem that PDP models have with scripts: New situations or exceptional ones cannot readily be handled (whereas symbolic approaches can detect the anomaly and call a special-purpose procedure to take care of it).

Miikkulainen (1993b, p. 259) emphasized, however, that

> there is an important distinction between scripts (or more generally,
> schemas) in symbolic systems. . . and scripts in subsymbolic sys-
> tems[.] In PDP, schemas are based on statistical properties of the train-
> ing examples, extracted automatically during training. The resulting
> knowledge structures do not have explicit representations.

This observation is most evident in Golden and Rumelhart's (1993) model of
schema-based story understanding:

> A point in situation-state space is specified by a collection of proposi-
> tions, each of which can have the values of either "present" or
> "absent". A trajectory in situation-space is a temporally ordered
> sequence of situations. . . . A multistate probabilistic (MSP) causal
> chain notation is also introduced for conveniently describing the
> knowledge structures implicitly represented by the subjective condi-
> tional probability distribution. A story is represented as a partially
> specified trajectory in situation-space, and thus, story comprehension
> is defined as the problem of inferring the most probable missing fea-
> tures of the partially specified story trajectory. . . The comprehension
> process is modeled by beginning with a story that has already been
> parsed into a situation-state space trajectory.

In other words, comprehension is reduced to probabilistic recognition (read
matching) of learned schemas. Van den Broek and Lorch (1993) discussed a
similar model that uses a network representation rather than a linear chain
model.

Finally, Miikkulainen (1993b) developed at length, **DISCERN**, a script-
based approach to text understanding (without syntax) that is interesting in
that all rules of interpretation are learned. In other words, it attempts to build
a text understanding system from the bottom up, with specific tasks handled
by separate PDP networks. The model includes a total of 8 modules (namely
for sentence and story parsing, for the lexicon, episodic memory, sentence and
story generators, cue former and answer producer). Each module is trained
separately and in parallel, using backpropagation (see McClelland, & Rumelhart, 1986), except for the lexicon and episodic modules. The latter are responsible for storing and retrieving patterns and are implemented with feature
maps. They implement the memory of the system. Miikkulainen explained
that backpropagation, a supervised learning technique, is not adequate for
modeling long-term memory (1993b, p.104). More generally, he added
(1993b, pp. 44-45):

> Backpropagation is not a panacea for several reasons. It is not always
> possible to specify optimal targets for each input situation. . . . For

> example, processing natural language is only possible after a theory
> for representing linguistic structures as fixed-length vectors is devel-
> oped. . . . It would [also] be useful to know what knowledge the net-
> work acquires in the learning process. . . . However, to this date there
> is no general method for extracting knowledge from the network. The
> network is a statistical pattern transformer, incapable of providing
> explanations for its decisions.

The whole work has the virtue of pointing out a multitude of technical problems with PDP networks, which lie beyond the scope of the present book (e.g.,
external bias unit, learning rate, number of hidden layers, external learning
rule). As mentioned in the Preface, in my opinion, **DISCERN**'s fundamental
drawback is that it requires developing an architecture that coordinates several
PDP networks using "prespecified, structured representations [of the] input
and output layers [of these networks.]" (Miikkulainen, 1993b, p. 99). In other
words, the tasks of these networks, as well as their interactions, are not learned
nor grounded in "neurons", but are arbitrarily established by the designer.
Thus, ultimately, as with symbolic approaches, the model relies on prespecified patterns of interpretation, the learned schemas against which the input is
matched. Bookman (1992, pp. 180–181) elaborated:

> A strong telling point of distributed representations is their ability to
> characterize the environment by encoding statistical correlations from
> the training set. It is these statistical correlations that give the PDP
> models the ability to generalize. If however, the training set has been
> carefully pre-selected, as is the case for the PDP systems [discussed
> above], the PDP training schemes will have eliminated by default a
> great many other possible characterizations and therefore will have
> built representations that are very specific to a given task. Even worse,
> their lack of real training data (i.e., data from corpora) will result in a
> failure to capture an adequate notion of meaning that is necessary for
> comprehension. . . . [These] systems can only process script-based
> related stories. And it is unclear how to represent other forms of non-
> scriptal text[.] Does one need different PDP modules for different
> kinds of text?. . . . This is a bad idea.

In the end, when considering the three scripts (each with three "tracks") used
to train **DISCERN**, I am reminded of Habel's (1983) previously quoted comment on schema-matching approaches: PDP models substitute probabilistic
matching for schema-matching, but, once the networks have been trained with
a small set of hand-crafted examples, "comprehension" boils down to matching, just matching. Also, I have some hesitations with respect to the relevance
of supervised learning for text interpretation. Such a technique presupposes

the existence of an optimal (i.e., correct) solution that the network is trying to learn, but this is irreconcilable with a diachronic view of meaning and understanding: A text may have several interpretations. Thus, it seems that despite the ability to ground PDP architectures into idealized neurons, PDP networks are relevant only to individual facets of comprehension and are not sufficient to address the whole of the problem of interpretation. In particular, it appears that they do not eliminate the notion of macrostructures.

2.3.3 General Objections to PDP

The small number of computational steps assumed for hard recognition problems (such as letterform recognition) has led connectionist researchers to postulate the existence of large, pre-connected networks of simple computing elements operating in *parallel*. It is generally accepted that the human brain also works in a highly parallel fashion. Conversely, the von Neumann computer used by most existing computational models of NLP is sequential. However, the issue at hand is not whether parallelism is essential for understanding but, as Pylyshyn (1984a, 1984b) remarked, whether or not cognition should be *characterized* in terms of a formal computation, that is, in terms of symbols and rules. Smolensky's (1988) answer to this question was simple and unambiguous: Subsymbolic networks have properties that cannot be captured at a "higher" symbolic level.

The debate between connectionist and information-processing architectures is not new, and I will not even attempt to summarize the different viewpoints here. Several of the technical problems initially identified (e.g., see Barnden, 1983; Birnbaum, 1985) have now been addressed, but opponents of PDP models (e.g., Fodor, & Pylyshyn, 1988; Lachter, & Bever, 1988; Pinker, & Prince, 1988) and proponents (e.g., Chalmers, 1990; Elman, 1989; Fetzer, 1992; van Gelder, 1989) still contradict each other. Some go as far as comparing connectionism with behaviorism in that, for both paradigms, only the output of the system matters, not the way in which it is obtained. Even a connectionist researcher such as Sun (1989) argued against both rule-based connectionism and PDP models (for the latter use oversimplified "neurons" that lack states and actions). Indeed, the neuron is an incredibly complex machinery, transforming synaptic inputs into action potentials. There is a multitude of factors involved in this transformation of inputs into outputs including time, refractory periods, chemical interactions, and so forth. (see Levine, 1991; Squire, 1987). "Yet connectionism only focuses on wired cells and forgets the more frequent 'glial', as well as the hormonal brain" (Rastier, 1991, p. 42). Therefore, it is possible that PDP models may be missing a complexity which is essential to the modus operandi of the brain. This possibility is exemplified in Smolensky's (1988) argument against equating connectionist with true neuronal modeling.

The debate between connectionism and information-processing is a specific instance of a more general and philosophical question, the *mind–body* problem (Johnson, 1987), which Thagard (1986) described:

> The currently dominant position in the philosophy of mind is *functionalism*, which says that mental states are to be understood in terms of their functional relationships to other mental states, not in terms of any material instantiation. . . . The rejection of a direct mind-matter link distinguishes functionalism from the *mind-body identity theory*, according to which types of mental states such as thoughts are identical to types of states in the brain. . . . In computational terms, functionalism is the claim that only software matters to the mental. The argument for multiple instantiation [on which functionalism is based] says that we can ignore hardware in characterizing the mental, since the same software can run on any number of different kinds of hardware: It is the functional performance of the software which is crucial.

The information-processing paradigm corresponds to a functionalist approach, whereas the mind-body identity theory underlies connectionism.

Functionalism has not been without its critics, even in philosophy. For example, Churchland (1985) advocated *eliminative materialism*, which claims that advances in neuroscience will lead us to a very different set of categories for describing mental states, eliminating the old ones. A similar argument is developed in Butler's (1994) work. The idea of a biochemical computer (Nelson, 1983) or of a molecular one (Conrad, 1985) proceeds from such a standpoint. In fact, even Chomsky's (1965) famous "language organ" can be rooted in this "biological" view of cognition, whose most notorious advocate is Millikan (1987, 1993).

Is there an obvious, verifiable solution to the mind–body problem? Thagard (1986) wrote:

> My conclusion is that we currently know too little about the human mind and brain and about the range of possibility of other kinds of intelligence to form a plausible solution to the intelligence-matter [or equivalently, mind-body] problem. Any answer offered at this point would be a generalization from one ill-understood instance, the brain.

In other words, our current understanding of the brain allows us only to *assume* a certain organization for the mind and the brain of a reader. In essence, we know what some of the areas of the brain are responsible for, and we can observe some of the low-level operating principles. However, experimental psychology, genetics, and neurology are a long way from verifiable and well-accepted cognitive theories. For example, we still cannot locate "memory" per se. Also consider, this remark from Farah (1994):

> When cognitive neuropsychologists make inferences about the functional architecture of the normal mind from selective cognitive impairments they generally assume that the effects of brain damage are local, that is, that the nondamaged components of the architecture continue to function as they did before the damage. This assumption follows from the view that the components of the functional architecture are modular, in the sense of being informationally encapsulated. In this target article it is argued that this "locality" assumption is probably not correct in general.

Thus, all current cognitive theories have one or more basic metaphors underlying them, as suggested earlier. Mac Cormac (1985, p. 17) warned us that "metaphors can be dangerous, not only in bewitching us into thinking that what they suggest really does exist, but also in leading us to believe that the attributes normally possessed by any of the referents in the metaphor are possessed by the others".

2.4 ON RASTIER'S WORK

In his most recent book, Rastier (1991) presented an extensive scholarly attack on the basic metaphors underlying what he calls "orthodox cognitivism". A fascinating aspect of this work is its historical perspective. Throughout the book, the author demonstrates that the debates and dominant metaphors of current cognitive theories can often be traced back through the centuries to problems Plato, Aristotle and the grammarians considered. It follows that the idea of a "cognitive revolution" (Gardner, 1985) is promptly discarded. Indeed, the existence of a "cognitive science" that is, of a science of the cognition (e.g., Posner 1989; von Eckard, 1992) is questioned. According to Rastier, only the functionalist postulate gives unity to cognitive science. However, the interdisciplinary nature of the field does not grant it de facto the status of a science, and thus Rastier quickly disposes of the expression "cognitive science" in favor of the more prudent "cognitive investigations" (my translation of "recherches cognitives"), where the plural subtly marks the disparity of the research fields studying cognition.

In this section, I do not attempt to summarize these historical observations, but rather overview some of the other arguments put forth by Rastier. (All quotes from his book are my translation.) However, before we get to the work of Rastier, we must first understand the role of classification and algorithms in cognitive theories.

2.4.1 Beyond Algorithmic Competence

Recall that the conduit metaphor views linguistic expressions as containers for meanings. The role of the reader is to retrieve the *determinate* meaning placed in a text by the writer. To do so, it is postulated that the reader must bridge from one sentence to the other by generating inferences: "The crucial problem of story understanding is inference" (Kass, 1986). As discussed in the previous section, most of the existing computational NLP models consider only these bridging inferences. In the context of *text* comprehension, this assumption presents the disadvantage of being too compartmentalized, that is, of ignoring the problem of the perception of subject matter: The bridging inferences presented in those models are restricted to the level of local coherence. This is not enough, as Dyer (1983, Preface) remarked:

> In-depth understanding means being able to do more than simply extract the facts of a narrative and infer causal connections between them. An in-depth understander must be able to recognize what was memorable about a narrative, what episodes were of significance, and what the point of the narrative was—that is, why the narrative was worth telling in the first place. Finally, if a narrative is significant in some way, the memory must be updated so that it will come to mind in appropriate future situations.

As previously observed, current information-processing theories that consider the problem of subject matter generally postulate a fixed set of macrostructures that, in essence, specify the possible gists of a text. The use of macrostructures constitutes a *structuralist* approach to comprehension. Let me first quote at length Norris's (1982, p. 2) summary of what structuralism is generally taken to be:

> The concept of *structure* serves to immobilize the play of meaning in a text and reduce it to a manageable compass. This process can be seen at work in the reception of a book like Jonathan Culler's *Structuralist Poetics* (1975), regarded as a sound and authoritative guide to the complexities of structuralist thought. . . . The proper task of theory, in [Culler's] view, is to provide a legitimating framework or system for insights which a 'competent' reader should be able to arrive at and check against his sense of relevance and fitness. . . . His argument becomes strained when it tries to link this notion of readerly 'competence' with an account of the manifold conventions—or arbitrary codes—that make up a literate response. On the one hand, Culler

appeals to what seems a loose extension of. . . Chomsky's argument:
that linguistic structures are innately programmed in the human mind
and operate both as a constraint upon language and as a means of
shared understanding. Thus Culler puts the case that our comprehension of literary texts is conditioned by a similar 'grammar' of
response which enables us to pick out the relevant structures of meaning from an otherwise inchoate mass of competing detail. On the other
hand, he is obliged to recognize that literary texts involve certain specialized codes of understanding which have to be acquired.

Any theory of text understanding adopts a a structuralist methodology as soon
as it postulates the existence of a (small) set of a priori rules of interpretations,
that is, as soon as they depend on some innate *competence*. Furthermore, some
of these theories may be *objectivist* if they attempt to decontextualize meaning
(Winograd, & Flores, 1986, p. 28):

For the objectivist school of hermeneutics, the text must have a meaning that exists independently of the act of interpretation. The goal of a
hermeneutic theory (a theory of interpretation) is to develop methods
by which we rid ourselves of all prejudices and produce an objective
analysis of what is really there. The ideal is to completely 'decontextualize' the text.

Structuralism (see Scholes 1974, Hawkes 1977 for an introduction) entails a
methodological outlook. Skousen (1985) explained:

A structuralist description can be broadly characterized as a system of
classification. The fundamental question that a structuralist description attempts to answer is how a general contextual space should be
partitioned. For each context in the partition, a rule is defined.

This need for a priori classification is apparent in the plethora of taxonomies
that have been proposed for knowledge in general (e.g., Mark, & Greer, 1991),
texts, inferences, and so forth.

The inherent danger with such classifications is in forgetting that they
constitute basic metaphors, that they immobilize their object of study only for
methodological purposes. For the computational cognitive scientist, the danger is being bewitched into reifying these metaphors in the form of static algorithms. Let me elaborate. The majority of the models of text comprehension
we have reviewed in the previous sections embed, in their architecture, specific algorithms that ultimately define what it is to correctly understand a text,
and what is understandable and what is not. This is most evident in the
schema-matching approaches (e.g., Dyer, 1983), but also pervades inference-

chaining models (e.g., Norvig, 1987), localist architectures (e.g., Lange, 1993) and hybrid models (especially in Kintsch's work, 1991, 1994).

An algorithm specifies a *formal* computation that itself defines a competence, that is, an implicit normative metric. Von der Malsburg (1985) remarked:

> It is the essence of an algorithm that all its qualitative aspects are premeditated and tested so that during its execution no ideas are necessary [and] no qualitative questions are left open. . . . Only quantitative decisions must be met, which can be handled in a mechanical way. . . . There is a very clear division between the qualitative and the quantitative aspects of an algorithm: The former is invented by the human mind and formulated as rules, the latter refers to the data handled by rules.

The point I want to make is that most existing NLP models unduly entrench rules of interpretation in fixed algorithms, as opposed to treating them as data. This observation holds both for models searching for a general mechanism for comprehension, and for systems that abandon such a general mechanism in favor of a very large number of loosely related experts. The latter approach is exemplified by the "word expert" model adopted by Small (1980, 1983; Small, & Rieger, 1982) for sentence parsing: Each word in the lexicon is represented by a procedure, and the parsing and semantic interpretation of a sentence are performed through the interactions of the concurrently running procedures. In both cases, the algorithms constitute (typically static) encodings of rules and schemas established by the programmers (Winograd, & Flores, 1986, p. 123):

> It must be stressed that we are engaging in a particularly dangerous form of blindness if we see the computer—rather than the people who program it—as doing the understanding.

Some philosophers (e.g., Odell, 1984; Searle, 1984) have argued against artificial intelligence as a whole on the basis of this observation. A more immediate difficulty with such an approach, I repeat, is that the resulting architectures are not grounded in "mindless stuff". Thus, it seems we must abandon any strategy that attempts to build a normative "understanding algorithm". On this topic, von der Malsburg (1985) observed:

> This conclusion [the abandonment of algorithmic control] creates a dilemma because surely the brain must follow some functional principle and surely this principle can be put into the form of an 'algorithm'.

> . . . The solution to this dilemma lies in the scheme of a *trivial algorithm*. All. . . rules, values, concepts, methods, procedures, etc., are treated by the trivial algorithm as data. The algorithm fixes the general form of operations on a fundamental level, and makes sure that organized states instead of chaos arise.

Because all theories must be expressed as data for the trivial algorithm, and because data is easily modifiable, such a strategy has the virtue of accounting for individual differences in reading: e.g., acquired dyslexia, eye movement control, iconic memory, differences in word recognition and phonetic recoding, differences in the use of syntactic and semantic constraints, differences in the accessing or knowledge of word meanings, differences in constructing and combining meanings, and so forth. The evidence for such differences is considerable in psycholinguistics (e.g., Mitchell, 1982, chapter 7; Oakhill, 1994; van den Broek, 1994) and in neuroscience (e.g., Vernon, 1994). In particular, Chen's (1990) observations on differences in lexical processing in non-native language users is specially interesting in that it acknowledges the diversity of natural languages.

Galloway (1983) remarked that if we recognize such differences, then recent theories in literary criticism, specially Iser's (1974) work, share many common interests and problems with computational theories of text interpretation. These theories, however, reject the conduit metaphor, that is, the view that the meaning of a text is placed in the words of the text by its author, and that text has a *single determinate meaning* that is obtained by a "competent reader", that is, one who possesses the *correct* set of a priori codes of interpretation. On the contrary, these theories acknowledge the *subjective* (or equivalently, *private* or *idiosyncratic*) aspects of the act of interpretation itself. Consider, for example, this remark by Frye (quoted in Hirsch, 1967, p. 1):

> It has been said of Boehme that his books are like a picnic to which the author brings the words and the reader the meaning. The remark may have been intended as a sneer at Boehme, but it is an exact description of all works of literary art without exception.

"Among the many developments in literary criticism in the past two decades has been the emergence of a group of German critics, who operate under the banner of *reception theory*, and a less cohesive group of American critics, who operate under the umbrella term *reader response criticism*. Both German and American critics of this persuasion have displayed a shift in concern from the author and the work to the text and the reader" (Plantinga, 1986). Holub (1984, p.149) elaborated:

> The conception of an objective and eternal work of art with a unique
> structure and a single, determinate meaning was replaced by a variety
> of models in which the essence of the work is a never-completed
> unfolding of its effective history, while its meaning is constituted by
> the interaction between text and reader.

In other words, the *act* of interpretation becomes central; comprehension is taken to proceed from the *private response* of a reader to a text: This constitutes a *reader-based* approach to understanding. For example, Gadamer (1976) suggested that the act of interpretation be understood as an interaction between the *horizon* provided by the text and the horizon that the interpreter brings to it. Gadamer insisted that every reading of a text (whether "literary" or not, for one cannot presuppose a classification for texts) constitutes an act of giving meaning to it through interpretation. From this perspective, the text acts as a *stabilizing* factor in comprehension: The techniques employed by the author (e.g., the spacing of related episodes), *may* constrain the *idiosyncratic* interpretation of a reader. However, this comprehender is never seen as an autonomous, idealized individual: "He is neither an abstract phenomenological subject nor an ideal perceiver" (Holub, 1984, p.32).

This individualized act of comprehension can be modeled with a trivial algorithm because the data of this algorithm, which constitutes a reader's private horizon (i.e., knowledge and memories), is completely separated from the algorithm itself. The trivial algorithm does not constrain what horizon is used. It merely fixes the expression and processing of this horizon as data. Understanding is neither in the algorithm, nor in the text alone, nor in a reader's horizon alone: It results from the interactions between these three entities. It follows that the "traditional" notion of an "optimal reading" is abandoned: Comprehension is not viewed as a problem for which there exists a (correct) solution, but rather, as the idiosyncratic response of a reader to a text. Each comprehender brings his or her private horizon to the act of interpretation, the text providing a factor of uniformity across responses. Another important factor of uniformity stems from the linguistic and conceptual *conventions* a reader inevitably acquires. In other words, it is highly probable that two distinct users would construct knowledge bases that significantly overlap due to the numerous conventions that they were taught, either explicitly or implicitly, as members of a social community.

This last remark, however, brings us back to the question of the existence of macrostructures. Do such entities exist? Are they learned or innate? Rastier's viewpoint is summarized in the next two subsections.

2.4.2 Contra Universals

According to Culler's (1975) most conservative view of structuralism, the reader possesses an *innate competence* that allows him to perceive what is relevant and what is not. From this point of view, Culler is indeed very close to Chomsky's position on language and cognition (Piatelli-Palmarini, 1980, p.10):

> The environment per se has no structure, or at least none that is *directly* assimilable by the organism. All laws of order, whether they are biological, cognitive or linguistic, come from inside, and order is *imposed* upon the perceptual world, not *derived* from it. These laws of order are assumed to be species-specific, invariant over time and across individuals and cultures.

Do the apparent regularities in linguistic comprehension originate in innate rules or are they derived from the environment (and, in particular, from a culture and one or more linguistic communities)? Kant claimed that man must possess certain innate faculties of mind by virtue of which he imposes law and order on his experiences. The laws man discovers in nature are those he puts there himself. It is almost as if man created nature, a standpoint subject to one important proviso. Kant believed that underlying man's experiences are unknowable *things-in-themselves*, which would continue to exist even if there were no minds left. The role of the mind is to organize the things-in-themselves into forms that make experiences intelligible. The result is man's perception of nature. Kant regarded the active but unconscious mental powers of man to be a priori, that is, to exist in the mind prior to experience, although not as ideas since, he claimed, the content of ideas can come only from sensory experience. Norris (1982, pp. 4–5) remarked:

> It is not hard to see the parallels between Kantian thought and the structuralist outlook presented by a theorist like Culler. Both have their origins in a sceptical divorce between mind and the 'reality' it seeks to understand. In structuralist terms this divorce was most clearly spelled out by the linguist Ferdinand de Saussure. He argued that our knowledge of the world is inextricably shaped and conditioned by the language that serves to represent it. Saussure's insistence on the 'arbitrary' nature of the sign led to his undoing of the natural link that common sense assumes to exist between word and thing. . . . In his view, our knowledge of things is insensibly structured by the systems of code and convention which alone enable us to classify and organize the chaotic flow of experience. This basic *relativity* of thought and meaning. . . is the starting-point of structuralist theory.

The theme of the relativity of language and meaning is typified in what has come to be known as the "Sapir-Whorf" hypothesis. Whorf (1956, p. 213) wrote:

> We dissect nature along lines laid down by our native languages. The categories and types we isolate from the world of phenomena we do not find because they stare every observer in the face; on the contrary, the world is presented in a kaleidoscopic flux of impressions which has to be organized by our minds—and this means largely by the linguistic systems in our minds. We cut nature up, organize it into concepts, and ascribe significances as we do, largely because we are parties to an agreement to organize it in this way—an agreement that holds throughout our speech community and is codified in the patterns of our language.

The Sapir-Whorf hypothesis (e.g., Anderson, 1980, pp. 384–386) claims that the language of an individual *partially* determines the world view and the conceptual system of this individual. *Linguistic determinism* in its strictest interpretation hypothesizes that language determines our concepts. Whorf became convinced of this hypothesis after studying Hopi Indians who apparently had no implicit or explicit concept of time. In the same vein, Sowa (1984, p. 347) observed that English speakers can easily talk about hypothetical situations that have not happened, but Chinese has no syntactic form for expressing them and, therefore, the comprehension of conditionals (e.g., in English) is harder for a native Chinese speaker.

Against the Sapir-Whorf hypothesis Berlin and Kay (1969) claimed that the color vocabularies of various languages form a fixed pattern. Rosch (1974) extended this notion of "prototypicality" beyond color to other categories (e.g., facial expression of emotions), arguing that humans categorize according to *innate prototypes* rather than by analyzing the features of objects and classifying them abstractly (see Mac Cormac, 1985, pp. 71–72). From this evidence, most researchers dismiss the hypothesis. Anderson (1980, p. 386), for example, observes:

> The evidence tends not to support the hypothesis that language has any significant effect on the way we think or on the way we perceive the world. It is certainly true that language can influence us, . . . but its effect is to communicate ideas, not to determine the kind of ideas we can think about.

However, rejecting *linguistic* relativity does not solve the problem of *conceptual* (or mental) relativity that results from placing structure in mind: Do we all share a set of "conceptual primitives"? Do we all possess an innate ability to understand language and to interpret text?

Rastier (1991) rejected the existence of such an innate competence, regardless of whether it is rooted in brain or mind. Let us start by considering the first of these hypotheses: the brain metaphor. I have already quoted Rastier earlier on the oversimplicity of connectionist models and their inadequateness as genuine neuronal models. Rastier (chapter 9) went further and attacked the biological view of cognition (e.g., Millikan, 1987). Much like Thagard (1986), he emphasized that our current understanding of the brain does not allow us to postulate any particular innate cognitive structures or processes. His criticism extends to "theories of setting parameters". Consider, for example, Chomsky's notion of a "language organ" (1984, and in Piatelli-Palmarini, 1980) whose "parameters" are set through training. This metaphoric "organ" is genetically determined (Rastier, 1991, pp. 226–227):

> And thus linguistics can be reduced to biology. This innatism, or more precisely, this nativisim, intends to provide biological foundations to universalism (forgetting that the genetic heritage varies from one individual to the next, and that genetically determined characteristics such as hemophilia have nothing universal to them). . . . Recent findings in neuroscience [however] bring back [the organicist theory] to the domain of speculations.

These findings include the following evidence (pp. 228–229):

1. The connectivity of the brain is largely acquired, as opposed to innate.

2. Neuronal development is generally regressive, as opposed to evolutive.

3. The fine anatomic structure of the brain is constantly affected by new experiences.

Philosophical, psychological, and linguistic arguments against the organicist theory are also presented (e.g., "that all societies play games and have beliefs does not validate the hypothesis of a game or a belief organ" (p. 230)).

In the end, Rastier concluded (p. 236):

> "Natural languages" belong to nature only because they are maternal: they belong to the social environment in which children take their place by learning them. And this social 'tissue' determines, in epigenesis, the properties of cerebral tissues.

> Here the why (the desire) precedes the how (the grammar). A child
> learns any language, any system of signs, provided this learning is
> validated through an affective exchange. But from the irrefutable fact
> that learning dispositions are innate, one can certainly not conclude
> that this is also the case for what is learned. That a child can learn a
> language cannot entail in any way that a universal grammar is part of
> his genetic heritage.

Having disposed of universalist theories rooted in the brain metaphor, Rastier
turned his attention to universalism in general. He is not the only researcher to
contest such a theory. For example, Matsumi (1994) contended that such normative theories often have difficulties explaining the learning of a second language.

The diversity of languages is central to Rastier's argumentation: One can
study the unity of languages, but the scientific problem resides mainly in their
diversity, which is undeniable. One must also acknowledge the diversity of
texts, which receive multiple interpretations, and therefore doubt such diversity can be reduced to universals. Consequently, the existence of a "small" set
of "primitives" is taken to be merely a myth. It follows that systems that
openly depend on this myth, such as Schank's (1982) Conceptual Dependencies or microfeature-based models in which each concept is represented by the
vector of all primitives (e.g., Bookman, 1992), are quickly rejected.

Rastier subscribed to the thesis that to the diversity of languages corresponds a diversity of concepts. But what about linguistic relativity? What
about the relationship between language and thought, which brings us back to
the Sapir-Whorf hypothesis.

Rastier (1991, p. 95) was quick to point out that this fundamental debate
dates back to Epicure and has yet to be solved. Sapir and Whorf, as anthropol-
ogists, were credited with giving culture its due importance in linguistics,
despite their seeming linguistic determinism. But, as we will see shortly, Rastier did not endorse their unjustifiable hypothesis. However, he disputed (for a
whole chapter) the results of Berlin and Kay (1969) and thoroughly demol-
ished (the word is not strong enough) Rosch's (1974) "evidence":

> The scientific question is: are theories of categorization and typicality
> adequate to the description of the lexicon of languages? The cognitive
> approach [to lexical semantics] was triggered by psychological stud-
> ies on categorization (see Rosch's results on prototypes and base level
> terms) and taken over by linguists such as Lakoff, Fillmore and Lan-
> gacker. . . . The fundamental investigations on categorizations [how-
> ever] proceed from universalist hypotheses with biological overtones.
> . . . Color is [taken to be] a universal category so that experiences of

> perception and recognition can be carried out without depending on
> language. Such motivations are however far from being accepted by
> ethnolinguistic specialists. . . . Prototypes are the perceptually salient
> parts of the [color] spectrum; the basic color terms denotes these
> salient parts. The rest of the lexicon for colors is then organized
> around them. . . . This presupposes three theses, which guide the pro-
> tocol of experimentation as well as the conclusions drawn: i) the
> structure of the lexicon is determined by the structure of reality (not
> by the culture) ii) consequently, words are. . . labels. . . denoting
> things iii) languages are nomenclatures.   (Rastier, 1991, pp. 180–
> 183).

Beyond methodological objections (specially with respect to the priming of
the results by the experimenter through the context), each of these three theses
is then refuted at length. (see chapter 7 of Rastier, 1991 for details). In particular, it is clear that these theses depend on a problematic correspondence
between words and concepts (as discussed in subsection 2.2.4). Also, Rosch's
theory of categorization, as well as any linguistic (e.g., Givón, 1989) or computational (Peters, & Shapiro, 1987) theory of prototypes, depends on the lexicon being organized in a hierarchy, an assumption Rastier has exhaustively
disproved. Such theories also ignore the diachronic nature of language (that is,
its evolution in time), and are limited to "natural" categories since, as Rastier
has remarked (p. 190), "experiential universals" are indefensible. Other
researchers (e.g., Regier, 1992) have also rejected the notion of "innate universals" for categorization.

Ultimately the validation of a theory of categorization requires a solution
to the mind-body problem, a solution that escapes us. Therefore, for Rastier
(p. 12) "only the dogmatic rationalist, guilty of unwarranted theoretical reductionism, searches for methodological universals that he invents and reifies,
admiring himself for their discovery". Indeed, such an approach, which he
claimed underlies most of the existing work in artificial intelligence and cognitive science, corresponds to Kant's solution that "strives to keep skepticism
at bay by insisting on the *normative* or somehow *self-validating* habits of readerly 'competence'" (Norris, 1982, p. 5).

The observation that a universalist theory is self-validating is not new.
Consider, for example, a structuralist theory of text interpretation, which is
quite similar to Rosch's approach. Ultimately, the postulated macrostructures,
which constitute the universals (or primitives) of the model, are grounded in
the *expert* and his ability to *abstract* from data, that is, to extract *relevant* (or
salient) *patterns* that are assumed to exist independently of the expert's act of
interpretation. Meaning comes from this *objective* recognition of *distinctive*

features and *significant* contrasts. The expert can be viewed as creating a master code for the interpretation of text. Structuralism becomes in effect a natural extension or legitimating theory of what it is to read a text properly. It is hoped that the rules of a complete model will capture the structure of the competent reader, that is, the master code he uses to impose meaning.

Against such a view, Barthes (1977) remarked that the language of the expert, what he terms the *meta-language*, is itself an object of study. Norris (1982, pp. 9–10) explained:

> Barthes is well aware of the dangers and delusions implicit in a discourse that claims the last word in explanatory power. The semiologist may seem to exercise 'the objective function of decipherer' in relation to a world which 'conceals or naturalizes' the meanings of its own dominant culture. But his apparent objectivity is made possible only by a habit of thought which willingly forgets or suppresses its own provisional status. . . . The dream of total intelligibility, like 'structure' in its metalinguistic sense, belongs (he implies) to a stage of thinking that is self-blinded by its own conceptual metaphors.

The point to be grasped is that a universalist theory (e.g., an innate competence to understand texts) can only be grounded in the self-validating basic metaphor(s) of an "expert". This constitutes an inadequate response to the problem of conceptual relativity and leaves the door open for the radical skepticism of the deconstructionist movement (see Norris, 1982).

Rastier (1991, p. 12) did not subscribe to such radical skepticism, but he also flatly rejected universalism and the dogmatic rationalism it presupposes, as exemplified by Hobbes:

> Our skepticism is in agreement with the empirical tradition, which has always emphasized the relative nature of knowledge.

At this point of the discussion, let me quote at length Rastier's position (pp. 95–96):

> We shall adopt . . . this measured standpoint: the signifiés of languages and the mental representations are both the former and the latter cultural constructions. They cannot be conflated, and mutually condition each other. However, their unity is such that a dualist position that would admit the unilateral determination of the signifié to the representation, or the inverse determination, would not capture the complexity of their interrelations.
>
> To their distinction corresponds the autonomy of semantics and psy-

chology; to their interrelations, the cooperation between these two disciplines. In fact, if the sterile debate that still opposes after two and a half millennia thought to language inevitably concludes to the determination of the latter by the former, the new idea (only two centuries) of an inverse determination raises a necessary doubt; but this idea maintains a duality that must be overcome, specially given that the notion of determination is most likely too strong.

In our domain, we formulate the hypothesis that the semantic structures of a text *constrain* the psychic representations that come with its enunciation as well as its interpretation, without however determining them in the strong sense of the word. . . . It is as formations relative to a culture that 'language' and 'thought' find their unity: a language carries in its usages norms that are easily paired with representations inasmuch as they proceed from a same cultural system.

We explore this position in the next subsection.

2.4.3 On the Nature of Semantics

A complete answer to the question of the nature of semantics appears to be provided in authoritative books such as Frawley's (1992) *Linguistic Semantics*. But, because they follow the Chomskyan separation of semantics from other facets of language, the mentalistic theories found in these works ignore the problem of linguistic performance, if not language altogether. Psycholinguistics (see Foss, & Hakes, 1978; Gernsbacher, 1994) is also firmly rooted in the distinction between an a priori linguistic competence and actual performance. Consider, for example, this comment from Forster and Stevenson (1987):

Understanding how linguistic competence controls linguistic performance is the primary aim of experimental psycholinguistic research.

As explained earlier, the notion of innate linguistic competence constitutes a universalist theory, a theory that Rastier (1991) rejected, along with its philosophical underpinnings in Western idealism, which unduly separates mind from body. Rastier was specially skeptical of psycholinguistics where, as we will see later in this book, debates and controversies abound (pp. 177–178):

It is with quite worrying ease, that [psycholinguistics] has and still proves all successive versions of the Chomskyan theory, without being concerned with their contradictions. . . . Neurolinguistics and psycholinguistics share common preconceptions of language and meaning common to artificial intelligence as to the whole of cognitive

investigations: notably the reduction of the linguistic to the verbal
(utterance), the separation of the signifié from the signifiant favoring a
modular conceptualization of language, the assimilation of signifiés to
representations. These preconceptions naturally guide the experimental process.

In his opinion, linguistics is a descriptive, partially predictive social science
that must adopt an empirical rationalist approach in order to account for the
multiplicity of determinations proper to linguistic objects such as texts. Such
a view is not new (e.g., Bange, 1986).

Rastier pled for a humanist approach to linguistics, one, in particular, that
does not rely on the Chomskyan distinction between semantics (concerned
with the problem of reference) and pragmatics (concerned with the problem
of inference), because this separation not only logicizes semantics but, more
importantly, incorrectly conflates meaning and representation. This led Rastier
to discard all cognitive theories of meaning: denotational semantics including
possible worlds (e.g., Barwise, & Perry, 1983; Montague, 1974; Partee,
Meulen ter, & Wall, 1990) and procedural semantics (e.g., Woods, 1981),
primitivism (e.g., Schank, 1972, 1982; Wilks, 1975), propositionalism (e.g.,
van Dijk, & Kintsch, 1983), and so forth. In fact, Rastier rejected the traditional instrumental view of language based on the idealistic Aristotelian triad
of meaning, which "bans semantics from linguistics and makes it depend on
an ontology, sole entity able to link words to reality through the mediation of
concepts" (p. 90). Instead, in order to rehabilitate linguistics as a social science
and separate semantics from psychology, Rastier considered signifiés of languages and mental representations to be distinct, mutually conditioning, cultural formations. A non-deterministic relativism was adopted: "The semantic
structures of a text constrain the psychic representations that accompany its
utterance and its interpretation, without, however, determining its meaning in
the strong sense of the term" (p. 97). The possibility of multiple interpretations
of a text is at the basis of such a standpoint (p. 160).

An extensive theory of text interpretation based on this position is developed in two other books of Rastier (1987, 1989). In the rest of this subsection,
it is not my intention to summarize this theory (whose implementation using
IDIoT will be the topic of a future book), but instead to highlight some of the
fundamental mechanisms it assumes.

Differential semantics constitutes the basis of Rastier's approach (1991,
pp. 101–103):

The linguistic meaning is not (or not only) constituted by the *reference* to things, or by the *inference* between concepts, but also and

firstly by the *difference* between linguistic units. . . The signifié of a
'lexie' [that is, of a stable grouping of morphemes, forming a functional unit] is defined as a *value*, the differences [between semes] that
constitute this value determine its operational contents, that is, the set
of its possibilities for assembling in texts. . . . The operational contents
constrain the eidetic contents, without however determining it in the
strong sense.

D'Alembert, in the *Encyclopédie méthodique*, provided a simple example of
this theory with respect to synonymy:

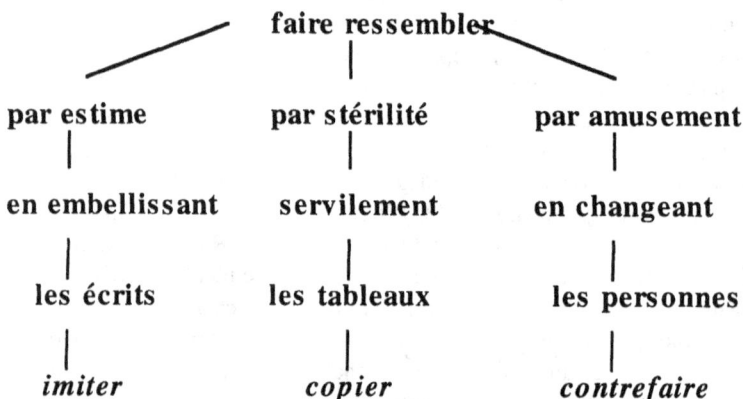

In essence, the goal behind such an decomposition is to highlight the subtle
differences between apparently synonymous words. Given such an analysis,
one can then establish one's preference for certain wordings. Consider, for
example, the phrase "servile imitation" used in *Harrap's New Shorter French
and English Dictionary* (1972, p. S:28). Its presence in this dictionary con-
firms its conventional usage in English. Yet, in French, its usage may be less
preferred than "servile copy" in which the recurrence of the feature "pejorative" in the two words constructs a stronger "impression" than for "servile imitation". A strategy that depends on an a priori competence could then lead to
the arbitrary decision that "servile imitation" is incorrect in French, a decision
Auroux (1984) defended! But this is nonsense. Instead, there are several
usages, and some may be perceived, by some reader, as more "felicitous" than
others, but no usages can be discarded a priori.

The example of synonyms emphasizes a first aspect of Rastier's theory:
the need for differential features. It is important to understand that these fea-

tures are relative to a language (Rastier, 1991, pp. 101–103):

> To say that a linguistic signifié is relative to a language defined as a
> system, is to assert that this signifié can be exhaustively analyzed with
> respect to relations of opposition. The latter are as much relation fea-
> tures that distinguish its class from others (generic features) as fea-
> tures that differentiate it within its class (specific features). The
> features that compose this signifié are themselves denominated by
> intralinguistic paraphrases that are themselves relative to the given
> language. They are elements of definition (not descriptions of the
> denoted object). For example, [in French, the feature] /for the dead/ is
> a semantic component (or *seme*) of 'scalpel' in contrast with 'bis-
> touri' which includes the reciprocal feature /for the living/. This is not
> the case in Polish, for example, where *skalpel* subsumes this opposi-
> tion.

It follows that a word is never defined in isolation, with respect to what it
refers to or denotes, but in relation to other words.

The second fundamental aspect of Rastier's theory is its dynamicity,
which is at the root of the modus operandi of **IDIoT**, as explained later. Let us
return to the example of D'Alembert. Rastier (p. 106) explained that neither
"imitate" nor "copy" possessed inherent evaluative features in the eighteenth
century. In other words, one could find either words in both pejorative and
meliorative contexts. However, because language is diachronic, at least the
pejorative use of "copy" got conventionalized over years. The point is that
only the context, that is, the interaction of the word to understand with surrounding words, determines meaning, that is, which feature is highlighted
(Rastier, 1991, p. 106):

> Contexts create local classes in which the typical senses are modified
> and one could say, transformed into instances.

Thus, meaning is constructed. This position is not new in itself. Consider, for
example, Lindsay and Manaster-Ramer's (1987) *teuchistic* approach to cognitive processes, which explicitly rejects the concept of a "correct" or "optimal"
interpretation:

> Our view is that [natural language] use involves processes which are
> neither algorithmic nor heuristic but, to coin a new term, **teuchistic**.
> Teuchistic processes construct a solution rather than search for one. . .
> We discard the concepts of *language* and *grammar*, replace the cus-
> tomary notion of linguistic competence with a concept of *potential
> behavior*, and view production and comprehension as nonmonotonic

problem-solving processes that satisfice rather than search out an optimal choice from a pre-established theoretical set of possibilities. We
further suggest that the multi-component constraint satisfaction model
serve as the basis of such problem solving. Comprehension is mod-
elled as a constraint driven satisficing process: information is selectively attended and used to constrain the generation of an
interpretation.

Rastier (1991, p. 106) suggested two distinct construction processes: assimilation and dissimilation. For assimilation, consider the phrase,

Example 2.4.3.1 *Drunks, women and burglars,*

which has the effect of transferring the feature /pejorative/, which is inherent
to "drunks" and "burglars", to "women" (which, I would hope, does not contain it a priori!). Similarly, consider the word "atoca" in these sentences:

Example 2.4.3.2 *Could I please have some atocas with my turkey.*

and

Example 2.4.3.3 *Apples, atocas and oranges are delicious.*

In the first example, "atoca" (a French "canadianism" for "cranberry", which
originates in Amerindian languages) will possibly receive the feature /eatable/
or remain undetermined. In the second example, it will likely obtain the
generic feature /fruit/.

For dissimilation, consider these sentences (p. 216):

Example 2.4.3.4 *attributive: A woman is a woman.*

Example 2.4.3.5 *disjunctive: There is music and music.*

Rastier (1991, p.216) remarked that such dissimilations could be codified into
a system of a priori semantic features (e.g., Katz, & Fodor, 1963), but that this
would bring us back to universals. For him, conventional transfers of features
would be acquired (and stabilized) over time in the form of associative paths,
whereas this dynamic process of assimilation and dissimilation would account
for the construction of all other meanings. The virtue of such a theory is that
it readily accommodates all interpretations, without relying on predefined distinctions such as figurative versus literal meaning.

At this point, I must emphasize that Rastier's theory introduces several
complexities (e.g., interpretative instructions at the micro-, meso-, and macro-
semantic levels, pp. 110–111) to account for the diversity of semantic phe-

nomena, as well as for addressing the interpretation of text. In particular, the notion of "parcours interprétatifs" (interpretative paths) seems very promising from a computational viewpoint. These details, however, still rest on the principle of feature highlighting and transfer, and therefore do not introduce any other aspects that can be readily grounded in the architecture I want to develop. Moreover, Rastier privileged an anti-computational stance (p. 206):

> We wish. . . to destabilize the problematic of the dominant semantics in cognitive investigations. To this paradigm dominated by symbolic logic (and called simply symbolic because logic seems obvious), [we oppose another] which does not subordinate the signifié to the concept, which refuses implicitly the compositionality of meaning, and admits the determination of the local through the global. . . We claim that this semantic treatment is generally closer to the recognition of forms than to a computation.

On this topic of the recognition of forms, Rastier (p. 114) saluted Smolensky (1988, p.16) for emphasizing the contextual view of meaning, but wishes to go further:

> To Pylyshyn who estimated that the connectionist representation of *coffee* was that of *cup of coffee* minus that of *cup without coffee*, Smolensky replies: 'the structure representing *coffee* in the context of *cup* is quite different than the one representing *coffee* in the context of *pot, tree, man.*' Thus, a representation is largely influenced by its context. This sensible conclusion marks an improvement of the classic paradigm. But we are still not talking about signifés: the discussion addresses the structure of constituents of *mental states*. If one admitted that *coffee* is not a concept but merely the signifié of the word *coffee*, then Smolensky would confirm our thesis that occurrences of [signifiés] are constructed by and in function of the context. So that . . we can defend the claim that semantic occurrence is a hapax, and complete it by asserting that any type is a reconstruction. This is the outcome of differential semantics: not only does there not exist two synonymous words, but there does not exist two identical occurrences of the same word.

The proposed theory is firmly rooted in Saussurian linguistics (1916). Such a theory is therefore exposed to the traditional objections that "unfortunately, this theory of signs, by completely neglecting the things that signs denote, [is] immediately cut from any contact with scientific verification methods" (Ogden, & Richards, 1923, p. 6). Such a comment, however, rests on the Aristotelian view of meaning, that is, on the instrumental of language and, in particular, on the truth-conditional nature of meaning, positions that Rastier rejected, as previously explained.

This led Rastier to reject the widely-used *semasiological* approach to meaning, which starts from the signifiant (i.e., the word) in order to understand the concept. This approach pervades artificial intelligence (e.g., Katz, & Fodor, 1963), including cognitive semantics (e.g., Lakoff, 1987; Langacker, 1987). For example, in order to define the concept of *ring*, Langacker felt compelled to interrelate the different meanings of "ring" and postulate some prototypical concept, an idea that again rests, as mentioned earlier, on universals. Instead, Rastier (p. 104) proposed an *onomasiological* theory that proceeds from signifiés to signifiants. The problem of inference is readily addressed by this theory (p. 110): It rests on the notion of an interpretative path that is guided by the principles of assimilation and dissimilation (see Rastier, 1987, 1989). As for reference, in essence, Rastier hypothesized (1991, p. 111) that once meaning has been constructed, it acts as a cue for the retrieval from memory of "referential impressions", In other words, the problem of reference is moved out of a problematic truth-conditional viewpoint and placed back in the field of psychology where it is taken to belong.

In the end, the point Rastier wanted to make was that a unified semantics for text comprehension based on the concept of difference is possible.

2.5 THEORETICAL FOUNDATIONS OF IDIoT

In light of the previous review, I conclude this chapter by establishing the fundamental postulates underlying a "grounded" approach to text comprehension.

First, such an approach is irreconcilable with any universalist theory of cognition, which is ultimately normative and self-validating. A biological discussion of the merits of the innatist hypothesis lies beyond the scope of this work. Let me simply remark that the debate between innatists and researchers who postulate some assimilation of ideas from the environment started more than 2500 years ago (when Aristotle rejected the *forms*, or universal archetypes, of Plato and advocated a tabula rasa) and still rages (see Piatelli-Palmarini, 1980; Lakoff, 1987). Piaget (1970) concisely summarized the issue when he remarked that the boundary between the *phenotype* and the *genotype*, that is, between the acquired (from the interaction of genetics with the environment) and the innate, is *floue* (fuzzy). Roughly put, the biological debate ultimately reduces to an interpretation of the role of *random mutations*, that is, to a debate on the paradoxical notion of probability "which has puzzled philosophers ever since Pascal initiated that branch of mathematics—and which von Neumann, the greatest mathematician of our century, called 'black magic'" (Koestler, 1978, p. 266).

In this chapter, I have argued that the innatist hypothesis subsumes the vast majority of symbolic and local connectionist architectures for text comprehension. This is most apparent in the more or less covert dependence of these models on predefined macrostructures for interpretation. However, innatism merely constitutes yet another basic metaphor, perhaps rooted in the brain but not "grounded in mindless stuff" (Minsky, 1986) because of no apparent reduction to such mindless principles. Conversely, with respect to text understanding, parallel distributed processing has been shown to apparently not scale up without the help of an overall symbolic control architecture, which is not grounded. In other words, the difficulty with such an approach is that, although PDP is rooted in mindless (yet) idealized neurons, the resulting models for linguistic comprehension are still not grounded.

Second, when considering again Thagard's (1986) warning that "any answer [to the mind-body problem] offered at this point would be a generalization from one ill-understood instance, the brain", we must accept that even a grounded architecture will originate in some basic metaphor (Mac Cormac, 1985). I choose to root the proposed architecture in the metaphor of human memory. Beyond the initial motivations mentioned in the Preface, this metaphor presents the advantage of bypassing the mind-body problem by respecting the Aristotelian inseparability of these two entities: Human memory is undeniably biological (Squire, 1987), but also intuitively acts as the medium for the storage and processing of elusive *mental* entities such as "ideas", "beliefs", "dreams", and so forth. From this perspective, because we can conceptualize memory as a mechanism for the assembling and storing of knowledge and experience, we will indeed obtain a grounded cognitive architecture if we can show how the complex mental operations hypothesized for linguistic comprehension can be reduced to purely mechanistic memory operations.

Third, a grounded perspective of cognition leads us to abandon the quest for the "correct" rules of interpretation, for the "correct" meaning of a text. Indeed, the rules and concepts presented in the rest of this work do not form a corpus of conventionalized knowledge or any sort of set of correct rules for comprehension. The suggested rules, features, and concepts are merely illustrative. In other words, our object of study is *not* the knowledge of the user, for by definition this knowledge does not lend itself to such a grounding. Instead, we investigate the modus operandi of a purely mechanistic model of memory for reader-based comprehension. This modus operandi takes the form of a "trivial" algorithm. This algorithm is trivial solely in the sense that it is strictly mechanistic, that is, free of heuristics, rules of interpretation, and other epistemological commitments. Consequently, there is no a priori competence, no a priori macrostructures, no predefined algorithm for understanding. Instead, I adopt a reader-based perspective for comprehension: The interpretation of a text depends on the user-specified knowledge and on the structural and processing characteristics of memory for that interpretation. The input text does not determine its interpretation; it merely constrains it (Gadamer, 1976).

Fourth, a reader-based approach to text comprehension emphasizes some fundamental postulates regarding language and understanding:

1. Meaning is a gerund; each word is a hapax: The interpretation of a word is always constructed, as opposed to being recognized.

2. Interpretation is non-deterministic:

   a) A text has multiple interpretations across several readers.

   b) A reader may fail to understand a text.

3. Interpretation is diachronic: For a single reader, a text may have different interpretations at different points in time depending on

   a) the evolution of the knowledge of this reader: The same text may lead to a radically different interpretation if the knowledge of the reader has considerably changed over time.

   b) the structural and processing characteristics of memory at a given point in time: The same text may lead to a radically different interpretation if a reader improves the capacity of her short term memory, or allows herself more time to infer, and so forth.

   c) the "life-span" of a trace in memory: Over time a trace of the interpretation of a text may become quite unretrievable if not completely forgotten.

Finally, the biological constraint, which emphasizes the real-time aspect of comprehension, is taken to impose the fundamental processing requirement on the proposed grounded architecture. More specifically, because we acknowledge the non-deterministic nature of interpretation, we assume that text understanding is a *time-constrained process—a race*. Let me elaborate briefly.

Lindsay and Manaster-Ramer (1987) suggested that linguistic comprehension consists in a teuchistic process constrained by

> a variety of factors, only some of which bear a close resemblance to the linguistic knowledge as normally conceived, whereas others involve factors such as the past processing that has been done by the system, interaction with other users of the language, and even physical characteristics of the language user. . . . People produce and parse rapidly a vanishingly small proportion of the theoretically possible utterances of a given language, and moreover, intend and understand only a vanishly small proportion of the theoretically possible interpretations of those utterances. Yet given sufficient time and effort, people seem to be able to increase these proportions significantly.

Of the multitude of possible factors that constrain linguistic comprehension, because of my choice of basic metaphor, I focus primarily in this work on the role and importance of processing *time*, that is, time as it pertains to memory management and memory processes such as retrievals (see Corriveau, 1987). I assume that the idiosyncrasies of interpretation observable between readers stem, in part, from differences between the private time constraints of these readers, that is, from differences in the comprehension time allocated by each one. This hypothesis proceeds not only from the biological constraint that emphasizes the short response times of humans for hard cognitive tasks (Feldman, 1985a; Gigley, 1985a, 1985b), but also from physiological (Zola-Morgan, & Squire, 1990) and psychological evidence suggesting that humans feel a determinative pressure to understand quickly (e.g., Márkus, 1983, for inference; Norris, 1986, for word sense disambiguation; van Dijk, & Kintsch, 1983, for text comprehension), possibly as the result of social demands and struggles (Peckham, 1979). From this viewpoint, the hypothesis considers both body and mind, in accordance with their postulated inseparability.

To conclude, I must emphasize that to assume that the biological constraint imposes computational constraints on cognition is not to claim the biological plausibility of the proposed architecture. Indeed, such a claim would seem to inherently presuppose a solution, which we do not have, to the mind-body problem. Thus, the proposed model of memory is metaphoric in that it does not attempt to account for existing anatomical, physiological, psychological, chemical, and neuropsychopharmacological evidence pertaining to human memory.

Part II
Design

Chapter 3

Designing a Grounded Architecture

3.1 IN SEARCH OF A STARTING POINT

The design of a grounded architecture rests, in my opinion, on two fundamental ideas introduced in the previous chapter:

1. Meaning is a gerund, a construction process, as opposed to an object to scrutinize in itself.

2. Linguistic comprehension is non-deterministic and diachronic.

In this chapter, I explore the consequences of these two observations on the design of a grounded architecture for linguistic comprehension. In order to do so, it is important to first understand that artificial intelligence per se is not a science, but rather a technique (Rastier, 1991, p. 10): Its object of study, cognition, belongs first to epistemology. Should we adopt a philosophical viewpoint to direct our design? Rastier (1991, p. 11, my italics) warned us:

> With the exception of epistemology, we will avoid general philosophy, though it has been presented as the prime of cognitive disciplines. And we shall be unjustly discrete regarding the philosophy that has spontaneously proceeded from 'cognitive research', the philosophy of mind: often finicky, speculative but lacking a reflective dimension, detailing *gratuitous experiences of thought*, it has inherited several of the besetting sins of analytical philosophy.

We also abandon a biological, if not genetic, outlook at cognition, for it presupposes a solution to the mind-body problem. It is one thing to explain the role of neurotransmitters with respect to the inhibition by the frontal lobe of "aggressive" impulses. It is another to understand the social and cultural factors that lead to the association of certain situations with an aggressive response. In other words, there is quite a bridge to cross between detailing biological mechanisms and correlating them to acquired mental experiences. Kanerva (1984) summarized this argument:

> When a system is sufficiently complex and very general, as are com-
> puters and even more so the [human] central nervous system, it is
> almost impossible to infer function from even the most detailed
> description of the structure.

In other words, any biological simulation, regardless of how detailed it is, fails at this point to scale up to the problems of cognition. Conversely, building a computational architecture resting on psychological or psycholinguistic evidence does not address the problem of grounding per se, nor the issue of the nature of meaning proper.

It is also important to understand that an implementation on a computer cannot validate by itself any cognitive theory: It is merely a tool for experimentation. In fact, even in an interdisciplinary field, a science cannot validate another. Rastier, (1991, p. 10) explained:

> When considering a technology such as artificial intelligence, we
> investigate, on the one hand, how its formalizations and procedures
> can be used in semantics, and, on the other hand, how semantics can
> contribute to the automatic processing of language. In sciences such
> as psychology or neurology, we search for correlates between seman-
> tic phenomena that can corroborate or weaken our hypotheses, with-
> out however expecting the former to validate or invalidate the latter.
> Regardless of fusionist conceptualizations of interdisciplinarity, a sci-
> ence cannot in fact validate another one, for, if they share the same
> empirical object (as with linguistics, psycholinguistics, neurolinguis-
> tics), they do not have the same object of understanding.

The need for tools of experimentation for cognition is exemplified in the following comment of Simon (1993):

> There has been a rather steady draft, in recent years, from articles
> describing and evaluating specific computer programs that exhibit
> intelligence, to formal, theoretical articles that prove theorems about
> intelligence though a large part of our understanding of intelligence—
> artificial as well as natural—will continue to depend on experimenta-
> tion[.]

With respect to linguistic comprehension, it seems, however, in light of the review of the previous chapter, that the computer scientist is condemned to depend on theories of interpretation resting on the problematic notions of innate competence and macrostructures. At the root of this difficulty, we find the incorrect conflation of signifiés with conceptual representations (if not with signifiants as in formal theories!). Instead, Rastier (1991, chapter 3) argued that signifiants must be distinguished both from signifiés and from concepts, and concludes that most of the work in AI, including mental models (see Garnham, & Oakhill, 1992) and connectionism (Smolensky, 1988), is concerned with conceptual representations. Beyond the underlying philosophical debate on the relation of language to thought, the point I want to make, which proceeds from Rastier's (1991, chapters 4 through 6) extensive comments on the semantics of networks and man-machine interfaces, is that a computer does not produce signifiés per se, but merely representations. Generally, these representations are taken to have a conceptual nature: Words refer to concepts. However, if we distinguish between signifiants, signifiés, and concepts, then the trace to be produced by **IDIoT** (see chapter 1) is not an interpretation per se, but rather, the representation of an interpretation. We are back to the remark of Winograd and Flores (1986): It is not the computer itself that does the understanding; it merely assembles a representation, in this case in a purely mechanistic way. Thus, the user of **IDIoT** must not only supply the knowledge used for the construction of this representation (as dictated by a reader-based approach to comprehension), but also read the generated trace in order to obtain a (personal) interpretation from it. There are no epistemological commitments entrenched in the architecture, no a priori normative theory of interpretation, no built-in notion of the acceptability of what is produced. Indeed, the "acceptability" of an interpretation, a metric that could be captured through a global multi-variable function to maximize, much like the minimization of global energy in relaxation models, is *not* addressed in this work, for it depends on a multitude of factors (e.g., social and cultural criteria) that lie beyond the scope of the present proposal. Consequently, in **IDIoT**, the reader is the sole provider of knowledge and sole judge of the appropriateness, acceptability, correctness, usefulness, and so forth. of the constructed trace. From this perspective, **IDIoT** is merely a mechanistic processor that reduces a large text to a smaller trace according to processes associated with the metaphor of memory. In other words, ultimately, **IDIoT** processes and produces signifiants: The trace is a representation of an interpretation, a representation that must still be apprehended by the user of the tool. We are a long way from viewing meaning as pertaining to some innate language, if not just syntax, of thought, and the question remains: How do we start the design of the proposed grounded architecture?

As previously discussed, existing computational approaches to comprehension generally adopt a *static* view of cognition. For the symbolic information-processing school, the "intelligent" system is programmed with the (often arbitrarily complex) data structures and algorithms for understanding. In the connectionist approach, the system goes through a (more or less) lengthy period of training to set weights in the network. In both cases, the system is only then considered to be ready for comprehension. From that point on, the way the system understands is typically fixed, and this system must generate repeatedly the same correct interpretation for a given input in order to be considered *reliable*. This strategy is taken to be desirable, if not mandatory, from a software engineering viewpoint: Comprehension is a problem, and there is a specific solution to it. The goal of the knowledge engineer is, therefore, to build a system that produces reliably this solution.

In my opinion, reducing reliability to the repeated production of the correct solution for a given input is problematic for cognitive systems, for it denies comprehension its diachronic and non-deterministic nature. It is my contention that acknowledging these characteristics of understanding leads us to a different set of software engineering requirements for a grounded architecture, requirements from which basic design assumptions and decisions can be extracted. The investigation of this thesis is carried out in the rest of this chapter.

3.2 FROM GENESIS TO REVELATION: DIACHRONIC INTERPRETATION

Let me start by illustrating, in this section, what I mean by diachronic interpretation.

The title of the first album of the group, Genesis, is "From genesis to revelation". When I first purchased this album, I did not pay a lot of attention to this title. In other words, I did not feel the need (see Peckham, 1979) to associate some kind of interpretation with it: It was merely a name for an album. For weeks, these words had *no* meaning per se as a whole; they only acted as a reference for something else. I then considered one day the illustration on the front of the album. Peter Gabriel, dressed as a flower, seemed in some sort of trance. Suddenly, a meaning for the title emerged in my mind: The music of Genesis leads to or induces an enlightenment, a revelation. This inference appears to depend on several facts:

1. The word "révélation" in French (my native tongue) corresponds to only the two first of the three possible meanings found in English (Webster, 1981): a) "an act of revealing divine truth" or b) "an astonishing disclosure". It does not refer to the apocalyptic writing of John, the last book of the New Testament. (This last book is called "Apocalypse" in French).

2. My "knowledge base" at that time did not include this third meaning for "revelation" in English.

3. My inferential apparatus apparently "made a link" between the illustration and the word "revelation" and proceeded to associate both with the name of the group via some sort of consequence or causality link suggested by the prepositions "from" and "to": From (the music of) Genesis, one can reach (i.e., go to) revelation.

4. The meaning of "genesis" as the first book of the Bible did not seem relevant, or at least, no interpretation relying on it was established, despite the fact that my knowledge base did include this meaning.

In the end, the meaning of the title at that point in time appears to have been nothing more than a *juxtaposition* of meanings for each of its component words. In other words, although an a posteriori explanation requires a lot of words to explain this interpretation, the latter boils down to the "packaging" of several other meanings as a whole.

I eventually learned the third meaning of "revelation" in English. This happened in a context that had nothing to do with music or Genesis. Consequently, the "meaning" for the title of the album remained the same despite this new piece of information. In other words, this new definition did not automatically get linked to the title although they both involve the same word, "revelation".

Finally, one day, years after the original purchase, both the third meaning of "revelation" and the title came to *coexist simultaneously* in my mind. This coexistence could have been the result of one of these two entities having sufficient time to "reach" the other, or it could have been contextual inasmuch as external inputs caused the separate activation of each of the two entities. Regardless, the coexistence led to a new inference: The title could merely be referring to the Bible, from its first to its last book. The "meaning" of the title would then reduce to nothing more than a reference. Arguably, this meaning could be considered a pun on the word "genesis", much like another title from the group, "Nursery Crime", constitutes a pun on "nursery rhyme" (another interpretation that took me, I confess, quite a lot of time to grasp, due to my poor knowledge of idiomatic English).

It would tempting to say that this last interpretation constitutes *the correct* meaning and that other possible interpretations (previous and future) are erroneous. Then, an understanding system with *all relevant* knowledge (as opposed to an incompetent reader like myself) could be built to generate this correct, definitive answer. There are several problems with this standpoint.

First and foremost, it relies on the notion of an innate competence, which I have rejected in the previous chapter. Second, applying the notion of correctness to the problem of interpretation too often adopts to a single-solution approach. In turn, this leads to the so-called "labeling problem". For example, a typical comprehension algorithm works only for a certain type of texts (e.g., "technical", "expository") and thus requires the input to be classified as such a priori. In other words, part of the solution, namely the kind of text, is needed before any processing occurs. Moreover, a single-solution approach certainly does not correspond to the history of human interpretation. For example, the Bible and Hamlet (a relatively short text) have generated countless interpretations, and our legal system is based on the interpretation of the law. This brings us to a final objection to the notion of "correct meaning". Beyond the undisputable reality of multiple acceptable interpretations (across a set of readers, cultures, ideologies, etc.), adopting a static approach to the ascription of meaning totally bypasses a fundamental characteristic of language and cognition, namely its diachronic nature. More specifically, change over time is inherent to meaning and understanding: An initial interpretation (or *absence* of interpretation, as in my example) can be challenged by a subsequent one, resulting in a choice between the older one and the new one (see Granger, & Holbrook, 1983), or even in a blending of the two into yet another interpretation. This mechanism is fundamental, in particular, to the understanding of specific types of texts such as mystery novels and laws. For example, the legal meaning of a "person" has evolved over centuries from denying humanity to Peruvian Indians to accommodating the legality of abortion. But the notion of "correctness" unduly forces an arbitrary a priori choice between interpretations. Were this choice acknowledged to be a posteriori, we would not talk of *correctness* but rather of *consensus*. Thus, returning to the example, correctness would require that I discard my first explanation.However, personally, because I find it intellectually more satisfying, I prefer this first explanation to the second! Furthermore, I certainly do not see them as mutually exclusive: Both have been remembered and can come back to mind.

Should it matter at this point what the *intended* "meaning" was, if any? Should it matter, for example, what Shakespeare wanted to convey in Hamlet? Should it matter that years after I had acquired both interpretations of the title of the album, I may have heard Peter Gabriel suggest an explanation akin to my own first interpretation? It doesn't if we adopt a *reader*-based approach to comprehension. Recall, for example, that according to Gadamer (1976), the text serves as a common constraining basis for all the interpretations derived from it, nothing more. As there is room for absence of interpretation, there must also be room for "mis-expression" of intended meaning, and thus for "mis-understanding" (in the eye of the writer, of what she intended). Legal texts again eloquently demonstrate this. For example, despite what the politicians intended, despite all the careful wording, the Canadian Charter of Rights has been successfully used by extremist groups to claim the right to exist and to express their controversial opinions, and by divorced women to not pay income tax on the pension they receive from their ex-husbands (even though the latter do not pay a cent on it either!). Thus, one cannot assume that the intended meaning, *if* it is known, is the correct one. Moreover, such a strategy would also deny the possibility of a diachronic "intended" meaning, that is, the possibility for the originator to modify, over time, what he intended to convey, a phenomenon politicians constantly rely on.

To the best of my knowledge, no existing computational system can tackle diachronic interpretation. This stems from the fact that this mechanism imposes new requirements on a cognitive architecture. These requirements are discussed in the next section.

3.3 REQUIREMENTS FOR A COGNITIVE ARCHITECTURE

3.3.1 Generation of Multiple Solutions

Several important implications stem from acknowledging that a cognitive architecture should allow the generation of a set of possible solutions.

First, the system should not hardwire any particular solution. More specifically, interpretation should not be reduced to the matching of the input with a predefined solution. As previously explained, such an approach suffers from being somewhat ad hoc in that it essentially fits the algorithm to the data. Approaches that construct several potential solutions but then rely on an evaluation mechanism to choose a winner between them present only a slight improvement: Interpretation still reduces to matching but, in this case, the system matches against pre-specified types of solutions as opposed to specific ones.

Second, the system must be able to take into account independent external factors that may influence cognition. For example, in the case of text comprehension, it is commonly accepted that the capacity of short-term memory (see next chapter) plays an important role with respect to understanding, and yet is independent of the input and of the comprehension algorithm. Consequently, the system must be designed so that such external factors are not hardwired, but rather user-specifiable. In turn, this allows the system to process the same input according to a multitude of combinations of values for these external factors. As previously suggested, we could thus model a reader processing a text with different levels of attention, possibly leading to different interpretations.

Third, the system must be provided with a stopping criterion. In other words, somehow the generation of possible interpretations must come to an end. However, this should not imply the use of a "semantic" evaluation criterion (which, in fact, defines a built-in competence). Mathematical equilibrium, as used in connectionist architectures (see Feldman, 1985b; McClelland, & Rumelhart, 1986), does not appear to work either because, by definition, it rules out the possibility of multiple solutions. But this is only partially true because, at least in theory, it is possible for a network to endlessly alternate between at least two states. However, this characteristic, which may be useful in modeling ambiguous visual effects such as the Necker cube, is generally regarded as undesirable, and, it fails to satisfy our third requirement inasmuch as it results from an absence of a stopping criterion, that is, from a pathological race condition.

3.3.2 Diachrony

From the absence of interpretation to the coretrievability of two interpretations, the previous example illustrates the diachronic nature of interpretation, which Rastier (1991) discussed at length. More specifically, the "meaning(s)" associated with the title of the album change(s) over time. To model this fundamental characteristic, we require that the system be able 1) to store a meaning, 2) to associate zero or more "meanings" with a mental entity, and 3) to retrieve these "meanings". Storing, retrieving, and associating all depend on time:

> 1. **Storage** (i.e., remembering) is not an all-or-nothing phenomenon: Some newly created associations will be ephemeral, whereas others will last a short or a long amount of time. Moreover, some associations that are remembered will eventually be forgotten (most likely due to a lack of retrieval). For example, I may eventually forget either or both of my interpretations of the title of the album, if not the latter itself!

> 2. **Retrieval** (i.e., recall) is highly "contextual": A mental entity is typically retrieved in a specific context (e.g., "genesis" as the first book of the Bible was not apparently retrieved in my first interpretation). Context, that is, what is in focus (and available for immediate consideration by the comprehension algorithm), constantly changes with time. Consequently, retrieval also indirectly depends on time. The example illustrates this: At the time the third meaning of "revelation" is acquired, neither the title of the album, nor its "meaning" are retrieved.

3. **Association** depends on the *co-existence in context* of two previously unconnected entities. It is, therefore, also dependent on time with respect to this co-existence.

In turn, **retrieval** entails a fourth operation:

4. **Matching** is required in order test for the presence *in context* of the features needed for the detection and subsequent retrieval of some entity. Clearly, matching is highly contextual by definition, and thus depends on time.

This set of primitive operations, which "grounds" the proposed cognitive architecture, is not new in itself. In particular, it is at the basis of Minsky's (1980) *k-line theory* of memory, which has been detailed in his *Society of Mind* (1986), and also roots my preliminary investigation of creativity (Corriveau, 1993a). The realization of these operations in **IDIoT** will be investigated in subsection 4.6.2. For now, it is enough to understand that, within the framework of a computational system manipulating representations, interpretation, that is ascription of meaning to text, consists in building a representation of a signifié and then *associating* it with the representation of a linguistic unit. For example, to "interpret" a word, **IDIoT** must build a representation of the signifié of this word in context and associate it with the word's representation. The same holds for a phrase (e.g., the title of an album), a sentence, and a text. Furthermore, the value of this association is not a single static value: It can change over time. Most importantly, the association can be multi-valued (i.e., have several values). For example, I have suggested that eventually two interpretations were associated with the title of the Genesis album. Another possibility is to have one interpretation replace another. More generally, a *resolution strategy* (see Corriveau, 1993b; Granger, & Holbrook, 1983) is required to manage how several interpretations are to be combined into a single association.

As an example of this case, consider ambiguous sentences such as these:

Example 3.3.2.1 *John watched the man with the telescope.*

Example 3.3.2.2 *The lawyer left the bar.*

In the first example, the prepositional phrase "with the telescope" can be attached to either the verb "watched" or to the noun phrase "the man". Out of context, both solutions are equally probable, and the ambiguity needs to be captured in the meaning of the preposition. One strategy could consist in ascribing *no* meaning to "with", leaving the sentence ambiguous in its representation. Another strategy could be to associate *both* attachments to the preposition, as will be further discussed in chapter 10. Similarly, the word "bar" in the second example could refer to "the bar in a court of justice" or to a tavern. Again, a multi-valued association may be required, in this case for lexical disambiguation, as explained in chapter 9. However, consider the following sentence:

Example 3.3.2.3 *The sailor ate the submarine.*

Despite the word "sailor" possibly preempting (or *priming*) the interpretation of "submarine" as ship, semantic constraints could force this interpretation to be replaced with that of "submarine" as sandwich. In other words, for this example of lexical disambiguation (see chapter 9), a resolution strategy that keeps the two possible interpretations is probably not adequate. Instead, the latest interpretation must replace the primed one.

Therefore, in summary, in order to model diachronic interpretation, we require that the grounded architecture offer primitive operations (namely, matching, storage, retrieval, and association) as well as some way of expressing a resolution strategy (to decide how to manage having several interpretations over time for the same linguistic unit).

Second, beyond interpretations, knowledge is itself generally diachronic: What we know changes over time. Even fundamental "laws of Nature", such as Newton's, are subject to revisions, enhancements, and so forth. This observation suggests that we, therefore, should refrain from hardwiring any knowledge into a software cognitive system. Instead, as previously mentioned, all knowledge should be treated as user-specifiable and user-modifiable data to the "understanding" algorithm. For example, each word has the potential to acquire new definitions over time (e.g., see Rastier, 1991, for an in-depth discussion of individual and cultural diachronic changes). Furthermore, in our Genesis example, if the third "meaning" of "revelation" is not stored in memory, then the second interpretation of the title of the album is not possible. Thus, as a user of **IDIoT**, I will have to input this new "meaning" of "revelation" in my knowledge base because this new meaning is neither built into the software nor inferable from other knowledge. As a corollary requirement, the format of the data in the knowledge base must be highly understandable to a user so that it can be easily modified. Moreover, if we envision the automatic integration of an interpretation into an existing knowledge base (see Bookman, 1992), we must also require that the system itself have the ability to modify a knowledge base.

Finally, we must acknowledge the diachronic nature of the understanding algorithm itself. In other words, how we understand may change with time.

This suggests that this algorithm be treated as data residing in the knowledge base because it is subject to change. Failure to do so inevitably leads to a static, if not a normative or innatist, view of comprehension. This requirement is not new. Lindsay and Manaster-Ramer (1987) have already suggested that we not think of an algorithm for understanding, but rather of several sets of (possibly inconsistent) rules that are selectively used to process the current input. The proposed requirement merely adds that these rules exist in the knowledge base rather than in the system itself.

3.3.3 Other Requirements

Cognitive architectures are software artifacts and, as such, should aim at the same software engineering goals as do other programs. However, generally, this has not been the case because artificial intelligence researchers that construct systems have been first and foremost concerned with "proving" their theories.

From a computational viewpoint, in my opinion, the most important requirement for cognitive architectures is tractability. Let me only briefly elaborate. Shastri (1993) distinguished between *reflexive* and *reflective* reasoning. The former is extremely fast, automatic, unconscious, and pervasive to human cognition. The latter requires "conscious deliberation, and at times, the use of external props such as paper and pencil (e.g., solving logic puzzles, doing cryptarithmetic, or planning a vacation)" (Shastri, 1993). Following Minsky (1986), it is my position that a general cognitive architecture should be based on reflexive cognition rather than on the more specialized reflective form. Indeed, reflective approaches to comprehension not only typically entail a normative theory of interpretation, but simply have little computational *or* cognitive relevance. This is exemplified in Levesque's (1984) trade-off between the expressiveness of a representational language and its computational tractability, a trade-off that erroneously presupposes that human cognition uses a truth-conditional (formal) theory of meaning (see 2.2.4.2). Instead, we want grounded cognitive systems that will offer an interpretation in a reasonable (read short) amount of time. Let us not forget that, despite all of its inherent complexity, we can understand language at the rate of several hundred words per minute (Shastri, 1993), as emphasized by the biological constraint (Feldman, 1984). However, not only do we require tractability with respect to time, but also with respect to space (see Shastri, 1993). In other words, the interpretation of a long text should not lead to a combinatorial explosion in the amount of space this interpretation "consumes".

A second important requirement is reusability (Jacobson, Christerson, Jonsson, & Overgaar, 1992; Sommerville, 1992): Ideally a single cognitive architecture should serve for the experimentation of several theories. For example, an architecture should be generic enough to accommodate several epistemological models. A corollary requirement of reusability is understandability: A program that can only be maintained and modified by its designer has extremely limited usefulness beyond the immediate experimentation led by this designer.

3.3.4 Summary of the Requirements

From the previous discussion, we have identified the following requirements:

1. The system should not hardwire any particular solution.

2. The system must be able to take into account independent external factors that may influence cognition.

3. The system must have a stopping criterion.

4. The architecture must be grounded in primitive operations (matching, storage, retrieval, and association) and allow the expression of a resolution strategy.

5. All knowledge (including the understanding algorithm itself) should be treated as user-specifiable and user-modifiable.

6. The format of the data in the knowledge base must be highly understandable to a user so that it can be easily modified.

7. The architecture must be tractable both in terms of time and space complexity.

8. The architecture must be reusable.

3.3.5 Conclusion

Without repeating all the objections of chapter 2 to the existing models of linguistic comprehension, a brief run-down of the previous list of requirements will emphasize the inadequacy of these approaches:

1. We have seen that existing systems generally depend on built-in macrostructures, that is, on a more or less hardwired solution.

2. Few systems let the user set external factors that may influence cognition. In appearance, this is merely a user-interface problem, but, in reality, it points to different design philosophies. Existing systems are typically not user-based, but rather programmer-based: They generally implement static theories of interpretation.

3. All existing systems have a stopping criterion. More precisely, information-processing approaches rely on a pre-specified semantic criterion (e.g., matching a schema, obtaining some sort of truth-conditional proof) and connectionism, on mathematical equilibrium. However, existing criteria typically do not allow the acquisition of several interpretations over time for a same text.

4. Existing architectures are not grounded, and very few models address the issue of a resolution strategy (see Granger, & Holbrook, 1983).

5. All information-processing approaches have built-in knowledge, as well as a fixed understanding algorithm. Knowledge entrenched by the designer in such systems is typically static (that is, not modifiable) and hidden from the user. Conversely, in PDP systems, the designer/ user generally specifies all knowledge by training the network. Modification to the knowledge embedded in the network is only possible through retraining. It is not clear, however, if incremental training is possible or if each set of modifications requires a complete re-training of the network. Furthermore, I have questioned in the previous chapter the relevance of training to the comprehension of text. Even more importantly, it appears that PDP models lack a genuine understanding algorithm and do not scale up by themselves to text comprehension. More specifically, it is not obvious how they could *construct* an interpretation, as opposed to merely recognizing one, without the help of a symbolic control architecture (for coordination between several PDP networks).

6. Information-processing systems can, at least in theory, accommodate a user-friendly format for the data in the knowledge base. Conversely, PDP models present the significant disadvantage of not having a separate knowledge base per se. Consequently, a user of a PDP network cannot readily understand what "knowledge" the network uses.

7. Shastri (1993) remarked that little consideration has been given at this point in time to time *and* space complexity. Information-processing models generally use arbitrarily complex algorithms and data structures, as previously mentioned. Some local connectionist approaches, such as the work of Bookman (1992), do address time complexity but violate space tractability (see Shastri, 1993, who remarked that some of these models even have quadratic space com-

plexity). As for PDP models, they may be tractable, but at the expense
of not addressing the difficulties of text comprehension.

8. Finally, neither information processing implementations nor PDP
networks are reusable, in the software engineering sense of this term.
Most information-processing models entrench too many specific
architectural details to be able to accommodate any other theory but
the one they implement. As for PDP systems, a network is trained
with respect to a specific "training set". Thus, a trained network is
typically not reusable beyond the task for which it was trained.

3.4 CHOOSING SPREADING ACTIVATION

With the conclusion that existing approaches to text comprehension fail to satisfy the requirements we have set forth, the question remains how do we start
the design of a grounded cognitive architecture.

First, it is essential to understand that the proposed design should not be
aimed at any particular interpretative theory. For example, Rastier's (1991)
differential semantics constitutes an extensive theory of interpretation, which
we have merely mentioned rather than explained at length. Indeed, we have
purposely avoided looking at the details of any particular theory of interpretation. We should not design **IDIoT** with respect to a specific theory, but instead
according to the requirements introduced in the previous section. Otherwise,
it is highly probable that we will build into the proposed architecture, techniques that are specific to given a interpretative theory. Such a strategy would
not only likely violate the purely mechanistic outlook of a grounded system,
but also possibly diminish its reusability.

Should we forget all existing work in AI as the previous section (and chapter) may seem to suggest? Quite on the contrary: The architecture to be developed should define a processing framework in which existing work can be
"integrated". In this context, "integration" does not mean direct reuse because
it would be utopian to design an architecture that readily accommodates all
existing systems! Instead, we want to provide a general experimentation
framework in which a large number of the existing models could be reimple-
mented with more or less effort, the actual integration effort varying according
to the "adhocness" of the model to reimplement. Such a strategy is possible in
IDIoT because we require that all knowledge exist in a knowledge base separate from the grounded architecture itself. In other words, any interpretative
theory can be accommodated, at least in theory, by **IDIoT** because this theory
is external to the architecture.

In fact, only the trivial algorithm, that is, the operational principle underlying the grounded architecture, imposes restrictions with respect to the expression and processing of existing (or future) models within the proposed framework. It follows that, in order for the framework to maximize reusability, the trivial algorithm must correspond to a general approach to the expression and processing of knowledge. *Spreading activation* (see Anderson, 1983; Hendler, 1989) constitutes such a general strategy. In essence, the mechanisms of spreading activation have remained almost unchanged since their introduction to AI in the sixties. In fact, as emphasized by Quillian (1967) and Fahlman (1979), the notion of spreading activation can be traced back to the early work of some psychologists on associative memory at the end of the nineteenth century.

Roughly put, spreading activation consists in having the *nodes* of a graph (taken to form a semantic network; see Sowa, 1991) exchange *signals* along (possibly weighted and directed) *edges*. All nodes are taken to be initially dormant and can be activated either directly from the input (to the model, such as a sentence for a natural language understanding system) or from receiving signals from their neighbors (i.e., their adjacent nodes). A signal corresponds to *activation* or equivalently, to *energy*: One node receives energy from some of its neighbors, processes it, and in turn, sends activation to some of its neighbors. We say activation is *spread* over a set of connected nodes that come to form a path. Each path of activation is assumed to correspond to an inference *constructed* from the semantic network.

Because nodes of the network are typically assumed to be concurrent processors, that is, because the semantic network is taken to be *massively parallel*, a multitude of inferences can be generated from the input. More precisely, each input token activates one or more nodes of the network, which, in turn, spread activation to numerous other nodes of the network, generating a multitude of inference paths.

This brief description of the spreading activation processing model emphasizes several of its characteristics that make it an attractive general theory for the expression and processing of knowledge:

1. Spreading activation underlies a multitude of models in artificial intelligence. In particular, semantic networks (Rastier, 1991, chapter 4; Sowa, 1991) are widely used as a representational scheme for natural language processing.

2. The basic processing model of spreading activation is simple and yet powerful. Bookman (1992) indeed observed that it underlies not only inference-chaining (or equivalently, marker-passing) systems but also local connectionist ones (see chapter 2).

3. Spreading activation can accommodate symbolic operations such as variable binding (e.g., Ajjanagadde, & Shastri, 1989, 1991). As a matter of fact, spreading activation models have been proposed for problems that were taken to inherently require a formal interpretative theory (e.g., Hendrix, 1979, for quantification). Indeed, if one believes the claim that semantic networks are reducible to propositions, a claim discussed and rejected by Rastier (1991, pp. 133–134), then, reciprocally, some truth-conditional approaches must be mappable, at least in theory, to spreading activation systems.

4. Through the interactions between the nodes of the network, spreading activation can construct (rather than merely recognize) an interpretation. In other words, not only can it model schema-matching (for it is rather trivial to re-express such a processing strategy in terms of activation over nodes that correspond to parts of patterns), but also constructionist theories of interpretation (see Meutsch, 1986), that is, theories that construct an interpretation.

Furthermore, with respect to **IDIoT**, I choose to adopt spreading activation because of its direct relevance to the basic metaphor of human memory and because spreading activation systems can be shown to address reflexive reasoning with adequate time and space complexity (Shastri, 1993), as will be discussed in section 4.7.

Spreading activation, however, also introduces a fundamental processing strategy that we must now investigate, namely massive parallelism.

3.5 CONCURRENT OBJECTS FOR SPREADING ACTIVATION

The biological constraint (Feldman, 1984) states that complex cognitive tasks must be performed in a few computational steps. From this observation, connectionist researchers (e.g., Miikkulainen, 1993b, p. 9; Shastri, 1993) hypothesize a massively parallel architecture for cognition, that is, a network of concurrent processors (or "neurons"). Indeed, some authors seem to go as far as claiming that there is an epistemological difference between parallel and traditional representation schemes and processing strategies (see Smolensky, 1988).

The question of the relevance of parallelism to artificial intelligence is not new (see Akker, Ablas, Nijholt, & Luttighuis, 1992; Kibler, & Conery, 1985; Kitano, Moldovan, Higuchi, Waltz, & Hendler, 1991). One the one hand, formalists have typically downplayed the importance of concurrency, arguing that it merely constitutes an implementation detail. On the other hand, a small group of visionaries (a word I use with its French meliorative connotation of one who foresees the future, as opposed to the pejorative connotation of "impractical dreamer"), I was surprised to find in the *Webster's*, 1981, p. 1299) have developed both hardware (e.g., Chung, & Moldovan, 1994; Kitano, 1991; Kitano, Moldovan, & Cha, 1991; Moldovan, Lee, & Lin, 1993) and corresponding cognitive theories that propose a new way of approaching some of the problems of artificial intelligence (Kitano, & Hendler, 1994). In particular, the *memory-based reasoning* (MBR) paradigm (Stanfill, & Waltz, 1986; Waltz 1990), which is close to case-based or example-based approaches (Kitano, 1993), has been shown to be very relevant to spreading activation (Tomabechi, & Levin, 1989) as well as to different facets of natural language processing such as parsing (e.g., Kitano, & Higuchi, 1991a) and translation (e.g., Kitano, & Higuchi, 1991b; Sato, & Nagao, 1990).

Waltz (in Kitano, Moldovan, Higuchi, Waltz, & Hendler, 1991) summarized the debate:

> I will argue that for nearly every domain of AI interest, MBR is likely to be more appropriate than rule-based methods. This is because most domains contain both regularities (that seem to encourage rule-based approaches) as well as large number of exceptions or idiosyncrasies (that demand item-by-item treatment). Unfortunately for those who favor rules, the ubiquity and sheer number of exceptions may cause the number of rules needed to handle all phenomena to become extremely large, so large that the number of rules is on the same order as the number of phenomena. MBR systems handle both regularities and exceptions in a uniform and simple-to-program fashion.

Evidently, the rejection of rules, much like Small's (1980, 1983) word-expert approach to NLP, and the acknowledgment of idiosyncrasies is in agreement with the reader-based approach I advocate. Nevertheless, MBR is also close to the design philosophy of **IDIoT** inasmuch as it respects the biological constraint and places memory at the foundation of intelligence rather than at the periphery. Consequently, I adopt the conceptualization of memory as a network of concurrent processors following a spreading activation processing strategy. From a design viewpoint, because of my upfront concern with reusability, I suggest that the concurrent processors be implemented as concurrent *objects*, in the object-oriented (OO) sense (Budd, 1991; de Champeaux, Lea, & Faure, 1993; Jacobson, Christerson, Jonsson, & Overgaar, 1992) of the term, and that spreading activation correspond to *message passing* between such objects.

This approach will be investigated in the next section. For now, I want to emphasize that a few researchers have already discussed the relevance of object-oriented programming (OOP) to artificial intelligence (e.g., Tello, 1989) and natural language processing. In particular, Cunningham and Veale (1991) presented **TWIG**, a blackboard architecture (see Anderson, 1983) for text understanding. This system, which integrates lexical and encyclopedic knowledge, uses a complex (read ad hoc) object-oriented architecture to tackle several facets of linguistic comprehension (such as anaphoric resolution, concept formation, parsing, composition, filtering). As with other blackboard systems (see Clancey, 1992), the system is not grounded and cannot model the interactions necessary to the construction of an inference, but it does take advantage of the semantic characteristics of object-oriented programming languages (e.g., polymorphism and inheritance between classes).

Object-oriented approaches to grammar (Zajac, 1992) and parsing (Brown, 1993; Lin, & Goebel, 1993) have also been proposed, and the role of inheritance (a key feature of OO) for natural language processing has been discussed at length in a recent special issue of the journal *Computational Linguistics* (Daelemans, Smedt De, & Gazdar, 1992).

It is my contention that, beyond the obvious correspondence between activation and messages on the one hand, and between processors and objects on the other hand, object-oriented programming (OOP) is particularly relevant to a *framework* for spreading activation architecture, as explained in the next section.

3.6 A REUSABLE FRAMEWORK FOR SPREADING ACTIVATION

3.6.1 On the Relevance of OO to Spreading Activation

Because, in OOP, objects and messages can be of arbitrary complexity, any kind of spreading activation system can be quite directly implemented. This is quite obvious for the simple signals and nodes assumed by connectionism (e.g., see Tello, 1989, for the implementation simple neural network), but even markers containing control information can be readily coded in OOP because messages can typically carry arbitrary pieces of code as parameters. For example, in the programming language Smalltalk (Goldberg, 1984), a block (of code) can be passed as an argument of a message and performed in the receiving object. Therefore, the issue is not the feasibility of an object-oriented implementation of a general spreading activation architecture, but its relevance to the design of such an architecture. In the rest of this subsection, I argue that, indeed, OOP is relevant to the design of a spreading activation architecture.

In essence, there are three main goals set forth by OOP: modeling, reuse, and refinement (Jacobson, Christerson, Jonsson, & Overgaar, 1992). All three appear to be pertinent to spreading activation.

First, modeling (i.e., the capturing of concepts, rules, and schemas using objects, classes, and messages) is directly applicable to the task of building a semantic network. The claim of OOP is that it provides standard notations and tools required for robust modeling (Jacobson, et al., 1992). Such a standardization in the description of semantic networks would be highly desirable in a field in which adhocness is an omnipresent problem, as we have witnessed in chapter 2. More specifically, OOP notations could be used for the specification of semantic networks (in terms of concepts and links between them) and for the design of spreading activation systems (i.e., for the processing architectures underlying the semantic networks). Such usage would likely minimize (both conceptual and architectural) idiosyncrasies and definitely favor a better understanding of the similarities and differences between such models.

Second, as previously suggested, reuse is also absolutely necessary in order to stop the proliferation of ad hoc models. In OOP, reuse is best realized through the use of a *framework* (in the OO sense of the word, see de Champeaux, et al., 1993), that is, as a set of reusable *classes* (Budd, 1991). The classes **Network, Node, Edge** and **Signal** are obvious candidates in order to standardize the specification of spreading activation models. The proposed framework consists of these classes as well as some prespecified subclasses that are discussed in the next subsection. For example, the nodes of a particular model would be *instances* of the class **Node**, or more probably, of one of its subclasses. The key idea of a framework is that the user either a) reuses one of the prespecified classes or b) subclasses them in order to introduce the specific characteristics of the chosen model.

Third, it seems that refinement, that is, the iterative development (de Champeaux, Lea, & Faure, 1993) of software, is at the heart of the development process for spreading activation models, if not of AI systems in general. More specifically, due to its experimental nature, any AI program inherently requires some "tweaking". For example, weights in local connectionist systems, learning rates, and number of "epochs" and of hidden layers (see Miikkulainen, 1993b) in PDP networks, and schema and rule interactions in information-processing models are generally obtained by trial-and-error. This is particularly true for domains, such as natural language processing, in which the adequacy of a particular solution cannot be formally proven, but only verified a posteriori by the user, a situation that entails a multitude of trials and corrections. In OOP, objects are ideally highly cohesive entities that are not highly coupled to each other (Jacobson, et al., 1992; Sommerville, 1992): Changes are ideally restricted (i.e., local) to an object (and invisible to the collaborators of this object). Such a design strategy allows the addition of objects to a design, as well as the refinement of an object (i.e., the addition or modification of functionality to this object by means of private attributes, or procedures), without catastrophic consequences to "surrounding" objects. Thus, an OO system can typically scale up painlessly from a small set of simple objects to a complex system, over several iterations. Each iteration, in essence, constitutes a development cycle, which includes requirement capture, analysis, design, implementation, and testing. A system that entails some trial-and-error design greatly benefits from such an iterative process because each iteration provides quality assurance feedback that is used to guide the next iteration. In other words, errors should be local to specific objects and should guide further development. Thus, in my opinion, object-oriented refinement not only improves the scalability but also the quality of a system whose development requires trial-and-error.

Furthermore, in OOP, modeling, reuse and refinement are supported by several technical mechanisms: encapsulation, classification, inheritance and polymorphism (see Budd, 1991, for a detailed discussion). Two of these mechanisms seem to be directly relevant to spreading activation and natural language processing.

First, several difficult programming problems (e.g., deadlock, starvation, etc.) are associated with concurrency (Burns, & Davies, 1993), and thus are relevant to spreading activation. Most of these problems proceed from attempting to share (as opposed to exchange) data between objects. *Encapsulation*, that is, the ability to hide inside an object its implementation (in terms of private data and procedures), explicitly discourages such sharing. In other words, in OOP, information must ideally be strictly local to objects or obtained by other objects through messages, a strategy that (is expensive from a performance viewpoint but) avoids coupling and concurrency problems. The adoption of encapsulation as a design guideline raises, however, the question of the implementation of global processes such as path evaluation or relaxation (see chapter 2) used respectively in marker-passing and connectionist architectures, as discussed in the next subsection.

Second, *classification* and *inheritance*, which are central to OOP's claim of producing reusable software, are also relevant to semantic modeling and natural language processing (see Daelemans, et al., 1992), as previously suggested. In fact, the treatment of classification, inheritance, and exceptions (called "overrides" in OOP) touches upon the problem of categorization (Lakoff, 1987): Because in OOP there is typically a direct mapping between conceptual categories on the one hand and implementation classes on the other, the choice of categories will ultimately affect the behavior of the software. For example, a poorly-designed category will lead to a class with poor cohesion (in the software engineering sense of the term, see Sommerville, 1992). In other words, semantic decisions will likely bear software engineering consequences, and thus could be evaluated according to software engineering principles, an intriguing idea that I explore elsewhere.

The point for now is that OOP is indeed relevant to the design of a general framework for spreading activation, if not for conceptual modeling in general as suggested by Kristensen and Østerbye (1994).

3.6.2 Overview of a Framework for Spreading Activation

Let us now briefly consider the organization of a framework for spreading activation. (The details of this framework will be discussed in a subsequent book that presents the implementation of the ideas of Bookman (1992, 1994), Dyer (1983), Norvig (1987, 1989) and Rastier (1987, 1989) using this framework.)

In order to design this framework, we must abstract away from the details of specific systems in order to identify the essential characteristics of spreading activation models. As previously mentioned, the classes **Network**, **Node**, **Edge** and **Signal** are obvious candidates for the standardization of the specification of spreading activation models:

1. The class **Network** implements all *global* processes of the model. These processes can be of arbitrary complexity. All processes not specified in **Network** must therefore be truly distributed processes that only rely on the exchange of signals between nodes. This class has currently two prespecified subclasses, classes **Marker-Passing-Network** and **Local-Connectionist-Network**. Each of these defines the characteristics of these specific types of networks. A **PDP-Network** class could also be supplied, although this is not the case in the current prototype. Path evaluation in marker-passing networks as well as global energy minimization through relaxation in connectionist networks (see Feldman, 1984, 1985b; Selman, 1985) constitute possible candidates for global processes. Decay could also be handled at the network level. In all cases, a global process takes the form of a *method* (see Budd, 1991) in the class **Network** (or one of its subclasses). For example, path evaluation could be implemented as the method **checkInference: aPath**, which any node in the network can invoke by sending this message to the class **Network** (or one of its subclasses). The **checkInference** method would examine the path supplied in the parameter **aPath** and either internally carry out further

actions or request the relevant node to do so (by sending a message to it). Subclasses of **Marker-Passing-Network** could then override this general method. For example, a subclass **Abduction-Network** could reimplement **checkInference** using an abductive algorithm, whereas the subclass **FAUSTUS** (Norvig, 1987)would have **checkInference** match the supplied path against a list of valid patterns (see chapter 2). Similarly, for connectionist networks, energy minimization would require that every node of the network send a message carrying this node's current energy level to the class **Network**. The method invoked in **Network**, call it **minimize: aFloat**, would accumulate these energy levels and monitor their minimization.

2. The class **Node** defines the general activities of any node in a semantic network, as well as the information such a node stores. For example, nodes of a connectionist network could individually store a threshold function, as opposed to using a global one stored in **Network** or one of its subclasses. Furthermore, the activities of a node take the form of the (arbitrary complex) methods of this class. In order to implement general distributed processes, I suggest that all nodes have the following methods:

a) a method **receive: aSignal**, which defines what to do upon receiving the signal **aSignal**. For example, in connectionist networks, the reception of a signal triggers the recomputation of an activation function and the comparison of its new value with a certain threshold.

b) a method **send: aSignal to: aNode,** which requests the sending of the signal **aSignal** to a specific node. In the most centralized design, all nodes would send only to the instance of the network (and ignore how to directly reach their collaborators), which then would send this message to its target destination. Conversely, in a totally distributed system, all nodes know how to refer to their collaborators.

c) a method **activate**, to spell out how the node becomes activated and which outputs are to be sent upon activation. In the simplest case, activate is merely a threshold function (with respect to a sum of input signals accumulated in a private variable of each node) and a list of output signals to send. More generally, **activate** consists of a constraint satisfaction step (defined with respect to the input signals and possibly involving complex processing) followed by an output step (which establishes output signals, possibly taking into account which activation constraint was satisfied). In turn, the constraint satisfaction step could be captured using a method **satisfy**, and the output step using **sendOutputs** (which merely consists of a sequence of invocation of the method **send**).

3. The class **Signal**, merely defines the format of the information exchanged between nodes. As previously mentioned, this information can be arbitrarily complex (possibly involving both data and control, because this is not a problem in OO). Typically, a specific subclass of **Signal** would be associated with a specific kind of network. For example, connectionist systems would use the subclass **NumericSignal**, which merely defines a range of valid numeric values for nodes to exchange in such networks. Other possible subclasses of **Signal** include **ControlMarker**, **DataMarker**, **ComplexMarker**, and so forth, and are quite self-explanatory.

4. The class **Edge** implements the communication links of the network. For generality, edges are weighted and directed, with the default weight being zero. Edges also have a communication delay set, by default, to zero.

The proposed framework leaves room for the designer to implement vastly different systems. For example, Norvig's (1987, 1989) **FAUSTUS** could implement path evaluation either

1. as a global process in its subclass of **Network** or

2. using a subclass of **Node**, called **PathEvaluationNode**, which would have a single instance implementing the evaluation process in its methods, or

3. as a truly distributed process, as suggested by Yu and Simmons (1989), which relies on complex messages carrying the paths to be evaluated. Such messages could be implemented as instances of a subclass, **PathSignal**, of the class **ComplexMarker**.

More generally, peculiarities of a given model (such as its anti-promiscuity rules, its modeling of short term memory, its learning strategy, etc.) merely have to be expressed as methods of the classes used to describe the system. Ideally, the designer should try to fit all characteristics of the target model into the framework established by the classes **Network**, **Node**, **Edge**, and **Signal**, and their descendant classes. For example, if a convergence strategy or a resolution strategy is adopted for a specific model, then if this strategy takes the form of a global process, it should be implemented as a public method of a subclass of **Network**. Conversely, if the resolution strategy can be entirely implemented using messages, it merely requires specialized methods in the relevant subclass of **Node**. And, finally, as with path evaluation, there is also the possibility of using a one-instance subclass of **Node** to localize the resolution strategy in a single node. The point to be grasped is that the framework does not constrain what a model can do, but rather the way it is implemented. Moreover, it should be noted that because we still do not have a solution to the mind-body problem, we cannot yet decide on which processes are truly distributed in the brain, and which ones rely on centralized centers. However, the use of a one-instance class such as **PathEvaluationNode** seems the least desirable implementation strategy, inasmuch as it is highly improbable from a neurological viewpoint that a node requiring total connectivity to all the other nodes of the network exists in the brain!

Finally, the programmer may even want to introduce subclasses of **Node** and/or **Signal** to capture in the framework the epistemological commitments of the model. For example, the classes of valid paths admitted by **FAUSTUS** could be explicitly captured as subclasses of the class **Path** itself a subclass of **ComplexMarker**, which is a subclass of **Signal**. Similarly, the subclasses of **Node** could be used to model a conceptual hierarchy (e.g., Animate, Animal, Mammal, Reptile, State, Event, Goal, Belief, etc.). The point is that the proposed framework does not constitute in itself a grounded architecture; we still need to address the requirements established in section 3.3. Indeed, Rastier (1991, p. 156) remarked that semantic networks still leave the door open to representational approaches (e.g., scriptal lexicons, lexical semantics [(Pustejovsky, & Bergler, 1991)], selectional constraints), which he considers problematic inasmuch as they treat context as prespecified in the knowledge encoded in the model, as opposed to something constructed and dynamically managed.

To conclude, I remark that this brief description of the concurrent object-oriented framework for spreading activation does not address some the difficult technical aspects of its realization, and in particular, its treatment of concurrency. I have deliberately adopted a user's viewpoint in the overview of the framework to avoid such technicalities which have the virtue of being encapsulated in the most abstract classes of the framework and thus of being essentially invisible to the user. For example, the spreading activation metaphor views nodes as concurrent processors. In turn, this implies concurrent exchanges of messages, synchronization, and so forth, but the treatment of nodes as concurrent processors and of message sends as concurrent processes is encapsulated in the classes **Network, Node,** and **Edge**. The programmer need not scrutinize the actual simulation of concurrency unless he or she specifically wants to modify it. Consequently, in the rest of this book, I shall motivate the design of **IDIoT** from the perspective of a user, not concerning myself with the technical difficulties experienced while developing the current prototype within this framework.

Chapter 4

Modeling Time-Constrained Memory

4.1 INTRODUCTION

We established at the beginning of this book that the proposed grounded architecture should be rooted in the basic metaphor of human memory (hereafter simply memory). Then in the preceding chapter, we selected spreading activation as the operational principle underlying this grounded architecture, but spreading activation does not make up this architecture per se; it does not constitute a model of memory by itself. Furthermore, the implementation of spreading activation as a concurrent object-oriented framework is essentially irrelevant to the design of a grounded architecture. The task at hand, then, is to understand how to model memory starting from spreading activation. In this chapter, I will first very briefly summarize the issues related to the modeling of human memory and then discuss the design of a model of time-constrained memory, a grounded model of memory using spreading activation as its operational principle and "on top of which" a conceptual analyzer can be constructed, as will be illustrated in Part III of this book.

4.2 HUMAN MEMORY AS METAPHOR

Research on memory constitutes a vast, complex, and controversial interdisciplinary field. Browsing, for example, the voluminous proceedings of the "Attention and Performance" conferences (e.g., Meyer, & Kornblum, 1993) will convince the reader of the breadth of phenomena considered in this domain; looking at specialized texts such as Horn's (1985) work on imprinting should demonstrate the depth of some of the issues associated with memory. Schacter (1989) provided a concise introduction to the field. It introduces several important notions:

1. working memory versus short-term memory versus long-term memory,

2. implicit versus explicitly memory,

3. semantic versus episodic memory,

4. multiple memories,

5. existence and role of a central executive and of an articulatory loop,

6. encoding, schemas, and

7. methodologies for studying memory.

I merely enumerate these phrases and refer the reader to Schacter's work or to more extensive introductions such as those of Baddeley (1976, 1986), Hockley and Lewandowsky (1991), and Parkin (1993) for details. I do not elaborate on these notions for one simple reason: There is still widespread disagreement with respect to the details associated with these terms. For example, Cowan, Keller, Hulme, Roodenys, McDougall, and Rack (1994) rejected Baddeley's model of "memory span". As a matter of fact, Greene (1992) explained that a few different schools of thought have confronted and continue to confront each other on a multitude of organizational and operational characteristics of memory. In the rest of this section, I briefly summarize some of these debates.

First, it is commonly accepted that memory has an omnipresent temporal dimension. However, modeling the mechanisms, such as attention, that subsume this dimension typically remains problematic. For example, Raymond, Shapiro, and Arnell (1992) supported the view of an opening and closing of an attentional gate to regulate the flow of perceptual visual information to the recognition centers of the brain. By closing this gate, one allows a refractory period akin to the one of neurons, during which further stimulus is ignored. When confusion is present, the attentional gate is both shut and locked, making the initiation of the next attentional episode a more time consuming process than if a locking operation had not been conducted. But what are these "recognition centres"; what is the capacity of the "attentional gate"; what is "confusion" in operational terms? Similar questions apply to the "articulatory rehearsal" process proposed by Longoni, Richardson, and Aiello (1993). In fact, psychological theories of attention often lack the mechanistic details required for computational modeling. This remark also holds for other theories that depend on intuitive notions such as "mood" (e.g., Perrig, & Perrig, 1988) that generally do not have mechanistic definitions.

Second, there is disagreement regarding the kinds of memories human beings possess. Schacter and Tulving (1994) summarized the viewpoint of neuroscience in a recent book, but, in fact, a multitude of different partitioning schemes have been proposed:

1. Nairne (1988), Penney (1989) and Speer, Crowder, and Thomas (1993) all argued, for example, for a distinction between auditory and visual memory, although they differed considerably on the modus operandi of these two systems.

2. Sebrechts, Marsh, and Seamon (1989) discussed the distinction between primary and secondary memory, which pertains to temporal, as opposed to modal partitioning. In essence, primary memory has an extremely short span, but how does it relate to short-term memory (Shiffrin, 1993), to implicit memory (Lewandowsky, Dunn, & Kirsner, 1989), and to working memory (Baddeley, 1986)? Moreover, are such distinctions strictly independent of the stimulus (see Bowers, 1994)? Furthermore, can we assume as Parkin, Reid, and Russo (1990) did, that there are actual processing differences between implicit and explicit memory systems?

3. Tulving (1983) suggested that episodic memory must be separated from semantic memory, a controversial distinction according to several researchers (see the comments at the end of Tulving, 1984). This separation has received recent support (e.g., Gardiner, & Java, 1990), but is still problematic for some researchers (e.g., Dosher, & Rosedale, 1991).

In the end, such distinctions are important but typically ignored from a computational viewpoint because of their lack of operational details. Short-term memory (STM) constitutes a notable exception to this observation. More precisely, although it is affected by several factors (e.g., age: see Gick, Craik, & Morris, 1988; Bäckman, 1991) that may be difficult to model computationally, several authors from psychology and artificial intelligence have proposed models of STM, models which generally support the notion of the decay of a trace. Even neural models of STM (e.g., Brown, 1989; Schweickert, Guentert, & Hersberg, 1989) have been put forth. Jones (1993) argued, however, that such neural perspectives do not proceed from recent evidence but rather can be traced back to ideas published in 1924. Moreover, fundamental characteristics of STM, especially its capacity (or "span"), remain quite controversial (see Schweickert, & Boruff, 1986; Ehrlich, Brebion, & Tardieu, 1994). Indeed, Martin, Shelton, & Yaffee (1994) even seemed to suggest that the issue of "span" ultimately rests on which kinds of partitions one adopts. As previously mentioned, however, the existence and functioning of such partitions are subject to debate. For example, Cowan (1993) proposed that STM "be depicted as a subset of the activated portion of long-term memory". This viewpoint is just one in the multitude put forth in the last 30 years (Schneider,

1993). In the end, we are forced to conclude, in accord with Cowan (1993) and Shiffrin (1993), that although STM is taken to be pervasive to any theory of human cognition, it is still a vague concept leading to metaphoric theories of cognition.

In turn, this observation leads us to question the role of STM with respect to comprehension. Several researchers (e.g., Just, & Carpenter, 1992) have proposed models of comprehension that hinge on the notion of STM capacity. Against this approach, Daneman and Green (1986) and Daneman (1987) remarked:

> It is not that individuals differ in structural temporary storage capacity, that is, in the number of 'slots' for passively storing items or chunks of information, as traditional [research on] short-term memory. . . would have us believe. Rather they differ in functional storage capacity, that is, in the amount of capacity that is effectively left over for temporary storage once the requirements for the computational or processing aspects have been met.

However, even such a functional (as opposed to structural) standpoint was rejected by Martin (1993), who questioned the role of STM altogether for comprehension.

Third, the unit for processing in memory ("items", "chunks", etc.) remains highly controversial. What is a chunk? Do we have hierarchical schemas (e.g., McKoon, Ratcliff, & Seifert, 1989; Schank, 1982), headed records (Morton, Hammersley, & Bekerian, 1985), scripts (e.g., Schank, & Abelson, 1977) "in our head"? Some psychologists (e.g., Alba, & Hasher, 1983; Thorndike, & Yekovich, 1980) have strongly argued against such complex entities as units of processing for memory. Others (e.g., Gernsbacher, 1985; Johnson, 1986) have remarked that too often we ignore the issue of the unit of loss, which may help us understand the nature of the unit of processing. In turn, this leads us to the problem of retrieval, which has been typically downplayed in the vast majority of existing computational models (with the works of Kolodner, 1988; Wharton, Holyoak, Downing, Lange, & Wickens, 1991; Lange, & Wharton, 1993 as notable exceptions). It is commonly accepted that recallability affects recognition (e.g., Gardiner, 1988), but the details of what is retrieved from memory, and how it is retrieved from it, remain problematic. Kintsch and Mannes (1987), for example suggested that scripts act as control structures for the ordered retrieval of information, rather than as precompiled structures, but such an approach says little about the role of surface information during retrieval, a role emphasized by Wharton et al. (1991). Furthermore, what about the so-called "recency effect" (see Baddeley, & Hitch,

1993), which is assumed to facilitate recognition? Can we conclude, as Whittlesea and Brooks (1988) did that "memory preserves information about the details of particular perceptual experiences, and that [recognition and retrieval] depends critically on the similarity of current demands and processing context to the demands and context of particular previous experiences"?

In the end, it appears that almost every facet of human memory is subject to some degree of controversy. In my opinion, this conclusion results from the current absence of a solution to the mind-body problem and, in particular, from our inability to pinpoint the "location" of memory in the brain. Ultimately, such a negative conclusion leads to the radical criticism of some researchers. For example, Malcolm (1977) presented a destructive treatment of both mentalistic and physiological theories of memory. For him, conjectures as to what takes place in our minds when we remember are illusory and self-defeating. More recently, Rosenfield (1988) strongly argued against the commonplace view that human memory is a kind of filing cabinet or database, that memories are permanent records, that remembering is retrieving something, that practiced behavior is reexecuting a program, and that learning, perceiving, and behaving are separate processes in the brain. Basing himself on work of the nineteenth century, this researcher rejected both information-processing and connectionist approaches to memory. Instead, much as Rastier (1991) did for linguistics, Rosenfield (1988) argued for a social approach to memory, an approach that is irreconcilable with the rigidity of "situated models" (e.g., Montague; 1974; Barwise, & Perry, 1983) and with the "behaviorist" outlook of connectionist models (which merely react to the stimulus and ignore the role of "internal values" in human cognition). Such virulent attacks on our current understanding of human memory have at least the virtue of asserting its metaphoric nature.

4.3 STARTING POINT

Several sophisticated models of memory have been developed over the years in psychology. Indeed, some of these models address the majority of the issues raised in the previous section. In contrast, computational models of memory generally remain relatively simplistic. My work is no exception. More precisely, the model of memory I now introduce is meant to be close, in spirit, to the work of Hintzman (1988) on memory. However, as it becomes apparent in the rest of this chapter, the current design of **IDIoT** is simplistic in that it completely abstracts away from several of the difficult problems tackled by psychological models (e.g., retrieval, chunking, etc.). This hopefully does not preclude the eventual refinement of **IDIoT** to address these issues.

The first simplifying design decision I make pertains to learning. Symbolic and local-connectionist models of comprehension are *programmable.*That is, their behavior is controlled by the designer. In information-processing models, programmability is achieved through the specification of data structures and algorithms. In "localist" models, through the direct modification of the weights of the connections of the network that, within the connectionist paradigm, encode all knowledge in the network. Conversely, PDP models, once trained, are *adaptable.* That is, their behavior is controlled by the network itself, which directly adjusts the weights of its connections (according to a predefined learning algorithm). As remarked in chapter 2, the typical consequence of such an approach is that the user cannot readily understand the internal representation of knowledge in a PDP network. Conrad (1985) observed that there is an inherent trade-off between programmability and adaptability: One must choose between the two. In this book, it is not my intent to develop a theory of human learning, but rather to construct a text comprehension tool based on a grounded cognitive architecture. Therefore, I do not focus on the mechanisms that shape human memory into the remarkable adaptable system it is, and I do not address the problems associated with adaptable systems (e.g., learning, chunking, proceduralization, categorization; see Schacter, 1989). Also, I strongly suspect that, much like the understanding algorithm itself, the mechanisms of learning are acquired and diachronic, and thus belong in the knowledge base. Instead, in accordance with both the reader-based strategy I adopt and the requirements put forth in the previous chapter (see subsection 3.3.4), the proposed model will be highly user-programmable and amenable to user scrutiny.

Still, it is a question how to derive a grounded architecture from the identified requirements. Shastri (1993) provided the initial answer when he demonstrated that "reflexive reasoning introduces a strong notion of tractability and necessitates the use of massive parallelism". Let me elaborate. First, I repeat, a cognitive architecture should not be designed from a specialized form of thinking (e.g., reflective), but rather should address the most general and common form of cognition, namely reflexive reasoning (which readily applies to such complex problems as text understanding). Second, the architecture must be tractable, both with respect to time and space, "though there have been very few attempts at developing a computational account of such inference" (Shastri, 1993). The design of **IDIoT** proceeds from acknowledging the biological constraint, that is, the real-time nature of linguistic comprehension. Thus, tractability with respect to time is the starting point of the design. Following Shastri (1993), I assume that strong tractability with respect to time requires massive parallelism and, consequently, I view memory as a spreading activation network with concurrently-executing nodes. In its most general form, this network could allow nodes to exchange messages of arbitrary complexity, as suggested in the previous chapter. There are at least two problems with such arbitrariness. First, as mentioned in chapter 2, such complex messages must have a predefined format known to the algorithm that processes them. This, in effect, hardwires part of the understanding algorithm in the software itself and thus is rejected, for such an approach is not grounded. Second, having a multitude of simultaneous messages of arbitrary complexity in a massively parallel architecture would likely violate the space tractability requirement: The space required to store all these concurrent messages will likely exceed a reasonable upper bound. Therefore, in the proposed grounded architecture, messages exchanged between nodes are restricted to simple (read numeric) values (each occupying constant space). We shall call such messages *signals*.

Viewing memory (that is, the knowledge base) as a network of concurrently-executing nodes exchanging simple messages only partly addresses the issue of time complexity. By itself parallelism does not guarantee strong tractability: We also require a stopping criterion, that is, some way of constraining how much work the architecture carries out for each input. The central idea of my work is that processing time constitutes this stopping criterion. Such an approach is not restricted to text understanding but seems to apply to a multitude of facets of cognition (e.g., Francini, 1993). Roughly put, each input triggers a limited amount of processing with respect to time. More precisely, a maximum amount of processing time is allocated to each input, but the processing of this input may not require all of this time (e.g., a word may quickly be disambiguated if already "primed", see chapter 9).

Recall that in general, neuronal models are relaxation models (see McClelland, & Rumelhart, 1986; Selman, 1985): Once inputs have been entered into the network, the computation terminates when the network reaches an equilibrium that is mathematically defined, typically as a global function to minimize (Feldman, 1985b). In other words, there are no rules to define the completeness of the computational process(es) used to solve a cognitive task, or rules to specify the correctness of the solution reached (Rumelhart, 1984): A solution emerges from a constraint satisfaction process rather than from a search through a space of solutions. In contrast, conceptual approaches rely on data structures, rules, heuristics, and algorithms that must cover every possible input, and thus define, in effect, the completeness of the processing algorithm and the "correctness" of the solution obtained. For the problem of text understanding, viewing linguistic comprehension as a time-constrained process eliminates the need to choose between relaxation mechanisms and arbitrary rules to stop the understanding process. Instead, the processing time becomes the essential stopping criterion: There is no correct interpretation, but rather an interpretation that is reached given a certain private knowledge base and a set of time-related memory parameters that characterize the "frame of mind" (Gardner, 1983) or "horizon" (Gadamer, 1976) of a particular individual. The details of this mechanism are the topic of this chapter. More specifically, the conceptualization of memory as a massively parallel network of simple computing units exchanging simple signals leads to the following issues to be addressed in the next sections:

1. the organization of memory,

2. the structure and behavior of the computing units of the network, and

3. the nature of signals and communication within the network.

Throughout this discussion, the omnipresent role of processing time (i.e., time as it pertains to memory management and memory processes such as retrievals) is emphasized. I also suggest how the construction (or teuchistic) process that underlies linguistic comprehension need not be implemented as a global algorithm of the semantic network but, rather, as a distributed process.

4.4 THE ORGANIZATION OF TIME CONSTRAINED MEMORY

As mentioned earlier, much like connectionist researchers, I view memory as a massively parallel network of simple computing units. This functional conceptualization is essential to the proposed model of time-constrained memory, yet incomplete in that it ignores the fundamental feature of conceptual analyzers, namely, the ability to construct "new" cognitive structures through processing. A construction process in memory suggests an intuitive and commonly accepted dichotomy between a priori "static" knowledge and "dynamically built" structures, that is, between a static and a dynamic memory. However, since these dynamic structures are ultimately composed of elements of static memory, the dichotomy is tenuous. Indeed, as Hinton and Plaut (1987) suggested, static memory can be thought of as a set of stable "slow" links between memory elements, whereas dynamic memory could consist of a set of fast, impermanent connections over the same memory elements. Such a standpoint essentially agrees with Cowan's (1993) view that STM is effectively a subset of LTM.

In the current prototype of **IDIoT**, the knowledge specified by the user is completely static, that is, it remains unchanged throughout the processing of an input text. The elements of the knowledge base (hereafter KB) are called *knowledge units* (KUs); they form the contents of the static atemporal memory. In contrast, the "created" structures, which shall be called *clusters*, exist in a separate dynamic memory and cannot be automatically integrated with static memory. This simplified organization will eventually be abandoned in favor of a truly homogeneous model of memory, as will be suggested in chapter 12.

Dynamic memory must also be organized with respect to time. That is, dynamic memory must be partitioned into temporal stages, as suggested by both neurological evidence (Squire, 1987; Zola-Morgan, & Squire, 1990) and psychological (Baddeley, 1976, 1986; Hockley, & Lewandowsky, 1991; Parkin, 1993) evidence. Generally, a short-term memory (STM) and a long-term memory (LTM) are postulated. STM is assumed to have a limited capacity, and its elements are taken to be, by definition, more readily accessible than those of LTM. In the simplest form, limits on STM capacity are captured by stipulating its maximum size, although more sophisticated approaches to STM capacity are possible (e.g., Schweickert, & Boruff, 1986). An element's belonging to STM is constantly reviewed with respect not only to STM capacity (in terms of elements) but also to the duration of the membership itself. More specifically, it is commonly assumed in computational models of memory that the elements of the STM have a certain "energy" (or activation) level that quickly (read exponentially) decays with time. Once the energy level of a member of STM falls below a certain threshold, it is either "moved" to LTM or forgotten (Graesser, & Clark, 1985). Conversely, elements of LTM decay at a very slow rate over days or years—a process that is irrelevant from a computational perspective. I adopt this common characterization of memory but, following the ideas of Baddeley (1986), I also identify a working memory (WM), which is the subset of STM whose elements are *"immediately"* and *simultaneously* accessible. In other words, the elements of WM are *necessarily* accessible. Furthermore, I assume that WM has a very limited capacity. I have adopted the traditional capacity of seven elements for WM.

Clusters "move" between WM, STM, and LTM. To "move" does not consist in a physical transfer between partitions of memory, but rather in a change of membership from one partition to another. I assume a cluster is constructed in WM and eventually decays to STM and LTM if it is not entirely forgotten (i.e., deleted from dynamic memory). Elements of STM all start with the same activation level and the same decay rate. Therefore, for memory management (i.e., enforcement of capacity limits and decay thresholds), it is sufficient to organize the elements according to their time of arrival in STM (not WM): The "oldest" clusters in STM are also the "weakest" (with respect to their level of activation), and thus the ones most likely to be "moved" to LTM during memory management. An ordering is not required in LTM, for which there is no capacity limit or decay, nor in WM, in which, by design, all elements are equally accessible, and since the proposed model of memory is to be strictly mechanistic, there is no need for qualitative (i.e., not grounded) partitions of memory (e.g., semantic *versus* episodic memory; see Tulving, 1983, 1984).

At any time, a cluster can be *retrieved* from LTM or STM and "moved" to WM. I postulate that a cluster must be in WM before a construction process can manipulate it. Following Baddeley's (1986, chapter 10) idea of a centralized executive, I hypothesize the existence of a *memory manager* responsible, among other duties, for verifying the membership of a cluster in WM and STM, and for "transferring" clusters back and forth between WM, STM, and LTM. (However, I make no effort to model some sort of articulatory loop in the current prototype.) In **IDIoT**, retrieval is viewed as an atomic operation performed by the memory manager, which *hides* all details of memory management (i.e., complex notions and processes for retrieval, such as *engrams* and *synergy,* are ignored). The focus is placed instead on the notion of *reachability*: Given a time-constrained process, that is, a process that must complete its execution before a certain deadline, a cluster can be retrieved by this process if, and only if, it can be accessed before the deadline of this process. In other words, within the paradigm of a time-constrained memory, the issue is not how a cluster is retrieved, but whether or not it can be reached for retrieval before the execution deadline of the particular process that wants to use it. The notion of reachability only applies to clusters (not KUs) and ties in with the organization of dynamic memory into temporal stages. By definition, all elements of WM are always reachable. For STM, the ordering of elements with respect to their time of arrival defines an ordering for reachability, the "oldest" clusters being the least reachable ones. This chronological ordering does extend to LTM although, typically, clusters in LTM are seldom reachable (Márkus, 1983).

The temporal partitions of dynamic memory need not correspond to anatomical or physiological separations in the brain, and clusters need not be physically moved from one temporal partition to another. Indeed, as previously mentioned, it merely suffices to have the memory manager keep track of the membership for the WM and STM. More precisely, when the memory manager decides that a certain cluster must be moved from one partition to another, it merely updates its internal membership list for STM and/or WM. For example, when moving a cluster from LTM to WM, the memory manager updates its membership list for WM and stores the time of arrival. Let me summarize the rules for "moving" between the partitions of dynamic memory in

IDIoT:

1. A cluster moves from WM to STM when it has sufficiently decayed.

2. Upon retrieving a cluster from STM or LTM, if the capacity limit of WM has already been reached, the "oldest" cluster of WM is moved to STM to "make room" for the new arrival in WM.

3. A cluster moves from STM to LTM when it has sufficiently decayed.

4. Upon "receiving" a cluster from WM, if the capacity limit of STM has already been reached, the "oldest" cluster of STM is moved to LTM to "make room" for the new arrival in STM.

5. A cluster in STM or LTM may be retrieved, that is, put in WM, if, and only if, this cluster is reachable by the retrieval process.

6. A cluster is said to be forgotten when it is deleted from STM and not moved to LTM.

Clusters are cognitive structures built during the processing of an input. In the current prototype, once in LTM, clusters constitute "passive" entities in that they cannot be retrieved later in the interpretation, a significant oversimplification. Ideally, as suggested in chapter 12, some clusters should become retrievable entities on their own. That is, some clusters should be able to automatically "mature" into retrievable KUs that can be reactivated later during comprehension. Furthermore, without immediately describing their exact nature, let me repeat that clusters are ultimately "composed" of elements of the KB. I use the word "ultimately", for I assume that the "components" of a cluster can be other clusters, but that, if we think of a cluster as a hierarchical (tree-like) structure, its leaves "correspond" to KUs. More precisely, because KUs permanently reside in static memory, they cannot be, in the current prototype, genuine components of clusters, which are elements of dynamic memory. Therefore, the leaves of a cluster merely refer (or point) to KUs.

4.5 COMMUNICATION IN THE NETWORK

Having adopted the conceptualization of the knowledge base as a static memory in the form of a massively parallel network of simple computing units, let us briefly focus on the exchange of signals between KUs. First, it is important to understand that, in the current prototype, the clusters of dynamic memory are not computing elements, but merely constructed cognitive structures, and therefore do not exchanges signals. Thus, communication is restricted to static memory.

Knowledge units communicate through what I shall call input and output "ports". Ports are merely required for simulation purposes, that is, to implement the queues entailed by the use of parallelism (e.g., several signals can be received simultaneously, even possibly from the same sender; signals decay over time, etc.). They are not part of the proposed model per se and, therefore, are not further discussed.

The role of time during processing is greatly emphasized by the assumption that, in **IDIoT**, the exchange of a signal between two KUs consumes time. More precisely, if the user specifies that a KU x sends a signal to a KU y, then the user must specify (in the KB) a time delay (or cost) for this exchange. Another (possibly different) delay may be incurred if y sends a signal to x. In other words, communication links are not necessarily symmetric with respect to their time delays. Furthermore, I introduce the intuitive notion of *familiarity* to define an a priori static order of "retrieval", with respect to communication, for the elements of the KB. Each KU needs a user-specified *retrievability coefficient*. If a KU sends a signal to two others, with the same communication delay for both, then the "most familiar" of the two receivers, that is, the one with the lowest retrievability coefficient, will receive the signal before the other one. More specifically, the *actual* (as opposed to the user-specified) delay of an exchange at time t is computed as the multiplication of the a priori delay of the exchange by the retrievability coefficient of the receiver at t.

Following evidence of the existence of both excitatory and inhibitory processes in the brain (e.g., Dagenbach, & Carr, 1994), two "high priority" signals are introduced in **IDIoT**. The signals, "forced activation" and "forced inhibition", are assumed to have a priority greatly superior to the other signals used in **IDIoT**, that is, to "instantaneously" reach their destination (regardless of the retrievability of this destination). "Instantaneous" communication, that is, communication that requires zero time, is only asymptotically possible and thus actually requires a minimum time quantum, which I call "epsilon".

Another fundamental time quantum used in **IDIoT** is the "character quantum", that is, the time it takes to read and recognize a character. In **IDIoT**, the time it takes to read and recognize a word is taken to be equal to the multiplication of the number of characters in this word by the character quantum. Consequently, a text of n characters is processed in n character quanta, thus emulating real-time processing. However, clearly, this is a significant oversimplification of the complex perceptual processes involved in reading.

4.6 THE INTERNAL STRUCTURE AND BEHAVIOR OF KNOWL-

EDGE UNITS

4.6.1 Knowledge Units As Feature Detectors

4.6.1.1 Forward Chaining Feature Detection

As mentioned above, KUs are the construction material for the distributed teuchistic process that builds clusters and is taken to underlie the task of linguistic comprehension. Neurological evidence suggests thinking of the elements of the network forming static memory as feature detectors (e.g., Squire, 1987), a viewpoint also adopted by connectionist researchers (e.g., Feldman, 1985b). A feature is a qualitative (i.e., not grounded) entity (e.g., a phoneme, a sememe, a syntax rule, an inference rule, etc.), and each computing element of the network, that is, each KU, is capable of recognizing several "configurations (or patterns) of features". It is left to the user to decide whether a localist representational scheme (which associates one KU to one feature) or a distributed one (which associates several KUs to one feature or several features to one KU) is more adequate. In this book, I have adopted, for both clarity and simplicity, a one-to-one mapping between KUs and features. Consequently, in the rest of this work, these two terms are used interchangeably.

A commonly accepted conceptualization in both connectionism and psychology (e.g., Norris, 1986) is thinking of a "configuration of features" as a weighted sum of the features. A *constraint* is formed of such a configuration together with a numeric threshold; the constraint is said to be satisfied once the weighted sum exceeds the associated threshold of detection. From local connectionism (Feldman, 1985b), I adopt the following characteristics:

1. Each KU has an input port for each distinct feature used in its constraint.

2. The value of a constraint at time t is computed using the value at t of the input port associated with each feature of the constraint.

3. Once a constraint is satisfied, its associated computing unit x notifies all other units whose constraints refer to the feature associated with x by sending out a *presence signal* whose "strength" varies from 0 to 1 and denotes the degree of presence of the feature.

In **IDIoT**, the KUs, whose associated feature is referred to in a constraint of a KU x, are called the *suppliers* of x. Similarly, those that have a constraint that refers to the feature associated with a KU x are called the *customers* of x. It follows that a KU has supplier and customer ports. For now, we will assume that KUs exchange only *presence signals*.

I make several enhancements to the local connectionist model; some are discussed in the paragraphs below; others will be introduced throughout this section. I must emphasize that these enhancements merely simplify the data specification task of the user (by providing intuitive labels for certain data), but do not improve the model of memory itself in any way. Moreover, no claims are made about the biological plausibility of the proposed enhancements.

First, in order to be capable of detecting several configurations of features, an element of the network, that is, a KU in **IDIoT**, is allowed to have several constraints, which are evaluated in parallel. Therefore, the number of constraints in a KU does *not* correlate to the time complexity of the constraint satisfaction step. In other words, we avoid the problems that could result from the sequential processing of a large number of constraints. Furthermore, for simplicity, in the current prototype, only one of these constraints can become satisfied at a given point in time. The order in which these constraints are specified by a user is important, for it defines the order in which simultaneously satisfied constraints will be considered. Once a constraint is satisfied, the KU is said to be *activated* and its associated feature(s) to be *detected*.

Second, again for simplicity, I assume that all constraints in static memory are evaluated with respect to a unique detection threshold (across the KB) initially specified by the user. Typically, a higher initial detection threshold will result in fewer features being detected, and thus in far less material being available for the construction process.

Third, I distinguish *triggers* and *exceptions* from the other suppliers of a constraint, which are simply called *inputs*. *Triggers* are those features that must be present in order for the constraint to be satisfied. They act as the preconditions of a constraint and, therefore, need not be weighted. Triggers can be ordered, in which case presence signals from their corresponding suppliers must be received in the specified order. (A presence signal that is not in order is simply ignored.) A constraint that has received all its triggers is said to be *triggered*. In the current prototype, only the first triggered constraint of a KU can be satisfied, and thus, I repeat, the order in which constraints are specified is extremely important. *Exceptions* are those features of a constraint whose presence decreases the possibility of satisfying the constraint. Exceptions are weighted, as the presence of an exception does not necessarily prevent the satisfaction of a constraint (e.g., the comprehension process manages to parse and understand "ungrammatical" sentences). As explained below, exceptions also delay the satisfaction process.

Fourth, decay is integrated with constraint satisfaction. More precisely, each supplier port of a KU is taken to hold a queue of presence signals received from its corresponding supplier. A presence signal starts decaying as soon as it is received. Signals that decay below a certain threshold are considered obsolete and are automatically purged from their queue. The value of a port at time t is computed as the sum of all presence signals stored in its queue at t. In other words, constraint satisfaction is implicitly limited by time: All required presence signals must be received within a short interval of time. Otherwise, some will have decayed so much that the constraint cannot be satisfied unless they are received again.

Finally, within the framework of time-constrained memory, feature detection is also made explicitly time-constrained by implementing it as a race process that is given a fixed amount of time to execute. More specifically, once a KU has one of its constraints triggered, it becomes a *candidate* (much as in the model proposed by Norris, 1986) and is given a fixed amount of time to satisfy the constraint. During a candidacy, only the triggered constraint can be satisfied, and its sum (i.e., its "value") is recomputed each time a new presence signal from a supplier is received. If, however, the triggered constraint has exceptions, then the sum is checked and satisfaction is possible only at the end of the candidacy's delay, in order to allow any signal from an exception sufficient time to reach the candidate KU. Otherwise, satisfaction is possible at any time within the interval of candidacy. At the end of the candidacy, regardless of success (i.e., satisfaction) or failure (i.e., the sum of the triggered constraint is below the detection threshold), a KU resets all its constraints by emptying the queues of its supplier ports.

We are now ready to consider a simple example illustrated in the figure below:

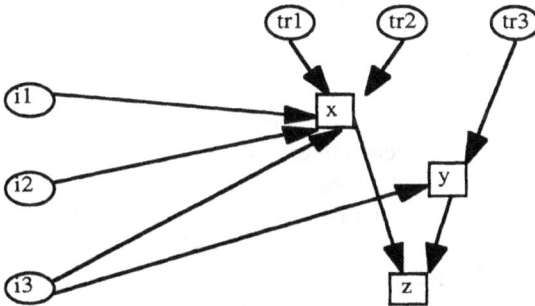

Figure 4.1: A simple example.

The definitions for the relevant KUs follow (The notation is that of the current implementation.):

KU x:
```
constraint c1:
 triggers: tr1, tr2
 inputs:
     i1 has a weight of 0.9
     i2 has a weight of 0.1
constraint c2:
 triggers: tr1, tr2
 inputs:
     i1 has a weight of 0.5
     i3 has a weight of 0.5
```

KU y:
```
constraint c1:
 triggers: tr3
 inputs:
     i3 has a weight of 1
```

KU z:
```
constraint c1:
 inputs:
     x has a weight of 0.5
     y has a weight of 0.5
```

KU x has two constraints, each one becoming triggered as soon as it has received a presence signal from both KUs $tr1$ and $tr2$ (in any order). Constraint $c1$ of x has two inputs $i1$ and $i2$. In the current prototype of **IDIoT**, the sum of the weights of the inputs of a constraint must be less than or equal to 1. Intuitively, the weight of an input defines its relative "necessity" with respect to the current detection threshold. In $c2$ of x, the inputs carry the same weight, and thus are equally "important" for the satisfaction of the constraint. Conversely, in $c1$ of x, $i1$ is far more needed than $i2$; with a detection threshold at 80 percent of the maximum detection threshold, $c1$ could be satisfied with only a presence signal from $i1$.

If x and y receive a presence signal on all of their trigger ports and on all of their input ports, then they become activated and send a presence signal to

z that, in turn, becomes activated. Because of the ordering of its constraints, x becomes activated through the satisfaction of its constraint $c1$.

4.6.1.2 Backward Chaining Feature Detection

The process of constraint satisfaction described so far requires only one signal, namely, the presence signal (whose value varies from 0 to 1), but only allows for the forward chaining of feature detections: A constraint cannot be satisfied, and thus, a feature cannot be detected unless its suppliers have been activated. I now introduce the notions of *submission, confirmation*, and *reinforcement*, in order to accommodate the backward chaining of feature detections. Intuitively, as soon as a feature has one of its constraints triggered (i.e., satisfies one of its sets of preconditions), it need not wait for signals from its inputs, but, rather, it may immediately ask the latter for "positive feedback", that is, for some confirmation of its "felicity" if it were activated. More specifically, I propose that when at time t a KU x becomes a candidate, it verifies the value of all the supplier ports referred to in its triggered constraint. A *missing feature* is one whose corresponding port in x has no queue of signals at t. A *submission signal* is sent by x to all the missing features of its triggered constraint. This signal acts as a conditional presence of x. Upon receiving such a signal, any KU y associated with a missing feature of x treats the signal as a maximum presence signal (i.e., the value 1) from x and checks whether one of its constraints would be satisfied by this input. If one would be satisfied, then y sends back a confirmation signal to x and starts waiting (for a short fixed amount of time) for a reinforcement signal from x but the feature associated with y does not become detected. If, on the other hand, y has one of its constraints triggered but not satisfied by the submission signal from x, then y, in turn, sends a submission signal to the missing features of its triggered constraint. In all other cases, the submission signal to y is ignored. Each KU z that is not the originating candidate and that sends a submission signal to the set of its missing features waits for a fixed amount of time for a confirmation signal from each member of this set. Once z receives all the required confirmations, it sends a confirmation signal to the KU from which it received a submission signal. If the candidate x receives a confirmation signal from all its missing features before the deadline of its candidacy, its triggered constraint is considered satisfied, and the feature associated with x is detected. Intuitively, x has received enough "positive feedback", *confirmation* of its felicity if it were activated. Upon its detection, x not only notifies its customers, but also sends a *reinforcement signal* to its missing features. Upon the reception of this reinforcement signal, the missing features first relay this reinforcement signal to the KUs that sent them confirmation signals, and then become themselves detected.

This process of submission/confirmation/reinforcement is somewhat similar to the spreading activation mechanisms of marker-passing models (e.g., Hendler, 1989; Norvig, 1989) but presents some advantages. Since only the missing features of would-be triggered constraints are used to relay submission signals, the number of possible chains or paths (of submission/confirmation signals) is far more constrained than in marker-passing systems, and, by design, a path of confirmation signals is always a "useful" path. Furthermore, there is no need for an often arbitrary or intractable mechanism for evaluating paths: For each missing feature, the path (of confirmation signals) that "wins" is simply the first one to send a confirmation signal back to the originator of the initial submission signal. Since the proposed scheme is time-constrained, the only restriction for a candidacy is that all required confirmation signals arrive at the initiating candidate *before* the deadline of the candidacy is reached Also, the proposed scheme does not use complex markers, but only three numeric signals (for submission, confirmation, and reinforcement). Finally, the submission/confirmation/reinforcement mechanism does not impose restrictions on the lengths of paths and captures the intuition that the most "reconstructible" knowledge is not necessarily put in dynamic memory. Let me explain. In **IDIoT**, contrary to typical marker-passing systems, a path of features does not become activated as a whole but, rather, is incrementally constructed through reinforcement signals, starting with the originating candidate x. Given a path of confirmation signals between a candidate x and a KU y (that sent back the first confirmation signal of the path), y waits a fixed amount of time for a reinforcement signal from the KU to which y sent a confirmation signal. Again, since communication consumes time, the longer the path (in terms of KUs) between x and y is, the longer the confirmation signal originated by y will take to be relayed to x, and thus, provided x becomes activated, the longer a reinforcement signal originated by x will take to be relayed to y. It is therefore possible that y (as well as some of the KUs that precede it in the path between x and y) will *not* receive the reinforcement signal it is waiting for before its waiting race expires, that is, before y stops "listening" for the signal. It follows that it is possible that only a few of the KUs forming the path between x and y become activated. However, this is not a problem because, given the same "context" (i.e., the same contents of dynamic memory and the same parameters of memory), the path can be reconstructed through the same process. Also, the more of the path that is already detected when the reconstruction is attempted, the faster the missing features will be detected because, in essence, part of the construction is already present. To clarify this discussion, let us consider a simple exchange of signals illustrated in Figure 4.2:

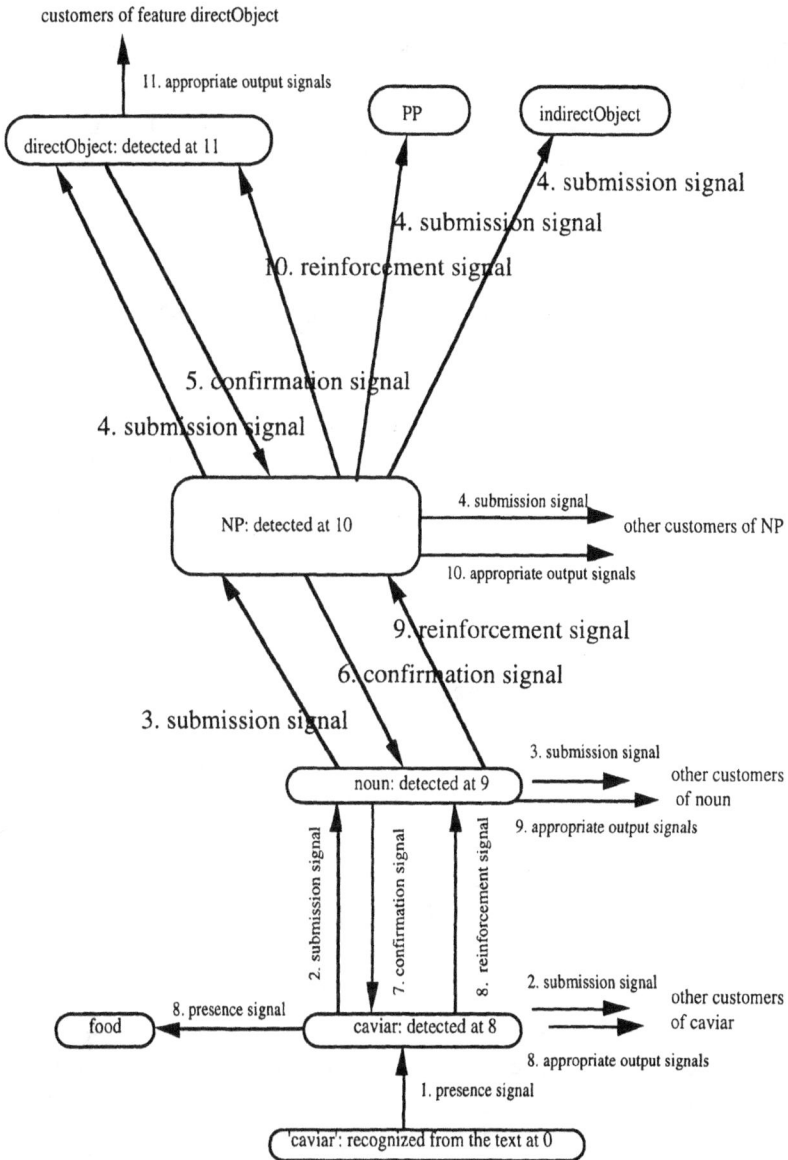

Figure 4.2: Submission, confirmation, and reinforcement.

Here is the corresponding sequence of events:

1. In the sentence "John eats caviar", the word "caviar" is recognized and triggers the candidacy of the feature **caviar** associated with the concept of caviar.

2. Feature **caviar** submits (i.e., sends a submission signal to) its only missing feature **noun**.

3. Feature **noun** relays the submission signal it receives from **caviar** to its customer **NP**.

4. Feature **NP** (noun phrase) relays the submission signal it receives from **noun** to its customers including **directObject, indirectObject, PP**, and so forth.

5. Feature **directObject** has its constraint (triggered earlier by the detection of a subject-verb relationship) satisfied by the submission signal received from **NP**. In essence, an NP following a verb is treated as the initial direct object. Feature **directObject** does not become detected, but instead sends a confirmation signal back to **NP**.

6. Feature **NP** relays the confirmation signal it receives from **directObject** to **noun**.

7. Feature **noun** relays the confirmation signal to **caviar**.

8. Having received a confirmation signal from all its missing features, **caviar** becomes detected. It sends a presence signal to its customer **food** and a reinforcement signal to **noun**.

9. Feature **noun** receives the reinforcement signal of **caviar**, becomes detected, and sends a reinforcement signal to **NP**.

10. Feature **NP** receives the reinforcement signal of **noun**, becomes detected, and sends a reinforcement signal to **directObject**.

11. Feature **directObject** receives the reinforcement signal of **NP** and becomes detected. It sends a presence signal to its customers.

If the candidacy of **caviar** expires before it receives a confirmation signal from **noun**, then the path between **caviar** and **directObject** is not used, and the candidacy fails. If, while waiting for reinforcement, **noun, NP**, or **directObject** has its race expire, then it do not become activated, and the reinforcement signal that will eventually reach them will be ignored. If we assume that this is the case for **directObject**, then given the same context, that is, the prior detection of a subject-verb relationship and the detection of **caviar** and **noun** and **NP**, **directObject** is readily reconstructible because its constraint can be directly triggered and satisfied.

4.6.1.3 Other Enhancements

The race processes and constraints briefly described in the previous sections form the essence of the internal organization and behavior of KUs. Several other enhancements to the conceptualization of KUs as feature detectors are made in the current prototype of **IDIoT** in order to simplify the knowledge specification task for the user. None are truly required because "tricks" can be typically used to replace them. However, these enhancements are included in the proposed model not only for simplification, but also to make visible some common intuitions about knowledge organization and use (as opposed to relying implicitly on the exact modus operandi of **IDIoT**).

First, I assume that every exchange of signals is routed through the memory manager (introduced in section 4.4). This is totally invisible to the user and has the advantage of bypassing the difficult problem of the implementation of an addressing scheme in memory (see Kanerva, 1984). More specifically, it is not reasonable to assume that arbitrarily long links between all communicating KUs physically exist in the brain. Indeed, there is speculation that the cortex may play the role of an addressing mechanism for human memory (Squire, 1987). Using the memory manager has the advantage of abstracting away from neurology and preserving the locality of information by having the memory manager, rather then the sender, compute the actual delay it takes a signal to reach its destination.

Second, as mentioned earlier, there are two high priority signals, namely, the "forced detection" signal and the "forced inhibition" signal (hereafter "inhibition"). At any point in time, a KU that receives a forced detection signal immediately becomes activated (i.e., its feature becomes detected) and sends a presence signal to its customers.

Conversely, at any point in time, a KU that receives an inhibition signal immediately stops its current process and reverts to its initial mode, which shall be called the idle mode (i.e., the KU does not have any process executing). Inhibition is taken to have precedence over forced detection. Both signals take epsilon time to be sent from their sender to their receiver, regardless of the retrievability of the receiver and of the a priori delay between both KUs. This is made possible by the previous assumption that all signals are routed through the memory manager (which simply assigns an epsilon delay to these high priority messages). Furthermore, in order to be instantaneously processed by their destinations, these signals are received on a special input port, called the *manager port*, that every KU has. As soon as a high priority signal is received on this port, it is immediately processed, regardless of the state of the KU at that point in time, and, for convenience, I allow the user of **IDIoT** to distinguish *associations* from the other customers of a KU. The associations of a KU are those customers to which it sends a forced detection signal upon its activation. For example, the feature **food** could be an association of **caviar** since caviar is necessarily an instance of the concept food. Although not absolutely necessary, associations have been found to be very helpful for implementing a *generalization* hierarchy (see Budd, 1991, section 6.3), as illustrated by the examples of word sense disambiguation shown in chapter 9.

Third, in order to account for the important phenomenon of expectations (which is akin to priming; see Tulving, 1983 for an introduction), I introduce one last special signal, the *expectation signal*. I view expectations as a mechanism for the speed-up of the detection of a feature. In other words, a feature that is expected will become activated more readily than a non expected feature. Within the framework of time-constrained memory, I suggest that, for a short fixed amount of time, the receiver of an expectation signal need not satisfy any of its constraints, but rather, merely obtain all triggers for one of its constraints in order to become detected. Intuitively, receiving an expectation signal guarantees the felicity of the receiver, which therefore, merely has to assemble its preconditions. Let us consider a simple example:

Example 4.6.1.3.1 *John eats at Maxim's. He orders caviar.*

Let us assume that the feature **actionDine** (associated, among others, with the action of eating at a restaurant) sends, upon its detection, an expectation signal to the feature **orderFood**. Then

> 1. having the verb **actionEat** with a well-known restaurant as a complement of location causes the eventual detection of the feature **actionDine**, which sends an expectation signal to **orderFood**.
>
> 2. feature **orderFood** receives an expectation signal.
>
> 3. the word "orders" triggers the feature **orderFood**, which immediately becomes detected, as it has received an expectation signal and merely needs to have one of its constraints triggered.

Table 4.1 summarizes the different numeric signals used in the current prototype of **IDIoT**.

As a fourth enhancement, I propose associating an *output strategy*, which can possibly be empty, with each constraint of a KU. So far, upon its detection, a KU sends a forced detection signal to its associations and a presence signal to its other customers. The user must specify for each non association customer a default signal to send. The enhancement consists in allowing the user to override the default output to be sent to a particular non association customer of a KU x if a particular constraint c of x becomes satisfied. This overriding is achieved by associating a set of (customer–signal) pairs to one or more of the constraints of x. Upon its detection, x checks which of its constraints was satisfied. If this constraint has an associated output strategy, then, for each customer referred to in the output strategy of the satisfied constraint, x sends the output signal specified by the output strategy rather than the default signal for this customer. This enhancement has been found to be extremely useful for a feature x in which a customer should be sent an inhibition signal or an expectation signal for only a few of the constraints of x.

Table 4.1: Signals in IDIoT

Signal	Value	Priority
presence	[0,1]	default
submission	-6	default
confirmation	-2	default
reinforcement	-5	default
expectation	-3	default
forcedDetection	-1	high
forcedInhibition	-4	high

Finally, I allow the user of **IDIoT** to specify the *candidates* of a KU. Anticipating chapter 9, I remark that the notion of candidates is especially intuitive and useful for word sense disambiguation. For example, the two KUs **alcoholicBeverageGin** and **cardGameGin** are candidates of their sole trigger, the KU **gin**. The presence of **gin** is not sufficient to have either of these candidates become detected. Instead, each could be defined to require receiving a confirmation from one of its customers (e.g., **toDrink** for the beverage, **toPlay** for the game) to become activated. Candidates have also been used as a possible approach to prepositional phrase attachment (chapter 10). At a non linguistic level, candidates are introduced in the proposed memory model to simplify the specification of non-deterministic races. More specifically, recall from the previous chapters that comprehension is taken to be non deterministic. It follows that, often, several different interpretations (for words, sentences, paragraphs) will be competing in parallel. Because these candidate interpretations are all time-constrained and because which one(s) will be selected is *not* pre-specified, they indeed correspond to non-deterministic races (with respect to time).

Let us now consider the behavior of such candidates in **IDIoT**. In the sub-mission/confirmation/reinforcement mechanism introduced previously, the chaining process is initiated by a KU missing one or more features in its triggered constraint, that is, in the constraint this KU must satisfy in order to become detected. In this process, a submission signal is not sent to the customers of the candidate for the simple reason that receiving a confirmation from a feature that would become detected if feature f were active does not entail that f ought to become detected. In other words, a confirmation from a customer is not sufficient evidence to cause the detection of a feature if it has a triggered constraint to satisfy. But what if the triggered constraint has only triggers? In this case, the constraint is satisfied as soon as all triggers are received. If this is generally acceptable, there may be features for which triggers are not enough and a confirmation (necessarily from a customer, as there are no missing features to the triggered constraint) is required. Such features are called the *candidates* of their trigger(s). More precisely, if KU x has KU y declared as a candidate, then when x becomes detected, it sends a confirmation signal to y. Once y has received a confirmation signal from all its triggers, it sends a submission signal to each of its customers and waits for a fixed amount of time for a confirmation signal from one of them. The KU y becomes active as soon as such a confirmation signal is received. The customers of y act exactly like any KU that receives a submission signal. In other words, the chaining process is the same as for backward chaining; only how this chaining is initiated differs: Whereas backward chaining is initiated by sending a submission signal to its missing features (in order to satisfy its triggered constraint), in the case of an explicit candidate x, x sends a submission signal to each of its customers as soon as it has received a confirmation signal from all its triggers, and x becomes detected as soon as it receives a confirmation signal from one of its customers.

These enhancements will be illustrated at the end of this chapter, as well as in Part III.

4.6.2   Knowledge Units as Cluster Builders

Recall that KUs are the construction material for the distributed teuchistic process that builds clusters and are taken to underlie the task of linguistic comprehension. The set of clusters constructed during the reading of the text constitutes the output of **IDIoT**, the interpretation that the user can examine. In this subsection, I focus on the process of the construction of clusters.

4.6.2.1   Organization of a Cluster

Let me start by elaborating on the nature of clusters. Recall that the proposed model of memory is strictly mechanistic, that is, deprived of any qualitative (e.g., semantic) information. Clusters must be general enough to allow the user to construct almost any kind of representation (e.g., parse trees, scripts, etc.) that is hypothesized for comprehension. Of the multitude of possible organizations for clusters, I have selected a very simple one: A cluster is defined as a non empty set of features, each feature *governing* a (possibly empty) set of clusters. In other words, a cluster is a hierarchical structure whose "leaves" are features.

Consider, for example, a cluster associated with the noun phrase "a park":

cluster <identifier1> with features:

```
KU NP

KU NPhead that governs:
 cluster <identifier2> with features:

  KU 'park'
  KU singular
  KU park
  KU noun
  KU 3rdPerson

KU NPquant that governs:
   cluster <identifier3> with features:

   KU determiner
   KU singular

KU NPmods
```

I emphasize that the contents of this cluster are assembled from the knowledge specified by the user, as shall be explained shortly. The "correctness" or "completeness" of a representation is not, I insist, the object of study in this book. In the example, the outermost cluster has 4 features: **NP, NPhead, NPquant** and **NPmods**. In turn, **NPhead** governs a cluster that holds the features associated with the word "park". Similarly, **NPquant** holds information for "the".

The clusters governed by a feature are called its *subclusters*. Also, each cluster has an identifier, that is, a unique address in dynamic memory, given in the form of an integer. Each subcluster can be shared by other clusters, as in the actual structure produced for the sentence "John watched the rabbit in the park", in which the prepositional phrase "in the park" is taken to be ambiguous, and is therefore attached to *both* the verb "watched" and the noun "rabbit", as illustrated in the following figure:

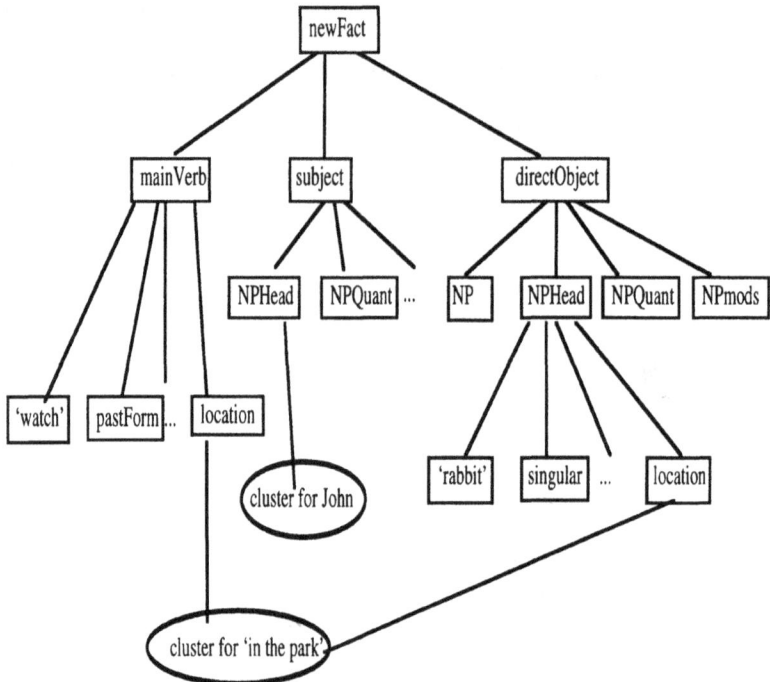

Figure 4.3: Cluster sharing.

```
cluster 16436 in working memory with features:

 KU newFact that governs:
   cluster 17620 in working memory with features:

   KU mainVerb that governs:
     cluster 15957 in working memory with features:
     KU 'watch'
     KU pastForm
     KU actionObserve
     KU verb
     KU activeMood
     KU verbComplemented
     KU location that governs:
       cluster 18999 in working memory with features:
       KU NP
       KU NPhead that governs:
         cluster 16207 in working memory with features:
         KU 'park'
         KU singular
         KU park
         KU noun
         KU 3rdPerson
       KU NPquant that governs:
         cluster 7987 in STM with features:
         KU determiner
       KU NPmods

   KU VPmods that governs:
     cluster 15005 in STM with features:
     KU 'close'
     KU adverb

   KU subject that governs:
     cluster 10935 in STM with features:
     KU NP
     KU NPhead that governs:
       cluster 17028 in STM with features:
       KU singular
```

```
    KU 'John'
    KU proper
    KU person
    KU male
    KU rational
    KU animate
    KU 3rdPerson
  KU NPquant
  KU NPmods


 KU directObject that governs:
   cluster 16183 in working memory with features:
   KU NP
   KU NPhead that governs:
     cluster 15035 in working memory with features:
     KU 'rabbit'
     KU singular
     KU noun
     KU rabbit
     KU animate
     KU 3rdPerson
     KU location that governs:
       cluster 18999
   KU NPquant that governs:
     cluster 17872 in STM with features:
     KU determiner
     KU singular
   KU NPmods
```

In this structure, the cluster 18999 corresponding to the prepositional phrase "in the park" is a subcluster of feature **location** in both cluster 15957 corresponding to the main verb and in the cluster 16183 corresponding to the direct object. The reader will also notice that the verb "to watch" has been interpreted as "to observe" with the modifier "close" in the cluster 15957 corresponding to the main verb of the sentence.

The levels of indentation of the structure correspond to the level of nesting of clusters. The structure consists of one cluster (16436) having only the feature **newFact**, which corresponds to the whole sentence. This feature governs one cluster (17620), which has the four features **mainVerb**, **VPmods** (for the modifiers of the VP), **subject** and **directObject**. Feature **mainVerb** governs cluster 15957, whose features mainly capture the fact that the main verb is **actionObserve** in the active mood, and that this verb has a location specified in cluster 18999. Feature **subject** governs cluster 10935, which corresponds to the NP "John". The feature **NPquant** is used to hold a determiner, if there is any. The feature **NPmods** keeps a list of the adjectives of the head of the NP. The knowledge inferred from the feature **John**, namely that this is a male rational animate, has been added to the cluster for the head of the NP. Similarly, feature **directObject** governs cluster 16183, whose features capture the fact that the object being observed by the subject is a rabbit in a park. This actual trace also indicates the membership of each cluster (with respect to the temporal partitions of dynamic memory) at the end of the interpretation of the sentence. It is important to understand that the structure of this cluster, that is, the structure resulting from the "parsing" and "semantic analysis" of this sentence is *not* prespecified within **IDIoT**, but rather produced from the activation of rules that I inputted in a knowledge base. As a matter of fact, there is no such thing as "parsing" and "semantic analysis" from the perspective of a grounded architecture, just the construction of clusters proceeding from the activation of KUs.

4.6.2.2   Expansion Procedures

Having briefly shown what a cluster looks like, I now turn to the problem of cluster construction. I suggest that once a KU becomes activated, it asks the memory manager to execute its *expansion procedure*. An expansion procedure is an ordered sequence of *cluster operations* that modifies the current contents of the dynamic memory. The cluster operations, which are introduced below, provide the basic functionality required for generic hierarchical data structures: access, addition, deletion, comparison, traversal, and so forth.

A KU does not execute its expansion procedure itself, for two reasons. First, having each KU able to execute cluster operations would violate the assumption that KUs are simple computing units. Instead, the use of a memory manager hides the details of complex processes such as cluster retrieval (e.g., with respect to memory management) within a single abstract entity. Second, having a single entity be able to execute expansion procedures avoids the complex problems associated with concurrency, that is, with several KUs *simultaneously* modifying the contents of memory. The memory manager executes a single expansion procedure at a time, in the order in which the corresponding KUs become activated. If two KUs are activated simultaneously, the memory manager executes their respective expansion procedures in a random order. (The parallel execution of expansion procedures is possible, in theory, provided "critical" mutually exclusive segments of procedures can be identified by the user. In practice, this could require that the user be able to identify exhaustively which KUs can be detected simultaneously. This is clearly unacceptable, for it essentially reduces to asking the user to determine a priori the behavior of the system, independently of the input. A more promising strategy would consist of having the memory manager dynamically establish the mutually exclusive segments of actual, as opposed to prespecified, concurrent expansion procedures. Because clusters can be shared, this approach is, however, significantly more complex than it may seem at first. Consequently, the current prototype does not address the concurrent execution of expansion procedures.)

Cluster operations do not refer to the actual addresses in memory of features and clusters (for these addresses do not exist at the time the operations are specified!). Features are referred to by their *unique* names (an operational requirement verified by the input mechanism), and in order for two instructions of a procedure to refer to the same cluster (e.g., to associate several interpretations with a same title), the supplied retrieval operations bind (i.e., associate) the retrieved cluster to a *user variable*, which consists of an alphanumeric string. As a whole, an expansion procedure is given a fixed amount of time to execute, and it either succeeds or fails. An expansion procedure fails as soon as any of its operations fails and succeeds if none do.

I now present the list of these operations for the current prototype of **IDIoT**. To do so, I use the following notation:

1. An item between square brackets is optional;

2. (feature) is a feature name, and

3. (uv1) and (uv2) are user variables.

Here are the operations:

1. **addFeature (feature) to (uv1)** Given the cluster uv1, add the specified feature to it. As a side effect, a forced detection signal is sent to the feature to ensure that it becomes detected, if it is not already.

2. **addFeaturesOf (uv1) to (uv2)** The features of cluster uv1 are added to the features of cluster uv2.

3. **addFirstSubCluster (uv1) to (feature) in (uv2)** Given the cluster uv2 with the specified feature, the cluster uv1 is added to the set of clusters governed by uv2. In fact, a feature governs a collection of subclusters that defines an order of traversal. This instruction makes uv1 the first element of the ordered collection of clusters governed by

the specified feature.

4. **addLastSubCluster (uv1) to (feature) in (uv2)** This is analogous to the previous operation.

5. **exit** Terminate with success the expansion procedure.

6. **findExactReference (uv1) to (uv2)** Search dynamic memory for a cluster with the exact same set of features and governed subclusters as uv2. If found, this cluster is bound to uv1. FindExactReference fails if multiple reachable referents are found during its time-span or if no reachable referent can be found within the time-span allocated to its expansion procedure.

7. **findInclusiveReference (uv1) to (uv2)** Search dynamic memory for a cluster with a set of features that includes all features and governed subclusters of uv2. If found, this cluster is bound to uv1. Failure conditions are the same as for findExactReference.

8. **getCluster (uv1) governedBy (feature) in (uv2)** Search dynamic memory for the first cluster that is a subcluster of the given feature in uv2.

9. **getCluster (uv1) governing (feature) [in (uv2)]** Search dynamic memory for the first cluster that governs the given feature. If the optional part of the operation is specified, then the search is limited to the subclusters of uv2.

10. **getNewCluster [(uv1)]** Create an empty new cluster in WM and bind it to uv1. If no argument is specified, then the predefined user variable "newCluster" is used.

11. **moveFeature (feature) from (uv1) to (uv2)** Move the specified feature and its subclusters from cluster uv1 to cluster uv2.

12. **moveSubClustersFrom (feature1) to (feature2) in (uv1)** Move the subclusters of feature1 to become those of feature2 in cluster uv1.

13. **removeCluster (uv1)** Remove the cluster uv1, without its subclusters, from dynamic memory.

14. **removeFeature (feature) in (uv1)** First delete all subclusters governed by the specified feature, and then delete the feature from the cluster.

15. **renameFeature (feature1) to (feature2) in (uv1)** This is self-

explanatory.

16. substituteCluster (uv1) for (uv2) Cluster uv1 is given the dynamic memory address of cluster uv2, which is then removed.

17. testAbsenceOf (feature) in (uv1) This succeeds if the specified feature is not in uv1.

18. testDifferenceOf (uv1) and (uv2) This fails if uv1 and uv2 recursively have the same features and the same subclusters.

19. testEquivalenceOf (uv1) and (uv2) This succeeds if uv1 and uv2 recursively have the same features and the same subclusters.

20. testPresenceOf (feature) in (uv1) This succeeds if the specified feature is in uv1.

These operations implement different forms of the four primitive memory operations identified in subsection 3.3.2: 1) to store a meaning, 2) to associate zero or more "meanings" with a mental entity, 3) to retrieve these "meanings", and 4) to match a set of features against a context. The following table groups the proposed operations according to these categories:

Table 4.2: Cluster Operations

storage and association	retrieval	matching
addFeature addFeaturesOf addFirstSubCluster addLastSubCluster	getCluster governedBy governing	testAbsenceOf testDifferenceOf testEquivalenceOf testPresenceOf
substituteCluster	getNewCluster	findInclusiveReference
moveFeature		findExactReference
moveSubClusters		
removeFeature		
removeCluster		
rename		

A great deal of flexibility is introduced in expansion procedures by having conditional instructions of this form:

if (constraint name) then (cluster operation)

In such an instruction, the specified cluster operation is attempted only if the specified constraint was the one whose satisfaction led to the activation of the KU that owns the executing expansion procedure. In other words, within the same executing expansion procedure of a KU x, different cluster operations can be attempted according to which constraint of x was satisfied (as will be illustrated shortly)

Let us conclude with some additional details of **IDIoT**. First, with respect to retrieval, the traversal of a cluster is performed breadth first, that is, each level of a cluster is visited completely before the next one is accessed. Each level costs increasingly more time to access, and thus, the deeper the structure, the more time it takes to reach the "lower" levels. Therefore, the time it takes to reach a cluster is determined by which partition of dynamic memory it resides in *and* by the number of levels that have to be traversed in order to reach it. Given that any expansion procedure is allocated a fixed amount of time to execute, a **getCluster** operation will fail if it cannot find a reachable satisfactory cluster in time.

Second, memory management is made completely invisible to the user of **IDIoT** by being encapsulated in the operations **getNewCluster**, **getCluster**, and **removeCluster**. In its present form, the memory management algorithm implements a simplistic first-in first-out storage/retrieval system for dynamic memory. Enhancements to the management of memory are discussed in chapter 12. For now, the point to be grasped is that, most importantly, all the complexities of the modus operandi of time-constrained memory (e.g., the complex implementation of the **findInclusiveReference** operation) are completely hidden from the user of **IDIoT** who specifies KUs without regard to this modus operandi. The net effect I have witnessed is that users believe that **IDIoT** is a simple, if not trivial, access system to the rules and concepts they specify. This is a most desirable illusion, because it favors the specification of knowledge completely independently from the exact workings of time-constrained memory. Nevertheless, it is also very important to understand that this illusion is just that, an illusion, for the clusters built during comprehension do not proceed solely from the knowledge base, but also depend on the parameters of memory (e.g., race deadlines, decay factor) and on the *context*, that is, on the contents of dynamic memory at a given point in the reading. In other words, the interpretation of a text results from the interactions between the knowledge base and the time-constrained memory.

Third, up to this point in the discussion of time-constrained memory, constraints have been specified by the user and depend on receiving signals from suppliers. In order to have the detection of a KU depend alternatively on context, that is, on a matching of the contents of the dynamic memory at a given point in time, I introduce the important notion of a *buildable feature*. A buildable feature is a feature whose expansion procedure contains a matching operation and acts as a *dynamic constraint* that can be satisfied within a short time interval with respect to the current context. If the expansion procedure of a KU does not include a matching operation, then the KU is not buildable, and an error is reported to the user if its expansion procedure fails. Conversely, the constraints of a buildable feature have only triggers, and its expansion procedure must include at least one of the following matching operations: **findExactReference, findInclusiveReference, testAbsence, testDifference, testEquivalence**, or **testPresence**. Once a constraint of a buildable feature x has received a presence signal for all its triggers, x does *not* become activated, but rather attempts, for a fixed amount of time, to have its expansion procedure succeed. Within the time interval allocated by x, the memory manager attempts the execution of the expansion procedure of x each time a new feature is detected, until either the procedure succeeds or time runs out. If the expansion procedure succeeds, x immediately becomes activated; if it fails, nothing happens, and if the deadline is reached, then x reverts to idle mode.

Finally, two other types of special KUs are now introduced strictly for convenience. First, *innate features* are KUs that are not buildable and that do not have any constraints. These KUs become activated by the presence of a string in the input text. Intuitively, the innate features are the recognizable (i.e., known a priori) words of the KB. Second, *relays* are KUs that have no constraints and no expansion procedure, just supplier and customer ports. Their role is limited to relaying the signal received from a supplier to all their customers. A relay groups a set of features under a common name that can be referred by a constraint, thus avoiding specifying a constraint for each member of the group. In the current prototype, it is left to the user to specify whether a KU is innate or a relay. In the future, however, it is conceivable that the implementation of **IDIoT** could identify such KUs by itself.

4.6.3 Examples of Knowledge Units

Here are a few examples of possible definitions for KUs. A line starting with a % is a comment and the ellipsis (. . .) is used to omit irrelevant details:

innate KU 'caviar':

```
% This innate feature recognizes the word 'caviar'
% and constructs a cluster with that feature for it
```

```
% An innate feature never has constraints.
 expansion:
% Use the built-in user variable called 'newCluster' which
% is set by the getNewCluster instruction with no argument.
     getNewCluster
     addFeature 'caviar' to newCluster
```

KU caviar:

```
% The KU food is a generalization of caviar.
% An association is used to immediately force the activation of the
% KU food when the KU caviar (not 'caviar') becomes detected.
 associations: food
% The 'concept' of caviar is triggered by the word 'caviar'.
% The constraint uses input KU noun to enforce the felicity of a
% noun at that point in the processing of the sentence.
% In other words, according to this definition, the KU caviar can
% only become detected if a noun would be 'grammatically correct'
% at that point in the processing of the sentence.
% An alternative approach, discussed in chapter 7, would be to
% activate the KU caviar as an association of the KU 'caviar' and
% then worry about the syntactic felicity of a noun at that point
% in the sentence.
 constraint 'caviar':
  triggers: 'caviar'
  inputs: noun has a weight of 1
```

```
% If the 'concept' caviar is detected, then the cluster that
% includes 'caviar' is updated to reflect the new information. This
% strategy is frequent using IDIoT.
% First the cluster governing the feature 'caviar' is bound to the
% user variable u1. Then the features caviar and noun are added to
% u1.
```

```
expansion:
     getCluster u1 governing 'caviar'
     addFeature caviar to u1
     addFeature noun to u1
```

```
ports:
      'caviar' has a delay of 1 and is a supplier
      noun has a delay of 1 and is a supplier
```

relay KU noun:

```
% This relay has all nouns of the KB as suppliers and only KU NP
% as a customer.
% All rules concerned with a noun refer to this relay rather than
% to each noun.
% The specification of such a relay is cumbersome and error-prone:
% it is the responsibility of the user to verify that all nouns
% are indeed suppliers!
 ports:
      bench has a delay of 1 and is a supplier
      box has a delay of 1 and is a supplier
      gin has a delay of 1 and is a supplier
      ...
      NP has a delay of 1 and is a customer
```

innate KU 'ate':

```
% The word 'ate' is associated with the verb eat.
 associations: actionEat
 expansion:
      getNewCluster u1
      addFeature 'eat' to u1
      addFeature pastForm to u1
 ports:
      pastForm has a delay of 1 and is a customer
```

KU actionEat:

```
% Most of the constraints of actionEat capture the different
% morphological forms of eat. Alternatively a relay could have been
% used.
 constraint 'ate':
  triggers: 'ate'
  inputs: verb has a weight of 1
 constraint 'eats':
  triggers: 'eats'
```

```
inputs:
    verb has a weight of 1
    ...
% However, the KU eat can be activated by other KUs that denote
% more specialized actions such as 'to dine' which has feature
% restaurant as an expectation.
% Notice the use of an explicit output strategy in this case
constraint dine:
  triggers: actionDine
  outputs:
    restaurant is sent signal expectationSignal
expansion:
% We use conditional instructions to handle the feature actionDine.
% The next 3 instructions are executed only if constraint dine was
% satisfied. In this case, the feature actionEat is added to the
% cluster containing the feature 'dine'. Notice the use of the
% instruction exit.
    ifConstraint dine then getCluster u1 governing 'dine'
    ifConstraint dine then addFeature actionEat to u1
    ifConstraint dine then exit
% If we are not dealing with actionDine then we want to associate
% the feature actionEat with the word 'eat' and mark it as a verb.
    getCluster u1 governing 'eat'
    addFeature actionEat to u1
    addFeature verb to u1
ports:
    'ate' has a delay of 1 and is a supplier
    'eats' has a delay of 1 and is a supplier
    ...
    actionDine has a delay of 1 and is a supplier
    verb has a delay of 1 and is a supplier
    eatFood has a delay of 1 and is a customer
```

KU missingDirectObject:

```
% Once at the end of a sentence, detect whether an obligatory
% transitive verb is missing its direct object. If so, flag a
% syntactic conflict.
% This feature captures a dynamic constraint and thus is
```

```
% buildable as indicated by the following line that is
% automatically generated by the system.
is buildable:
% syntacticConflict is a feature I use to capture all syntactic
% violations as explained in chapter 7.
 associations: syntacticConflict
% A constraint of a buildable feature only has triggers.
% In this case we insist on having established that a direct object
% is indeed still required and having reached the end of the
% sentence. Such a strategy will require that the KU
% missingDirectObject be inhibited as soon as a direct object is
% found.
 constraint c1:
  ordered triggers:
      compulsoryTransitive endOfSentence
  expansion:
      getCluster u1 governing newFact
      getCluster u2 governing mainVerb in u1
      getCluster u3 governedBy mainVerb in u2
      testPresenceOf compulsoryTransitive in u3
      getCluster u2 governing VP in u1
      testAbsenceOf directObject in u2
 ports:
      compulsoryTransitive has a delay of 1 and is a supplier
      endOfSentence has a delay of 1 and is a supplier
```

KU alcoholicBeverage:

```
% This KU illustrates another typical use of conditional
% instructions.
% More importantly, it illustrates a possible organization for a
% is-a hierarchy of KUs: the parent is triggered by its children.
% This organization of communication links must not be conflated
% with issues of retrieval. In particular, this organization DOES
% NOT imply that a parent (such as alcoholicBeverage can readily
% enumerate all its children (such as gin, scotch, etc).
% IDIoT simply does not address the issue of categorization.
 associations: aboutAlcoholicBeverages beverage
 constraint gin:
```

```
 triggers: alcoholicBeverageGin
constraint scotch:
 triggers: alcoholicBeverageScotch
expansion:
     ifConstraint gin
       then getCluster u1 governing alcoholicBeverageGin
       ifConstraint scotch
       then getCluster u1 governing alcoholicBeverageScotch
     addFeature alcoholicBeverage to u1
ports:
     alcoholicBeverageGin has a delay of 1 and is a supplier
     alcoholicBeverageScotch has a delay of 1 and is a supplier
```

4.7 BEYOND TIME TRACTABILITY

Up to this point in the discussion, the description of **IDIoT** has emphasized the pervasive role of processing time for ensuring tractability with respect to time. However, beyond time complexity, several other requirements were established in the previous chapter. Let us first consider space complexity. This problem requires that 1) the amount of space consumed during processing, and 2) the amount of space required for the constructed structures both be tractable. In other words, in both cases, it is unacceptable to witness an "explosion" of space requirements with respect to the size of the knowledge base, or of the input. Yet Shastri (1993) observed that this issue is generally ignored. For example, Bookman (1992, 1994) is one of the few researchers that explicitly addressed time complexity, but, like most "local" connectionist researchers, he considerably downplayed the enormous space requirements of his model space requirements that essentially disqualified his approach with respect to scalability.

Restricting messaging to numeric signals only addresses the first facet of space complexity. More precisely, because each message in **IDIoT** consumes an extremely small amount of space, no "space explosion" will result from a large number of concurrent messages, and thus, massive parallelism need not be constrained from this viewpoint. Conversely, if we were using complex markers (see subsection 2.2.2), we would have to consider the amount of space required by concurrent markers. In the worst case, there would be a trade-off between the size of a marker and the amount of parallelism (in terms of the number of concurrent markers) allowed in the system. In other words, the more complex these markers, the fewer of them would be allowed to be spread in the network.

To obtain complete space tractability in a grounded architecture, we must also guarantee that no "space explosion" (with respect to the size of the constructed structures) will occur at any point during processing, *regardless* of the size of the input text *and regardless* of the size of the knowledge base (Shastri, 1993). In essence, this requirement corresponds to the problem of *convergence* (see section 1.1 and Corriveau, 1994c), which consists in explaining how the multitude of inferences *potentially* generated by a text can be reduced to the small set that is put in the trace. **IDIoT**'s solution to this requirement proceeds from the following observations, which pertain to its time-constrained nature:

1. The activation of a KU depends on satisfying one of its constraints. In turn, constraint satisfaction relies on the reception of signals *within a short interval of time* (called a detection race).

2. Each KU has a diachronic retrievability coefficient that affects its reachability, that is, the time it takes for a signal to reach this KU.

3. Upon activation, the expansion procedure of a KU is allocated a maximum amount of time to build and modify clusters. This is called an expansion race.

4. Each element of dynamic memory has a retrievability coefficient corresponding to the cost of retrieving it (using a getCluster operation). Upon inclusion in WM through construction or retrieval, this coefficient is set for a short amount of time to an arbitrarily low value β and then gradually increases over time according to a decay rate π. Once a retrievability coefficient goes over a certain threshold, it is set to the default (initial) value Ω corresponding to the elements in LTM.

5. Clusters in LTM are essentially unretrievable due to the time-constraint associated with the execution of any expansion procedure.

6. STM (which includes WM) has a small maximum number of elements, which we will denote ¥.

7. Membership to WM and STM is time-constrained, as well as capacity-constrained.

8. For simplicity, in the current prototype, all cluster operations except retrieval ones are taken to be instantaneous.

From this list, we can establish the following facts with respect to space complexity:

1. Of the KUs that are triggered by the input or by other KUs, some will not satisfy one of their constraints during the timespan of their detection race, simply because their current retrievability coefficient prevents any signal from reaching them in time. In other words, the higher the retrievability coefficient of a KU, the less chance it has of becoming activated. Thus, combining communication delays with detection races constrains the number of potential inferences that are selected (through constraint satisfaction), that is, the number of triggered KUs that become activated.

2. Of the elements of dynamic memory at a given point in time, only the reachable ones with respect to the timespan of an expansion race can be modified by the corresponding expansion procedure. Consequently,

a) decay constrains how many clusters can be accessed by an expansion procedure.

b) an expansion race constrains the number of potential inferences that are selected through buildable features: Only reachable clusters can participate in the detection of a buildable feature, and thus the number of potential inferences that are selected (whether by constraint satisfaction or buildable features), that is, the number of triggered KUs that become activated, is constrained by the deadlines of races in **IDIoT**. (These deadlines are user-programmable for flexibility. However, experimentation with the current prototype has taught us that arbitrary, long deadlines inevitably lead to *chaotic interference* between the rules of the knowledge base. In effect, "far-fetched" paths are constructed and clutter the interpretation.)

c) a cluster has a maximal useful "size" of ¥ "components" because

• in order to be "manipulated" by an expansion procedure, a cluster needs to be accessed by means of a retrieval cluster operation which consumes time.

• there are at most ¥ elements in STM to be grouped into a cluster at any point in time. Thus, the maximal number of components at any level of a cluster is ¥.

• the maximal useful depth of a cluster is ¥ "levels":

Additional levels would be unreachable by definition.

• a cluster that has more than ¥ components distributed among its levels would necessarily have some
of these components unretrievable.

d) an expansion procedure having limited time to execute
and consuming some of this time to access the cluster(s) it
manipulates, cannot construct a cluster exceeding ¥ components.

e) an expansion procedure that constructs a cluster that
"monopolizes" STM decreases the likelihood of success for
the expansion procedure of a subsequent and totally independent KU. As an example, consider one or more KUs that construct a VP cluster that comes to occupy all of STM. Then, if
a subsequent KU x becomes detected but requires access to
the subject cluster that has been shifted into LTM as a result
of the monopolizing KU(s), then the expansion procedure of
x will fail, causing an error.

3. The number of KUs becoming detected being constrained and the
expansion procedure of each KU being constrained by time (through
the deadline of an expansion race and through decay of elements of
STM), we can conclude that no space explosion will happen in **IDIoT**.

It is important to understand that this list of postulates does *not* solve the issue
of space complexity in itself: It merely suggests that no space explosion will
occur in **IDIoT**. Experimentation does "confirm" that the amount of space
required by constructed structures in **IDIoT** is quite constrained: Either deadlines ensure convergence on a small set of clusters, or chaotic interference
resulting from long deadlines leads to the failure of an expansion procedure!
However, we are a long way from a computational theory of memory that
would explain

1. what are clusters, what are the "levels" of a cluster, what are the
"components" of a cluster, what is the "size" of a cluster, how clusters
combine with other clusters, and so forth.

2. how temporal and capacity constraints are "realized" in STM.

3. how the structure of a cluster (e.g., its depth) affects its retrievability.

4. how the familiarity of a cluster affects its retrievability.

5. how the next input (e.g., the next word of a text) "shifts" processing to it (see Gernsbacher, 1990).

6. how semantic considerations such as coherence (which will be discussed in Part III) affect retrievability.

Let me briefly elaborate. It is well accepted that the cognitive structures built during interpretation may not necessarily be retrievable by themselves, but only as components of larger structures (Gernsbacher, 1990). For example, one may not recall an episode from a Colombo movie by itself, but only when the whole storyline is retrieved, and, clearly, some of the structures constructed during processing will simply be forgotten (e.g., it is well accepted that we do not store the exact wording of a text although we process it). The point is that not all constructed structures have the same life span: Some will be replaced, deleted, or forgotten, whereas others will become "recallable" by themselves (a reflexive form of learning, as opposed to rote learning). In other words, both the components of an interpretation, as well as the interpretation as a whole, are diachronic. This facet of cognition is extremely complex. For example, what we remember has to do in part with what we already know, how often it is retrieved, how and when the new information was acquired (i.e., its context of acquisition), how we organize and integrate information in our knowledge base, and so forth. We require a theory of episodic memory, but such a theory often entails several epistemological commitments (e.g., with respect to categorization) and thus lies beyond the framework of a grounded architecture. From my viewpoint, it is important that the rules of "memorizing" subsuming such a theory be grounded, but this topic lies beyond the scope of this book.

Having addressed the tractability issue, we turn to the other requirements established in subsection 3.3.4:

1. The system does not hardwire any particular solution: **IDIoT** is a purely mechanistic model of memory. Furthermore, massive parallelism allows the generation of multiple solutions. To model this, we could assume that the input or the activation of a KU triggers several candidate KUs and, possibly, another KU acting as a resolution manager. Each candidate has a maximum amount of time to become activated. All candidacies proceed in parallel. The first candidate to become activated, if any, can possibly inhibit other candidates (if they are known to it) as well as the resolution manager. Otherwise, multiple winners are possible. Each winner notifies the resolution manager,

which coordinates how these multiple solutions are then reconciled (e.g., all can be inhibited or all become detected, or candidacies may be restarted with more time allocated to them). In other words, lack of interpretation, ambiguous interpretation and corrected interpretation can all be modeled in **IDIoT**.

2. The system is able to take into account independent external factors that may influence cognition. The user-specifiable parameters ß, Ω, π, and ¥ can be varied from one run to the other of the system, possibly leading to significantly different interpretations of a same input text.

3. The system uses processing time as its stopping criterion. This stopping criterion guarantees time tractability without making epistemological commitments.

4. The architecture is grounded in primitive operations (matching, storage, retrieval, and association). More precisely, the expansion procedure of a KU uses cluster operations that are merely user-friendly versions of these primitive memory operations. Also, **IDIoT** allows the expression of a multitude of resolution strategies as suggested in i). In essence, a resolution manager is a KU that "knows" about a set of candidates and manages their detection via the output strategies of its constraints. This KU may be inhibited by the first winner, as suggested in i). But this requires that each candidate knows all the others. A better strategy for allowing the detection of only the first winner consists in having the resolution manager have a constraint for each possible winner. Then the expansion procedure of the manager uses the output strategy of each constraint to inhibit all candidates except the one associated with the constraint.

5. All knowledge is treated as user-specifiable and user-modifiable. For better or worse, all knowledge, including all rules implementing the comprehension algorithm, that is, any entity requiring epistemological commitments is to be specified by the user and to reside in the knowledge base (as opposed to being entrenched in the cognitive architecture).

6. The format of the data in the knowledge base (i.e., the definition of KUs, see subsection 4.6.3) is quite understandable to a user and will be shown, in the next chapter, to be easily modifiable. In particular, expansion procedures abstract away from complex memory issues (such as the details of retrieval, association, juxtaposition, etc.). Furthermore, I introduce in the next chapter, tools that further simplify

the specification of KUs.

7. The architecture is tractable both in terms of time and space complexity.

8. The architecture is reusable by virtue of being implemented as a concurrent object-oriented framework (see section 3.6).

This list suggests that **IDIoT** does indeed constitute a grounded architecture for comprehension inasmuch as it satisfies the requirements established in the previous chapter. Within this framework, an interpretation consists of building a representation in the form of clusters for the signifiés of a text (e.g., words, sentences, etc.). These clusters are not static: They can constantly change during the interpretative process, and in the end, they do not constitute an interpretation by themselves but rather with respect to the user of **IDIoT** who will scrutinize them. In other words, the clusters produced by **IDIoT** act as triggers for the idiosyncratic interpretation of a user.

Chapter 5

A Prototype of **IDIoT**

5.1 INTRODUCTION

The previous chapters introduced **IDIoT** from the viewpoint of a cognitive scientist interested in developing a grounded architecture for linguistic comprehension. In this chapter, we rather adopt the perspective of a user of the current prototype. We survey the available interfaces of the tool, consider what experimentation has taught us, and follow an annotated trace of the processing of the sentence "John drinks gin". We also look at this prototype from an implementation's viewpoint by examining some of the details of the mechanisms presented in chapter 4.

The current prototype of **IDIoT** exists in three different versions of the programming language Smalltalk (Goldberg, 1984). These different versions differ in the specification and look-and-feel of user interfaces, as well as in their treatment of concurrency. In all three versions, the prototype represents about 300K of code, and the largest knowledge base used with the 89 running examples consumes 500K of storage for about 300 knowledge units. Given the simplicity of the example texts (both in terms of syntax and of inferences), the latter number suggests that a knowledge base for the interpretation of even "children stories" would be several orders of magnitude larger than the current one.

I abstract away from these details in the rest of this book. Also, I omit discussing partial prototypes in C++, as well as a prototype currently being developed in the experimental concurrent object-oriented language ABCL/R2 (Matsuoka, Watanabe, & Yonezawa, 1991). Not only does this prototype lack the user interfaces of the Smalltalk versions, but also, it serves a different goal. Whereas the Smalltalk versions are meant to be tested by actual users, the ABCL/R2 version only aims at exploring the use of reflection (see Maes, 1987) in a cognitive architecture. Should reflection turn out to be useful, it will be ported to the Smalltalk versions.

5.2 THE BASIC USER INTERFACES

The current prototype of **IDIoT** includes several knowledge specification tools. In this section, we look at the three different *browsers* (in the Smalltalk sense of this word, see Goldberg, 1984) initially developed for the specification of knowledge units (with actual screen captures from the original prototype implemented in Smalltalk-80 from ParcPlace Systems, CA). Roughly put, a browser is a menu-driven interactive window allowing for both the inspection and modification of information. More recent interfaces are discussed in section 5.7.

The *knowledge base browser* (see Figure 5.1) allows the user to create a KU and assign it a retrievability coefficient. Through the command "verify", the whole KB can be scanned to ensure that no KU refers to a nonexistent one. The commands "load" and "save" allow a verified KB to be loaded from or saved to a disk. The knowledge base browser consists of a single scrollable list pane providing a view on the KB. It has a single menu.

Having selected a KU in the knowledge base browser, a *knowledge unit browser* (see Figures 5.2 through 5.6) can be opened. It allows the user to define the associations, candidates, expansion procedure, and ports of a KU, and indicate whether the KU is innate or not, a relay or not. The user can also specify the names and order of constraints. Automatic checks force the user to enter a syntactically correct expansion procedure. In particular, the system verifies that a user variable is bound to a cluster (through a **getCluster** or **get-NewCluster** operation) before it is referred in another operation. For conditional instructions, the specified constraint must already exist. The system also verifies that all KUs referred to in the constraints of a KU have delays assigned to them. The knowledge unit browser consists of five top buttons, two bottom buttons, and a large scrollable list pane in the middle. The mutually exclusive top buttons drive both the menu and contents of the list pane. The two bottom buttons merely act as on/off toggles.

Selecting a constraint, the user can open a *constraint browser* (see Figure 5.7), which allows the specification of the triggers, inputs, exceptions, and outputs of a constraint. The triggers can be marked as ordered or not. When defining an output, the user is prompted for a target KU and then for a signal to send.

Menu entries for all these browsers should be self-explanatory.

5.2.1 The Knowledge Base Browser

I emphasize the fact that the knowledge base browser cannot be closed if any KU refers to an non existent KU. In other words, the system enforces referential integrity throughout a KB.

Knowledge Base Browser

accessToFood
actionBe
actionCelebrate
actionCommand
actionCry
actionDie
actionDine
actionDiscuss
actionDrink
actionEat
actionGive
actionKick
actionLike
actionMan
actionObserve
actionOrder
actionPick
actionPlay
actionPlayAGame
actionPlayAMusicalInstrument
actionPut
actionSit
actionSleep
actionSpill
actionSpillLiquid
actionSunbathe
actionWatch

Create
Copy
Rename
Browse Definition
Modify Familarity
Delete
Load
Verify
Verify and Save
Print

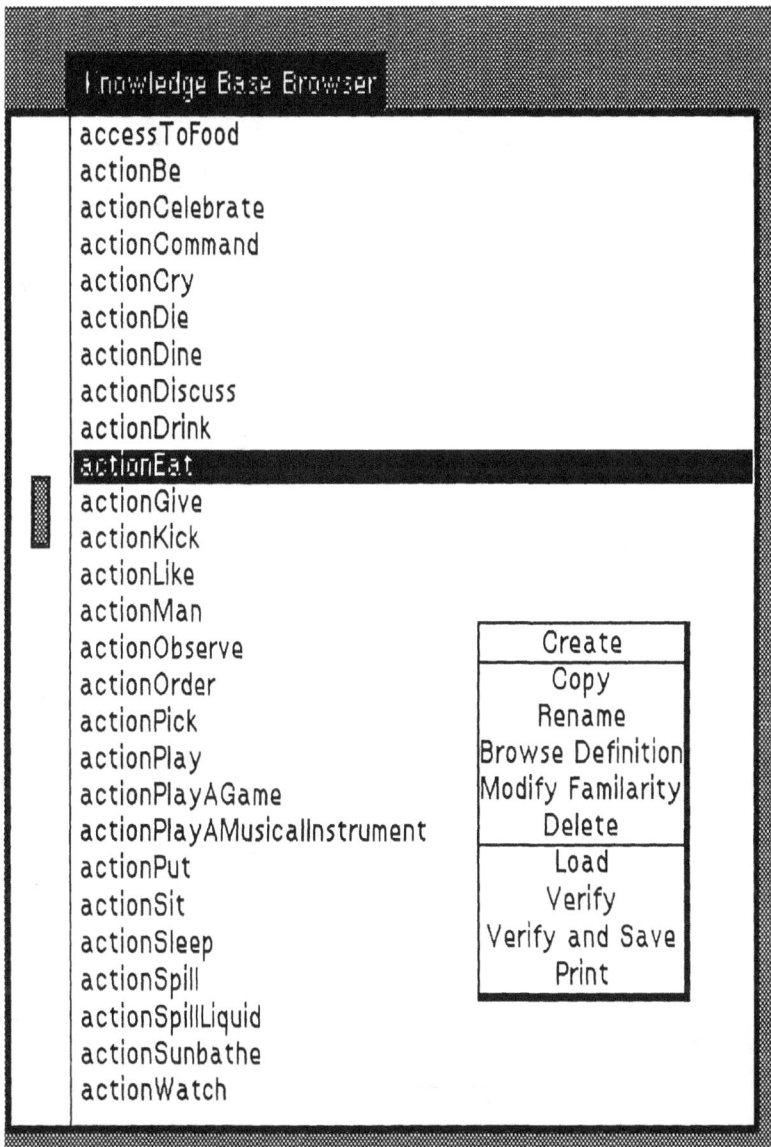

Figure 5.1 The Knowledge Base Browser.

5.2.2   The Knowledge Unit Browser

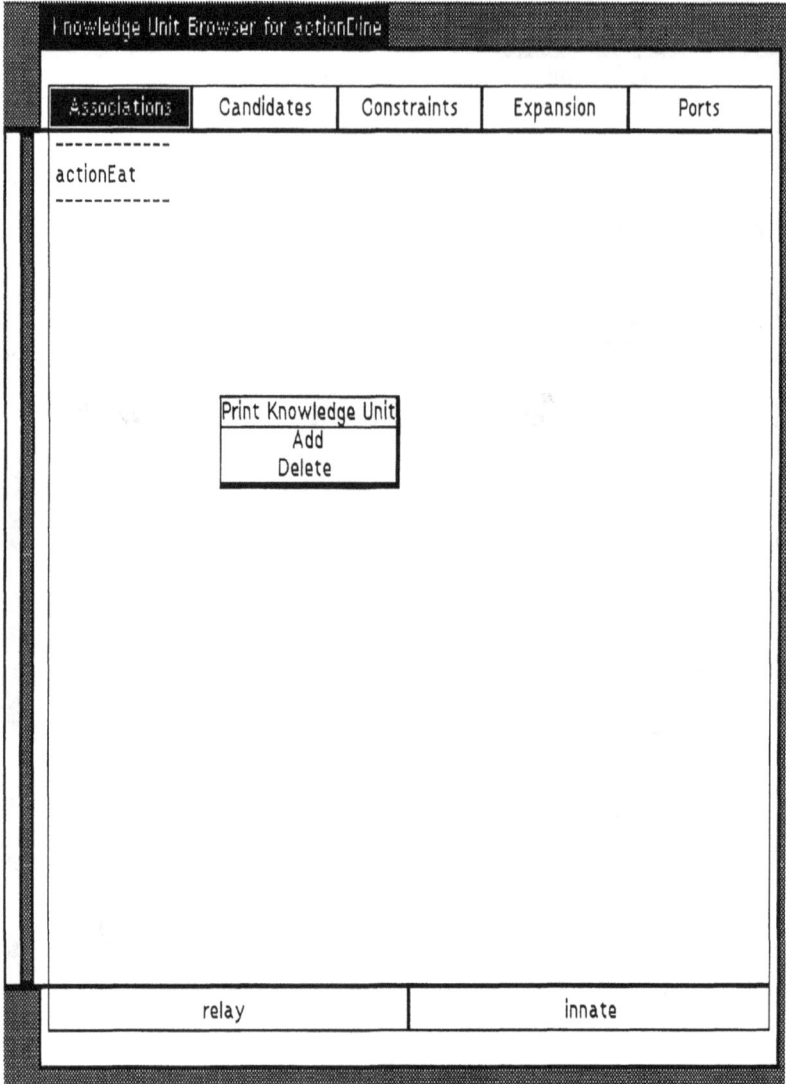

Figure 5.2 The Knowledge Unit Browser: Associations Menu.

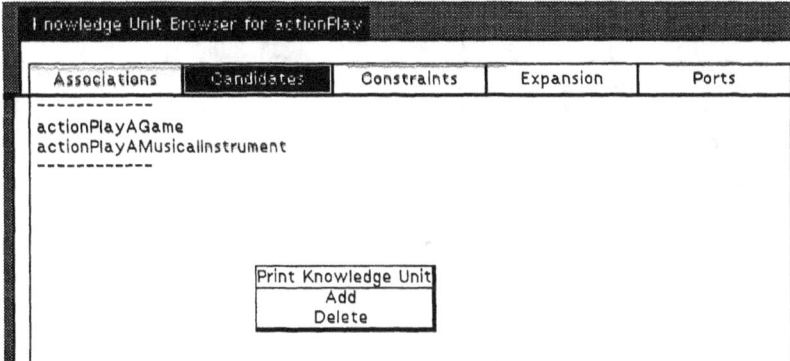

Figure 5.3 The Knowledge Unit Browser: Candidate Menu.

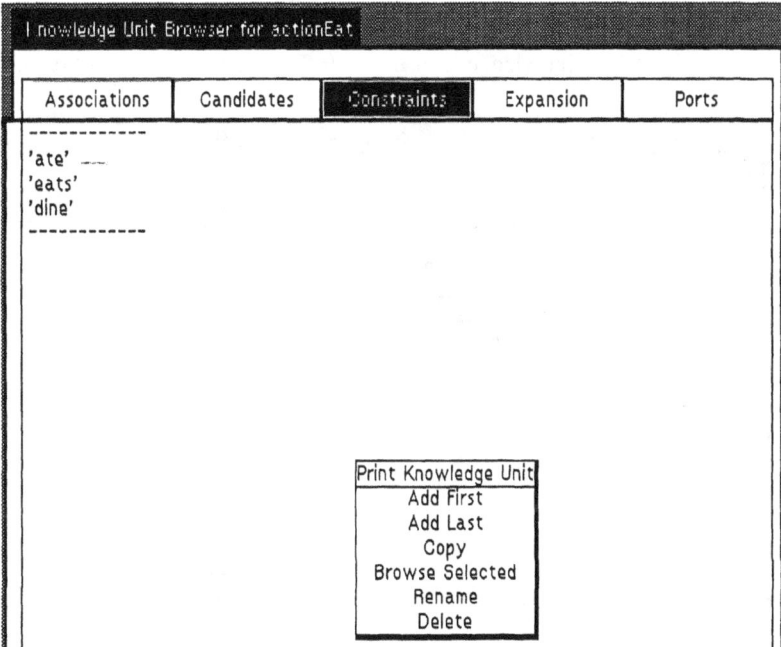

Figure 5.4 The Knowledge Unit Browser: Constraint Menu.

| Associations | Candidates | Constraints | E·pansion | Ports |

```
------------
ifConstraint 'dine' then getCluster u1 governing 'dine'
ifConstraint 'dine' then addFeature actionEat to u1
ifConstraint 'dine' then exit
getCluster u1 governing 'eat'
addFeature actionEat to u1
addFeature verb to u1
------------
```

```
Print Knowledge Unit
       Add
    Add First
    Add Last
     Modify
     Delete
```

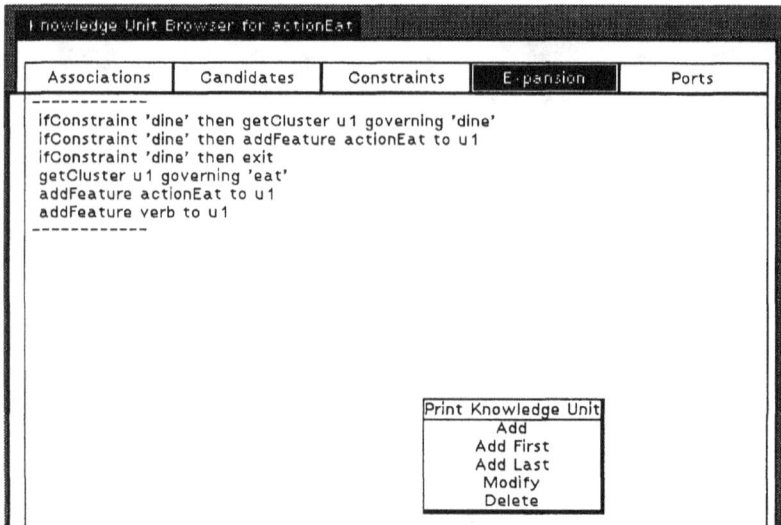

Figure 5.5 The Knowledge Unit Browser: Expansion Procedure Menu.

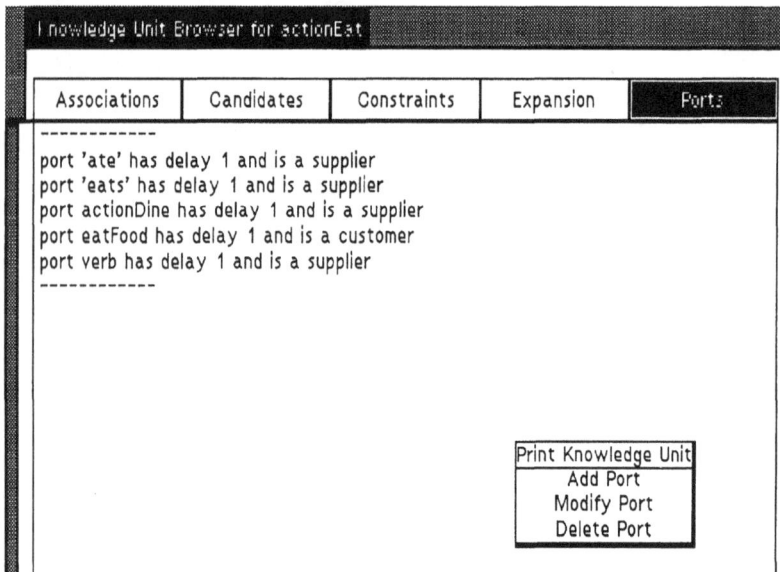

| Associations | Candidates | Constraints | Expansion | Ports |

```
------------
port 'ate' has delay 1 and is a supplier
port 'eats' has delay 1 and is a supplier
port actionDine has delay 1 and is a supplier
port eatFood has delay 1 and is a customer
port verb has delay 1 and is a supplier
------------
```

```
Print Knowledge Unit
     Add Port
    Modify Port
    Delete Port
```

Figure 5.6 The Knowledge Unit Browser: Ports Menu.

5.2.3 The Constraint Browser

Here is a constraint browser opened on a possible constraint for the KU **onTime**. In this case, the user has specified four ordered triggers, no inputs, no exceptions, and one output to the KU **forced-VP-PP-Attach**. Through the use of the different menus, the user can edit this constraint. In particular, specifying a KU as one of its own triggers may be problematic and thus, in this example, the triggers most likely need to be revisited. The current prototype does not detect such problems.

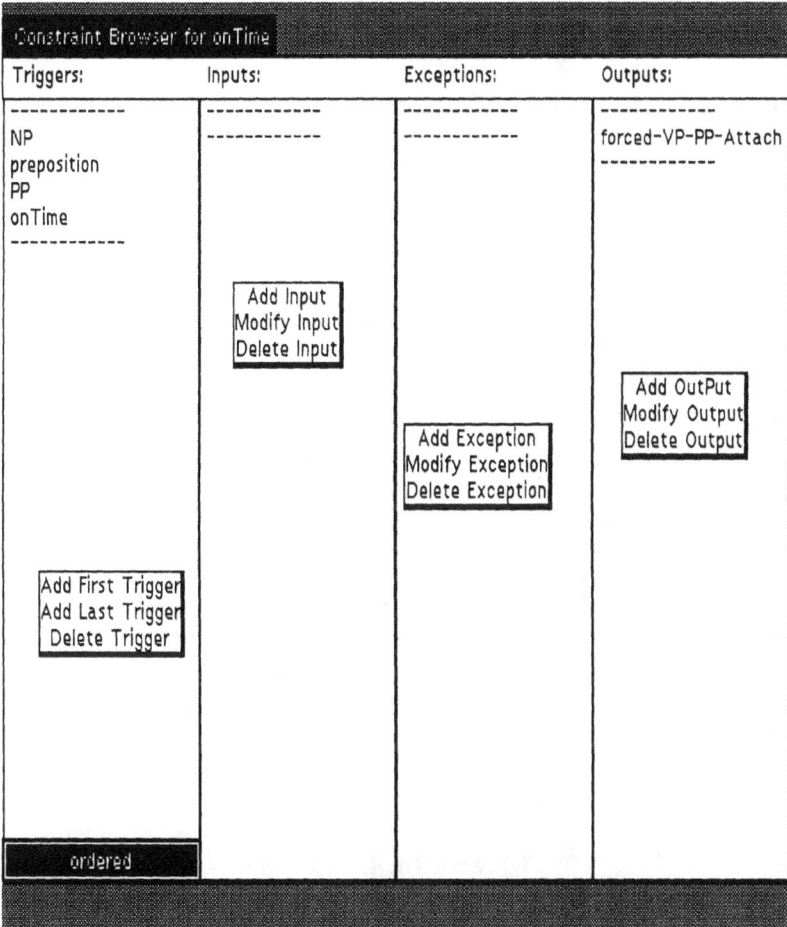

Figure 5.7 The Constraint Browser.

5.2.4 The Trace Browser

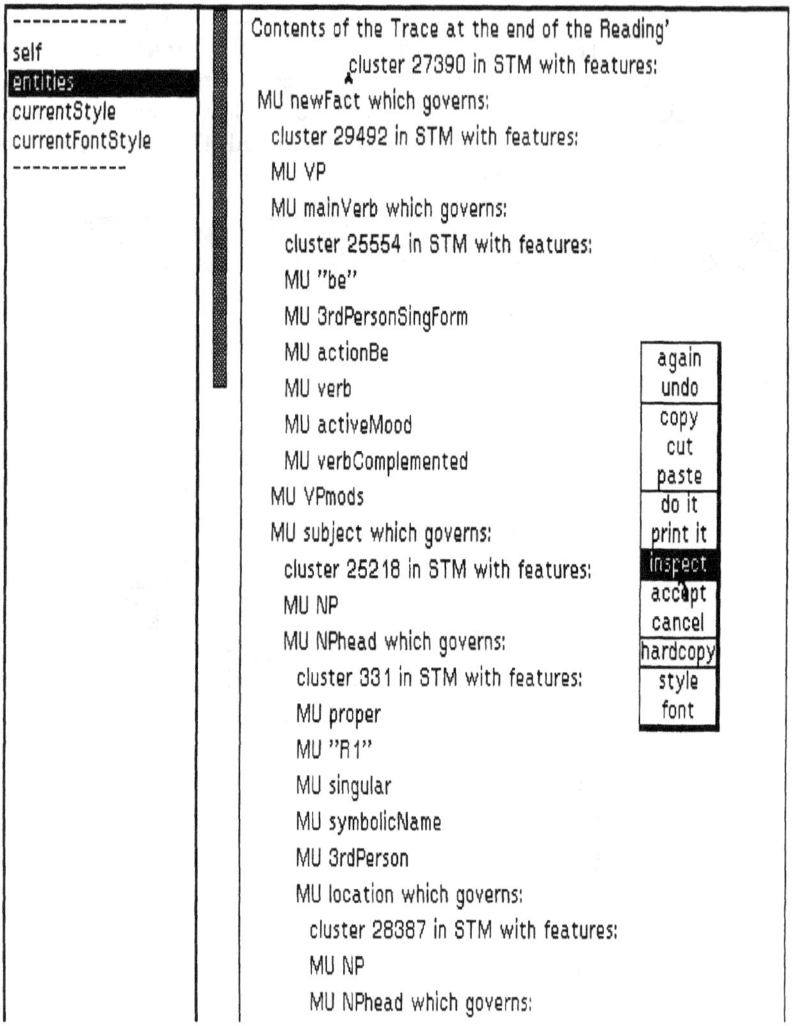

```
-----------        Contents of the Trace at the end of the Reading'
self                        cluster 27390 in STM with features:
entities                MU newFact which governs:
currentStyle              cluster 29492 in STM with features:
currentFontStyle          MU VP
-----------               MU mainVerb which governs:
                            cluster 25554 in STM with features:
                            MU "be"
                            MU 3rdPersonSingForm
                            MU actionBe                    again
                            MU verb                        undo
                            MU activeMood                  copy
                            MU verbComplemented            cut
                          MU VPmods                        paste
                          MU subject which governs:        do it
                            cluster 25218 in STM with features:  print it
                            MU NP                          inspect
                          MU NPhead which governs:         accept
                            cluster 331 in STM with features:  cancel
                            MU proper                      hardcopy
                            MU "R1"                        style
                            MU singular                    font
                            MU symbolicName
                            MU 3rdPerson
                            MU location which governs:
                              cluster 28387 in STM with features:
                              MU NP
                              MU NPhead which governs:
```

Figure 5.8 The Trace Browser.

In its current form the Trace Browser is merely a Smalltalk inspector on the
data structure produced by **IDIoT** (an ordered collection of clusters in the cur-

rent prototype).

5.3 KNOWLEDGE UNIT SPECIFICATION

A user of **IDIoT** uses the browsers of the previous section to input the specification of individual KUs. These specifications are stored in a knowledge base
(KB). The user may manage several knowledge bases but must select a single
one at the start of each interpretation. The selected KB constitutes the contents
of the static memory of the system for the current interpretation. The ports of
all KUs in the selected KB define the topology of the network of KUs forming
static memory.

The information specified in a KU is strictly local to it, that is, independent of any other KU and of any global (network-wide) information. The
knowledge base browser allows the user to create a new KU in a KB by giving
it a unique name. A new or existing KU can have its definitions modified by
the opening of a knowledge unit browser on it.

Once opened on a KU x, the knowledge unit browser allows the following
actions:

1. By selecting the "Associations" button, the user can see the list of
associations of x, KUs to which a forcedDetection signal is sent upon
the detection of x. The user may add or delete associations to the list.

2. By selecting the "Candidates" button, the user can see the list of
candidates of x, KUs to which a confirmation signal is sent upon the
detection of x. The user may add or delete candidates to the list.

3. By selecting the "Constraints" button, the user can see the ordered
list of the names of the constraints of x. A constraint browser must be
opened to examine the contents of a specific constraint. The user may
add a constraint to the beginning or the end of the list. Constraints
may also be deleted.

4. By selecting the "Expansion" button, the user can see the ordered
list of cluster operations that form the expansion procedure of x. The
user may add an instruction to the beginning or the end of the procedure, or after a selected instruction. An instruction is inserted in the
procedure if, and only if, it has a valid syntax. A conditional instruction must refer to an existing constraint of x, and all non retrieval
operations (i.e., all instructions except for those of the **getCluster**
series) must refer to user variables for which a retrieval operation
existed in the procedure previously. (The first user variable of a "find"
instruction does not obey this rule because it is set to a retrieved clus-

ter.) For example, the instruction

> addFeature actionEat to u1

is valid only if

> getCluster u1 . . .

precedes it in the expansion procedure. This rule is also enforced when an instruction is deleted from an expansion procedure. Failure to comply with this rule results in the display of an appropriate warning to the user, as well as the rejection of the instruction.

Also, recall that the system automatically establishes whether a KU is buildable from the presence of "test" or "find" instructions in the expansion procedure of this KU. A buildable feature may have only triggers and outputs in its constraints.

5. By selecting the "Ports" button, the user can see the list of ports of x. The customer ports of a KU are those ports that are used to send out a signal to another KU the supplier ports, to receive a signal from another KU. From the constraints of x, the system can infer which ports are suppliers (corresponding to the triggers, inputs, and exceptions of the constraints of x) and which are customers (corresponding to the output strategy of the constraints). Additional customer ports corresponding to KUs not referred to in the constraints of x may be specified: Regardless of the satisfied constraint, a presence signal is sent to these ports upon the detection of x. Also, a KU may receive a signal from itself, in which case the port is considered to be a supplier port. Modifications to the constraints of x cause the system to recategorize all its ports. A delay must be specified for each port of a KU before the knowledge unit browser can be closed. Ports can be added or deleted, or have their delays modified.

6. By selecting the "innate" button, the user indicates that the KU corresponds to an innate feature, that is, to a feature that is automatically activated (i.e., becomes detected) if its name is found as a string of characters (delimited by spaces or punctuation signs) in the input text. For example, the feature **"John"** is an innate feature that is automatically activated when the word "John" is read from the input text.

Recall that an innate feature has no constraints, as it is directly activated by the input text. It may have associations, to which a presence signal, not a forcedDetection signal, is sent. At least one association must be specified before the knowledge unit browser of an innate feature can be closed. An innate feature may also have candidates, an expansion procedure, and ports.

7. By selecting the "relay" button, the user indicates that the KU is a relay, and thus must consist only of ports. Therefore, for relays, the system only allows the specification of ports, which must be explicitly identified as either supplier or customer ones. An innate feature cannot be a relay.

Finally, the constraint browser of a KU allows the user to specify the triggers, inputs, exceptions, and output strategy of a particular constraint. Triggers may be considered ordered or not through the use of the "ordered" button, and to specify an output of a constraint, the user must give the target KU and the signal to send it. A constraint browser cannot be closed unless at least one trigger is specified.

5.4 SOME IMPLEMENTATION DETAILS

In order to start an interpretation, the user selects an input text (in an ASCII file) and a knowledge base. The default settings for the different parameters of memory (see section 4.7) can then be altered. Once these parameters have been specified, a special event is sent to the memory manager to start the reading. The memory manager reads the input text one character at a time, each character "costing" one character quantum of time. A word is considered to be a string of characters delimited by spaces or punctuation signs. Each time a word is found, the memory manager checks whether an innate feature of that name exists. If not, a warning stating that the word is unknown to the system is displayed, and the reading continues. Conversely, if the word is recognized, the memory manager sends a forcedDetection signal to its corresponding innate feature. This signal will cause the innate feature to send signals to its customers and request the execution of its expansion procedure by the memory manager. In turn, the signals sent out by the innate feature will eventually lead to the activation of other KUs, which, upon their detection, will send out signals to their customers and have their respective expansion procedures execute. The execution of an expansion procedure constructs or modifies clusters in dynamic memory. Once the text has been completely input, a *trace browser* opens on the interpretation generated for the text, that is, on the contents of the dynamic memory at the end of processing (see Figure 5.8).

In order to handle sentences in a simple way, the current input process of the memory manager considers that a sequence consisting of a period followed by one or more spaces, followed by a capital, indicates the end of a sentence and the beginning of a new one. Since all "knowledge" is user-specifiable, the current prototype expects the user to define the features **end-OfSentence** and **startOfSentence**, as well as features corresponding to the punctuation signs. Otherwise, punctuation, which does play a role in the timing of reading, will simply be ignored.

Each exchange of signals in the system is routed through the memory manager, which computes the actual arrival time of a signal from the following:

1. The delay associated with the port on which the signal is sent.

2. The retrievability coefficient of the receiver.

3. The nature of the signal.

Recall that a forcedDetection or forcedInhibition signal takes epsilon time to reach its destination. In other cases, the actual delay is computed as the multiplication of the specified delay by the retrievability coefficient of the receiver. The memory manager keeps a schedule of all signals to be received and their time of arrival to their destination. This schedule is used to simulate real-time processing of communications in memory. It is also at the basis of **IDIoT**'s simulation of concurrency. Ideally, this schedule should be replaced by a more direct use of the concurrency support offered by the language of implementation.

Independently of inputting the text, the memory manager has the responsibility to execute sequentially the expansion procedures of the KUs that become detected. Procedures are executed on a first-requested–first-executed basis. In order to execute an expansion procedure, the memory manager attempts the instructions of the procedure in order. Should an error occur (e.g., failed **getCluster** operation, non-existent feature in a **moveFeature**, non existent cluster in a **removeCluster** operation), the system will report to the user the simulated time of the error, the KU whose expansion procedure crashed, and the guilty instruction. It will then open a trace browser on the contents of the dynamic memory in order for the user to debug the procedure. The current prototype abandons further processing of the text in the event of such an error. Still, on the topic of expansion procedures, all data structures and algorithms for cluster operations are specific to a particular implementation of **IDIoT** and thus are taken to be of little interest to the reader.

The rules controlling the membership of a cluster to one of the partitions of dynamic memory are enforced by the memory manager. Both the capacity and membership constraints of these partitions are reviewed only after the execution of **getCluster** and **removeCluster** operations.

The memory manager is also responsible for trying to execute the expansion procedure of a buildable feature once this KU has a triggered constraint. Requests from a buildable feature to the memory manager asking to attempt to execute its expansion procedure are treated as follows:

1. If the expansion procedure of a buildable feature succeeds, the memory manager sends the KU a forcedDetectionSignal, and the feature does not request, upon its detection, the execution of its expansion procedure (because this procedure has been executed!).

2. If the expansion procedure of the buildable feature fails, then the manager registers it on a list of buildable features waiting to be built, marking down the time after which the feature should be purged from the list. In other words, the manager ensures that a buildable feature has only a short amount of time to have its expansion procedure succeed. Failure to do so corresponds to the situation in which the dynamic constraint that the buildable feature embodies fails. Given that an expansion procedure has a very short amount of time to execute, the list of buildable features waiting to be satisfied is always very short.

3. in order to avoid having to "restore" the contents of dynamic memory after the failure of the expansion procedure of a buildable feature, the system insists that dynamic memory not be altered by a buildable feature before all its test operations have succeeded. In other words, the contents of dynamic memory cannot be modified by a buildable feature before its expansion procedure is guaranteed to succeed. In essence, this avoids any form of backtracking in **IDIoT** and restricts a dynamic constraint to apply only to clusters in context, which is precisely what we want.

4. Within the time allocated to a buildable feature to be successfully expanded, the memory manager will attempt to execute the expansion procedure of this buildable feature each time a new feature has its expansion procedure executed, that is, each time the contents of the dynamic memory change.

5. Finally, the memory manager may receive a request to attempt to execute the expansion procedure of a buildable feature that received a submission signal for some of its triggers. In this case, the memory manager attempts this expansion procedure only once and sends back a forcedDetection signal in case of success, or a forcedInhibition signal in case of failure. In other words, whereas a buildable feature with

genuine triggers can have its expansion procedure attempted several times, a buildable feature that has received a submission signal for one or more of its triggers is given only one chance of succeeding.

This description should convince the reader that **IDIoT** is definitely not as trivial as it may seem, and that several design decisions are still open to more investigation. To further demonstrate this point, the detailed algorithm of a knowledge unit is presented in the rest of this section. More specifically, I now present the signal processing algorithm that all KUs (which run asynchronously and in parallel) obey.

Each KU executes the following basic reception algorithm each time it receives one or more new signals:

1. It receives all new signals at time t. Once the memory manager has computed the actual time of arrival of a signal, it places the signal and its time of arrival in the queue of incoming signals of the receiving port. Each KU keeps a queue of pairs of the form *<incomingSignal, arrivalTime>* for each of its supplier ports. A KU receives all new signals at time t by retrieving all signals of its input port queues that have t as their arrival time. The signals received at t are called the current signals.

2. Independently of its current mode, the KU verifies that it has not exceeded the current deadline of its mode. If it has, it immediately reverts back to *idle mode*. In other words, at a given point in time, a KU is in a certain mode (waiting for certain signals and ignoring others). All modes, except idle mode, last a fixed amount of time. Once the time allocated to a mode has been reached, the KU automatically reverts back to idle mode.

3. If the current signals include a forcedInhibition signal, then the KU immediately reverts back to idle mode and ignores all other current signals.

4. ElseIf the current signals include a forcedDetection signal, then the KU immediately goes to *detected mode*. Both forcedInhibition and forcedDetection signals are always routed by the memory manager to the manager's port of a KU (see 4.6.1.3).

5. Else, the KU goes to the algorithm of its current mode.

The algorithm for the *detected mode* follows:

1. If the KU is a relay feature, it sends a presence signal to its customers.

2. If the KU is an innate feature, it sends a presence signal to all its associations. Otherwise, it sends a forcedDetection signal to all its associations.

3. The KU sends a confirmation signal to all its candidates.

4. The KU sends a reinforcement signal to all KUs to which it initially sent a submission signal and that have sent back a confirmation signal. This step corresponds to the reinforcement of all missing features of the triggered constraint, if there are any.

5. The KU sends the specified signals to the customers listed in the output strategy of the satisfied constraint, if there any.

6. The KU sends a presence signal to customers to which it is not sending a reinforcement signal and that are not part of the outputs of the satisfied constraint.

7. The KU requests the execution of its expansion procedure by the memory manager and reverts back to idle mode.

The algorithm for the *idle mode* follows:

1. If the current signals include expectation signals, then follow the algorithm of the *expecting mode*.

2. ElseIf the current signals include submission signals, then execute the "process submission input" method.

3. ElseIf the current signals include confirmation signals, then execute the "start candidacy" method.

4. Else, execute the "process all presence signals" method.

5. If the KU is a marker, then relay the current signals to the customers.

6. ElseIf a constraint is triggered (i.e., has received a signal for one or more triggers), then execute the "start satisfaction race" method.

7. Else, remain in idle mode.

All presence signals received by a KU start decaying upon reception. Each supplier port of a KU keeps a queue of presence signals individually associated with their time of reception. The "value" of a supplier port for constraint satisfaction purposes is the sum of all its decayed presence signals at a particular point in time. Presence signals that decay below a certain threshold are automatically purged from their queue. The "process all presence signals" method consists of computing the new value of all customer ports of a KU that receive new presence signals.

The "process submission input" method follows:

1. Set submission mode deadline.

2. Process all presence signals.

3. If a constraint is fully triggered (i.e., has a presence or submission signal for all its triggers), then

    a) if this is a buildable KU, then

        • request an attempt to execute the expansion procedure.

        • if the attempt is successful, then

            - send a confirmation signal to submitters, that is, to the KUs from which a submission signal was received.

            - set mode to toBeReinforced.

        • else (the attempt failed): Ignore submission signal and continue the idle mode algorithm.

    b) else (this is not a buildable feature)

        • if the triggered constraint is satisfied, then

            - send confirmation signal to submitters.

            - set mode to toBeReinforced.

        • else (the triggered constraint is not satisfied)

            - send submission signal to the missing features of the triggered constraint.

            - set mode to toBeConfirmed.

4. Else (no fully triggered constraint): Stay in idle mode and continue the idle mode algorithm.

The "start candidacy" method follows:

1. Set candidacy mode deadline.

2. Process all presence signals.

3. If there is no fully triggered constraint, then stay in idle mode.

4. Else (there is a fully triggered constraint), then

   a) if this is a buildable KU, then request attempt to execute the expansion procedure.

   b) else: Send a submission signal to customers.

5. Set mode to directImmediateCandidate.

The "start satisfaction race" method follows:

1. Set satisfaction race deadline.

2. Process all presence signals.

3. If the triggered constraint has exceptions, then

   a) if this is a buildable KU, then

      • request attempt to execute the expansion procedure.

      • set mode to toBeBuiltImmediate.

   b) else (this is not a buildable KU):

      • send submission signal to missing features and to customers.

      • set mode to endCandidate.

4. Else (the triggered constraint has no exceptions):

   a) if buildable, then:

      • request attempt to execute the expansion procedure.

      • set mode to toBeBuiltImmediate.

   b) else (not buildable):

- send submission signal to missing features and to customers.

- set mode to immediateCandidate.

The algorithm for the *directImmediateCandidate mode* has the KU waiting for a confirmation signal from a customer. Upon reception of such a signal, the KU becomes detected. All other signals are ignored.

The algorithm for the *directEndCandidate mode* is the same as the preceding one except for the fact that input signals are processed only at the end of the time allocated to the race of this mode.

The algorithm for the *immediateCandidate mode* follows:

1. Process only confirmation signals.

2. If a constraint has received a confirmation signal from each of the suppliers it sent a submission signal to, then it becomes detected.

3. Else remain in this mode.

The algorithm for the *endCandidate mode* is the same as the preceding one except for the fact that input signals are processed only at the end of the time allocated to the race of this mode. The algorithm for the *toBeReinforced mode* ignores all signals but reinforcements signals. Once the KU has received a reinforcement signal, it relays this signal to the KUs from which it received a confirmation signal and changes its mode to detected.

The algorithm for the *toBeConfirmed mode* follows:

1. Ignore all signals but confirmations signals.

2. For each confirmation signal;

   a) if this is the last confirmation needed, then

      - send confirmation signal to submitters.

      - set mode to toBeReinforced.

   b) else (this is not the last confirmation): Take it out of the list of KUs from which the KU still needs confirmations.

The algorithm for the *toBeBuiltImmediate mode* simply ignores all signals except for a forcedDetection signal from the memory manager. Similarly, for the *expecting mode*, a KU ignores all signals but presence signals for its triggers. The KU goes to detected mode as soon as it has received all the triggers for any of its constraints.

Because the algorithm followed by all KUs can be expressed using simple finite state machines, it is highly testable by itself, that is, without considering natural language understanding.

5.5 LESSONS FROM EXPERIMENTS

Given the details of the previous section, this section summarizes some of the lessons we have learned using the different prototypes of **IDIoT**.

5.5.1 Organizing KUs on the Retrievability Axis

Recall that the actual delay associated with an exchange of a signal is computed as the product of the a priori delay with the retrievability coefficient of the receiver. The coefficient is not an integer but a floating point number. Because the current prototype does not support the dynamic modification of a KU's coefficient by another KU, the user can set the retrievability of KUs by following a simple heuristic such as assigning a coefficient of 1 to "independent concepts" and only using this coefficient to define an ordering among "related concepts". For example, the words "pen" and "plane" are likely to be equally retrievable, but the interpretation of "pen" as a male swan may be far less familiar than other "meanings" of the word, granting it a significantly higher retrievability coefficient (e.g., a value of 2 to make it twice as long to retrieve as more "common" senses). Experiments suggest that the difference between the values of two coefficients must be several times (i.e., at least an order of magnitude) larger than the epsilon quantum (see chapter 4) in order to become significant with respect to processing. Also, depending on the time-span of candidacies, too high a retrievability coefficient may make a KU systematically unreachable, and thus irrelevant for the interpretative process.

From a grounded (non semantic) viewpoint, tracking the "relatedness" of two KUs is a difficult task. At a superficial level, it simply consists in checking whether or not their respective transitive closures (of reachable supplier and customer KUs) intersect. However, this is not sufficient; for example, KUs that access the same cluster may also be considered to be "related" (e.g., the KUs for recognizing the direct and indirect object of a bitransitive verb). A fundamental goal of the familiarity axis is to minimize, through ordering, the risks of conflicting concurrent detections of "related" KUs. This is particularly important for a problem such as word sense disambiguation (see chapter 9). Other strategies to avoid such conflicts include refining or reordering constraints, using inhibition signals to implement a winner-take-all strategy, and using exceptions, as discussed in Part III. The point is that ordering KUs along the familiarity axis constitutes a simple (if not simplistic) approach to reducing the risk of erroneous interactions resulting from a large number of simultaneous "related" detections. This ordering also affects the interpretative process by indirectly creating an order of reachability (e.g., for syntactic and semantic preferences) on which the construction of clusters is based.

5.5.2 Using Associations, Candidates, and Buildable Features

First, experiments suggest that associations are best limited to archetypal generalizations along the conceptual "is-a" hierarchy, as previously mentioned. For example, the fact that a cat is a mammal suggests that the KU **cat** have the KU **mammal** as an association. A presence signal should be used to capture the "strength" of a (i.e., less automatic) "weaker" generalization. Otherwise, because associations are sent forcedDetection signals (and exceptions, forced-Inhibition signals), an inherent danger in the abuse of associations (and exceptions) is the creation of a communication network where all timing aspects are in essence bypassed. In other words, an excessive dependence on priority signals at the detriment of the user-specified communication delays and retrievability coefficients decreases the time-constrained nature of the system.

Second, experiments suggest that the use of candidates is best limited to sets of mutually exclusive KUs (e.g., for word sense disambiguation, see chapter 9).

Third, buildable features should be used with caution because it is hard to determine exactly when they become detected. Consequently, working out the "timing" of collaborating features is significantly harder than for non buildable features.

5.5.3 Varying the Strength of a Presence Signal Output

In order to notify a customer of its presence, a KU typically sends it a presence signal varying in value from 0 to 1, corresponding to the "strength" of the sender's presence with respect to the receiver. For example, along the conceptual "is-a" hierarchy, it is possible that a child would "strongly" classify (e.g., send an output of 0.8 or more) a dolphin as a mammal and "weakly" classify (e.g., send an output of 0.3 or less) it as a fish. Experiments suggest that a user should avoid "in-between" presence signals (e.g., between 0.3 and 0.8) so that an accumulation of relatively weak signals does not lead too quickly to the satisfaction of a constraint. Choosing the strength of presence signals, the weights to use in constraints, and the delay to assign to exchanges constitutes the trickiest task for the user of **IDIoT**, a task I have found quite akin to the "tweaking" of weights in local connectionist networks. However, only the setting of communication delays has been found to have an immediate and significant effect on the processing of the current examples.

5.5.4 Race Deadlines

First, the candidacy deadline applies to constraint satisfaction. It defines the amount of time a KU has to satisfy its triggered constraint and become activated. Experiments suggest that a "short" candidacy length typically reduces the number of detections dramatically, and thus the extent of the final interpretation. Conversely, a long candidacy length has little effect, especially if decay is significant. More specifically, in this case, decay will effectively set the upper bound on the time allowed for a chain of clusters to become activated. Also, because both the recognition of innate features and the exchange of signals consume time, the length of a candidacy should be several orders of magnitude larger than the epsilon quantum in order to take into account the next word(s) of the input.

Second, the expectation delay defines the amount of time a KU has to receive one of its triggers and become activated. The setting of this parameter depends entirely on the role that the user is willing to grant to expectations. An excessively short delay (i.e., close to the epsilon quantum) will not allow any expectations. An average delay (e.g., a few orders of magnitude larger than the epsilon quantum) will allow consideration of further input and some immediate expectations (e.g., for "priming effects", see Part III). A longer delay will allow for more complex expectations (e.g., involving inferences). An extremely long delay may lead to the detection of somewhat "far fetched" conceptual links.

Third, the deadline of a submission race defines the amount of time a KU has to receive all appropriate confirmation signals from a set of suppliers and send a confirmation signal to the KU that initially sent it a submission signal. Experiments suggest setting this delay, which defines the time span of backward-chaining, to the same order of magnitude as the candidacy deadline, which defines the time span of forward chaining. Because of the larger number of exchanges of signals required by backward-chaining, I typically have set the length of a submission race to at least twice that of a candidacy race. Variations have basically the same effect as with the candidacy length. In both cases however, arbitrarily long delays seem psychologically implausible.

5.5.5 Other Timing Factors

First, all memory parameters pertaining to time are based on the epsilon quantum that, in essence, defines the unit of granularity of time for memory. Further investigation of psychological and neuronal evidence is required before the establishment of a non arbitrary value for this parameter. In other words, at this point in my research, this quantum is strictly metaphoric.

The character quantum defines the cost of inputting and recognizing a letter. In the current prototype, this quantum is oversimplified in that it is arbitrarily set to be an order of magnitude larger than the epsilon quantum, and also because it is uniform across letters, which does not seem to be psychologically plausible (see Gernsbacher, 1994).

Both psychological and biological evidence (Gernsbacher, 1994) suggests the importance of decay. In particular, it is an essential facet of the convergence problem. Experiments suggest leaving it at a rate of zero until all other parameters have been "tweaked" to the user's satisfaction. This will make for traces whose sequences of events are a lot simpler to follow. Once an acceptable interpretation is generated, the user may want to introduce decay in order to find out which conceptual links are more tenuous, that is, which links will be removed from the interpretation because of decay. Only truly exponential decay is psychologically plausible, but experiments demonstrate that, although "slow" decay is basically insignificant, "fast" decay has dramatic repercussions on the final interpretation. Indeed, "fast" decay seems to implicitly define a time span upper bound for all memory processes in that clusters become unreachable far more quickly, thus significantly constraining the interpretative process.

The capacity of WM is also crucial because it defines the number of "instantaneously" reachable clusters. A minimum value of 1 is required in order to handle retrievals correctly. Although implausible, a high limit (e.g., more than 50 percent of STM) will not greatly affect understanding because, in the current prototype, access to the clusters in STM is, by default, only one order of magnitude slower than access in WM. Further investigation of the role of WM, but also consideration of the "size" of clusters, is required before suggestion of a plausible value for this parameter.

Finally, because in the current prototype access to LTM is considerably "slower" than access to STM, the capacity limit of STM seems to define, much like decay, an upper time limit on all memory processes inasmuch as once in LTM, clusters become unreachable. Experiments suggest that a limit of less than 25 clusters does not allow for the interpretation of a short "simple" sentence. Conversely, a psychologically implausible, extremely large STM (e.g., a few hundred clusters) will possibly generate an "in-depth" interpretation (i.e., an interpretation in which even complex inferences have been used) but, unless "knowledge" is extremely well-organized, it will most likely lead to unexpected and undesirable interactions (i.e., catastrophic interference) between KUs that incorrectly remain reachable. For example, an erroneous inference may be drawn between the current word and one that was encountered several sentences back. Much as with the capacity of working memory, further investigation is required in order to understand the trade-off between solving the convergence problem and unduly limiting the interpretation (because of overly fast unreachability). In particular, we need to study the *shift processing hypothesis* of Gernsbacher (1985), which suggests that upon each new input, resources are shifted from processing/integrating previous inputs to attending to this new input. This hypothesis not only addresses the convergence problem but also has the virtue of being easily implemented in the memory manager and solving the space complexity issue: There is no space explosion simply because the next input essentially "kills" any on going construction processes.

5.5.6 Simulating Different Readers

During experiments with the current prototype, several configurations of parameters were systematically tried with the input texts. All assumed, for simplicity, an insignificant rate of decay and an STM of 50 clusters. Separate experiments were conducted to assess the repercussions of variations of decay rate and of STM capacity on understanding. These repercussions have been briefly discussed previously. Let me now summarize my observations regarding the "standard" configurations of parameters I used with the examples:

- **Reader 1** has an "average" KB (i.e., a KB that does not include KUs for some of the complex inferences required in some of the examples) and is given "average" time (in terms of the time spans of races). This configuration generated the interpretation against which those resulting from more extreme configurations of parameters were compared.

- **Reader 2** has the same KB as reader 1 but extremely short races. This reader generated interpretations that lacked all of the more "time-consuming" conceptual relationships such as causal inferences. In essence, this reader could barely do more than the simplest parsing.

- **Reader 3** has the same KB as reader 1 and long races. This reader generated interpretations that were similar to those of reader 1, mostly because there were no complex inferences in the KB to be detected, regardless of the time available. Furthermore, the longer races led to the discovery of some undesirable interactions between KUs that do not occur with reader 1.

- **Reader 4** has a "poor" KB (i.e., a KB with only the simplest parsing rules). Regardless of the values of the memory parameters, the
interpretations generated by this reader were extremely superficial
and incomplete with respect to those of reader 1.

- **Reader 5** has a "rich" KB (i.e., one that includes complex inferences) and is given "average" time. Because of lack of time, the
"richness" of the KB is not systematically exploited, and interpretations are typically similar or marginally more "complete" than those
produced by reader 1.

- **Reader 6** has a rich KB and extremely short races. This reader is
identical to reader 2.

- **Reader 7** has the same KB as reader 5 and long races. This reader
generates the most "complete" interpretations of all the readers, but
also required the most "rule tweaking" because of unwanted interactions. Also, recall that arbitrarily long races violate the initial
assumption that comprehension is a real-time process.

In conclusion, experimentation with the current prototype of **IDIoT** demonstrates that there are still too many unanswered questions to suggest what
"good" values for the different parameters of the model may be.

5.6 AN ANNOTATED EXAMPLE

To briefly recapitulate the different facets of the proposed model of time-constrained memory, let us consider the processing of the sentence "John drinks
gin". All my linguistic examples follow a simple grammar derived from that
of Winograd (1983). For the sake of simplicity, I will consider only two of the
meanings of "gin": the card game and the drink. Also, some of the KUs used
in this example have been presented in subsection 4.6.3, and the structure of
most the others can be inferred from the exchange of messages. Finally, I want
to highlight only the most important aspects of the processing, and thus I have
taken out several exchanges of messages not germane to the discussion at
hand.

Once the user of **IDIoT** has started the system and given an input text, he
or she can modify the defaults of the different parameters of time-constrained
memory. Here are the default settings for the examples of this book:

Table 5.1: Default settings

deadlines and quanta	time units	other factors	value
Candidacy	200	decay	0
Expectation	100	STM capacity	50
Submission	50	WM capacity	7
epsilon	0.01		
character	1		

I emphasize that these values are arbitrary and do not proceed from psychological evidence. They have been chosen to simplify the understanding of the examples as much as possible by having a large STM, long races, and no decay. Also, for the sake of simplicity, the presence signals used by the KUs of this example have systematically been given their maximum value of 1.

The system is designed to automatically activate the innate feature **startOfSentence** at the beginning of the text and after each period. Another innate feature, **endOfText**, is automatically activated at the end of the text. Both of these features must be defined in a knowledge base used for processing a text. And both require arbitrarily 3 time units to become activated. The processing of the text thus starts at time 0 with the recognition of **startOfSentence**, which sends a presence signal to its customers (which I have defined as grammatical rules). Then, at time 3, the word "John" is recognized. Here is its simple definition:

innate KU 'John':

```
associations: johnPerson
expansion:
     getNewCluster u1
     addFeature singular to u1
     addFeature proper to u1
     addFeature person to u1
     addFeature male to u1
     addFeature 'John' to u1
```

. . .

The features **singular**, **proper**, **person**, and **male**, are defined elsewhere in the KB. For example, **proper** is a relay with all known proper nouns as suppliers and all rules relevant to proper nouns as customers.

All features referred to in the expansion of "John" are sent a forced detection signal (as shown in the portion of the actual execution log that follows and that is obtained by switching on the debug mode of the current prototype of **IDIoT**):

> **innate KU 'John' read in at 3**
>
> **is recognized**
>
> **manager expands**
>
> **manager sends forcedDetectionSignal from manager to singular arriving at 3.01**
>
> **manager sends forcedDetectionSignal from manager to proper arriving at 3.01**
>
> **manager sends forcedDetectionSignal from manager to person arriving at 3.01**
>
> **manager sends forcedDetectionSignal from manager to male arriving at 3.01**

Throughout this log, "manager" refers to the memory manager, and the phrase "manager expands" means that the memory manager executes the expansion procedure of the corresponding KU.

The feature **person** will in turn lead to the detection, at 3.02, of its two associations, **rational** and **animate**. At 3.01, feature **proper** becomes detected and sends a presence signal to its customers, one of which is **NP**. Given an a priori delay of 1 between these two features (as with the vast majority of KUs in this example), at 4.01, **NP** receives this signal, which triggers and satisfies its constraint called **proper**. Among the many customers of **NP** that are sent a presence signal is the feature **s-Start**. This feature was triggered by **startOf-Sentence**. Once the presence signal from **NP** is received, **s-Start** becomes detected, capturing the fact that the sentence starts with an NP (as opposed, for example, to a verb that could indicate the imperative mood). Through the expansion of **s-Start**, the cluster associated with the NP has features **topNP** and **subject** added to it. (The feature **topNP** keeps track of the most referable NP of a sentence as suggested in chapter 8.) The feature **subject** captures the intuition that the first NP of a non imperative sentence will be assumed to be the subject unless subsequently proven otherwise. At this point in time (5.01), dynamic memory contains a cluster for the NP with **NPhead** governing the cluster associated with John.

Each letter of the word "John" takes a character quantum, in this case 10 time units, to read. Hence the next word is input 40 time units after "John", at time 43. The innate feature **"drinks"** sends a presence signal to the feature **actionDrink** whose definition follows:

KU actionDrink :

```
constraint 'drinks':
 triggers: 'drinks'
 inputs:
      verb has a weight of 1
expansion:
      getCluster u1 governing 'drink'
      addFeature actionDrink to u1
      addFeature verb to u1
ports:
      'drinks' has a delay of 1 and is a supplier
      drinkBeverage has a delay of 1 and is a customer
      verb has a delay of 1 and is a supplier
```

Feature **actionDrink** receives the presence signal from **"drinks"** at 44 and becomes a candidate. It sends a submission signal to its missing feature **verb**. Feature **verb** simply relays the submission signal to its customer **VP**. This is used for encapsulation, that is, in order to avoid having every known verb of the system have **VP** as a customer. This constitutes a typical role for relays, as previously mentioned.

VP relays the submission signal received from verb to its numerous customers including feature **subj-verb-rel** which captures the subject-verb relationship. The latter feature has already been triggered by the feature **subject** and, once it receives the submission signal from its input VP, has one of its constraints satisfied. At that point, **subj-verb-rel** does not become activated, but rather sends a confirmation signal back to **VP**. This confirmation signal is relayed from **VP** to **verb** to **actionDrink**. Since the triggered constraint of **actionDrink** does not have exceptions, **actionDrink** can become detected as soon as it receives a confirmation signal from all features to which it sent a submission signal, that is, from **verb**. At this point, **actionDrink** checks the deadline of its candidacy and forgets it since it has not been exceeded, becomes detected, and sends a reinforcement signal to **verb** and a presence signal to its customer, **drinkBeverage**. The features **verb**, **VP**, and **subj-verb-rel**, eventually become activated:

> **KU actionDrink in mode immediateCandidate works at 50**
> receives confirmationSignal on verb
> confirmers are verb
> manager sends reinforcementSignal from actionDrink to verb
>   arriving at 51
> becomes detected at: 50
> forgets end of race deadline
> manager expands
> manager sends presenceSignal from actionDrink to drinkBeverage
>   arriving at 51
> **KU drinkBeverage in mode idle works at 51**
> receives presenceSignal on actionDrink
> **KU verb in mode toBeReinforced works at 51**
> receives reinforcementSignal on actionDrink
> manager sends reinforcementSignal from verb to VP arriving at 52
> becomes detected at: 51
> **KU VP in mode toBeReinforced works at 52**
> receives reinforcementSignal on verb
> manager sends reinforcementSignal from VP to subj-verb-rel
>   arriving at 53
> becomes detected at: 52
> manager expands
> manager sends forcedDetectionSignal from manager to activeMood
>   arriving at 52.01
> manager sends forcedDetectionSignal from manager to mainVerb
>   arriving at 52.01
> manager sends forcedDetectionSignal from manager to VPmods
>   arriving at 52.01
>   ...
> **KU subj-verb-rel in mode toBeReinforced works at 53**
> receives forcedDetectionSignal on VP
> becomes detected at: 53
> manager expands
> manager sends forcedDetectionSignal from manager to clause
>   arriving at 53.01

**manager sends presenceSignal from subj-verb-rel to directObject
    arriving at 54**
**manager sends presenceSignal from subj-verb-rel to newFact
    arriving at 54**
manager sends presenceSignal from subj-verb-rel to sva-1 arriving at 54
manager sends presenceSignal from subj-verb-rel to sva-2 arriving at 54

As a result of the expansion of **subj-verb-rel**, dynamic memory contains a
cluster having the single feature **clause**. This feature governs a subcluster corresponding to the VP and another subcluster corresponding to the subject. The
two customers, **sva-1** and **sva-2**, of **subj-verb-rel** are buildable features used
to verify that the subject and the verb agree. They are discussed in chapter 7.
As for feature **direct-Object** it has its constraint triggered by the presence signal received from **subj-verb-rel**.

At time 103, the word "gin" is input and sends a presence signal to **gin**.
Feature **gin**, sends a submission signal to **noun**, which relays it to **NP**, which
sends a submission signal to **directObject**. A definition for **directObject** follows:

KU directObject:

```
% This feature takes the most reachable NP and makes it
% the directObject of the verb if the latter is not
% intransitive. It also makes this NP the top NP of the
% clause. The next line is automatically generated by the
% system to indicate the KU is buildable.
is buildable
 constraint c1:
  ordered triggers: subj-verb-rel NP
 expansion:
      getCluster u1 governing VP
      getCluster u2 governing topNP in u1
      removeFeature topNP in u2
      getCluster u2 governedBy mainVerb in u1
      testAbsenceOf intransitive in u2
      addFeature verbComplemented to u2
      getCluster u2 governing NP
      addFeature directObject to u1
      addSubCluster u2 to directObject in u1
      addFeature topNP to u2
```

```
ports:

    . . .
```

Feature **directObject**, is buildable and therefore, upon receiving the submission signal from **NP** and having one of its constraints satisfied, requests that the memory manager check whether **directObject**'s expansion procedure succeeds. This procedure succeeds if the verb admits of a direct object. In the example, the expansion of **directObject** succeeds and **directObject** sends a confirmation signal back to **NP**:

> **KU directObject in mode idle works at 107**
>   **receives submissionSignal on NP**
>   **in submission, a triggered constraint is c1**
>   **satisfaction of c1 against threshold 1**
>   **manager attempts dynamic construction for submission at 107**
>   **manager sends confirmationSignal from directObject to NP**
>   **arriving at 108.26**

The confirmation signal will ripple from **NP** to **noun** to **gin**, which becomes detected. Feature **gin** has two candidates, **cardGameGin** and **alcoholicBeverageGin** to which it sends a confirmation signal in order to have their candidacies start. Each candidate sends a submission signal to its customers. The submission path, **alcoholicBeverageGin, alcoholicBeverage, beverage, drinkBeverage**, will eventually be built and lead to the confirmation of **alcoholicBeverageGin**, whereas a path from **cardGameGin** will reach a dead end because of the absence of feature **actionPlayAGame**. Further explanations for this scenario are provided in Part III. At the same time that these candidacies occur, the features **noun** and then **NP**, will be reinforced and become activated. Feature **NP** will reinforce **direct-Object**, which also becomes detected. The following segment of the execution log captures this sequence of events:

> **KU gin in mode immediateCandidate works at 110.26**
>   **receives confirmationSignal on noun**
>   **confirmers are noun**
>   **manager sends reinforcementSignal from gin to noun**
>   **arriving at 111.26**
>   **becomes detected at: 110.26**
>   **forgets end of race deadline**
>   **manager expands**

manager sends confirmationSignal from gin to cardGameGin
  arriving at 111.26
manager sends confirmationSignal from gin
  to alcoholicBeverageGin
  arriving at 111.26

KU alcoholicBeverageGin in mode idle works at 111.26
  receives confirmationSignal on gin
  start direct candidacy race ending at 311.26 for constraint gin
  manager sends submissionSignal from alcoholicBeverageGin
    to alcoholicBeverage
    arriving at 112.26

KU cardGameGin in mode idle works at 111.26
  receives confirmationSignal on gin
  start direct candidacy race ending at 311.26 for constraint gin
  manager sends submissionSignal from cardGameGin
    to cardGame
    arriving at 112.26
  manager sends submissionSignal from cardGameGin
    to rulesOfGin
    arriving at 112.26

KU noun in mode toBeReinforced works at 111.26
  receives reinforcementSignal on gin
  manager sends reinforcementSignal from noun to NP
    arriving at 112.26
  becomes detected at: 111.26

KU alcoholicBeverage in mode idle works at 112.26
  receives submissionSignal on alcoholicBeverageGin
  in submission, a triggered constraint is alcoholicBeverageGin
  satisfaction of alcoholicBeverageGin against threshold 1
  manager sends submissionSignal from alcoholicBeverage
    to aboutAlcoholBeverage
    arriving at 113.26
  manager sends submissionSignal from alcoholicBeverage
    to beverage
    arriving at 113.26

KU NP in mode toBeReinforced works at 112.26
  receives reinforcementSignal on noun
  manager sends reinforcementSignal from NP to directObject
     arriving at 113.26
  becomes detected at: 112.26
  manager expands
  manager sends forcedDetectionSignal from manager to NPhead
     arriving at 112.27
  manager sends forcedDetectionSignal from manager to NPquant
     arriving at 112.27
  manager sends forcedDetectionSignal from manager to NPmods
     arriving at 112.27
  manager sends forcedDetectionSignal from manager to 3rdPerson
     arriving at 112.27
  manager tries dynamic construction of sva-1 at 112.26
  manager tries dynamic construction of sva-2 at 112.26
     ...

KU cardGame in mode idle works at 112.26
  receives submissionSignal on cardGameGin
  in submission, a triggered constraint is cardGameGin
  satisfaction of cardGameGin against threshold 1
  manager sends submissionSignal from cardGame to game
     arriving at 113.26
  manager sends submissionSignal from cardGame
     to aboutPlayingCards
     arriving at 113.26

KU rulesOfGin in mode idle works at 112.26
  receives submissionSignal on cardGameGin
  in submission, a triggered constraint is cardGameGin
  satisfaction of cardGameGin against threshold 1

KU game in mode idle works at 113.26
  receives submissionSignal on cardGame
  in submission, a triggered constraint is cardGame
  satisfaction of cardGame against threshold 1
  manager sends submissionSignal from game to actionPlayAGame
     arriving at 114.26

KU beverage in mode idle works at 113.26
 receives submissionSignal on alcoholicBeverage
 in submission, a triggered constraint is alcoholicBeverage
 satisfaction of alcoholicBeverage against threshold 1
 manager sends submissionSignal from beverage to drinkBeverage
  arriving at 114.26
 manager sends submissionSignal from beverage to liquid
  arriving at 114.26

KU aboutAlcoholBeverages in mode idle works at 113.26
 receives submissionSignal on alcoholicBeverage
 in submission, a triggered constraint is c1
 satisfaction of c1 against threshold 1

KU aboutPlayingCards in mode idle works at 113.26
 receives submissionSignal on cardGame
 in submission, a triggered constraint is c1
 satisfaction of c1 against threshold 1

KU directObject in mode toBeReinforced works at 113.26
 receives reinforcementSignal on NP
 becomes detected at: 113.26
 manager expands
 manager sends forcedDetectionSignal from manager
  to verbComplemented arriving at 113.27
 manager sends forcedDetectionSignal from manager
  to topNP arriving at 113.27
 manager sends presenceSignal from directObject to coi
  arriving at 114.26
 manager sends presenceSignal from directObject to newFact
  arriving at 114.26

KU drinkBeverage in mode idle works at 114.26
 receives submissionSignal on beverage
 in submission, a triggered constraint is c1
 satisfaction of c1 against threshold 1
 manager attempts dynamic construction for submission at 114.26
 manager sends confirmationSignal from drinkBeverage
  to beverage arriving at 115.52

KU actionPlayAGame in mode idle works at 114.26
receives submissionSignal on game

Eventually, the path of features that led to the detection of **alcoholicBeverage-Gin** will also become detected, and the period of the sentence combined with the innate feature **endOfText** will complete the processing. The resulting structure in dynamic memory, as observable from the trace browser, is shown in the following:

```
KU newFact that governs:
    cluster 12565 in working memory with features:

    KU VP
    KU mainVerb that governs:
      cluster 14282 in working memory with features:
      KU 'drink'
      KU 3rdPersonSingForm
      KU actionDrink
      KU verb
      KU activeMood
      KU verbComplemented
    KU VPmods

    KU subject that governs:
      cluster 10317 in working memory with features:
      KU NP
      KU NPhead that governs:
        cluster 257 in working memory with features:
        KU singular
        KU 'John'
        KU proper
        KU person
        KU male
        KU rational
        KU animate
        KU 3rdPerson
      KU NPquant
      KU NPmods
```

```
KU directObject that governs:
   cluster 10186 in working memory with features:
   KU NP
   KU NPhead that governs:
      cluster 7652 in working memory with features:
      KU 'gin'
      KU singular
      KU gin
      KU noun
      KU 3rdPerson
      KU alcoholicBeverageGin
      KU tasteOfGin
      KU alcoholicBeverage
      KU aboutAlcoholBeverages
      KU beverage
      KU liquid
      KU aboutLiquids
   KU NPquant
KU NPmods
```

5.7 GENERATING KNOWLEDGE UNITS

The basic user interface of **IDIoT,** which consists of the browsers presented earlier in this chapter, offers a monostratal view of knowledge units. In other words, all knowledge units are treated uniformly. Often however, users will want to think of the KUs used for linguistic comprehension as belonging to certain intuitive categories (e.g., grammar rules, polysemous words, etc.) that do not and should not be part of a grounded architecture. Also, experimentation demonstrates that users would prefer more "conventional" interfaces for the specification of knowledge, interfaces that would be responsible for inputting the rules of these users and generating corresponding KUs for these rules. It is in this spirit that some of my students (namely, Shu Hung Chan, Susanna Chan, Conlinh Chau, and Meng Hang Kan), recently developed the two simple tools that are briefly presented in the rest of this section. The details of these tools are of little import in the context of this book, and I will not justify their epistemological and design choices. These tools should rather be viewed as initial case studies for the promising idea of having interfaces that allow intuitive definitions of rules to be "translated" into knowledge units.

5.7.1 The Grammar Tool

This tool preempts the topic of grammar specification, which is addressed in chapter 7.

The idea of the tool is to let the user define a "template" cluster for the parsing of a clause and then to express syntactic rules with respect to the features of this template. The feature definition window is used to build the template cluster (see figures 5.9 and 5.10):

1. The user defines the feature governing the cluster for a clause or sentence (using the "add starting feature" button). In Figure 5.9, the sentence cluster thus far governs only a **subject** subcluster. This cluster consists of an NP, whose features are exhaustively defined. A "+" marks optionality (e.g., a quantifier is optional), a "*", multiplicity (e.g., we can have several adjectives). Also, the word "or" identifies an exhaustive list of alternatives (e.g., **singular** or **plural**). Figure 5.10 shows a partial definition for the VP. The user can then add definitions for the direct object, indirect object, and so forth. The tool assumes that each feature's name is unique. Therefore, if the **directObject** subcluster governs the feature **NP**, the tool will automatically supply the definition for **NP** given under the **subject** subcluster.

2. The user adds (and can remove) subfeatures in the cluster.

3. The user selects the "input patterns" button to input rules. As will be explained in chapter 7, rules are either static (in the form of syntactic patterns) or dynamic (in the case of contextual rules that verify the construction of a cluster built in STM).

The pattern definition window (Figure 5.11) allows the user to define either kind of rule, with some automatic verification. More specifically, using the add pattern button, the user can write static syntactic rules. Then, using the parse button, the user will automatically obtain how the rule maps onto the template defined for the sentence. For example, the rule "NP VP PP" allows for the multiple parses partially displayed in Figure 5.12. Put simply, the PP can be, in theory, attached to the NP or the VP. In practice, however, in English, only VP attachment is possible. It is the responsibility of the user to select the parses that are allowed in the target language, using the validation window shown in Figure 5.13. Most importantly, several parses can be selected in order to specify multiple interpretations. For example, the pattern "NP VP NP PP" can correspond to VP attachment or direct object attachment as will be explained in chapter 10. The tool merely generates in a brute force way all possible mappings of the pattern onto the template (for a sentence or a clause) and lets the user decide which ones to keep.

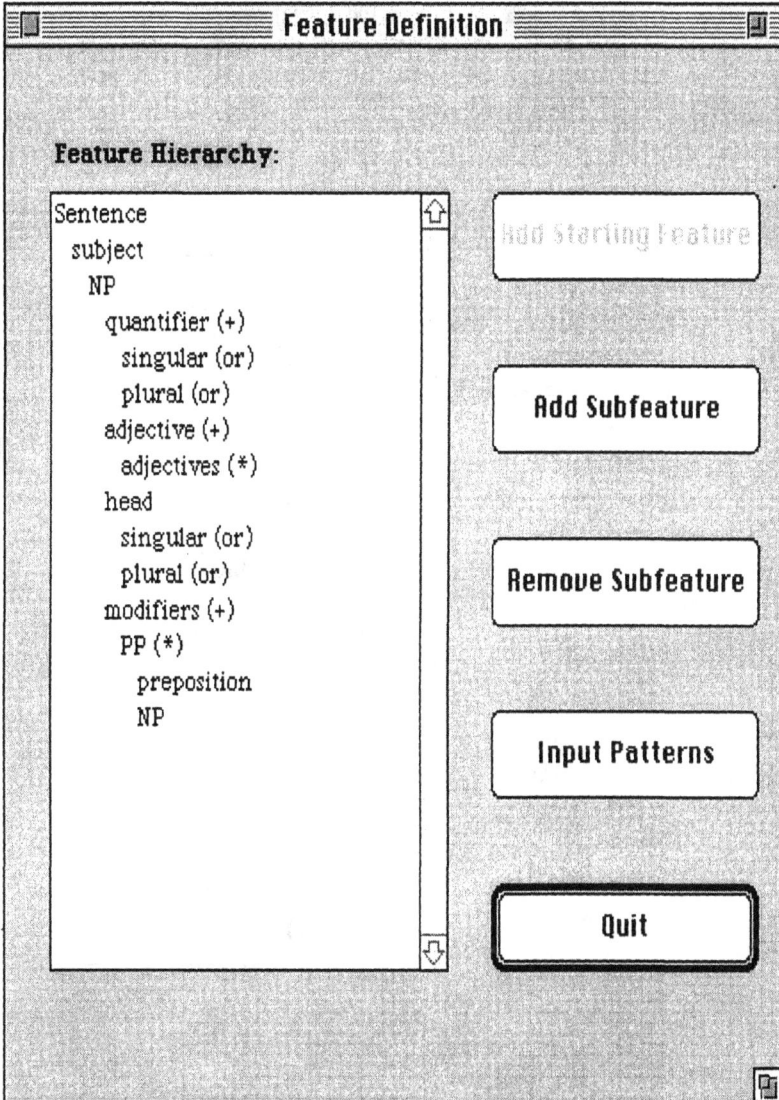

Figure 5.9 The feature definition window showing the definition of an NP.

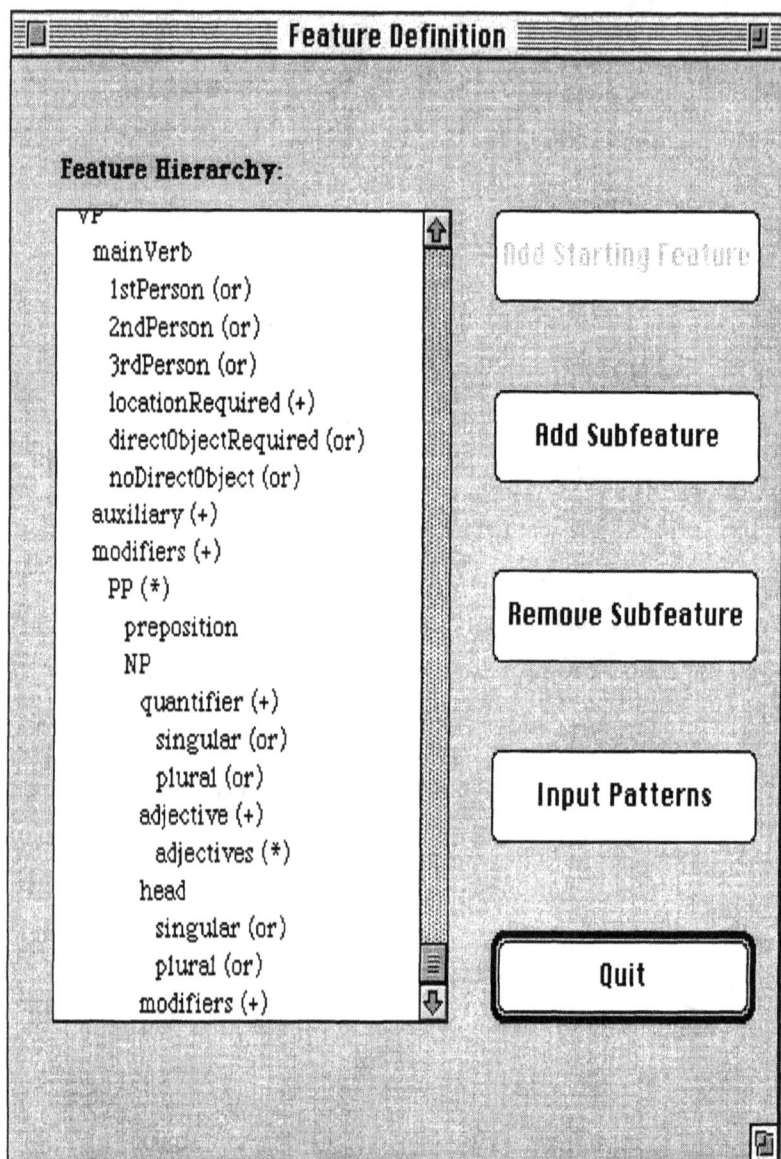

Figure 5.10 The feature definition window for a VP.

Pattern Definition

Patterns added:

Sentence->NP VP
Sentence->NP VP NP
Sentence->NP VP PP
Sentence->NP VP NP PP

Add Pattern

Remove Pattern

Feature Hierarchy:

Sentence
  subject
    NP
      quantifier (+)
        singular (or)
        plural (or)
      adjective (+)
        adjectives (*)
      head
        singular (or)
        plural (or)
      modifiers (+)
        PP (*)
          preposition
          NP

Parse Pattern

Dynamic Rules

Quit

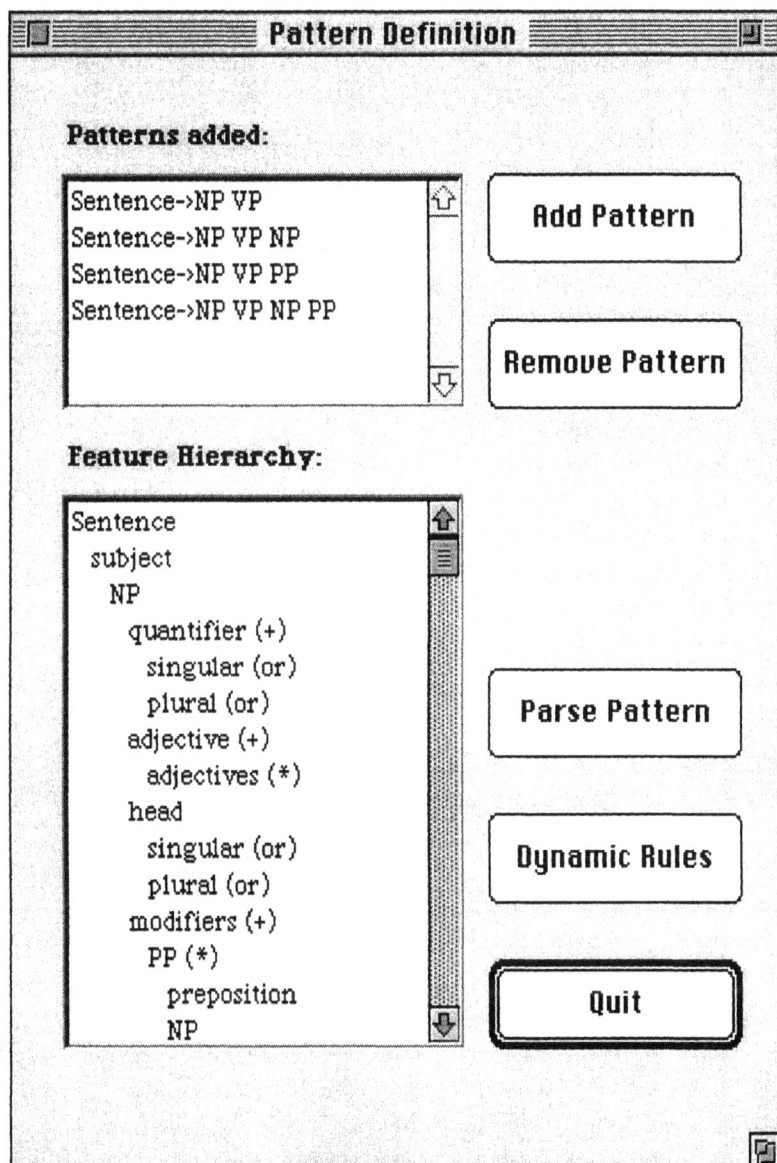

Figure 5.11 The pattern definition window.

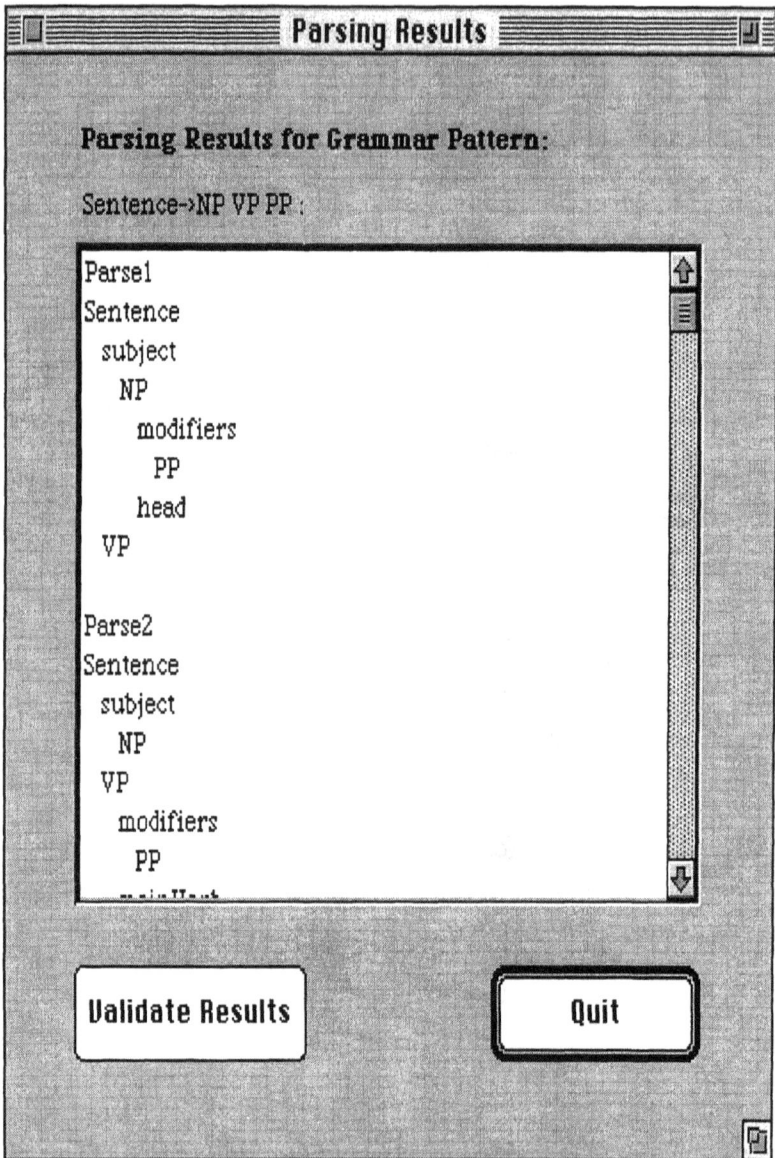

Figure 5.12 Possible parses for a pattern.

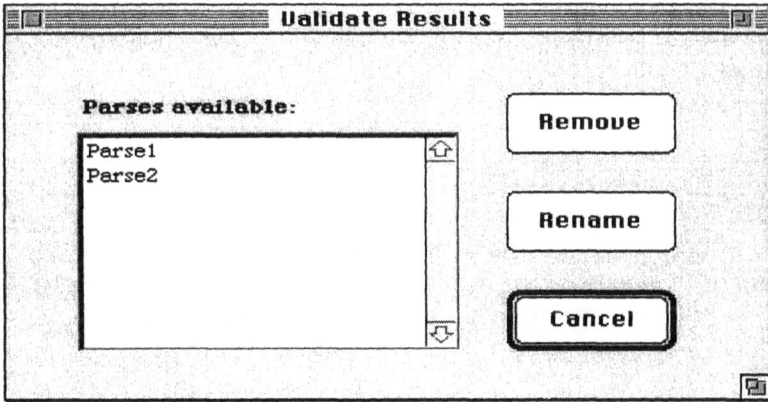

Figure 5.13 Selecting between possible parses.

Dynamic rules (e.g., used for syntactic conflicts, see chapter 7) are merely buildable features that check for the presence or absence of a certain combination of features in STM. They are added from their own definition window (Figure 5.14).

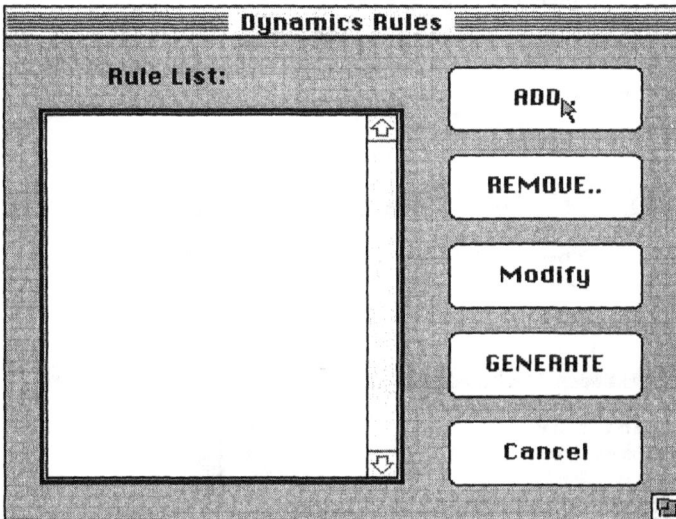

Figure 5.14 The definition window for dynamic rules.

As an example, a number agreement rule could check that if the quantifier of an NP marks the singular, then we have a conflict if the head of the NP is, in fact, plural. Without presenting all the windows used for the definition of such rules (see details in Corriveau, 1994d), let me simply say that the idea of the tool is to display the structure defined for a clause and allow the user to select features in this structure or its subclusters, and, for each of these, a test cluster operation (i.e., presence, absence, etc.). The following figures illustrate this process.

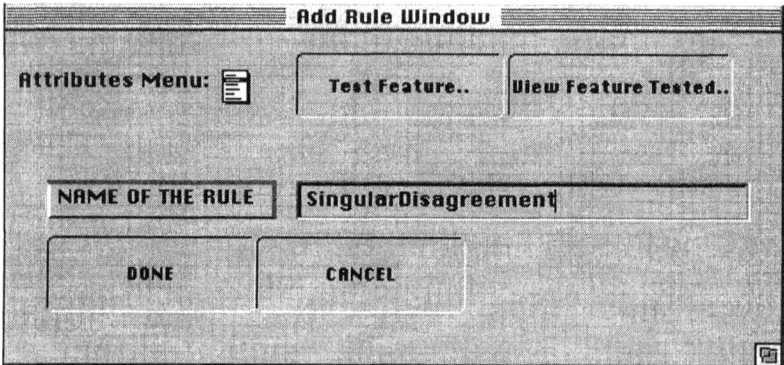

Figure 5.15 Adding a rule for singular disagreement.

To specify a dynamic rule, the user must first name this rule (see Figure 5.15) and determine what is the governing feature of the cluster in which the testing occurs (see Figure 5.16).

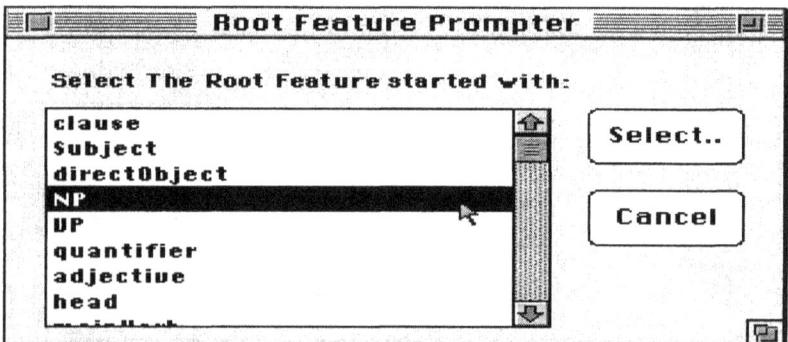

Figure 5.16 Selecting the root feature for the dynamic rule.

For number disagreement, each NP needs to be checked. Pressing the "select" button (in Figure 5.16), the user opens a "test procedure" window (see Figure 5.17) on the list of features governed by **NP**, (e.g., head, modifiers, quantifier, adjectives, etc.). In our example, we want to test features in both the head and the quantifier subcluster. For the latter, we test the presence of the feature **singular**.

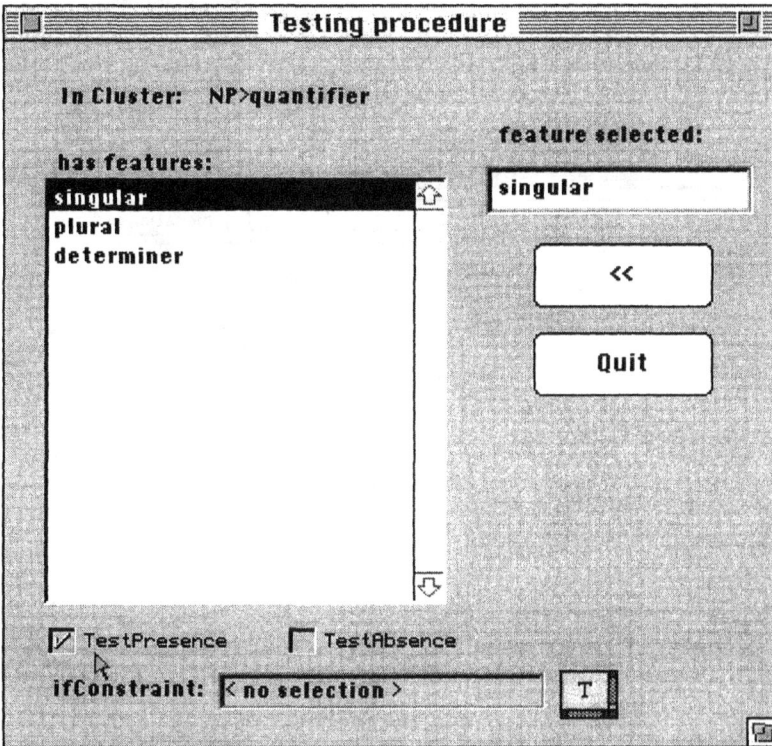

Figure 5.17 The test procedure window.

The "ifConstraint" field allows the user to specify a constraint in order to make a conditional test. This considerably improves the flexibility available for the specification of such dynamic rules. The << button allows the user to return to the list of features for the **NP** cluster. To complete our example rule, we would test for the presence of the feature **plural**, under the head of the NP. Once this is done, we could use the "view features tested" of the addition window (Figure 5.15) to view all the features and the test relevant to the rule at hand.

Finally, I emphasize that the usefulness of this tool comes from the fact that is automatically generates the knowledge units corresponding to the rules specified by the user.

5.7.2 The Lexical Disambiguation Tool

This tool preempts the topic of lexical disambiguation, which is addressed in chapter 9. Also, this tool addresses both word recognition and word sense disambiguation. However, I will offer here only a very brief overview of what the tool does (again, see Corriveau, 1994c for details). The opening window (Figure 5.18) summarizes the functionality of the tool:

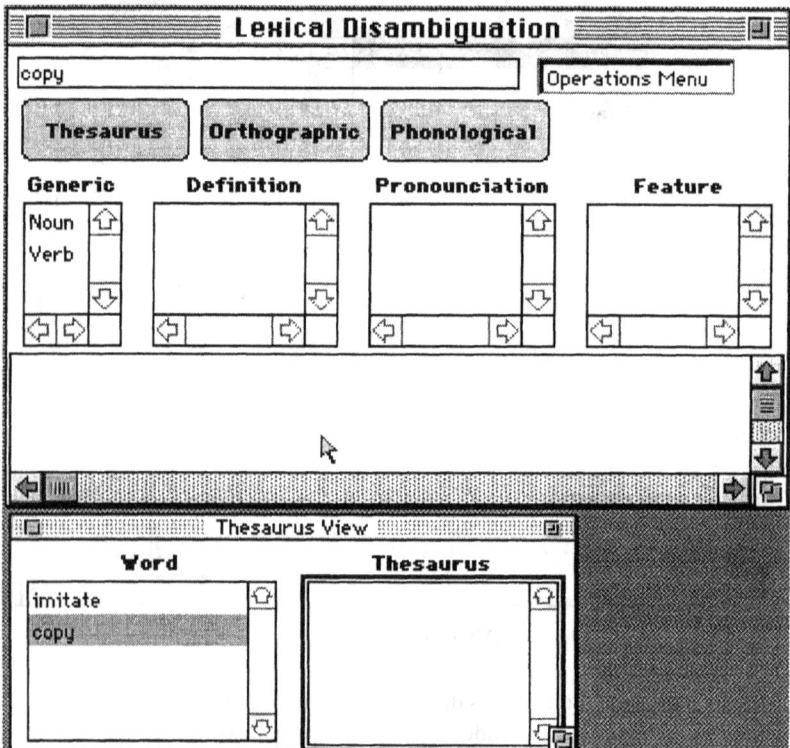

Figure 5.18 The lexical disambiguation window.

For word sense disambiguation, the tool allows the user to define the different "shades of meaning" of a word. In Figure 5.18, the word "copy" has been defined as a noun and a verb. (The term "generic" is used instead of the longer "parts-of-speech"). For each possible part-of-speech, several definitions can be specified. A thesaurus is used to automatically keep track of which words share common definitions or are expressed one in terms of the other.

For example, consider the definition of the verb "imitate" (see Figure 5.19):

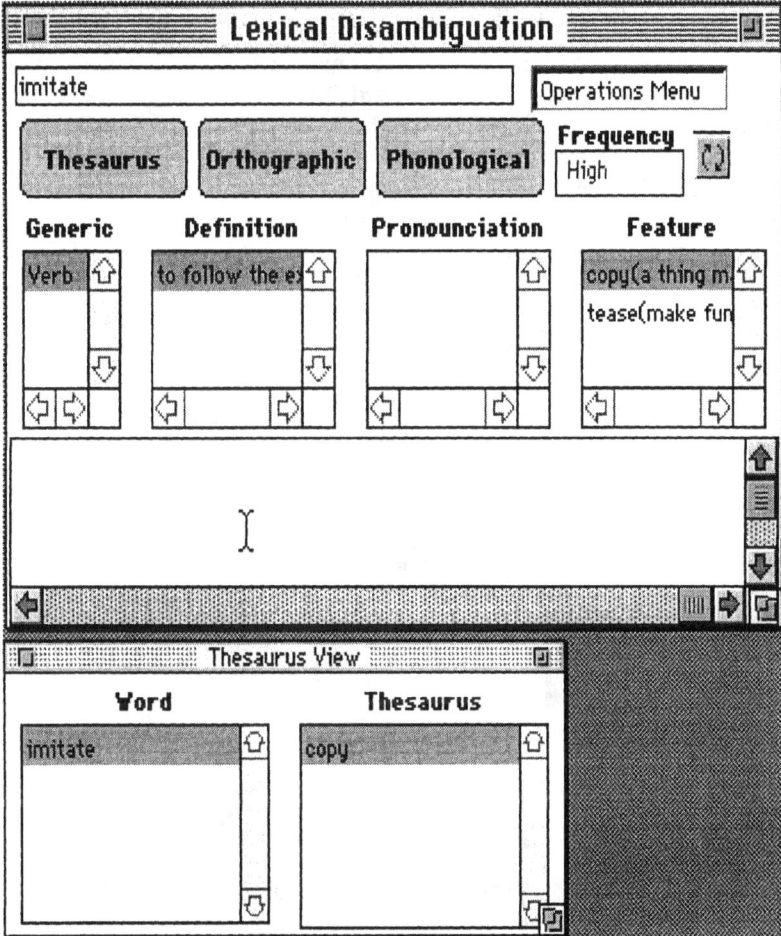

Figure 5.19 Defining the word "imitate".

Here "imitate" has been defined as the action of making a copy of something or as the action of making fun by copying. A frequency level (low, medium, or high) must be assigned to each definition in order to possibly specify preferences between them. Given these definitions, the thesaurus automatically shows that "copy" is a word related to "imitate". Finally, through several menus, the user can add, modify, and delete not only the definitions of words, but also the links created by the thesaurus. Once satisfied with these definitions, the user can request the automatic production of corresponding knowledge units.

For word recognition, the user must give both an orthographical and a phonological specification for each word. The orthographical representation merely consists of the string of letters that make up the word. In other words, by defining a new word, the user also de facto supplies its orthographical representation. By selecting the "orthographical" button in the lexical disambiguation window, the user can query the system with respect to the orthographical neighborhoods of a word. For example, the words "dig", "dog", and "dug" are at a distance of 1. That is, they differ by one letter. The system can determine orthographical neighborhoods (i.e., sets of words that differ by the number of letters specified as the distance) automatically (see Figure 5.20):

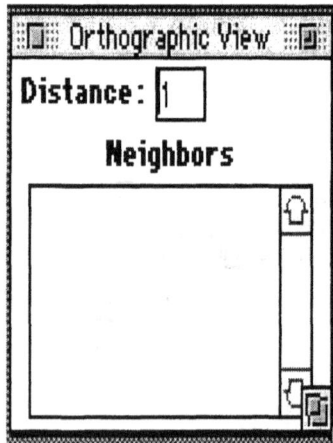

Figure 5.20 Query orthographical neighborhoods.

For the phonological definition, a set of phonological symbols (those found at the beginning of any dictionary) is supplied and can be modified by the user. The phonological specification of a word consists of a sequence of these characters, combined with the encoding of stress. This definition is entered into the system using the phonology palette (see Figure 5.21):

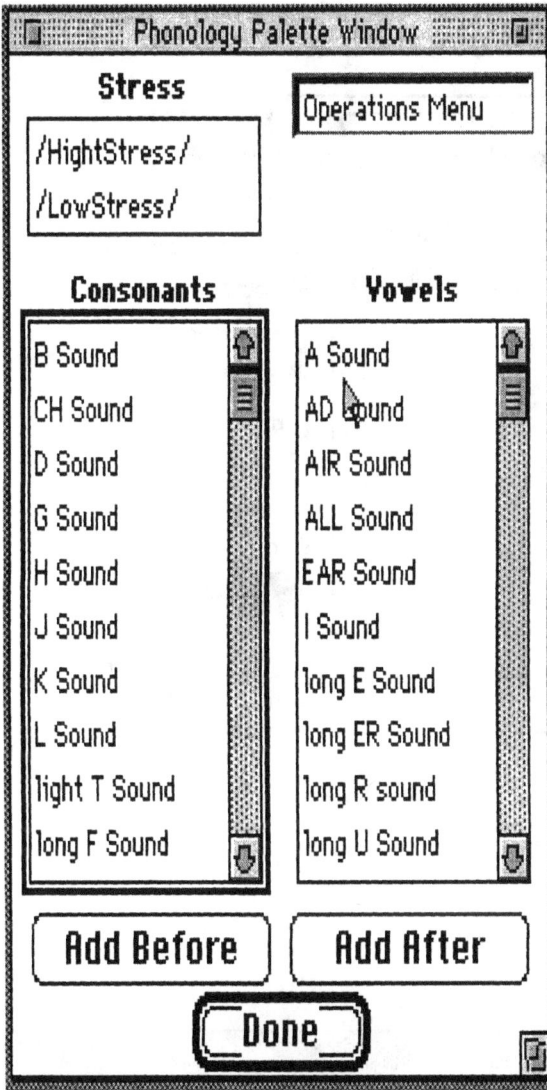

Figure 5.21 The phonology palette.

For example, the phonological definition of the word "contest" is given in Figure 5.22:

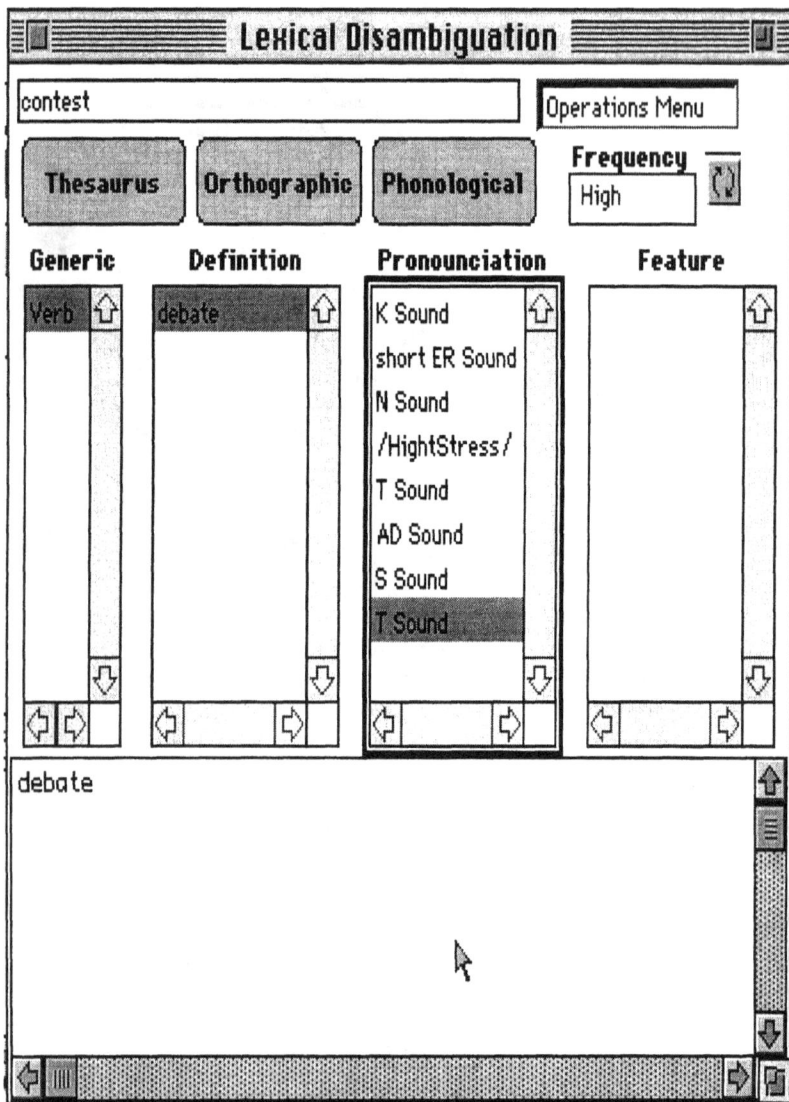

Figure 5.22 The phonological definition of "contest".

If we define phonetically the words "dog", "dig", "dug", and 'dock" as follows:

1. dog: <"D Sound" "OD Sound" "G Sound">,

2. dig: <"D Sound" "short E Sound" "G Sound">,

3. dug: <"D Sound" "short UN Sound" "G Sound">,

4. dock: <"D Sound" "OD Sound" "K Sound">,

then we get the following neighborhoods for the words "dug" (see Figure 5.23):

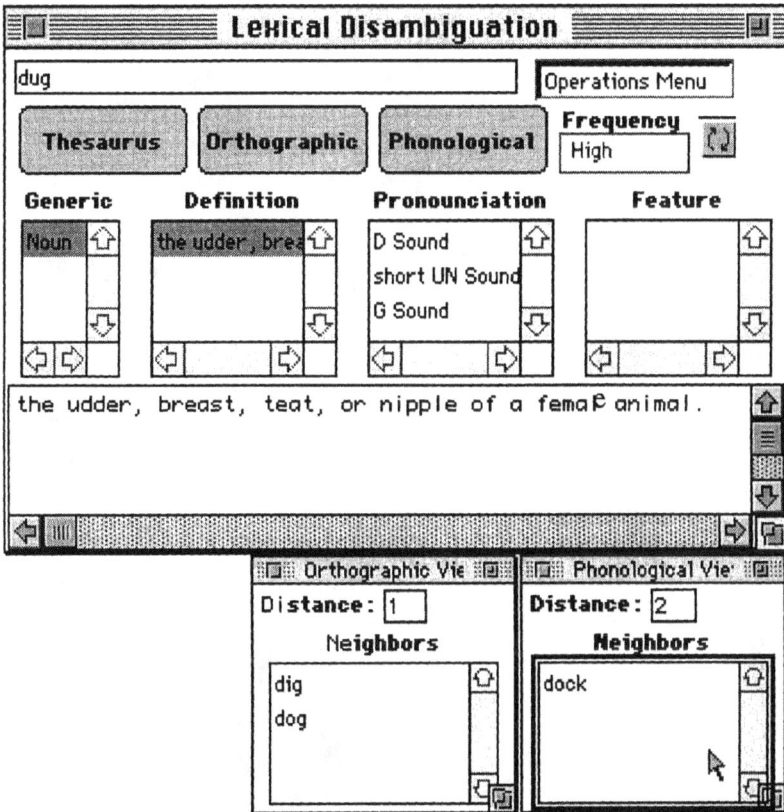

Figure 5.23 Neighbors of "dug".

At a distance of 3, "dock" is found as the orthographical neighbor of "dug".

Once again, the user can request the automatic production of corresponding knowledge units.

Part III
Linguistic Comprehension with IDIoT

Chapter 6

On Linguistic Comprehension

6.1 INTRODUCTION

In the third part of this book, I suggest that the grounded architecture developed in the previous chapters can be used to specify the rules of a text comprehender. More specifically, for some of the key facets of text interpretation, I want to

> a) briefly overview existing computational and psycholinguistic work on this facet.

> b) discuss the expression of typical rules of interpretation with the representational scheme of **IDIoT**.

> c) demonstrate the processing of typical examples with **IDIoT**.

It is important to understand that it is *not* my intention to present here a model of comprehension per se, because this task would require making a multitude of epistemological commitments that would obscure the fundamental point of this book, that is, the need for a grounded architecture for linguistic comprehension. Rather, the task at hand consists of first identifying the "key" facets of text understanding, and then discussing how typical rules associated with each facet can be realized using **IDIoT**. Once more, recall that all examples are strictly illustrative and that the "correctness" of these rules is essentially irrelevant for my purpose: The user of **IDIoT** remains the sole judge of the adequacy of the information placed in the knowledge base.

In order to identify the "key" facets of text comprehension, I focus more extensively, in this chapter, on three archetypal models. However, before doing so, I want to briefly comment, in the next section, on psycholinguistic research pertaining to text understanding.

6.2 PSYCHOLINGUISTICS MODELS OF READING

The interpretation of written text involves not only the problems of "natural language processing" (NLP), but also those of reading per se (e.g., Balota, Flores d'Arcais, & Rayner, 1990; Gernsbacher, 1994; Mitchell, 1982; Underwood, & Batt, 1995). In both domains, research has addressed not only general issues, but also more specialized topics (e.g., for NLP, see Wilks, 1989; Pereira, & Grosz, 1994; and for reading, see Britton, & Black, 1985; Britton, & Glynn, 1987). In this section, I restrict the discussion to the more general models of reading and text comprehension proposed by psycholinguists. From chapter 2, recall that these models generally lack an underlying grounded cognitive architecture. For example, Goldman and Varnhagen (1986) relied on story categories, goal hierarchies, causal structures, and so forth. that were shown (in chapter 2) to constitute a priori macrostructures.

The **READER** model put forth by Just and Carpenter (1987) epitomizes the psycholinguistic approach to text understanding:

1. It uses schemas and reduces meaning to propositions (using explicit "production" rules.)

2. It assumes the immediacy of an interpretation (as opposed to the delayed hypothesis; see Haberlandt, & Graesser, 1990).

3. It postulates parallel processing with sharing of constructed structures in working memory.

4. It is based on eye-fixation experiments.

5. It acknowledges but minimizes the idiosyncrasies found in reading.

Most psycholinguistic models for text comprehension fit this "mold", typically insisting on one or the other of these facets. For example, Kintsch (1991, 1994) proposed a strictly bottom-up construction of an interpretation and emphasizes the propositional aspect of meaning, an approach carried to its extreme in the work of Le Ny (1991), who considered decay and forgetting to be irrelevant to comprehension. Some however, such as Chafe's (1990) "functional linguistic" approach to meaning, differ significantly in my opinion and shall be studied in detail when I present, in a separate book, the implementation in **IDIoT** of the model of Rastier (1991).

For now it is important to understand that the hypotheses of **READER** define the scope of the problems generally addressed by psycholinguistic models for text comprehension, but are not widely accepted per se.

First, as becomes apparent in later chapters of this book, methodological quarrels abound (see Graesser, & Clark, 1985, on question-answering protocols; Dark, 1988, on viewing priming as facilitation; Wilson, Rink, McNamara, Bower, & Morrow, 1993, on the interference of consciousness on the study of word recognition; and Haberlandt, 1994, for a survey of methodological issues in general). In particular, with respect to **READER**, Masson (1986) questioned the relevance of eye-fixation experiments for understanding the processes of linguistic comprehension.

Similarly, although it is widely accepted that structures are built in memory during interpretation (e.g., Ballstaedt, & Mandl, 1991), some researchers question the so-called "integration hypothesis" adopted by the majority to solve the problem of convergence. For example, Gernsbacher (1985) identified three strategies for the convergence problem:

1. *The linguistic hypothesis*: Surface information loss is the result of performing grammatical transformations.

2. *The memory limitation hypothesis*: Surface information loss is the result of exceeding short-term memory limitations.

3. *The integration hypothesis*: Surface information loss is the result of integrating information into gist.

After arguing that these strategies (which underlie most of the existing models) are incomplete, Gernsbacher proposed a fourth alternative, which I have mentioned in the previous chapter, the "shift-processing" hypothesis:

1. Decay is not sufficient to explain convergence: It is known that immediately upon overhearing a homograph, all its meanings are activated. However, only the contextually relevant meaning remains activated 200ms later. The responsible process resembles suppression (i.e., inhibition of the other candidates) as opposed to simple activation decay.

2. Apart from the passage of time and the need to attend to subsequent material, the constituent structure of the material greatly affects memory for its surface form. For example,

a) information about original surface form becomes markedly less available just after comprehension has crossed the boundary of one constituent into another.

b) in a two-clause sentence, comprehenders have greatest access to the most recent clause. However, at some point in time, the first clause becomes more accessible because the structures representing it serve as a foundation for the whole sentence-level representation. In other words, the representation of the sentence requires that the structures of the first clause be retrieved before it can be completed. (see Gernsbacher, Hargreaves, & Beeman, 1989, for details.)

3. It is not only the quantity of information contained in STM or the duration it might have been held there that predicts the probability of loss of this information. In fact, it is hypothesized that the less congruent the incoming information is, the less likely it is to interact with the current contents of STM, and the less readily it can be added onto the structure currently being developed in STM. Instead, the construction process shifts from actively building the current structure(s) to initiating the elaboration of a new one.

The point to be grasped from this summary of competing hypotheses for convergence is two fold:

1. It is generally the case that psycholinguistic models entrench epistemological commitments as well as linguistic (e.g., Trabasso's (1991) a priori distinction between facts, episodes, etc.) and pragmatic (e.g., the reader goals and task demands of Wilson et al., 1993; the role of expectations in the work of Taraban, & McClelland, 1988) considerations.

2. There is no consensus at this point in time on these commitments and considerations. We are still relying on experts looking for norms, as explained in chapter 2.

Graesser (1993) demonstrated this second point when he remarked, for the problem of inferencing (which we will revisit in chapter 11):

> Inference generation has been one of the controversial topics in the field during the last 10 years. Researchers have disagreed on what inferences are generated during the process of comprehension, as well as when they are generated. According to some theories, very few inferences are generated 'on-line' (i.e., during comprehension), whereas many inferences can be reconstructed 'off-line' (i.e., during a subsequent retrieval task). At the other end of the continuum, some theories assert that many inferences are generated on-line. There are many positions in between these two extremes[.] Researchers have also substantially disagreed on methodological and metatheoretical issues. For example, there are heated debates over what experimental

methods provide convincing tests of whether a class of inferences is generated on-line. Some researchers are even skeptical about whether it is possible or productive to study scientifically the problem of inference generation.

Finally, one remarks, as I have done in chapter 2, that few of these models address the problem of global coherence. It is widely recognized that global coherence involves several sources of knowledge (e.g., Reyna, & Kiernan, 1994), much like everything else in linguistic comprehension, but the discussion generally stops there, and this observation merely serves as an excuse to introduce a plethora of prespecified rules, data structures and algorithms, if not preprocessors as in McRoy (1992). We are still a long way from a grounded psycholinguistic model of comprehension.

6.3 DYER'S THEMATIC ABSTRACTION UNITS

Dyer's (1983) **BORIS** system uses a demon-based control structure to match many different classes of knowledge structures in a text, corresponding to different types of inferences. Each input must search memory in order to explain itself, rather than wait for some top-down process to interpret it. **BORIS** first builds a conceptual dependency (CD) representation (Dyer, 1983, pp. 379–382) of the current proposition in the working memory by accessing the lexicon. The selected lexical entries or the current configuration of the CD representations may trigger the recognition of a higher level of representation for the current input. For example, the word "restaurant" will trigger the "restaurant" scenario, the "restaurant" MOP (memory organization packet), and a service triangle knowledge structure. In total, **BORIS** has seventeen knowledge structures and twenty-eight legal interactions between them. Each link between two knowledge structures corresponds to a group of demon processes: Whenever a knowledge structure is recognized (i.e., matched), demons are spawned for each of its links. If a demon fires (i.e., has its preconditions satisfied), then the old representation is reinterpreted in terms of the new one. This strategy allows **BORIS** to infer multiple connections between concepts in the story. In other words, there are no principles that constrain the inferencing process. However, Dyer's set of heterogeneous knowledge structures and associated links have been criticized as being ad hoc, incomplete, and incorrect (Norvig, 1987, p. 38). In contrast, Wilensky (1983b) proposed the following "story understanding principles": coherence, concretion, least commitment, exhaustion, parsimony, and poignancy. Norvig (1987, p. 40) however remarked that "the difficulty with applying these principles to any particular text is that they contradict each other, and it is never clear how to resolve the contradictions."

For Dyer, "understanding" is organized around situations in which "failures" occur due to error(s) in planning. Those situations are represented in thematic abstraction units (TAUs), each of which represents a possible failure and its outcome. TAUs organize cross-contextual *episodes* that involve similar failures in planning: Provided the correct TAU is selected, **BORIS** is "reminded" of old expectations from previous similar narratives. More precisely, a TAU consists of the plan used, its intended effect, the reasons for failure, and knowledge of how to avoid or recover from this type of failure. Goal and expectation failures and planning choices may trigger the matching of TAUs. To decide whether or not a planning failure has occurred, Dyer proposed eleven planning metrics (e.g., **RISK, VULNERABILITY, LEGITIMACY**, etc.). When a character in a story selects a plan, each of these metrics is checked against an a priori norm, and the resulting analysis determines the presence or absence of a planning error. For example, if John owes money and can either take out a loan or play Russian roulette to pay it back, a planning error will be detected, under the **RISK** metric, if he elects to go for the second alternative. The determination of these metrics is context-sensitive in that it highly relies on how much of the story has been processed up to that point in time. This approach is taken to be more powerful than strict metaplanning (see Wilensky, 1983b): The inherent trade-offs are defined within the narrative rather than as general principles; a bad solution can sometimes be the only alternative.

"Stories" are assumed to deal with characters and their reactions to events. Dyer claims that affective reactions of the characters reveal the underlying goal situations at an abstract level. Therefore, since **BORIS** must track these goal situations, it must somehow represent "emotions". For this task, Dyer suggested an **AFFECT** structure (1983, chapter 4), which allows the (positive or negative) emotional affective state of a character to be represented. More precisely, as with the detection of a planning error, a priori rules define how an affective state can be computed by comparing *metrics* to *norms*: Complex psychological phenomena and their bodily facets are reduced to a simple a priori computation by ad hoc metrics.

6.4 NORVIG'S UNIFIED THEORY OF INFERENCE FOR TEXT UNDERSTANDING

Norvig (1987, 1989) rejected models, such as Dyer's, that concentrate on particular types of knowledge structures (such as TAUs) and construct an algorithm fitted to process those particular types of structures. Instead, Norvig advocated a unified approach to inference, one similar to mine, in which the complexity is shifted from the algorithm to the knowledge base. This approach is formalized in a program named **FAUSTUS**, which is capable of drawing the *proper* inferences, that is, the ones intended by the author of the text, and avoiding improper ones. A proper inference is taken to be an assertion that is implicit, plausible, relevant, and "easy" (i.e., obtained without conscious effort). It is also stated that a "suitable" KB is a prerequisite to making proper inferences. Consequently, a distinction is claimed between proper and idiosyncratic inferences. Such a dichotomy is quite irreconcilable with reader-based hermeneutics, because the notions of plausibility, relevance, and ease are relative to the reader, as Norvig himself admitted (1987, p. 3).

When **FAUSTUS** is given a text, input sentences are first converted to representations by a conceptual analyzer or by hand. The understanding component, **FAUSTUS**, takes in representations and immediately stores them in a story memory. In addition, it makes inferences, based on what is known about the story so far, as well as what is in the general knowledge base. More precisely, **FAUSTUS**'s algorithm (Norvig, 1987, pp. 8–9) consists of the following steps:

- **Step 0**: Construct a knowledge base.

- **Step 1**: Construct a semantic representation of the next piece of the text.

- **Step 2**: Pass markers (see chapter 2) from each concept in the semantic representation of the input text to adjacent nodes, following along the links in the semantic network.

- **Step 3**: Suggest inferences on the basis of marker collisions. For each collision, look at the sequence of links along which markers were passed. Each link has a primitive link type associated with it, and the list of primitive link types determines the shape of the marker path that led to the collision. If the total path shape matches one of the pre specified shapes (see later), then an inference is suggested by placing the path in the agenda.

- **Step 4**: Evaluate the potential inferences that are on the agenda. The result is either to make the suggested inference, to reject it, or to defer the decision by keeping the suggestion on the agenda. If there is explicit contradictory evidence, an inference can be rejected immediately. If several potential inferences are competing with one another, as when there are several possible referents for a pronoun, then the decision is deferred if none of them is more plausible than the others. If there is no reason to reject or defer, then the suggested inference is accepted, and new concepts are added to the model of the text.

- **Step 5**: Repeat steps 1 to 4 for each piece of the text.

- **Step 6**: At the end of the text there may be some suggested inferences remaining on the agenda. Evaluate them to see, as in step 4, if they lead to any more inferences.

Unlike the Conceptual Dependency primitives that underlie Dyer's Thematic Abstraction Units, **KODIAK** (Wilensky, 1986), the representation language used by Norvig, is both language- and application-independent and has no semantic primitives per se. Representations in the **KODIAK** language are composed of instances of three types of primitive objects and eight primitive associations between objects. The primitive object types are (Norvig, 1987, p. 59):

- **Absolutes** — concepts, e.g., person, action, purple, government.

- **Relations** — relations between concepts, e.g., actor-of-action.

- **Aspectuals** — formal parameters for the relations, e.g., actor.

The primitive link types are these:

- **Dominate** — a concept is a subclass of another class.

- **Instance** — a concept is an instance of some class.

- **View** — a concept can be seen as another class.

- **Constrain** — fillers of an aspectual must be of some class.

- **Argument** — associates aspectuals with a relation.

- **Fill** — an aspectual refers to some absolute.

- **Equate** — two concepts are co-referential.

- **Differ** — two concepts are not co-referential.

From these eight types of links, five different path shapes and six inference classes are established (Norvig, 1987, p. 101). The path shapes are regular expressions (in the sense used in formal language and automata theory) that each specify a valid sequence of links. An inference class consists of a pair of path shapes that must be matched to the two halves of the total path of a marker collision.

Throughout his dissertation, Norvig insisted on the following fact (1987, p. 7):

> Declarative knowledge, when organized properly, can be used in several ways, while procedural knowledge by definition can only be used one way. . . . Because the knowledge base and the possible inferences are in a declarative form, it is relatively easy to combine them, to consider several inferences at the same time (as when two or more possible inferences each suggest a referent for the same pronoun). If the knowledge needed to make inferences were represented procedurally, it would be more difficult to inspect, compare, and merge inferences together. If the procedures were going to have any interaction, they would have to be written as co-routines, and would have to know some of the details of other procedures. This is often confusing and difficult, and would probably require the knowledge base modeler to modify existing inference rules to interact with new rules as they are added. . . . The complexity has not disappeared; it has just moved from the algorithm to the knowledge base.

Reader-based hermeneutics lead to an extreme version of this strategy: In **IDIoT** *all* qualitative data required for an interpretation are specified by the user.

Norvig (1987, p. 77) also introduced the notion of *views*, that is, of links that support the idea of viewing one concept as another. He acknowledged the fact that several AI systems provide support for such an idea but claimed that "**KODIAK** is the first representational language to have [as] a design goal the explicit representation of views that prescribe how certain concepts can be interpreted as others". The important point he emphasized is that views need to be represented explicitly, rather than have the modeler rely on some general processing mechanism that would derive such analogical or figurative interpretations. However, such general mechanisms for mapping one concept into another have been proposed by several researchers in philosophy, psychology, and artificial intelligence (see Mac Cormac, 1985). Much like the debate between Small's (1980, 1983) word expert parsing and general parsing mechanisms, this is a "religious" debate (Hirst, 1987, section 4.2.4), which ultimately depends on one's belief in the existence of general rules.

Views may be chained. Consider, for example, the following sentence (Norvig, 1987, p. 76):

Example 6.4.1   *The Kremlin took offense at Reagan's latest remarks.*

The word "Kremlin" should be explicitly mapped to the concept "soviet-government" using the view link "place-for-organization", and "soviet-government" to "soviet-leaders" by applying the "organization-for-people" view, rather than having a single general rule that would create this conceptual connection.

A major drawback of **FAUSTUS** is that it fails for *ambiguous* input, although it may succeed for *vague* sentences. Norvig explained this distinction by considering the following sentence:

Example 6.4.2   *They saw her duck.*

He suggests (1987, p. 79) that the sentence is ambiguous inasmuch as there are two possible interpretations for it:

1. They saw a water fowl belonging to some female.

2. They saw a female quickly bow.

Moreover, even if we make the assumption that "*duck* refers to a water fowl[,] the sentence is still vague, in that it does not specify if the duck is male or female, large or small, alive or cooked" (Norvig, 1987, p. 79). In other words, from my understanding, a concept is vague if some of its attributes are left unspecified. Norvig blamed **FAUSTUS**'s strict pipeline process of syntactic analysis first, inference second, for this limitation, and acknowledged that the representation of an ambiguous input was bypassed by typically hand-coding his "best guess as to what the semantic analysis would have been, had [the parser] been able to make the *correct* choice" (Norvig, 1987, p. 80).

Another important limitation of **FAUSTUS**, and of spreading activation models in general, is that the number of possible inferences dramatically increases with the complexity of the knowledge base. Charniak (1986b) suggested not passing markers to nodes that exceed a maximal number of links. Instead, Norvig adopted the *dynamic anti promiscuity solution* (Norvig, 1987, p. 98):

> First run the algorithm on a representative sample of texts. Then count
> the markers that accumulate at each concept, and declare the *m* con-
> cepts with the most markers as promiscuous concepts. . . . Both solu-
> tions have an element of arbitrariness.

Also, **FAUSTUS** is based on the assumption that the input will be coherent.
The program does not generate expectations, has no forward or top-down
inferencing, and does not tackle the problem of global coherence. The important conclusion of Norvig's research is that "both script- and goal-based processing can be reproduced by a system that has no explicit processing
mechanism aimed at one type of story or another, but just looks for connections in the input as they relate to what is known in memory" (Norvig, 1987,
p. 139).

6.5 GRAESSER AND CLARK'S MODEL OF COMPREHENSION

I previously remarked that, typically, the few schema-based models that address the problem of global coherence specify a small set of a priori macrostructures. In contrast, Graesser and Clark (1985) have presented an extensive
model of comprehension that focuses mainly on the generation and management of *bridging inferences*. Although they did not directly tackle the problem
of the perception of subject matter, they suggested, much like Kintsch and van
Dijk (1978, 1983), that coherence relies on, among other things, a schema for
the narrative "genre". The existence of such a macrostructure is briefly justified (Graesser, & Clark, 1985, p. 249):

> Adults have knowledge about the general composition of narrative
> passages. A typical story starts out with a description of the setting,
> including information about characters, the time frame, the spatial
> scenario, and some background episodes. Then the story proceeds
> with the plot. The order of episodes usually follows the chronological
> order of the episodes that the characters enact. Stories usually have a
> point which may be summarized in the form of an adage.

This obvious dependence on an "omniscient" (with respect to the set of possible structures of a text) reader (which explains the necessity of the word
"adult") directly proceeds from earlier schema-based approaches to subject
matter such as story grammars and thematic abstraction units. Indeed,
Graesser and Clark claimed that their model includes most of the previous
research done on the comprehension of *simple narratives*. It is not my intent
to discuss at length their (strictly cognitive) model of understanding. How-

ever, since their model is very general (mostly because it is not implemented), in this section I focus on some of its fundamental characteristics.

Graesser and Clark proposed procedures to model comprehension, recall, summarization, and question answering. These procedures work on *generic knowledge structures* (GKSs) represented by *conceptual graphs* (see Sowa, 1984) that they traverse and *match* in order to generate the bridging inferences that make a text locally coherent, as well as other inferences (called *projections*) that capture the reader's *expectations*. "GKSs are structured summaries or abstractions of sets of exemplars[; each one] constitutes an atheoretical data base with general knowledge about a concept" (Graesser, & Clark, 1985, p. 34). (Due to the use of conceptual graphs, the components of a GKS are referred to as *nodes* and can be thought more or less of as propositions.) The fundamental claim made is that most inferences produced during comprehension *match* information contained in those GKSs. Finally, in order to minimize the role of the components left out (e.g., reader's horizon, language, global coherence), Graesser and Clark had to resort to passages that are short (less than 15 lines and 10 propositions) and "simple" (read "artificial"). Thus, like other information-processing approaches, non artificial text and its possible differences in interpretation are banished in order to discover processing regularities.

The foremost characteristic of the model is this claim (Graesser, & Clark, 1985, p. 41):

> Narrative comprehension is best viewed as a mechanism which dynamically composes a knowledge structure from nodes and structured chains that already exist in the associated GKSs. Existing GKSs "rub up against each other" in systematic ways and eventually converge on a reduced set of nodes which end up being the passage inferences.

In other words, comprehension is a *dynamic* process that *constructs a representation* of what is understood. This construction process does not reduce (at least in theory) to the *exact* matching of *a* predefined schema, but instead results from the *interactions* between several GKSs. From this viewpoint, Graesser and Clark's proposal is mostly a schema-matching model with some limited inference-chaining abilities. What sets their work apart is the fact that they address the convergence problem. That is, they provide a description of the mechanisms they assume in order to explain how a small set of adequate bridging inferences is eventually generated. Most importantly, their solution is plausible from a psychological point of view, for it is primarily rooted in the dichotomy between a working memory and a less accessible "secondary memory" (Graesser, & Clark, 1985, p. 41):

> Our model of comprehension adopts the distinction between working
> memory and secondary memory. Secondary memory is a vast store-
> house of specific knowledge structures, generic knowledge structures,
> and active symbolic procedures. Working memory is a limited capac-
> ity workspace where procedures and processes are executed when a
> person interacts with the world. For example, the process of construct-
> ing a passage structure during comprehension takes place in working
> memory; the new passage structure is eventually passed to secondary
> memory. . . . Given that working memory is limited in capacity, there
> are limits to the number of GKSs that can occupy working memory at
> any point in time.

Specifically, Graesser and Clark assumed that at a given point in time, the
reader processes one clause (in the intuitive linguistic sense of the word); all
the GKSs associated with that clause are said to be *active* in the working memory. To justify the activation (and the transfer to the working memory) of *all*
these GKSs, Graesser and Clark (1985, p. 41) observed that "a GKS is usually
an automatized, overlearned conceptualization, at least those GKSs that are
relevant to simple narrative passages". In other words, familiarity has bound
the GKSs associated with a concept together, and thus they are accessed as a
unit. Graesser and Clark also assumed that both the GKSs of the previous
clause and a "topic" list (which contains automatically "recycled" GKSs such
as those concerning spatio-temporal or "genre" information (Graesser and
Clark, 1985, p. 198)) are kept in the *foreground* of the working memory.
Finally, the structures obtained for the other clauses and "episodes" processed
so far are stored in the *background*, which is separate from the working memory.

Comprehension consists in constructing both bridging inferences and
"some" projection inferences between the active GKSs and the ones in the
foreground or, on very few occasions, the ones in the background. Convergence relies mostly on the content and capacity constraints of the working
memory to limit the generation of inferences: "Comprehension suffers when
the comprehender is expected to reinstate explicit propositions and inferences
from several clauses earlier" (Graesser and Clark, 1985, p. 42). In other words,
the strictest linear coherence between clauses is required.

A second source of convergence comes from the fact that the GKSs have
intersecting nodes: Graesser and Clark claimed that 90 percent of the bridging inferences involve nodes that intersect or are close to an intersection
between one active GKS and another GKS. In other words, convergence is
possible because the reader possesses all the GKSs necessary to match or

chain the current clause to some existing knowledge.

The third and final source of convergence involves text coherence and bridging inferences. It is assumed that bridging inferences are generated during comprehension and that the projection inferences resulting from the reader's expectations play only a minor role at reading time.

Now that we have enumerated the principal assumptions of the model, let me quote at length Graesser and Clark's description of the comprehension process (1985, p. 43):

> When an incoming clause N is interpreted, the old passage structure (created from clauses 1 to N-1) is modified and a new structure is constructed. According to our model, four procedures accomplish this modification. These four procedures may be accomplished in the order that we list and describe them. During procedure 1, a check is made for a direct match between clause N and an existing node in the old structure. For example, a match occurs when a prior expectation is confirmed by the incoming clause N. During procedure 2, a set of bridges are [sic] formed between clause N and the old passage structure in working memory. When a bridge cannot be formed, the comprehender attempts to reinstate old passage nodes in working memory and then construct a set of bridges. Alternatively, the comprehender concludes that a new topic or episode is introduced. After the bridging procedure is executed, the pruning procedure is executed (procedure 3). The erroneous nodes in the old structure are deleted in light of new information and constraints posted in working memory. During procedure 4, projection nodes are constructed. The projection nodes include expectations and elaborations. The construction of projection nodes is particularly sensitive to the comprehender's goals and many of these nodes may not be constructed during comprehension. When the four procedures are considered as a whole, we refer to the construction mechanism as the *matching-bridging-pruning-projection* mechanism (abbreviated MBPP).

The final structure produced by the **MBPP** algorithm consists of a set of separate and distinct "episodes"; the scope of an episode entirely depends on the linear coherence assumed between the clauses of a text. Because the model is not implemented, it is difficult to grasp the exact nature and scope of an episode. It appears that the final representation of each episode consists of *all* the GKSs and the bridging inferences that were still active at the end of the processing of that episode. This aspect of the model is not explicitly dealt with because, from my standpoint, the four simplistic passages used as examples each consist of a single episode. Thus, I repeat, Graesser and Clark's model can only account for the strictest linear form of clausal coherence.

It is clear that the **MBPP** algorithm does not deal with the perception of subject matter. Indeed, this problem is postponed to retrieval time: The reader is assumed to *reconstruct* subject matter only when asked to recall, summarize, or answer questions about the narrative. This reconstruction process assumes an a priori macrostructure for the text and a *central content selector* that traverses the (extremely rich) passage structure obtained (for each episode) at comprehension time and selects nodes and bridging inferences with respect to their content. Although this selection is content-dependent, Graesser and Clark assumed the existence of three general principles that underlie this process:

1. The principle of inferability: Typically, information that can be inferred or reconstructed is not selected (Kintsch, & van Dijk, 1978, 1983).

2. The principle of structural centrality: *Pivotal* information (Lehnert, 1983) is selected.

3. The principle of pragmatic communication: Information that conveys a major message or point (Wilensky, 1982, 1983a) is selected.

In summary, Graesser and Clark's model of comprehension consists of the generation and pruning of a multitude of bridging inferences in working memory.

6.6 THE PROBLEMS OF TEXT INTERPRETATION

The models of understanding summarized in the previous sections introduce most of the typical issues that must be addressed by a theory of linguistic comprehension. In this section, I wish to establish a partial list of these issues to be tackled in the rest of this book.

First, I remark that none of the reviewed models draw on work in formal semantics, a field that currently occupies a large portion of the research spectrum in philosophy and artificial intelligence. Indeed, recall from chapter 2 that the relevance of formal semantics to text understanding is generally rejected (e.g., Norvig, 1987, p. 20; Graesser, & Clark, 1985, p. 23). Also remember that several researchers (e.g., Minsky, 1975; Braine, 1978; Johnson-Laird, 1982; Rastier, 1991) have emphasized the inadequateness of logical formalization (e.g., using propositions) with respect to the fundamental goal of cognitive science, that is, the understanding of human cognition: Formal reasoning is taken to account for only a small portion of adult thinking. In my opinion, "human reasoning" seems to consist of the ability to apply an inferential schema that specifies a rule defined over abstract symbols. The immediacy of the application of such a rule depends on

1. the individual's ability to abstract.

2. the intellectual resources that may be brought into play by an individual in order to apply the rule. Intuitively, it appears that the more abstract (or complex) a mental operation is, the more memory resources it requires (up to the point where pencil and paper become necessary), and the more time it takes to execute (possibly due to the hypothesis that the manipulation of abstract symbols is inherently sequential).

3. the retrievability of the rule itself.

In other words, not surprisingly, I suggest that the ease and frequency of use of reasoning techniques can be somewhat idiosyncratic. Since reading does not allow, in general, sufficient time to make such complex inferences (see Garrod, 1985), I will not investigate this topic further.

Second, some of the hypotheses of the reviewed models belong, in my opinion, to the grounded architecture proper:

• Although **FAUSTUS** (Norvig, 1987) does not handle expectations, they are typically assumed to play a role in comprehension. For Graesser and Clark (1985), projections, which result from the reader's expectations, are extremely idiosyncratic with respect to the reader and thus constitute only a minor facet of their **MBPP** algorithm. Conversely, expectations are omnipresent in **BORIS** (Dyer, 1983). They are crucial, for example, for the detection of a planning error or the determination of an affective status. In **IDIoT**, expectations are handled through the use of expectation signals. In other words, their mechanics are defined in the grounded architecture, but their use is left to the user.

• The problem of convergence, which is typically ignored by schema-matching approaches to text understanding but central to Graesser and Clark's discourse, does not belong to a model for text interpretation so much as to a model of memory, as I have argued in the previous chapters.

• As explained in chapters 2 and 3, complex markers and sequential path evaluation are problematic in the context of a grounded architecture. Instead, we require a unified approach to processing, and more specifically, a non semantic model of spreading activation. Furthermore, this model should not be limited (as **FAUSTUS** and **BORIS** are) to bottom-up processing but rather accommodate both forward and backward chaining.

From the discussion of linguistic comprehension presented in chapter 2, we can therefore establish the following list of linguistic issues to address in the next chapters:

1. the role of grammar and syntax, which is significantly downplayed in psycholinguistic models.

2. the problem of reference resolution, which has also been significantly downplayed.

3. the general problem of disambiguation (see Hirst, 1987), which involves, at least, the issues of lexical and structural disambiguation.

4. the problem of inferencing, which is generally taken to be central to comprehension of larger textual units.

5. beyond local coherence, the problem of global coherence and the perception of subject matter. In particular, we need to investigate the intuitive notions of "fact", "event", and "episode".

Chapter 7

On Grammar and Syntax

7.1 A BRIEF INTRODUCTION

Syntax has come to dominate linguistics, as well as, to a lesser degree, computational linguistics, as I have observed in chapter 2. A plethora of syntactic theories have been proposed:

1. Government and binding: Chomsky (1980, 1982, 1984)

2. Generalized Phrase Structure Grammar (GPSG): Gazdar, Klein, Pullum, and Sag (1985)

3. Head Phrase Structure Grammar (HPSG): Pollard and Sag (1988)

4. Definite clause grammars: Pereira, Gazdar, Pulman, Joshi, and Kay (1987)

5. Other types of unification grammars, for example, JPSG, LFG, FUG; see Gazdar and Mellish (1989, p. 281)

6. Functional linguistics, for example, Fox, 1989; Chafe, 1990; Givón, 1993a

Clearly, the notions of a linguistic grammar and of a parsing mechanism pervade existing approaches to natural language processing (see Mitchell, 1994). Beyond the more traditional syntax-first models (e.g., Marcus, 1980, 1984; Allen, 1987; Delisle, Copeck, Szpakowicz, & Barker, 1993) to the more "semantic" strategies (e.g., Dyer, 1983; Lytinen, 1984), most researchers have acknowledged the existence of some syntactic processing, either before or concurrently with semantic processing. However, if these two notions are generally accepted, their realization differ very significantly from one approach to the next. Consider, for example, these recent proposals:

1. Bouma (1992), who suggested a unification-based grammar with nonmonotonic extensions.

2. Fraser and Hudson (1992) who introduced a word grammar that relies on inheritance.

3. Eizirik, Barbosa, and Mendes (1993) whose work mixed syntax with case analysis and probabilities.

These proposals offer vastly different viewpoints on the nature and modus operandi of a grammar. Indeed, as with most aspects of human cognition, open problems and controversies abound.Consider these examples:

1. Forster and Stevenson (1987) summarized the methodological debate surrounding the processing of ungrammatical sentences.

2. Levin and Pinker (1992) argued that syntactic constructions are sensitive to the words they contain, an observation that leads them to reject formal approaches to grammar (which abstract words into context-independent symbols).

3. Both van der Linden (1992) and Hemforth, Koniecny and Strube (1993) questioned existing approaches because these approaches either downplay or ignore the incremental (e.g., word-by-word) nature of linguistic comprehension.

4. Shapiro and Nagel (1993) proposed a strategy whereby lexical information is used during the initial analysis of a sentence to set up *possible* paths the parser might take. When the structure of the sentence is incongruent with a subject's preference, sentence processing performance is disrupted and reanalysis must occur. Such an hypothesis leads to a reevaluation of the role of syntax for linguistic comprehension.

5. Osterhou and Swinney (1993) emphasized the role of processing time (that is, a *performance* issue) even for specific facets of syntax (namely, gap-filling in verb passives). Similarly, Millis and Just (1994), stressed the importance of the functional role of connectives in sentence comprehension.

In the end, these debates lie beyond the scope of this book, which is not to say that we should ignore syntax. Therefore, we briefly discuss this topic with respect to **IDIoT** in the next section.

7.2 SYNTAX WITH IDIoT

As explained in chapter 2, several researchers have criticized the relevance for linguistic comprehension of the conceptualization of a grammar as a set of consistent rules defining the well-formedness of a parse tree: As explained when story grammars were discussed (see subsection 2.2.1), text interpretation is *not* an issue of well-formedness. Also, recall that most computational models for text understanding either ignore or systematically downplay the importance of syntax. More importantly, existing theories of grammar are typically grounded in the conduit metaphor and its implied inaccessible (and self-validating) notions of competence and language, which I have abandoned in favor of reader-based comprehension. For example, Lindsay and Manaster-Ramer (1987) wrote:

> Almost all computational work on natural languages, in and out of AI, has adopted the conception of language, derived from traditional grammar and structural linguistics, according to which there exists a body of knowledge which defines the primitives of which the language is composed, the principles by which these primitives may be combined, and the meanings associated with each primitive and with each principle of composition. This conceptual homogeneity has been obscured by the controversies surrounding virtually every other question in NL processing, such as the debate over models which postulate syntactic and/or logical levels of analysis in addition to the meaning (conceptual) representation, . . . as opposed to models which relate utterances to meanings in an integrated fashion, . . . which has sometimes been viewed as involving a contrast between grammar-based and knowledge-based methodologies. . . . [A]lmost all models purport to simulate the idealized user of a given language, conceived as an expert on his native language, . . . and consequently assume that there is such a thing as a definite knowledge of *what* a native speaker does in the way of assigning some structural representations.

It should be clear from the discussion of chapter 2, that I discard the notions of linguistic competence of an idealized user, and of a correct set of rules of understanding, and thus, of a grammar as a set of consistent rules of composition. In this book, I focus on the idiosyncratic performance of a reader. From my viewpoint, regardless of its expression, knowledge, including grammar, is always idiosyncratic in that it is acquired, owned, and managed by a specific individual who is the sole judge of the acceptability of an interpretation. The mind's ability to often understand so-called "ungrammatical" sentences and to misunderstand or simply not understand grammatical sentences seems to reinforce this standpoint.

Because I adopt this perspective, I do not develop a grammatical theory, and I do not consider the complexities studied by linguists. From my standpoint, grammar is not a system of consistent rules of composition, but merely an *acquired* system consisting of often-inconsistent conventions used to *constrain* the arbitrariness between signifiant and signifié that de Saussure (1916) took as the fundamental principle of linguistic communication. It is essential that a majority of the users of a language share a large number of graphological, grammatical, and even lexical conventions, in order for the inherent arbitrariness of communication to be constrained, and thus for comprehension to be made possible. This sharing of conventions does *not* imply an innate "competence" but merely attempts to limit the arbitrariness of reading to the "semantic" level(s), and does not *necessarily* eliminate it at the grammatical and lexical levels. In other words, I suggest that grammar merely constitutes a conventionalized linguistic mechanism to *speed up* the recognition of certain semantic cues. Because I view comprehension as a time-constrained process for which past processing plays an important role, I feel particularly close to Lindsay and Manaster-Ramer (1987) when they explained:

> If there is such a thing as a grammar, only parts of it will be accessed at any given point in time in real-time processing. As a result we would be able to explain how a speaker can consider a sentence ungrammatical for a time and then decide, upon further reflection (i.e., when more of the grammar is considered) that it is grammatical, or vice versa.

Within the framework of **IDIoT**, any grammatical rule must be specified by means of the associations, candidates, constraints, and expansion procedures of one or more features (see chapter 4). Because knowledge units (which implement features) and their communications both consume time (to be retrieved and to transmit a signal, respectively), it is possible to model rules that require a long time to retrieve and which, therefore, can be missed if the time-span allocated to produce an interpretation is too short, the phenomenon described by Lindsay and Manaster-Ramer. Furthermore, it is important to understand that all rules are treated equally in **IDIoT**, that is, as data for the trivial algorithm. Thus, there is no need to assume separate algorithms and data structures for the processing of syntax. Indeed, the organization of short-term memory in the proposed model of time-constrained memory implements de facto a stack, which is often used in conventional parsers. Also, since candidacy races span an interval of time after having been triggered, they can consider subsequently processed information without having to resort to counterintuitive look-ahead mechanisms. In other words, some of the characteristics hypothesized for conventional parsers are readily available in **IDIoT**. Most importantly, there is no need to assume that syntax is processed before semantics or vice versa, as the distinction between syntax, semantics, and pragmatics becomes irrelevant in the framework of a grounded (mechanistic) architecture. It follows that, contra Lytinen (1984), it is not even necessary to keep syntactic and semantic knowledge in separate KBs.

Let us turn to the specification of a grammatical rule using **IDIoT**. The triggering mechanism of any KU allows the user to specify the static preconditions of a rule. The triggers (which may be ordered) are those features that must always be present in order for a rule to apply (i.e., become detected). Through the use of the **testEquivalenceOf**, **testDifferenceOf**, **testPresenceOf**, and **testAbsenceOf** instructions, the dynamic preconditions of a rule may be checked using buildable features. For example, the candidacy of a feature, called say **forcedPP-Attach**, which attaches a locative PP (e.g., "on the beach") to a verb, may be triggered by the presence of both a verb and such a PP but may require that the verb in question does not have another locative PP already attached to it at that point in time. If we assume that a locative PP is attached as a subcluster under feature **location** (as illustrated in 4.6.2.1) in the cluster **u1** associated with the verb, then **forcedPP-Attach** can verify this dynamic constraint using the following instruction:

```
testAbsenceOf location in u1
```

which ensures that if feature **location** is absent from u1, then the expansion procedure of **forcedPP-Attach** proceeds; otherwise, this procedure immediately fails.

The use of weights, especially for exceptions, allows a rule to admit a certain degree of "ungrammaticality". For example, a constraint that attaches the subject and verb of a clause may be specified in such a way that it can become detected even if the feature **SVA** that detects a subject-verb agreement is absent (i.e., has not been detected): All that is necessary is for a smaller weight (with respect to the detection threshold) to be assigned to **SVA**.

Any "transformation" (i.e., modification) of the current context (i.e., of the current set of reachable clusters) can be specified through the expansion procedure of a rule, the proposed set of instructions for such procedures allowing for all the basic data structure operations. Let me elaborate. Recall that a particular cluster can be accessed through one of the features it contains. For example, all verbs denoting an action could have feature **actionVerb** put in the cluster constructed by their expansion procedure. Then, using the instruction:

```
getCluster u1 governing actionVerb
```

a rule can access the most reachable cluster associated with an action verb, independently of the actual verb itself. Once u1 is bound to this cluster, it is possible to add features and subclusters to it, rename features, and so forth. Since an expansion procedure can access several clusters, it is possible for a single detected feature to arbitrarily modify all the clusters it accesses. Experimentation with the current prototype of **IDIoT** suggests that access to the relevant clusters of a rule constitutes one of the tasks that must be well thought out by the user. For example, as illustrated in the examples of the next section, the clusters associated with the different NPs of a sentence should contain features that precisely identify the role of each NP in the sentence: A feature that captures a rule does not want to access the direct object of the verb or the noun phrase of a PP if it is the subject NP that is relevant to the rule. Experimentation also suggests that relays (i.e., KUs that simply relay signals from their suppliers to their customers; see chapter 3) are very useful to handle more "general" rules. For example, if feature **actionVerb** is a relay with all action verbs as suppliers and all rules relevant to such verbs as customers, then each time an action verb becomes detected, all the rules that apply to action verbs in general will be notified through **actionVerb**. For example, if the word "eat" eventually leads to the detection of **actionEat**, then all rules specific to **actionEat** will be notified because of this detection, and all rules for action verbs in general will be subsequently notified through the detection of **actionVerb** that results from the detection of **actionEat**. It should be clear that these considerations are not limited to grammatical rules, but, in fact, hold for all rules. Thus, there is no need to postulate a separate methodology for grammar: All grammatical rules are specified using KUs, and a parse tree is merely a cluster. Furthermore, since rules are implemented as KUs of a time-constrained memory, parsing is necessarily a time-constrained process (both with respect to the retrieval of use and with respect to the construction of some sort of parsing structure).

Incidentally, the importance of punctuation must be stressed with respect to such time-constrained parsing: Not only does a punctuation sign require some time to process, but it may also provide a clue with regards to the end of a clause. For example, a period followed by a space and a capital can denote the end of a sentence and the start of another one. Upon detecting the end of a sentence, some of the existing candidacies could be interrupted and a particular parse adopted. (On this topic, remember the shift-processing hypothesis of Gernsbacher (1985), which was discussed in the previous chapter.)

Finally, I remark that some syntactic cues such as the tense of verbs will play an important role for text interpretation (as explained in chapter 11) and that the phenomenon of the loss of surface information (Gernsbacher, 1985) will be very simply explained by having most syntactic rules being more retrievable, and thus more readily detectable, than complex thematic rules.

7.3 EXAMPLES OF SYNTACTIC PROCESSING WITH IDIoT

In **IDIoT**, several approaches to parsing are possible. For example, the use of relays and confirmation paths in the following examples could be replaced by a set of rules in which detection is possible only through the satisfaction of expectations. It is not my goal to explore the different representational strategies, but, instead, to propose an approach to some typical problems associated with syntax.

Let us start with the first steps involved in the processing of a word. For example, consider the words "woman" and "women", to which correspond the innate features **"woman"** and **"women"**. Let us assume that the words are associated with a single signifié, namely the feature **woman**. There are several different ways of specifying these features. Here are three possible sets of definitions:

Possibility 1: Using an "empty" (or dummy) feature **rootWoman** to capture the morphological root shared by the two words and ignoring agreement rules:

```
innate KU 'woman':
 associations: woman
 expansion:
      getNewCluster u1
      addFeature rootWoman to u1
      addFeature singular to u1

innate KU 'women':
 associations: woman
 expansion:
      getNewCluster u1
      addFeature rootWoman to u1
      addFeature plural to u1


KU woman:
 constraint c1:
  triggers: 'woman'
```

```
inputs:
     noun has a weight of 1
constraint c2:
 triggers: 'women'
 inputs:
     noun has a weight of 1
 expansion:
     getCluster u1 governing rootWoman
     addFeature person to u1
     addFeature female to u1


KU rootWoman:
```

Possibility 2: Identical to possibility 1, but moving the constraints from **woman** to **rootWoman** for which the former becomes a customer port:

```
innate KU 'woman':
 associations: rootWoman
 expansion:
     getNewCluster u1
     addFeature rootWoman to u1
     addFeature singular to u1


innate KU 'women':
 associations: rootWoman
 expansion:
     getNewCluster u1
     addFeature rootWoman to u1
     addFeature plural to u1


KU woman:
 constraint c1:
  triggers: rootWoman
  inputs:
     noun has a weight of 1
 expansion:
     getCluster u1 governing rootWoman
     addFeature person to u1
     addFeature female to u1
```

```
KU rootWoman:
 constraint c1:
  triggers: 'woman'
 constraint c2:
  triggers: 'women'
 port:
      woman has a delay of 1 and is a customer
```

Possiblity 3: Using conditional instructions and eliminating **rootWoman**:

```
innate KU 'woman':
 associations: woman
 expansion:
      getNewCluster u1
      addFeature 'woman' to u1
      addFeature singular to u1


innate KU 'women':
 associations: woman
 expansion:
      getNewCluster u1
      addFeature 'women' to u1
      addFeature plural to u1


KU woman:
 constraint c1:
  triggers: 'woman'
  inputs:
      noun has a weight of 1
 constraint c2:
  triggers: 'women'
  inputs:
      noun has a weight of 1
 expansion:
      ifConstraint c1 then getCluster u1 governing 'woman'
      ifConstraint c2 then getCluster u1 governing 'women'
      addFeature person to u1
      addFeature female to u1
      addFeature noun to u1
```

Each set of possible definitions corresponds to a different level of data specificity, but also to a different sequence of exchanges of signals. In the first set, the feature, **rootWoman**, is detected through the expansion procedure of **"woman"** or **"women"**. More specifically, since **rootWoman** is not specified anywhere else in the definition of these innate features but in an addFeature instruction of their expansion procedure, **rootWoman** is sent a forced detection signal and immediately becomes detected upon receiving this signal. In the second set, since **rootWoman** is explicitly specified as a "forced detection" of the innate features, it is merely sent the presence signal of the detected innate feature. Upon receiving this presence signal, **rootWoman** does not immediately become detected, but instead starts its candidacy. Since the constraints of **rootWoman** have only triggers, and since it is not buildable, the triggered constraint will necessarily be immediately satisfied, thus leading to the detection of **rootWoman**. The third set of definitions illustrates the use of conditional instructions to regroup in a single expansion procedure the actions associated with the detection of several distinct features. In this set, the clusters constructed by **"woman"** and **"women"** do not share a feature, and thus conditional accesses (i.e., combinations of **ifConstraint** and **getCluster** instructions) are required in the expansion procedure of **woman** in order to access the cluster of its triggering feature.

In all three sets of definitions, **woman** has the limitation that it can be detected only if its syntactic category, that is, the feature **noun** is felicitous at that point in the processing of the clause. Feature **noun** is a relay with all possible nouns as suppliers, and all general rules of valid noun usages (e.g., **NP**) as customers. The latter rules capture where a noun (any noun) is felicitous in a clause: after a determiner, after an adjective, after a transitive verb, and so forth. Such valid sequences can be detected using ordered triggers, expectations, and, if necessary, even buildable features.

In all three sets of definitions, the problem of number agreement is ignored, number information being directly constructed by the innate features. One solution could consist in having **woman** "submit" (i.e., send a submission signal to) **nounSingular** if triggered by **"woman"** and **nounPlural**, if triggered by **"women"**. The difficulty with this approach is that the syntactic category and the number agreement of a word do not seem to have the same importance: A sentence can be intelligible even if number agreement is violated. As an alternative, **woman** could submit **noun** with a weight of 0.9, for example, and **singular** with a weight of 0.1. This approach may be more intuitive, but it still has a flaw: Features **singular** and **noun** are treated as equals when, in fact it seems to me that the detection of **singular** should only be relevant once **noun** has been detected. In other words, number agreement first requires establishing the syntactic category of a word. In view of these observations, I suggest that agreement be handled after word recognition. Again, several strategies are possible: Are agreements detected, or disagreements, or both?

A disagreement constitutes an ungrammaticality. On the one hand, some models of NLP attempt to correct these ungrammaticalities but, as remarked by Lindsay and Manaster-Ramer (1987, p. 101), such corrections are hazardous if they ignore the context. On the other hand, linguists simply reject the sentence. In the case of the human mind, the reader may notice (i.e., become aware of) a disagreement, possibly infer a correction or re-read the passage in question, and continue reading. From that viewpoint, a syntactic disagreement constitutes one kind of *conflict* in the interpretation, a topic we address in chapter 11. The point for now is that the detection of a disagreement will lead to the detection of a conflict feature that handles such problems. To illustrate this point let us focus on how a disagreement may be detected. Continuing with our example, let us study number disagreement for the following sentence:

Example 7.3.1 *A women cries.*

I suggest the following scenario:

1. Feature **startOfSentence** is detected. This feature captures the processing of a new sentence, as explained in chapter 5.

2. The word "A" leads to the detection of **aArticle** whose cluster contains features **singular** and **determiner**, which also become detected.

3. Feature **determiner** is a trigger of **NP**.

4. The word "women" constructs a cluster including **plural**, and triggers **woman**, which submits **noun**.

5. Feature **NP** is a customer of **noun** and thus receives a submission signal from **noun**.

6. Feature **NP** has one of its constraints consisting of the ordered triggers, **determiner** and **noun**, satisfied, and thus sends a confirmation signal back to **noun**, which becomes detected and sends a reinforcement signal to **NP**.

7. Upon receiving reinforcement from **noun**, **NP** becomes detected and notifies, among others, for example, **numberAgreement**, **numberDisagreement**, **validNPUsage** and **invalidNPUsage**.

8. Feature **numberDisagreement** is a relay with **NP** as its supplier and **singularDisagreement** as one of its customers.

9. Feature **singularDisagreement** is a buildable feature with customer **syntacticConflict**:

```
KU singularDisagreement:
% This feature checks that a singular determiner and a plural noun
% are in the same NP.
is buildable
 associations: syntacticConflict
 constraint c1:
     triggers: NP
 expansion:
     getCluster u1 governing NP
     getCluster u2 governing determiner in NP
     testPresenceOf singular in u2
     getCluster u3 governing noun in u1
     testPresenceOf plural in u3
 ports:
     ...
```

Other disagreement features (if any) and the corresponding agreement feature(s) (if specified) are all similar to **singularDisagreement**.

10. Feature **singularDisagreement** has its expansion procedure successfully built into the current context, and thus becomes detected, leading to the perception of a conflict (i.e., to the detection of **syntacticConflict**).

11. Feature **validNPUsage** is a relay with **NP** as its supplier and **validSentenceStart** as one of its customers.

12. The ordered triggers, **startOfSentence**, **NP**, satisfy a constraint of **validSentenceStart**, which becomes detected.

The proposed scenario also addresses the syntactic felicity of an NP in a sentence by the features **validNPUsage** and **invalidNPUsage**. The latter could have **NPfollowingIntransitive** as a customer. In its simplest form, this feature would have a constraint with only the ordered triggers **intransitive** and **NP**. It would become detected if an intransitive verb was followed by an NP, and would lead to the perception of a syntactic conflict.

It should be noted that the handling of number agreement is designed independently of adjectives that could be inserted between the determiner and the noun. Consider, for example, the NP, "a short beautiful young women", for which I suggest the following scenario:

1. The word "A" and its number agreement with the word "women" are handled exactly as in the previous example.

2. The word "short" leads to the candidacy of **short**, which submits **adjective**.

3. Feature **adjective** is a relay with **adjectivesStart** as a customer.

4. The sequence **determiner, adjective**, satisfies a constraint of **adjectivesStart**, which sends a confirmation signal to **adjective**.

5. Features **short, adjective**, and **adjectivesStart** all eventually become detected.

6. The expansion procedure of **adjective** makes the cluster associated with **short** a subcluster under feature **adjectives**, in the cluster associated with the determiner.

7. The word "beautiful" leads to the candidacy of **beautiful**, which submits **adjective**.

8. Another customer of **adjective** is **adjectivesSuite**, which has one of its constraints satisfied from the co-occurrence of **adjectiveStart** and **adjective**. Thus, **adjectivesSuite** sends a confirmation signal back to **adjective**.

9. Features **beautiful, adjective**, and **adjectivesSuite** all eventually become detected.

10. Again, the expansion procedure of **adjective** makes the cluster associated with **beautiful** another subcluster under feature **adjectives** in the cluster associated with the determiner.

11. The word "young" is processed like the previous adjectives, with the only difference being that **adjectivesSuite** would send a confirmation signal to **adjective** through the satisfaction of another of its constraints with only the ordered triggers, **adjectivesSuite, adjective**. In other words, the sequencing of adjectives is handled by a recursive constraint.

12. Upon the eventual detection of **NP**, the clusters associated with the determiner, the adjectives, and the noun can be reorganized into a

single cluster that is easier to manipulate.

Anticipating our discussion of lexical disambiguation (in chapter 9), I suggest the following (still very incomplete, especially in that possible agreement and disagreement features for verbs, with respect to person, tense, etc., are not considered) definitions for the more complex case of the words "man" and "men" ("man" can be a noun or a verb):

```
innate KU 'man':
% This feature handles the recognition of the word 'man'
 associations: nounMan, actionMan
 expansion:
      getNewCluster u1
      addFeature 'man' to u1


innate KU 'manned'
% This feature handles the recognition of the word 'manned',
% which is known to be a verb in the past form.
 associations: actionMan
 expansion:
      getNewCluster u1
      addFeature 'man' to u1
      addFeature pastForm to u1


innate KU 'mans':
% This feature handles the recognition of the word 'mans',
% which is known to be the third singular person of a verb.
 associations: actionMan
 expansion:
      getNewCluster u1
      addFeature 'man' to u1
      addFeature 3rdPersonSingularForm to u1


innate KU 'men':
% This feature handles the recognition of the word 'men',
% which is known to be a plural.
 associations: nounMan
```

```
expansion:
      getNewCluster u1
      addFeature 'man' to u1
      addFeature plural to u1


KU nounMan:
% This feature corresponds to the concept of man as a noun.
% The different morphological forms of the concept define
% its constraints.
% If 'man' leads to the detection of nounMan,
% then actionMan can be inhibited.
 constraint 'man':
  triggers: 'man'
  inputs:
      noun has a weight of 1
  outputs:
      sends inhibitionSignal to actionMan
 constraint 'men':
  triggers: 'men'
  inputs:
      noun has a weight of 1
 expansion:
      getCluster u1 governing 'man'
      addFeature noun to u1
      addFeature person to u1
      addFeature male to u1
      ifConstraint 'man' then addFeature singular to u1
      ...
 ports:
      ...


KU actionMan:
% The different morphological forms of the verb define
% its constraints. The different meanings of the word
% are the customers of this feature.
 constraint 'mans':
  triggers: 'mans'
  inputs:
      verb has a weight of 1
```

```
constraint 'man':
 triggers: 'man'
 inputs:
     verb has a weight of 1
 outputs:
     sends inhibitionSignal to nounMan
constraint 'manned':
 triggers: 'manned'
 inputs:
     verb has a weight of 1
     ...
expansion:
     getCluster u1 governing 'man'
     addFeature actionMan to u1
     addFeature verb to u1
     addFeature compulsoryTransitive to u1

ports:
     'man' has a delay of 1 and is a supplier
     'mans' has a delay of 1 and is a supplier
     'manned' has a delay of 1 and is a supplier
     manAShip has a delay of 1 and is a customer
     actionSupplyWithMen has a delay of 1 and is a customer
     ...
```

If desired, these definitions could handle more details at the expense of being more complex. For example, the expansion procedure of **nounMan** could build a more complex structure to reflect that **male** is a type of **sex**.

The problem of subject-verb agreement should probably not act as a gating factor for the detection of a subject-verb relationship, and can be treated much in the same way as number agreement: Once the subject and the verb have been established, features similar to **singularDisagreement** can be used to check that the number of the subject agrees with the person of the verb. Consider the following two features for detecting subject-verb disagreements:

```
KU sva-1:
% This feature becomes detected if the subject is in the 3rd
% person and the verb is not in 3rd person nor in past tense form.
```

```
is buildable
 associations: syntacticConflict
 constraint c1:
  triggers: subj-verb-rel

 expansion:
      getCluster u0 governing clause
      getCluster u1 governing subject in u0
      getCluster u2 governedBy subject in u1
      getCluster u3 governedBy NPhead in u2
      testPresenceOf 3rdPerson in u3
      testPresenceOf singular in u3
      getCluster u3 governedBy mainVerb in u1
      testAbsenceOf pastForm in u3
      testAbsenceOf 3rdPersonSingularForm in u3
 ports:
      subj-verb-rel has a delay of 1 and is a supplier


KU sva-2:
% This feature becomes detected if the verb is in 3rd person
% form, but the subject is not.
is buildable
 associations: syntacticConflict
 constraint c1:
  triggers: subj-verb-rel
 expansion:
      getCluster u0 governing clause
      getCluster u1 governing mainVerb in u0
      getCluster u2 governedBy mainVerb in u1
      testPresenceOf 3rdPersonSingForm in u2
      testPresenceOf singular in u3
      getCluster u1 governing subject in u0
      getCluster u2 governedBy subject in u1
      getCluster u3 governedBy NPhead in u2
      testAbsenceOf singular in u3
 ports:
      subj-verb-rel has a delay of 1 and is a supplier
```

The point to be grasped is that syntactic disagreement (e.g., subject-verb disagreement) should not prevent the establishment of syntactic categories and semantic relationships. Ungrammaticality should not prevent understanding.

Let us now consider the recognizing of the direct object of a verb. Observe the following sentence:

Example 7.3.2 *John likes.*

With no implicit direct object in context, the KU **missingDirectObject** is triggered. This buildable feature, whose definition is given in section 4.6.3, will have its expansion procedure succeed and will become detected, notifying the KU **syntacticConflict**.

Also, consider this sentence:

Example 7.3.3 *John gives the girl red roses.*

Once the direct object has been detected, the sequence, **actionVerb, directObject, NP**, triggers the KU **indirectObject**. Feature **indirectObject** could be a buildable feature that checks that the verb is bitransitive and already has a direct object. Upon its detection, **indirectObject** has its expansion procedure first move the existing direct object cluster under the new feature **indirectObject**, which is added to the cluster governing the verb, and then add the most reachable NP cluster (i.e., "red roses") under feature **directObject**. Here is a possible expansion procedure to achieve this:

```
getCluster u1 governing mainVerb
getCluster u2 governedBy mainVerb
testPresenceOf bitransitive in u2
testPresenceOf directObject in u1
addFeature indirectObject to u1
moveSubClustersFrom directObject to indirectObject in u1
getCluster u2 governing NP
addSubCluster u2 to directObject in u1
```

Note that since there is no look-ahead in **IDIoT**, the cluster associated with the words "the girl" is first assumed to be the direct object, and then, as a result of the detection of the indirect object, is "corrected" to being governed by feature **indirectObject**. As an alternative, it is possible that the indirect object rule becomes detected and inhibits the not-yet-detected direct object rule if the former is specified as an exception of the latter. In other words, the indirect object rule would be faster and would establish both the direct and the indirect objects by relying on the fact that the most reachable NP is the direct object, and the second most reachable one, the indirect object. A different language could have a different rule.

Continuing with our example, once the syntactic cues direct- and indirect-object have been established, word expert feature(s), that is, features associated specifically with **actionGive** (much as in Small's approach, 1980, 1983), can be used to modify the cluster of the verb. For example, the indirect object is the *recipient* of the action, and the direct object, the *given*. Even the **subject** feature could be renamed to **giver**. The point is that since no definitive and exhaustive list of syntactic cases exists (see chapter 2), each verb may establish its own. These modifications can be trivially implemented with the **renameFeature** instruction as follows:

```
KU giveTo:
 constraint c1:
  triggers: actionGive
 expansion:
        getCluster u0 governing clause
        getCluster u1 governing actionGive in u0
        testPresenceOf indirectObject in u1
        renameFeature indirectObject to recipient in u1
        testPresenceOf subject in u0
        renameFeature subject to giver in u0
        testPresenceOf directObject in u0
        renameFeature directObject to given in u0
```

It is also possible that other rules associated with **actionGive** bypass completely the need for **directObject** and **indirectObject** to be detected and, instead, directly recognize **given**, **giver**, and **recipient**.

Finally let me briefly address the handling of a simple prepositional phrase attachment (a problem studied in chapter 10) in the following sentence:

Example 7.3.4 *The cat sits on the mat.*

I propose the following very sketchy scenario:

1. The words "the cat" cause an NP cluster to be built.

2. The word "sits" leads to the detection of **actionSit** and of the subject-verb relationship.

3. The word "on" leads to the detection of **onPreposition** which trig-

gers the candidacy of all its possible interpretations. The feature **prepositionNP** becomes expected.

4. The words "the mat" lead to the construction of an NP cluster. Through this process, the feature **prepositionNP** is triggered and becomes detected as it was expected. As a consequence, the cluster associated with "the mat" is made a subcluster of the cluster constructed for "on". In other words, the cluster resulting from the processing of the words "the mat" is attached to the cluster of preposition "on".

5. All candidate interpretations of **onPreposition** fail except **onObjectLocation**, which eventually causes (directly or through a general attachment feature) the cluster associated with "on" to be attached as a subcluster under feature **location** in the verb cluster.

Evidently, all the features presented here are still very simplistic. Yet, the previous discussion, which proceeds from experimentation with the current prototype of **IDIoT**, suggests that knowledge units *do* offer an adequate vehicle for the expression of syntactic rules. In particular, the distinction between constraint satisfaction through signals and through buildable features seems very promising for the definition of a set of rules that allows and processes ungrammaticalities. Furthermore, it appears that the grammar tool presented in section 5.7.1 considerably simplifies the task of specifying such rules in **IDIoT**.

Chapter 8

Reference Resolution

8.1 INTRODUCTION TO REFERENCE RESOLUTION

Rastier (1991, p.111) remarked that the problem of *reference* is central to linguistic comprehension. Indeed, "reference resolution" spans not only the resolution of noun phrases (e.g., definite NP resolution, that is, resolution of noun phrases starting with the determiner "the"), but also several other complex linguistic issues commonly regrouped under the term *anaphoric resolution*. Let us first briefly summarize the introduction (with examples) of Hirst (1981) who suggested that anaphora is a "linguistic device of making in discourse an abbreviated reference to some entity or entities in the expectation that the perceiver of the discourse will be able to disabbreviate the reference and thereby determine the identity of the entity".

Anaphora may involve an "explicit" referent:

Example 8.1.1 *Mary watched* **the boy** *crossing the road.* **The boy** *fell down and dropped all* **his** *books.*

note that "the boy" is repeated. Also, consider the "explicit" referent in this example:

Example 8.1.2 *John carried a pencil and a pencil case to put* **it** *in.*

The word "it" here is taken (by means of an inference) to refer to the pencil.

More frequently, the *referent* is not explicitly mentioned:

Example 8.1.3 *Mary gave each student a pencil.* **They** *use* **them** *to write* **their** *names.*

Here the personal pronouns "They", "them" and "their" refer to "each student", "pencils" and "each student's" respectively.

The implicitness of a referent introduces a certain non-determinism in the resolution process. More specifically, a certain reader may perceive a certain anaphoric reference to be genuinely ambiguous (either due to an absence of a potential referent in context or to the existence of several potential referents). Hirst (1981) indirectly acknowledged this observation when he introduces in his classification (of the different types of anaphoric references) the category "strained anaphora", for which he proposes the following examples:

Example 8.1.4 *Peter became a pianist because he thought that* **it** *was a lovely instrument.*

Example 8.1.5 *Peter became a flutist because he thought that* **it** *was a lovely instrument.*

According to Hirst, a strained anaphora is an anaphoric reference whose "felicity" is debatable. In the above examples, "it" respectively refers to "piano" and "flute", rather than to "pianist" and "flutist", with the consequence that a certain awkwardness *may* be perceived, but, should we consider the first of the two examples to be more "felicitous" than the second? On the other hand, should either one be unacceptable? I think not, for this would presuppose the existence of an a priori norm (as discussed in chapter 2). Furthermore, any general rule of resolution for anaphora would likely ignore the role of context in the resolution of reference. As an example of a contextual anaphor, assume that a reader has just read about a person admiring, at an automobile show, a car in front of her. In the text, a salesperson comes up and says this:

Example 8.1.6 *Do you like* **it***?* **It** *is an excellent choice.*

In this example, the salesperson can use "it" to refer to "the car" because the referent is obviously the car in front of the potential customer "in context", that is, the one that the reader has just read about.

The previous examples suggest that the word "it" is typically anaphoric, and that it can be involved in different types of anaphora, such as in the following temporal reference:

Example 8.1.7 *In 1970, Mary gave birth to a baby, John.* **It** *was then that John brought a lot of happiness to his family.*

Yet, "it" can also be non-referential:

Example 8.1.8 **It** *is so nice that I can meet you* **here.**

Clearly, with the word "here", example 8.1.8 demonstrates that an anaphora is not limited to the use of "it", or more generally, of pronouns. Also consider these examples:

Example 8.1.9 *Mary looked at a landscape and then at a portrait, and claimed that she rather preferred* **the former***.*

Example 8.1.10 *Since Paris is a romantic and famous place, many people want to travel* **there***.*

Furthermore, it should be obvious, from the following, that an anaphoric reference does not necessarily refer to a specific entity:

Example 8.1.11 *Computers help* **one** *save time and work faster.*

In this example, "one" refers to "any person using a computer". Similarly, note the use of "such" in the next example:

Example 8.1.12 *John was waiting for a girl who has purple hair, but he could not find* **such** *a girl.*

The word "such" refers "a girl with purple hair". Also consider the use of "so" to refer to a specific action:

Example 8.1.13 *Don't start the exam until you are told to do* **so***.*

The verb "to do" is of particular interest in that it can be anaphoric, or mean "to perform an action", or be a meaningless auxiliary, as illustrated in the following examples:

Example 8.1.14 *John bought a burger and a coke like Mary* **did** *too.* (anaphoric)

Example 8.1.15 *Mary did her homework.* (action verb)

Example 8.1.16 *John does not like classical music.*(auxiliary)

The point, again, is that the use of general rules for reference resolution may be much more problematic than a "word expert" strategy (Small, 1980, 1983). Indeed, the context may make the usage of a certain word anaphoric, as "the eleventh" in the following example of a surface count anaphora:

Example 8.1.17 *On the twelfth day of Christmas my true love gave me eight ladies dancing, six drummers drumming, eleven songbirds singing, nine pipers piping, fifty lords a-leaping, seven federal agents, a swarm of swans a-swimming, five pogo sticks, four cauliflowers, three French fries, two cans of*

*yeast and a parsnip in a pear tree. I returned all but the **eleventh** to the store
the following morning.*

Finally, an ellipsis probably constitutes the hardest form of anaphora from a
computational standpoint, because the referent must be found from a "gap"
(indicated below by __) in the text:

Example 8.1.18 *Sam brought a hamburger and Mary __ a cheeseburger.*

Example 8.1.19 *Who is the winner in this competition? Sam __*

The above discussion demonstrates the pervasiveness of the phenomenon of
reference in language. Consequently, a plethora of computational models have
been proposed. Consider these, for example:

1. the "syntactic" approaches:

   a) the tree-oriented algorithmic approach of Ingria and Stallard (1989) for the resolution of pronouns and of Prust and
   Scha (1990) for verb anaphora.

   b) the algorithms of Lappin and McCord (1990) using a slot
   grammar.

   c) the work of Merlo (1993), using Chomsky's (1982) theory of government and binding.

2. the logic-based approaches (e.g., Hobbs, 1977;   Ardissono, Lesmo, Pogliano, & Terenziani, 1991):

3. other computational (read algorithmic) approaches:

   a) the general rules proposed by Fox (1989), which however
   admit counterexamples.

   b) the algorithm of Godden (1989) for "computing" referents.

   c) the work of Kronfeld (1990), which is based on the
   notion of goals and attempts to integrate reference resolution within speech act theory, but which was criticized by
   Barnden (1990).

   d) the model of Dohsaka (1990), based on "pragmatic constraint interpretation" for the resolution of zero-pronouns in
   Japanese.

    e) the ad hoc representation for indefinite noun phrases of
Ali (1993).

These models are not grounded in that they inevitably rely on more or less ad
hoc rules of resolution. For example, let us briefly discuss a typical system
such as the one of Alshawi (1987, sections 3.2 and 6.5), which I have reviewed
at length elsewhere (see Corriveau, 1988). This author proposes a general
"context mechanism" that is used to find references: First, the constraints of
the referent are derived and marked in a semantic spreading-activation network; second, if these constraints do not lead to a single referent (i.e., a node
where all the activated markers intersect), then the context mechanism is used
to choose between the possible candidates. This simple mechanism can be
thought of as a generalization of Grosz's (1977) notion of "global focus".
More precisely, in Grosz's work, focus information is used for resolving definite references made in task-oriented dialogues between an expert and a nov-
ice being taught how to construct an air compressor. Focus consists of a set of
nodes in the semantic network that are highlighted on the basis of relevance.
Conversely, in Alshawi's work, the initial candidates for reference resolution
are the nodes with an activation level above a certain threshold in the network.
If the search in this initial set fails, then the search is widened to nodes outside
this "focus space". More precisely, the focus space is augmented with nodes
that are taken to be *implicitly* in focus (e.g., all subparts of the objects or par-
ticipants that are in focus). The most serious flaw of this approach stems from
this notion of implicitness that corresponds to a sort of a priori semantic priming of relevant features. For example, Alshawi explained (1987, p. 102) that
for a noun in focus, all entities below it in both the assumed specialization and
"correspondence" hierarchies are deemed implicitly in focus, and that for the
pronoun "it", all entities below the concept "inanimate" are also considered
implicit. Such a tactic is not only ad hoc but fundamentally irreconcilable with
the philosophy of reader-based comprehension, which rejects any form of a
priori relevance rules. Moreover, given a large knowledge base, it seems probable that an unmanageable number of features would have to be marked, especially when considering the purpose of Alshawi's correspondence hierarchy,
which is to capture correspondences of the form "role C1 of owner D1 is a
role-specialization of role C2 whose owner is D2". Moreover, inference-
chaining models in general (including marker-passing models such as
Alshawi's) do not correlate "focus" to the notion of reachability (and to STM
constraints), and, most importantly, cannot consider clues that come after the
reference in the text. Also, it is important to understand that these models often
suffer from the "labeling problem" (see section 3.2) in that they postulate special algorithms that presuppose the need for reference resolution. Conversely,

in existing models of text understanding, the problem of reference is typically ignored (e.g., by schema-matching models such as those of Dyer, 1983, and of Graesser, & Clark, 1985) or oversimplified (e.g., Norvig, 1987, reduced it to a single rather simplistic inference class).

Finally, existing computational work is typically simplistic when one is considering the insights obtained from

1. **psychology**:

> a) the work of Grosz and Sidner, (1986) and others (e.g., Gordon, Grosz, & Gilliom, 1993) on the importance of the centering of attention for pronoun comprehension.

> b) the experiments of Matthews and Chodorow (1988), Lucas, Tanenhaus, and Carlson (1990), Macdonald and MacWhinney (1990), Garrod and Sanford (1990), and Garrod, Freudenthal and Boyle (1994) emphasizing the importance of time with respect to reference resolution.

> c) the theory of Greene, McKoon and Ratcliff (1992), which emphasizes the role of context and suggests that automatic process may *not* always identify a unique referent for a pronoun.

> d) the work of van Dijk and Kintsch (1983, p. 161) and of Stevenson, Crawley, Wilson, and Kleinman (1990), and Stevenson, Nelson, and Stenning (1993) on the strategic nature of pronoun comprehension, that is, on the existence of different strategies for resolution.

2. **neurology** (e.g., the work of Friederici, Weissenborn, and Kail (1991) on aphasia and pronoun comprehension).

3. **linguistics**:

> a) Kleiber (1981) and Givón (1989, 1992) for reference in general.

> b) Bosch (1983) for pronoun comprehension.

> c) Hofmann (1989) on the importance of paragraph boundaries with respect to the resolution process.

8.2 REFERENCE RESOLUTION WITH IDIoT

For Rastier (1991), once meaning has been constructed in STM, it acts as a cue for the retrieval from memory of "referential impressions". In other words, the problem of reference is moved out of a problematic truth-conditional viewpoint (see chapter 2) and placed back in the field of psychology where it is taken to belong. The point to be understood is that reference is intimately tied to memory, and more specifically to the notion of "context". Given this observation, in the rest of the section, I merely use simple examples (running in the current prototype) to illustrate the adequacy of **IDIoT** for simple reference resolution. (The more complex facets of reference resolution, and in particular, quantification, are currently under research by the author and Saba (1995). They are briefly addressed in the next section).

Let us first consider the problem of pronoun comprehension, for which I suggest the following general strategy in **IDIoT**. When a pronoun is read, do the following:

- Check its syntactic felicity at that point in the clause. In other words, verify the syntactic constraints associated with the pronoun.

- Use a **findInclusiveReference** instruction to establish whether there is one or several possible referents for it. A possible referent is a cluster that matches the pronoun's "essential" features (e.g., number, gender, etc.).

- If there is a single referent, replace the pronoun's cluster with the cluster of the referent. Then check for semantic disagreements (e.g., the referent must be a person in the case of a personal pronoun). These disagreements capture ungrammaticalities, that is, features that do *not* prevent referent resolution but whose violation signals a syntactic conflict.

- If there are several possible referents, treat the pronoun as an ambiguous word (see the next chapter). During the short interval of time associated with the disambiguation feature, information from subsequent words and clauses may lead to the selection of one of the possible referents.

Possible definitions for the pronoun "he" implementing this tactic follow:

innate KU "he":

```
% This feature recognizes the word 'he'
 associations: hePronoun
 expansion:
     getNewCluster
     addFeature 'he' to newCluster
```

KU hePronoun:

```
% This feature verifies the syntactic felicity of a pronoun at that
% point in a sentence. If the pronoun is felicitous, the feature
% marks the cluster of 'he' as an unreferenced (ie toBeMatched)
% pronoun.
 constraint 1:
 triggers: 'he'
 inputs:
     personalPronoun has a weight of 1
 expansion:
% Add a cluster, under feature toBeMatched, that will contain the
% features that must be matched by a referent to the pronoun
% through the use of the findInclusiveReference instruction of
% personalPronounMatch. Also add feature unsolvedPersonalPronoun
% to the pronoun cluster to allow subsequent retrieval.

     getCluster u1 governing 'he'
     renameFeature 'he' to hePronoun in u1
     addFeature toBeMatched to u1
     getNewCluster
     addFeature noun to newCluster
     addFeature male to newCluster
     addFeature singular to newCluster
     addSubCluster newCluster to toBeMatched in u1
     addFeature unsolvedPersonalPronoun to u1
 ports:
     . . .
```

KU ambiguousPersonalPronoun:

```
% A pronoun is ambiguous if, and only if, the buildable feature
% personalPronounMatch fails, which indicates
```

% that a unique reference for the pronoun was not found.
% In this case, further inferences will have to disambiguate this
% pronoun.
% The use of personalPronounMatch constitutes a typical use of
% exceptions in IDIoT.
 constraint c1:
  triggers: personalPronoun
  exceptions: personalPronouMatch
 ...
 expansion:
      ifConstraint c1 then getCluster u1 governing
          unsolvedPersonalPronoun
      removeFeature toBeMatched from u1
 ports:
      personalPronoun has a delay of 1 and is a supplier
      personalPronounMatch has a delay of 1 and is a supplier
      ...

KU personalPronounMatch :

% This buildable feature tries to find a single referent for an
% unsolved pronoun. It could also inhibit ambiguousPersonal
% explicitly.
is buildable

 constraint 1:
  triggers: hePronoun
 constraint 2:
  triggers: shePronoun
 constraint 3:
  triggers: iPronoun
 constraint 4:
  triggers: himPronoun
 ...
 expansion:
      getCluster u1 governing unsolvedPersonalPronoun
      getCluster u2 governedBy toBeMatched in u1
      findInclusiveReference u3 to u2
      substitute u3 to u1

```
ports:
    ambiguousPersonalPronoun  has a delay of 1 and is a customer
```

KU personalPronounDisagreement:

```
% This feature is triggered only if a personal pronoun has been
% solved.
% In this case, it checks whether the referent is a person. If it
% is not, a syntactic conflict is detected.

is buildable
 associations: syntacticConflict
 constraint 1:
  ordered triggers: hePronoun, personalPronounMatch
 constraint 2:
  ordered triggers: himPronoun, personalPronouMatch
 ...
 expansion:
% the most reachable NP is necessarily the referent at this point.
% The noun of this NP must be a person.
      getCluster u1 governing NP
      getCluster u1 governing noun in u1
      testAbsenceOf person in u2
      addFeature syntacticConflict in u1
 ports:
    ...
```

The purpose and details of these KUs are given in their comments. Moreover, these definitions do not tackle the role of expectations in reference resolution because there is currently no agreement on the importance of syntactic and topical expectations. Also, in the case of an ambiguous pronoun, the ambiguity is left to be possibly solved by inference, that is, by other KU(s).

To illustrate this tactic, let us look at a few simple examples, starting with a passage, in which there is only one possible referent:

Example 8.2.1 *John eats. He sleeps.*

In this example, once the resolution process has terminated, the cluster associated with "he" will be replaced by the cluster of "John". I remark, however, that this resolution may not be as immediate as it may appear and that, in fact, in this example, it may depend on establishing an implicit temporal inference between the two clauses (e.g., John sleeps after eating). This observation suggests that, in general, a non referential inter clausal relationship (such as this temporal inference) may be required in order to enable or to confirm the actual resolution. In other words, the expansion procedure of **personalPronoun-Match** would have to include cluster operations to check that the action of the referent comes before the action of the pronoun. The specification of such inferences is discussed in section 11.2. Compare with the following passage:

Example 8.2.2 *John eats. He then sleeps.*

In this passage, the temporal inter-clausal relationship is made explicit by the connective "then". In this case, it appears that the resolution of "he" to "John" is "stronger" (i.e., less provisional, more readily confirmed) than in the preceding example, mostly because the explicit temporal link necessitates less time to establish than does its implicit counterpart.

Temporal relationships are not the only inter clausal links that may confirm or enable reference resolution. Consider this passage:

Example 8.2.3 *John eats at a restaurant. He orders caviar.*

The semantic link (in the form of spreading activation or expectations) between the concepts "eating at a restaurant" and "ordering food" may help in associating "he" with "John".

The definitions given above could easily be enhanced to take inter clausal relationships into account. The importance of these inter clausal relationships becomes more apparent in examples with multiple referents, such as this one:

Example 8.2.4 *From his hotel room, John watched the old man in the park. He envied his freedom.*

In this case, syntactic expectations (especially for agentive NPs that start clauses; see van Dijk, & Kintsch, 1983, p. 167) may lead the reader to disambiguate "he" to "John" (i.e., to the subject or equivalently *agent* of the first sentence). Similarly, topical expectations could also favor "John" as the referent of "He" (i.e., the focus of the context is on John, not on the old man). Yet, the actual resolution could possibly only be confirmed through further inference, and it is possible that a reader may perceive the passage as being ambiguous.

The tactic suggested above also works for relative pronouns because the latter are typically simpler to disambiguate than personal pronouns since they are generally limited to prior referents. Consider, for example, a sentence in which there is only one antecedent for the relative pronoun:

Example 8.2.5 *John, who is hungry, eats.*

In this case, the cluster associated with "who" is replaced with the cluster for "John". As with personal pronouns, the substitution will be carried out even in the case of ungrammaticalities such as these:

Example 8.2.6 *The elephant who is hungry eats.*

Example 8.2.7 *John which I hate eats.*

Experimentation with the current prototype suggests that, in **IDIoT**, the difficulty associated with reference resolution consists in identifying which features are required for a resolution and which merely need to be checked afterwards by a disagreement feature. Consider, for example, this passage:

Example 8.2.8 *A man with a red hat, who was jogging nearby, saw the burglar escape.*

It is clear that the referent should at least be an animate entity in order for "red hat" to *not* be considered as a possible referent. In other words, the feature **"animate"** needs to be matched, but the more restrictive feature **"person"** may be checked only after resolution, that is, merely for noticing a disagreement with a convention.

Let us now turn to the general problem of definite NP resolution. The user of **IDIoT** may use a tactic quite similar to the one suggested for pronoun comprehension: Each definite NP triggers the candidacy of the buildable feature **referredNP**, whose expansion procedure tries to find a reference (i.e., a complete and *unique* cluster match). If several clusters are found as possible referents, the **findInclusiveReference** instruction fails, the candidacy of **referredNP** aborts, and the definite NP is left ambiguous. There can be several concurrent candidacies of **referredNP**, one for each definite NP to be resolved. Moreover, when a PP (or any other syntactic unit) is attached to a definite NP, the resulting complex definite NP needs to be resolved as a whole. Thus, the attachment of an NP as a subcluster of another NP inhibits the search for a reference for either initial NPs and triggers a new candidacy of **referredNP** for the new complex NP. In other words, it is the cluster associated with the complex NP (and which includes as a subcluster, the cluster associated with the PP) that will be matched.

Here are possible definitions (with the proviso that the actual reference resolution scheme I use in the current prototype of **IDIoT** is somewhat more complex):

KU definiteNP:

```
% A definite NP is an NP that starts with 'the'.
 constraint 1:
  ordered triggers: theArticle, NP
 ports:
       referredNP has a delay of 1 and is a customer
```

KU referredNP:

```
 constraint 1:
  triggers: definiteNP
% The second constraint recognizes the attachment of a PP to a
% definite NP. Note that the NP that is part of the PP does not
% have to be a definite NP and is not resolved by this case.
% Other similar constraints are not shown.
 constraint 2:
  ordered triggers: definiteNP, NP, attachPPtoNP
 ...


 expansion:
       getCluster u1 governing NP
       findInclusiveReference u2 to u1
       substitute u2 for u1
```

To illustrate this discussion, let us first consider Haddock's (1987) example:

Example 8.2.9 *the rabbit in the hat*

In the context there are three rabbits (R1, R2, and R3), two hats (H1 and H2), and one box (B1), where R1 is not in any container, R2 is in H1, and R3 in B1.

Despite the fact there are several rabbits in context, the NP is taken to have a unique referent. Haddock remarked that "any compositional accounts of NP semantics, . . . would judge [example 8.2.9] to be infelicitous" because they would fail to consider the referential context. Instead, he proposed an incremental interpretation stemming from a strictly word-by-word, left-to-right evaluation of the phrase (as is psychologically and intuitively well supported):

> If we assume that a hearer *incrementally* evaluates a semantic representation—after each word, say— the empty hat in the scene will never really be considered a viable candidate for the inner NP. When the word *rabbit* is reached, a hearer can collect together in his mind the set of rabbits in the context. After the preposition, this set can be refined to contain only rabbits which are *in* something and, most important, the hearer can start thinking about another set of objects, those which have rabbits in them. There is only one hat in this new set and so by the time the inner NP is processed a definite determiner sounds natural.

Haddock's approach seems to depend heavily on the unambiguous attachment of "in" to "the rabbit" since it is suggested that the preposition *immediately* restricts the set of rabbits to those that are *in* something. From my viewpoint, this restriction should not occur before the attachment of "in" to "the rabbit" is established. Therefore, to the best of my understanding, it is not clear how, in the same context, the following two sentences would be disambiguated by Haddock:

Example 8.2.10 *Put the rabbit in the car.*

Example 8.2.11 *Put the rabbit in the hat.*

In the first sentence, because the NP "the rabbit in the car" has no referent in context, but also because the verb "put" requires a direct object, the PP should not be immediately attached to the NP "the rabbit", but to the verb "put", and thus any one of the three rabbits is a possible referent for the NP "the rabbit". In other words, the syntactic and semantic constraints of the verb must be considered by the reference resolution process. Similarly, in the second sentence, if the PP is attached to "the rabbit", then the NP "the rabbit in the hat" has a unique referent, but the verb "put" is left without an obligatory direct object. Alternatively, if the PP is attached to the verb, then the NP "the rabbit" has several possible referents and is therefore ambiguous.

IDIoT's strategy does not require the complex symbolic mechanisms assumed by Haddock (e.g., extension variables, combinatory grammar and its functions and arguments, etc.) and does not resolve definite NPs by set attrition. Instead, I have specified KUs that grant precedence to verb constraints over referential felicity, but otherwise have used the **referredNP** feature to disambiguate NPs. More specifically, I introduce a feature, **forcedVPAttach**, for verbs that require a direct object (such as "to put"). This feature explicitly inhibits the feature **attachPPtoNP** if it becomes activated (as explained in chapter 10). Consequently, the attachment of the PP "in the hat" to the NP "the rabbit" being prevented, the feature **referredNP** only looks for a reference for "the rabbit", not for "the rabbit in the hat".

Using the same context as in the preceding examples, here is a rough scenario in **IDIoT** for the following sentence:

Example 8.2.12 *The rabbit in the hat is young.*

1. The definite NP "the rabbit" triggers the candidacy of **referredNP**. Since there are multiple possible referents for this NP, this candidacy fails.

2. Another candidacy of **referredNP** is triggered by "the hat". Again, since there are several hats in context, this candidacy fails.

3. When, and only when, the PP "in the hat" is attached to "the rabbit", a new candidacy of **referredNP** corresponding to "the rabbit in the hat" is triggered from the second constraint of **referredNP**. A unique referent is found for this NP, and the expansion procedure of **referredNP** replaces the cluster constructed for "the rabbit in the hat" with the cluster found as a reference. This substitution ipso facto resolves both definite NPs involved in the example. From this perspective, the suggested resolution strategy is not incremental in Haddock's sense, even though it proceeds in a word-by-word left-to-right order.

4. The rest of the sentence is processed.

Here is a list of similar independent examples working with the current prototype of **IDIoT**:

Example 8.2.13 *RB1 is the rabbit. RB2 is the rabbit. The rabbit eats.*

There is just one rabbit found. Much like the NP "the mayor" corresponds to a unique role. The two first sentences are taken to refer to the same unique rabbit.

Example 8.2.14 *RB1 is a rabbit in a hat. The rabbit in the hat eats.*

In the second sentence, the PP is attached to the NP "the rabbit", and then a unique referent is found.

Example 8.2.15 *RB1 is a rabbit. RB1 is in a hat. The rabbit eats.*

A unique referent is found.

Example 8.2.16 *RB1 is a rabbit. RB2 is a rabbit. The rabbit eats.*

Multiple referents are found, and thus there is no resolution.

Example 8.2.17 *RB1 is a rabbit. RB2 is in a box. RB1 is in a hat. RB2 is a rabbit. The rabbit in the box eats.*

A unique referent is found for "the rabbit in the box", not just for "the rabbit".

Example 8.2.18 *The young rabbit eats. The rabbit sleeps.*

A unique referent is found because the resolution process currently ignores adjectives.

Example 8.2.19 *RB1 is a rabbit in a hat. Put the rabbit in the hat.*

In the second sentence, a reference is found for "the rabbit" (to RB1) and the PP is attached to the verb. The PP is *not* attached to "the rabbit".

Example 8.2.20 *Put the rabbit.*

A syntactic conflict is detected.

Example 8.2.21 *Put the rabbit in the hat.*

As explained in chapter 10, the PP is attached to the VP, which blocks, in this case, the PP from being attached to the NP. No reference resolution occurs for "the rabbit".

Example 8.2.22 *RB1 is a rabbit. RB2 is a rabbit. Put the rabbit in the box.*

In the third sentence, the PP is attached to "put". Consequently, the NP "the rabbit" is the sole reference to resolve. In this case, given there are multiple referents (RB1 and RB2), resolution fails and "the rabbit" is left ambiguous.

Example 8.2.23 *RB1 is a rabbit in a hat. RB2 is a rabbit. Put the rabbit in the hat in the box.*

The third sentence is interpreted as "Put in the box the rabbit that is in the hat" (using more complex PP-attachment rules).

It is important to understand that these examples are simplistic. In particular, as with pronoun comprehension, inferences are extremely important for the task of definite NP reference resolution. Consider these examples:

Example 8.2.24 *John was pale: The boy was sick.*

Example 8.2.25 *John was pale. The boy was sick, and John feared he would die.*

Example 8.2.26 *John was pale. The boy was sick, and John feared his son would die.*

In the first example, "the boy" *could* be taken to refer to John, especially given the role of the colon. However, this becomes less probable in the second example, in which the explicit reference to John appears to eliminate the possibility of having John refer to "the boy". And in the third example, it seems unacceptable that John could refer to "the boy", mostly because of the probable inference that "the boy" is John's son. Such inferences greatly complicate the reference resolution process. For example, such inferences could dynamically modify the cluster to be matched during the resolution process. In the example, the cluster associated with "the boy" eventually gets to reflect that the boy is the son of John. Therefore, referential resolution of "the boy" to John would become invalid, even if it had already happened. In other words, the inference would either block the resolution or force this resolution to be "undone", a complex task to achieve, as experimentation has taught us! The "safest" strategy consists of adopting the delayed hypothesis (see Haberlandt, & Graesser, 1990) and waiting until the end of a sentence to actually carry out reference resolution. This is easily achieved in **IDIoT** but somewhat psychologically less plausible in my opinion. Yet another strategy, the hypothesis/verification approach, is quite difficult to realize in the current prototype of **IDIoT**: Some temporary resolution would eventually have to be finalized, but currently **IDIoT** does not accommodate the notion of temporary cluster operations.

Furthermore, I want to emphasize that such dynamic inferences should not be confused with expectations, especially with expectations due to *schema-matching*. Consider this passage:

Example 8.2.27 *John enters the park. He sits on the bench.*

One possible scenario consists of having a reader build an inference between "park" and "bench". In this case, "the bench" would be resolved to "the bench in the park". Alternatively, a reader may expect a bench after having read the word "park". In essence, this expectation short-circuits the need for any resolution, "the bench" is prespecified as "the bench in the park". Similarly, in the following example, "the waiter" may be expected:

Example 8.2.28 *John dines at the restaurant tonight. He orders caviar and savors it slowly. He then leaves a big tip for the waiter and walks out.*

More specifically, the features **orderFood**, **eatFood**, **payFood**, **leaveTipFor-Waiter**, and **exitRestaurant** are perceived as substeps of the schematic feature **eatAtRestaurant**, that is, are organized as subclusters of the latter feature. In this case, the NP "the waiter" is not referentially resolved but, instead, expected by virtue of belonging to the schema **eatAtRestaurant**. Consequently, in the current prototype of **IDIoT**, an NP that becomes detected as a result of an expectation does *not* trigger the candidacy of the feature **referredNP**.

Finally, complex issues such as the treatment of cataphoric or deitic pronouns are beyond the scope of most of the existing models of reference resolution. Yet, cataphoric pronouns (i.e., pronouns that have a referent *after* them) can be readily tackled in **IDIoT** because candidacies last a short amount of time, thus making it possible to have the referent *after* its referring NP. As for deitic pronouns, van Dijk and Kintsch (1983, p. 162) claimed that the treatment of this type of pronoun is quite similar to that of more usual ones, but this remains to be proven in general, and, in particular, with the current prototype of **IDIoT**. In other words, deitic pronouns remain an open issue at this point in time.

8.3   COGNITIVE QUANTIFICATION

This section reports on work currently undertaken by Walid Saba (Corriveau and Saba, 1995) under the supervision of the author, addressing the issue of quantification within the framework put forth by **IDIoT**. The current prototype of **IDIoT** will require some enhancements in order to support the proposed solution.

Virtually all computational models of quantification are based on some variation of the theory of generalized quantifiers (Barwise, & Cooper, 1981) and Montague's (1974) "proper treatment of quantification" (henceforth PTQ). Using the formal tools of intensional logic and possible-worlds semantics, PTQ models are able to cope with certain context-sensitive aspects of natural language by devising interpretation relative to a context, where the context is taken to be an *index* denoting a possible-world and a point in time: The *intension* (meaning) of an expression is taken to be a function from contexts to *extensions* (denotations). For example, the word "president", is ambiguous, unless interpreted relative to a place and a point in time. Within this framework of *indexical semantics*, models need not be limited to a single index. For example, Kaplan (1979) suggested adding other "coordinates" (i.e., indices) defining speaker, listener, location, and so forth. Using this extended model, he showed how an utterance such as "I called you yesterday" expresses a different content, whenever the speaker, the listener, or the time of the utterance is changed.

The intensions (meanings) of *quantifiers* (e.g., "every", "each", "some", "the", "a", etc.), however, as well as other functional words, such as sentential connectives (e.g., "and", "or", etc.), are taken to be constant. That is, the interpretation of such words is the same *regardless* of the context (Forbes, 1989). In such a framework, all quantifiers have their "meaning" grounded in terms of two logical operators: $\forall x$ (for all), and $\exists x$ (there exists) (which themselves can be expressed using disjunction, conjunction, and negation). Consequently, all quantifiers are modeled, indirectly, by two simple logical connectives: negation and either conjunction or disjunction. From this standpoint, quantifier ambiguity is often reduced to "scoping" ambiguity, a problem that has been extensively studied by formal semanticists (Cooper, 1983; Le Pore, & Garson, 1983; Partee, 1984) and computational linguists (Moran, 1988; Alshawi, 1990; Pereira, 1990; Harper, 1992). The problem can be illustrated by the following examples:

Example 8.3.1 *Every student in CS404 received a course outline.*

Example 8.3.2 *Every student in CS404 received a grade.*

The syntactic structures of these examples are identical, and thus, according to Montague's PTQ, both sentences would have identical logical translations. Hence, the translation in PTQ of the second sentence would incorrectly state that students in CS404 received different course outlines. Instead, the desired reading is one where "a" has a wider scope than "every", resulting in a translation that asserts that there is a single course outline for the course CS404, an outline that all students received. Clearly, such resolution depends on general knowledge of the domain: Typically, students in the same class receive the same course outline, but different grades. However, PTQ models, due to their strict *compositionality* (i.e., the meaning of the whole is the sum of the meanings of its parts), cannot cope with such inferences. Consequently, a number of *syntactically* motivated rules for resolving scoping ambiguities are typically suggested. Generally, these rules define an ad hoc (see Moran, 1988) "semantic" ordering between functional words, that is, an ordering fitted to a particular set of examples.

Such an approach is problematic, in my opinion, for several reasons:

1. From chapter 2, following Rastier (1991), I reject propositional (logic-based) approaches to language. Recall that Rastier remarked that there is quite a long way between trying to reduce context to indices and determining *how* to set these indices.

2. As argued by Zeevat (1989), the scope of quantifiers is usually given by the "linguistic context rather than by the linguistic rule that is responsible for their appearance in a sentence".

3. Partitioning a priori quantifier ambiguity into scoping and other "types" of ambiguity inevitably leads to the labeling problem (see section 3.2) and to ad hoc rules that are too specialized to address the general problem of quantification.

Not surprisingly, I instead suggest that a quantifier be treated as an ambiguous word whose interpretation is always contextual and highly dependent on time and memory constraints. More specifically, I propose reconciling quantification with both the non deterministic and time-constrained nature of linguistic comprehension. To use Shastri's (1993) terminology, we need a *reflexive* model of quantification resolution, as opposed to the existing *reflective* models. This seems possible if we view a quantifier as an ambiguous word whose interpretation is not only contextual, but also may involve complex time-dependent inferences. Lexical disambiguation is discussed in the next chapter, but given the exploratory nature of this section, let me briefly elaborate on viewing quantifiers as ambiguous words here.

First, we have already seen (in examples 8.3.1 and 8.3.2) that the interpretation of a quantifier ("a" in this case) may depend on an inference. More precisely, I suggest that

1. *in example 8.3.1:*, an inference, in the form of a path between features **student** and **courseOutline** disambiguates the determiner "a" to mean "the". In other words, "a" is ambiguous. That is, it has several possible *candidate* interpretations, one being selected through the inference. Through further inferencing associated with reference resolution, "the course outline" is interpreted as "the outline of the course taken by the student". In other words, the outline is recognized as an attribute (i.e., a feature of the cluster) of the course taken by the student (in this case CS404).

2. *in example 8.3.2:*, an inference in the form of a path between **student** and **grade** not only again disambiguates the word "grade" (which has several potential interpretations), but also disambiguates the determiner "a" to mean "a unique". In other words, in this case,

the grade is recognized as an attribute of the student.

The point to be grasped is that my current research with Saba (1995) suggests that there is no need to introduce ad hoc rules to handle the scoping of the quantifiers. Rather, the latter act as ambiguous words. Given that in **IDIoT**, inferencing participates in lexical disambiguation (see next chapter), quantifiers can therefore be disambiguated through inferencing. Furthermore, the interpretation of a quantifier can itself trigger further interpretation (e.g., through reference resolution, as in example 8.3.1).

Second, we propose that the quantifiers "most", "some", and "all" be grounded in memory, that is, have a strictly contextual interpretation dependent on timing and memory constraints. Consider, these examples:

Example 8.3.3 *Most Cubans like rum more than vodka.*

Example 8.3.4 *All Cubans like rum more than vodka.*

Example 8.3.5 *Some Cubans like rum more than vodka.*

In contrast to PTQ models, we claim that these examples are typically not processed extensionally, that is, by doing an exhaustive search over the set of Cubans to determine some truth value. Instead, we introduce the notion of a *referential set* with respect to both the capacity of STM and the timespan of the race associated with the disambiguation of these quantifiers. Intuitively, a referential set is the set of all instances of a "concept" that are *reached* within the timespan of a candidacy race. For example, the referential set for the previous examples consists of the instances of Cubans reachable in a particular context (with respect to expectations, contents of memory, race deadlines, decay rate, etc.). We suggest that the interpretation of "most", "some" and "all" (and most likely of similar words such as "many", "several", "each", "every", etc.) depends on the cardinality of this referential set. In **IDIoT**, this set is to be implemented as a buildable feature whose expansion procedure

1. accesses the top NP (i.e., the most recent NP) that follows the quantifier.

2. uses repeatedly (through a looping mechanism not yet supported in **IDIoT**) a **findInclusiveReference** instruction to retrieve the instances corresponding to this NP.

3. for each retrieved instance, increases the strength of its output presence signal (i.e., the looping mechanism correlates the number of time it succeeds with the output signal of the feature).

Given this feature, **buildReferentialSet**, here is a possible tactic for processing "most":

1. Trigger **buildReferentialSet** once both the word "most" and the NP that *follows* it have been detected. (I am not considering here phrases such as "most of all", which should probably be treated as idioms).

2. The feature **buildReferentialSet** assembles the referential set and sends a presence signal to the feature **mostCheck**. Most importantly, the "strength" (see chapter 4) of this signal is proportional to the cardinality of the referential set.

3. The feature **mostCheck** is strictly a threshold feature. In other words, it becomes detected if, and only if, the presence signal from **buildReferentialSet** is "strong" enough. If this is the case, then the quantifier of the top NP is disambiguated to feature **majorityQuantifier**.

4. Because quantifiers are being treated in **IDIoT** as ambiguous words, the word "most" has at least one other candidate interpretation. This default interpretation simply disambiguates "most" to **indeterminateCardinalityQuantifier** as the quantifier of the top NP. More precisely, **mostDefault** also receives the output signal from **buildReferentialSet** but has an extremely low threshold (i.e., it is easy to satisfy). However, it also has **mostCheck** as an explicit exception (in order to give the preference to the latter). The feature, **mostCheck**, explicitly inhibits **mostDefault** if it becomes activated. Thus, **mostDefault** will only become detected if **mostCheck** fails.

The same implementation strategy appears to be directly applicable to "some" and "all" (and similar words). In essence, only the threshold of **someCheck** and **allCheck**, respectively, differs, the former having a lower ("easier") threshold than **mostCheck**, the latter, a higher one. Furthermore, in order to account for apparent infinite (or more exactly, indeterminate) sets, I suggest that a cluster associated with a concept have the attribute (i.e., the feature) **indeterminateCardinality** if

1. the number of known instances associated with this concept (with respect to a *specific* reader) exceeds STM capacity (In other words, a concept will acquire the attribute, indeterminate cardinality, if not all its instances can be retrieved within the timespan of a candidacy race),

2. or the concept itself cannot be exhaustively searched (e.g., the concept of "men", or "cubans").

The feature **buildReferentialSet** would then first check if the top NP has indeterminate cardinality, and then *weaken* its output signal if **indeterminateCardinality** was indeed present in the cluster of the top NP. In other words, the cardinality of **buildReferentialSet** becomes less relevant if we are dealing with an indeterminate number of instances. For example, if I don't know any Cuban(s), but I know there is a large number of them, then I will probably be more hesitant to interpret "all cubans" as "all instances of cubans". More likely, I will either leave the quantifier ambiguous (see chapter 9) or disambiguate it to some default interpretation such as the one for "some". Should I fail to notice that my set of Cubans has indeterminate cardinality, that is, should this feature not be reached in time (by **buildReferentialSet**), it is also possible that I would base my interpretation of "all" on only a few quickly retrieved instances. In essence, in this case, I would "jump to conclusions" using very partial "evidence", a very human sin. Interestingly, such a strategy is in agreement with the findings of psychological experiments on children ages 5 to 12 (e.g., Freeman, & Stedmon, 1986) that suggest that quantification is often dependent, among other things, on the size of the quantified concept. Our use of feature **indeterminateCardinality** is also close in spirit to Johnson-Laird's (1994) argument that an appropriate model must allow sets of possibilities to be considered in a "highly compressed way" due to the processing limitations of STM.

The key idea of this proposal remains to treat quantifiers as ambiguous words that have a default interpretation. For example, "a" could be left ambiguous (i.e., unresolved) or default to "there exists" to signal its inherent indefiniteness. To illustrate this point with another quantifier, consider the following examples:

Example 8.3.6 *This room is full of overambitious accountants. Everyone works at least 14 hours.*

Example 8.3.7 *John's report on Japanese professionals is remarkable. Everyone works at least 14 hours.*

It seems probable that, through a combination of disambiguation and reference resolution, "everyone" will be interpreted as "each accountant" in example 8.3.6, but as "most" in example 8.3.7, given that the set of Japanese professionals has most likely indeterminate cardinality for most readers.

Also, consider sentences such as these:

Example 8.3.8 *Cubans like rum more than vodka.*

Example 8.3.9 *Students in CS404 are not allowed to work in groups.*

Example 8.3.10 *A Frenchman is trustworthy.*

Example 8.3.11 *A child starts to talk around two years.*

Here we must deal with "implicit" quantifiers. In example 8.3.8, the probable interpretation would be "most cubans like rum more than vodka", whereas in example 8.3.9, we likely have an implicit "all". I suggest that all plural and indeterminate NPs always trigger an implicit quantifier (which is generally explicit in French). By default, this implicit quantifier will be interpreted as "some", that is, as the least determinate of the quantifiers. Other possible candidate interpretations for this implicit quantifier include "most" and "all", disambiguation depending on the use of **buildReferentialSet** as with other quantifiers.

In the end, our proposal is still oversimplified and needs further research. For example, Saba is currently investigating how a cognitively plausible approach to quantification should avoid contradicting "valid" inferences. More precisely, his goal is to develop a model that would preserve a number of formal properties that are generally attributed to quantifiers:

1. Persistence (left increasing monotonicity),

2. Right increasing monotonicity,

3. Left decreasing monotonicity,

4. Reflexivity, and

5. Symmetry.

Formal definitions of these properties can be found in a recent paper (Corriveau, & Saba, 1995). According to the symmetry property, for example, if "some man from Detroit owns a 1965 Corvette" is true, then the set of "those who own a 1965 Corvette" must include "some man from Detroit".

To conclude, I must agree with the argument of Fauconnier (1994) that logic usually abstracts a solution that could work rather well in some idealized and controlled situation (referred to as "models" in formal logic), but fails to capture the idiosyncratic nature of human languages. In other words, to me, the notion of "valid" inferences remains problematic because it abstracts away from human performance. However, I do add that our proposed strategy for quantification does not preclude the use of "logical schemas" or "mental models" to process specific *patterns* of inferences such as syllogisms (e.g., Johnson-Laird, 1982). Indeed, Shastri (1993) suggested that formal reasoning can be handled within the framework of a spreading activation.

Chapter 9

Word Sense Disambiguation

9.1 INTRODUCTION TO LEXICAL DISAMBIGUATION

"Ah yes, the word! The word is as central to psycholinguistics as the cell is to biologists" (Balota, 1994). The task of word (or lexical) perception can be decomposed into two separate facets (Gernsbacher, 1994):

1. **word recognition**: perceptual recognition, whether spoken or visual.

2. **word sense disambiguation**: apprehension of meaning.

These facets have been extensively studied in psycholinguistics (e.g., Marslen-Wilson, 1989; Balota, Flores d'Arcais, & Rayner, 1990; Balota, 1994; Lively, Pisoni, & Goldfinger, 1994; Simpson, 1994) and, consequently, I will merely summarize here some of the issues.

9.1.1 On Word Recognition

Neither spoken nor visual word recognition are addressed in the current prototype of **IDIoT**. Yet the latter problem (see Balota, 1994) is definitely relevant to the understanding of written text and thus will be briefly discussed here.

The problem of letter recognition in itself constitutes a formidable challenge (see Hofstadter, 1985) from a computational viewpoint. Most likely, we must possess some sort of prototypical pattern (often called a *demon*) for each letter, a pattern that defines what is an "a", a "b", and so forth. in terms of lines, angles, curves. However, even for this specific aspect of visual perception, it appears that norms cannot account by themselves for the vast spectrum of "readable" hand-writing styles.

Closer to the problem of text understanding, the fundamental question of word recognition asks how we get from letters to words. After decades of research, we essentially still do not know the answer. As a matter of fact, controversies abound in word recognition literature. In particular, there is widespread disagreement on the role of phonology during lexical access (see Johnston, Rugg, & Scott 1987). More specifically, the *dual route* hypothesis states that two processes equally participate (most likely in parallel) in word recognition:

1. The *assembled route* recognizes a word by assembling together the sounds corresponding to the syllables of this word. In this case, phonological neighborhoods (i.e., sets of words with similar pronunciation) are important to understanding mistakes such as confusing "live" and "leave".

2. The *direct route* recognizes words from their orthography, that is, from the actual strings of characters forming them. In this case, orthographical neighborhoods (i.e., sets of words with similar spelling) are important in accounting for misreading "butler" for "butter" in the sentence, "The butter did it".

Some researchers have argued for no predominance between the two routes (e.g., Roderick, 1986). Others (e.g., Williams, 1993) contended that the phonological route is the dominant one of the two, and yet others (e.g., Martin, & Jensen, 1988; Radeau, Morais, & Dewier, 1989) minimized (if not simply rejected) the role of phonology in word recognition.

This dilemma is complicated by several other issues:

1. the possible differences in the time-course of each route (see Williams, 1993), the phonological one typically being viewed as the fastest of the two.

2. the possible role of context during word recognition and its effect on the time-course of word recognition:

a) Some researchers (Masson, 1988, 1989; Till, Mross, & Kintsch, 1988) assumed that perceptual analysis is independent of context and precedes the apprehension of meaning. In other words, the context may *prime* (see Ratcliff, 1987), that is, set up the expectation, of a certain meaning, but such semantic priming is taken to come after and be independent of word recognition per se.

b) Others (Colombo, & Williams, 1990; Tabossi, & Zardon, 1993; Kim, & Goetz, 1994) instead hypothesized an omnipresent *interaction* between context and word recognition processes. In other words, the context may prime the recognition of a given word: Word recognition and word sense disambiguation are then assumed to intimately work together.

3. the effect of familiarity (e.g., Mandler, 1987), word frequency (e.g., Grainger, 1990; Allen, McNeal, & Kvak, 1992) and other variables (see Balota, 1994) on the time-course of word recognition (either directly or through the organization of the lexicon). For example, does a word that has several higher frequency neighbors take more time to be recognized?

4. the choice between two distinct classes of models for word recognition (in which some models such as the one of Norris (1986) more or less fit):

> a) the *activation* models based on Morton's (1969) logogen model (including recent connectionist offsprings) in which frequency is coded via resting level activations (see Balota, 1994). The high-frequency words will have higher resting level activations than low-frequency words. Therefore, in order to surpass a word recognition threshold, the high-frequency words will need less activation than the low-frequency words.

> b) the *ordered search* models exemplified by Forster's (1979) work in which the lexicon is serially searched with high-frequency words being accessed before low-frequency ones.

5. the idiosyncracy of neighborhoods (e.g., Holligan, & Johnston, 1988), an obstacle that raises methodological problems for psycholinguists.

In the end, this list of difficult questions may explain why models of text understanding have generally ignored the problem of word recognition, but some appear to already have the "hooks" to address this problem. In particular, in **IDIoT**, the existence of activation thresholds and retrievability coefficients, as well as the use of parallel spreading activation, suggest that an activation model could be readily implementable. Moreover, the notion of time-constrained candidacies appears to be very close to the candidacy model proposed by Norris (1986).

9.1.2 Introduction to Word Sense Disambiguation

The problem of lexical ambiguity is often regarded as a touchstone for theories of linguistic comprehension (e.g., Birnbaum, 1985). A word (or a sequence of words) may have more than one interpretation. For example, the noun, "ball", can be interpreted as "spherical object", "baseball", "testis", and "formal dance", among other definitions. This problem of lexical disambiguation (see Ratcliff, 1987; Kawamoto, 1993, for an introduction; and Gorfein, 1989; Simpson, 1994, for details) raises two difficult psycholinguistic questions:

- The problem of *lexical access*: "Do people consider (unconsciously) some or all of the possible meanings of an ambiguous word, or do context and/or expectations take them straight to the 'correct' meaning?" (Hirst, 1987, p.85).

- The problem of the *decision point*: "If more than one meaning is accessed, how and when is a choice made?" (Hirst, 1987).

Hirst (1987, section 4.3) suggested that alternatives for the lexical access problem are the following:

1. the context may limit the process to a single access or influence disambiguation only after all possible interpretations have been accessed, or

2. interpretations are accessed in order of frequency of usage, the disambiguation process stopping as soon as an acceptable meaning is found.

As for the decision-point problem, he adds (Hirst, 1987, p. 85) that there are three possibilities: "that the choice is virtually immediate; that it does not happen until the end of the clause (or some smaller syntactic unit), with the several meanings remaining around until then; and that it happens as soon as enough information is available, whether this be immediately or later".

Hirst concluded (1987, pp. 94–95):

> There are clearly many questions yet to be resolved in the study of human lexical access and disambiguation. However, this much seems clear: in many cases, more than one meaning of an ambiguous word is accessed. Semantic priming and frequency of a particular sense can facilitate lexical access and disambiguation, and in some cases cause one meaning to be accessed to the exclusion of others.

This simplified account of the issues of lexical ambiguity, however, does not reflect the multitude of difficulties associated with this problem. Consider these, for example:

1. The absence of consensus on the role of the "dominant" meaning for disambiguation: Some researchers (e.g., Simpson, & Krueger, 1991) have argued for the importance of this "dominant" meaning, whereas others (e.g., Millis, & Button, 1989) have significantly downplayed it.

2. The role of syntactic judgments (e.g., Warner, & Glass, 1987; Eizirik, Barbosa, & Mendes, 1993) and "commonsense" inferences (e.g., Gerrig, & Littman, 1990) during disambiguation: In particular, the interaction between "the" grammar and the context remains problematic. For example, Frazier and Rayner (1987, 1990) suggested that "semantic commitments are minimized, occurring only when mutually incompatible choices are presented by the grammar or when forced by the need to maintain consistency between the interpretation of the current phrase and any already processed contextual material". Most researchers, however, do not adopt such a grammar-first approach to disambiguation.

3. The importance of memory constraints with respect to lexical ambiguity: Contrast, for example, Martin (1993), who rejected such importance, to Miyake, Just, and Carpenter (1994), who contended that readers with a large WM capacity ("high-span" readers) can maintain multiple interpretations of an unresolved lexical ambiguity longer than those with a small WM capacity ("low-span" readers).

4. The language specific aspects of ambiguity (see Schogt, 1976) and, in particular, the time-course for understanding different kinds of words (e.g., Taft, 1990 for functional words).

5. The role and organization of the lexicon: Some models, such as the one of Pustejovsky and Bergler (1991), attempt to handle all complexities of disambiguation within the lexicon. Such an approach is typically quite problematic. For example, Sharkey and Sharkey (1989) rejected the model of Kintsch (1988), which essentially hard-wires context into the lexicon.

6. The role of emotions during disambiguation (see MacLeod, & Cohen, 1993).

7. The relevance of aphasia and, more generally, of evidence from neuroscience to models of lexical disambiguation (see Gigley, 1988).

Not surprisingly, such difficulties have been generally ignored in computational models of lexical disambiguation, especially in text understanding systems. Lexical disambiguation is typically reduced by schema-matching approaches to the recognition of a particular context with respect to a set of knowledge structures that specify a priori all recognizable contexts. For example, in **BORIS** (Dyer, 1983, p. 181) the word "gin" is interpreted as **LIQUID** if the context "involves" the semantic primitive **INGEST**, and as **CARD-GAME**, if the context involves **COMPETITIVE-ACTIVITY**. Dyer (1983) added that a word may be disambiguated in either a top-down or a bottom-up fashion. In the top-down case, disambiguation corresponds to the satisfaction of an expectation set up by the words preceding the ambiguous one. In the bottom-up case, the ambiguous word is assumed to spawn a disambiguation demon that searches the current context for a match with one of its disambiguation rules. Hirst (1987, section 4.1) explained that the choice of the knowledge structure(s) (e.g., scripts, MOPS, etc.) corresponding to a given context constitutes the major difficulty of such an approach to disambiguation in that it ignores the local syntactic and semantic cues provided by nearby words. Both spreading activation (e.g., Cottrell, 1984, 1989; Alshawi, 1987) and PDP (e.g., Mayberry, & Miikkulainen, 1994) approaches to lexical disambiguation appear to be better at accounting for such local disambiguating cues and at handling context. In particular, I must emphasize the richness of Kawamoto's (1993) PDP model.

However, in the end, we are back to the conclusions of chapter 2: Symbolic approaches, whether they specify more or less complex rules (e.g., Wilks's (1975) preferences) or instead reject general disambiguation rules in favor of a vast number of loosely related sets of rules associated with each individual word (e.g., Small, 1980, 1983; Taft, 1990), are not grounded. On the other hand, PDP models do not scale up to the complexities of the problem at hand.

In order to illustrate this absence of grounding, let us briefly review the model put forth by Hirst (1987, 1988a, 1988b), which I feel is close in spirit to the approach adopted in **IDIoT**.

Hirst proposed the notion of *Polaroid Words* (*Polaroid* is a trademark of the Polaroid Corporation) for lexical disambiguation. Such words are fully integrated with his **ABSITY** semantic interpreter. Upon reading an ambiguous word, Absity is given a "fake" semantic object that acts like a self-developing Polaroid photograph of the disambiguated concept. Hirst elaborated (1987, p. 97):

> By the time the sentence is complete, this photograph will be a fully developed picture of the desired semantic object. And even as the picture develops, Absity will be able to manipulate the photograph, build it into a structure, and indeed do everything with it that it could do with a fully developed photograph, except look at the final picture.

> Moreover, like real Polaroid photographs, these will have the property
> that as development takes place, the partly developed picture will be
> viewable and usable in its degraded form.

A Polaroid Word (hereafter PW) consists of a disambiguation procedure, one
PW existing for each syntactic category. When a new PW is needed, an
instance of the appropriate type is cloned and is given a packet of knowledge
about the word for which it will be responsible. These packets contain only
lexical knowledge in the case of nouns but include some "world knowledge"
in the case of verbs, since these "can get quite idiosyncratic about their case
flags" (Hirst, 1987, p. 106). Upon its instantiation and, if required, each time
a new word is input, the PW attempts to narrow down its possible interpretations by looking for "strong" paths built by the marker passing component of
the model and by communicating with its "friends":

> Verbs are friends with the prepositions and nouns they dominate;
> prepositions are friends with the nouns of their prepositional phrase
> and with other prepositions; and noun modifiers are friends with the
> noun they modify. In addition, if a prepositional phrase is a candidate
> for attachment to a noun phrase, then the preposition is a friend of the
> head noun of the NP to which it may be attached. . . . The intent of
> friendship constraints is to restrict the amount of searching for infor-
> mation that a PW has to do; the constraints reflect the intuition that a
> word has only a very limited sphere of influence with regard to selec-
> tional restrictions and the like (Hirst, 1987, subsection 5.3.2).

The PW eliminates any of its meanings that are incompatible with those of its
friends. As for the paths supplied by the marker-passing component, their
"strength" is evaluated with respect to "magic numbers" set with respect to the
two following heuristics (Hirst, 1987, subsection 5.6.3):

1. the shorter the path, the stronger the path.

2. the more arcs that leave a node, the weaker the connections through
that node.

Summarizing, Hirst (1987, p. 111) wrote:

> Polaroid Words with marker passing are not a replacement for infer-
> ence and pragmatics in word sense and case disambiguation; rather,
> they serve to reduce substantially the number of times that these must
> be employed.

The current implementation of Polaroid Words does not have such an inference or pragmatics system available to it and does not use syntactic cues nor the "global context" (for which there is no representation). Also, the treatment of figurative language remains problematic in that such usage typically violates the rules of disambiguation postulated for literal English (Hirst, 1987, section 5.4).

Again, the major drawback of such symbolic approaches is that the complex algorithms, "magic numbers" and data structures they use are not grounded.

9.2 LEXICAL DISAMBIGUATION WITH IDIoT

As explained in chapter 2, and in accordance with reader-based hermeneutics, my research does not focus on some abstract language specified by a dictionary, nor on some "literal English", but rather on the *idiolect* of a specific user. In other words, the notion of a "universal lexicon", that is, a correct and exhaustive list of all possible meanings for any given word in a language, is abandoned. It is the user who must decide on the "boundaries" (or conceptual distance) between concepts. Similarly, it seems that existing models that statically capture rules for disambiguation, are limited to a literal interpretation of words and can never take into account the actual run-time context of a reading. I attempt to address these problems later in this chapter. First, let me comment on the general approach I adopt.

As previously mentioned, Small (1980, 1983) viewed language as being too irregular for generalizations above the lexical level. Instead, he suggested the coding of an individual and large disambiguation procedure for each word, an approach that requires a lot of time, reflecting the idiosyncratic nature and long apprenticeship of linguistic communication. Such an approach displeases those researchers who search for regularities in language. Although Small's strategy is undeniably inconvenient from an engineering point of view, I feel very close to it because, in the spirit of reader-based comprehension, it is based on the acceptance of human idiosyncrasies rather than on the quest for the correct set of rules and algorithms. The fundamental difference between **IDIoT** and Small's work is that I attempt to "de-proceduralize", that is, to avoid the use of a priori static algorithms for the specification of his word experts by instead having the user express them as knowledge units (see chapter 4). Furthermore, given this grounded standpoint, the notions of polysemy, homonymy, and categorial ambiguity (see Schogt, 1976) are not considered useful here because they introduce semantic distinctions that are irrelevant to a trivial algorithm. It is left to the user of **IDIoT** to specify features corresponding to rules that would or would not take these distinctions into account.

The proposed model of memory is particularly well-suited to implement a disambiguation strategy similar in spirit to Hirst's (1987) Polaroid Words. In **IDIoT**, words are disambiguated over a period of time, that is, the set of candidate interpretations for a given word w may shrink over time. Let me elaborate.

If the word w is ambiguous, then, at the time of its detection, all possible interpretations of w are notified and can become candidates for detection. This is easily realized by having these interpretations specified as the candidates (see chapter 4) of w. Recall that each candidate has a certain retrievability at that given point in time, and that communication is taken to be asynchronous. Therefore, all possible interpretations of w become candidates, *but* these candidacies do not necessarily start at the same time. Furthermore, in the case where one of the possible interpretations of w is already being expected, if the signal received from w triggers it, then it immediately becomes detected. Also, the expectation mechanism in **IDIoT** can be used to model the phenomenon of semantic priming, as illustrated in the next section.

Because candidacies may span the processing of a few words (or even clauses) after the input of an ambiguous word w, they are not limited to considering the context existing at their start, but in fact can take into account the context as it is modified over their time span. In other words, both the evidence existing at the start of a candidacy and the information established from subsequent words can affect disambiguation.

Also, if candidate x has candidate y specified as an exception of its triggered constraint, then the candidacy of x necessarily takes its maximum time span in order for y to be given the opportunity to become detected and possibly inhibit x. Because exceptions are not automatically reciprocal, y may not have x as an exception and therefore may become detected at as soon as it can be. Thus, the user may specify through the exceptions of the possible interpretations of w a disambiguation strategy that favors some candidates over others by having the former being immediately detectable whereas the latter must take the maximal time allocated to a candidacy. (The ability for one KU to dynamically modify the retrievability of another, an enhancement discussed in chapter 12, would make this strategy more dynamic.)

In **IDIoT**, disambiguation may also occur through the process of reference resolution. Detection by referencing is possible only if the ambiguous word is explicitly repeated after having been disambiguated in the nearby context, as in the following example:

Example 9.2.1 *John poured the gin but Mary refused: she had always hated* *gin.*

In this example, the first occurrence of "gin" is disambiguated to the feature **alcoholicBeverageGin** by constructing a path to the verb "pour." If the STM capacity allows for a context that spans at least a few words, then a reference is quickly found for the second occurrence of "gin", which is thus also disambiguated to the feature **alcoholicBeverageGin**. This referencing ability, which does not appear to exist in other models of lexical disambiguation, seems to be a plausible psychological approach, one where a repetition sufficiently "close" (with respect to time and STM capacity) to the original disambiguation, is not treated as an ambiguity but as a readily detectable reference. In support of this tactic, Hirst (1987) remarked that using two (or more) different senses of a same content word in the same sentence usually leads to a garden path effect (see Marcus, 1980), that is, to a perceived semantic awkwardness.

The act of disambiguation per se proceeds in **IDIoT** from the execution of the expansion procedure of a possible interpretation that becomes detected. This procedure first accesses the cluster with the original ambiguous word w, and then proceeds to modify this cluster. At an abstract level, if x is a possible interpretation of w that becomes detected, then the expansion procedure of x could either rename the feature **w** to **x**, or simply add **x** to the cluster of w.

Subsequent instructions of the expansion procedure of x could typically add the features that define x, as well as specialize some of the features associated with w. For example, disambiguating the word "gin' to the beverage could replace the feature **"gin"** with the feature **alcoholicBeverageGin** in the cluster created by **"gin"** and add some information about **alcoholicBeverageGin**. Because all "knowledge" is user-specified, the word "gin" may be disambiguated to a more general feature **alcoholicBeverage** that would govern another cluster capturing the kind of alcoholic beverage, as in the following expansion procedure:

```
getCluster u1 governing 'gin'
addFeature alcoholicBeverage in u1
getNewCluster u2
addFeature kindOf to u2
addSubCluster u2 to u1
getNewCluster u3
addFeature gin to u3
addSubCluster u3 to u2
```

In summary, the disambiguation step per se simply consists of accessing the cluster of w and modifying it to reflect the disambiguation of w to x; the specificity of the resulting cluster depends entirely on a user's KB.

Similarly, it is left to the user of **IDIoT** to decide on a feature-by-feature basis which candidates "know" about and can affect the candidacy of the others. More precisely, if candidate x is an exception to the triggered constraint of candidate y, or if x is explicitly sent an inhibition signal by the output strategy of the triggered constraint of y, then the detection of y will inhibit the candidacy of x.

Given that several candidacies may succeed, a *resolution strategy* is typically needed. More specifically, I do not assume that a single candidate must be the winner. Clearly, it is always possible that no candidacy succeeds. Conversely, there could be several "winning" candidates. A resolution strategy (implemented as a KU managing a set of candidates) could then decide to deactivate all candidates (leaving the input truly ambiguous), or it could invoke (i.e., trigger) some specific rule (i.e., yet another KU) which, in turn, would choose the winner. These different strategies are grounded in that they only involve having some KU(s) inhibit others. Several semantic resolution strategies have also been suggested (e.g., Granger, & Holbrook, 1983), and it has been stressed that not only different readers may use different strategies, but also, that a reader may use different strategies for different tasks and even for the same subtask at different points in time (e.g., because of a different context). The modeling of such semantic strategies lies beyond the scope of this book and will be addressed in the future.

IDIoT's approach to disambiguation is similar to Hirst's (1987) Polaroid Words in that

1. a semantic object, namely the cluster constructed by w, is initially associated with the ambiguous word w.

2. this semantic object is just another element of STM, and thus is fully integrated with the rest of the context and can be manipulated by other KUs.

3. this semantic object ends up containing a developed picture, that is, the disambiguated feature, if any.

However, in **IDIoT**, there is no need for a priori rules constraining how much of the context can be considered. Also, with respect to lexical access, in **IDIoT**,

1. a single access is possible according to a winner-take-all strategy (e.g., resulting from a triggered expectation or from a quickly retrieved candidate which inhibits all others).

2. multiple access is possible and constitutes the default scenario,

given that candidacies will likely overlap in time.

3. frequency and familiarity are accounted for in the retrievability coefficient and communication delay of each of the possible interpretations of an ambiguous word.

As for the decision-point problem, there is no need to postulate either the highly problematic "immediate decision" approach or any arbitrary semantic criterion. In **IDIoT**, the decision point is not specified a priori and, instead, results from the workings of the grounded architecture with respect to a certain text. More specifically, when, exactly, a word is disambiguated is unpredictable and depends on the multitude of factors (e.g., STM capacity, candidacy deadlines, retrievability coefficients, context set up by previous inputs, etc.) affecting the likelihood of detection of each of the candidates.

9.3   EXAMPLES OF LEXICAL DISAMBIGUATION

Let us start by considering the problem of semantic priming, although I emphasize that, in view of the recent criticism of Norris (1986), no claim is made with regards to the psychological reality of this phenomenon. Let us consider the following sentence:

Example 9.3.1 *John plays gin.*

A feature x is said to prime a feature y if, upon the detection of x, an expectation signal is sent from x to y, which lowers the retrievability coefficient of y and places it in expectation mode.

Let us make the following assumptions regarding the KB:

1. The innate feature **"plays"** eventually triggers the feature **actionPlay**.

2. The feature **actionPlay** primes **cardGame**. (In fact, **actionPlay** would also probably prime all other types of games, which would result in a KB with a high degree of specificity. The KB could be even more specific if **actionPlay** directly primed **cardGameGin** and all other known games, as may be the case for a child.)

3. The feature **cardGame** is an association of **cardGameGin**; **game** is an association of **cardGame**.

4. The feature **"gin"** has **alcoholicBeverageGin** and **cardGameGin** as candidates.

5. Both **alcoholicBeverageGin** and **cardGameGin** are triggered by "**gin**".

Upon the detection of **actionPlay** (from the word "plays"), **cardGame** is primed and becomes expected. After the word "gin" is input and detected, **alcoholicBeverageGin** and **cardGameGin** are triggered and become candidates. Feature **cardGameGin** sends a submission signal to its association **cardGame**. Upon receiving this signal, **cardGame** is triggered, has its expectation satisfied, and thus, since this a submission, sends a confirmation signal to its submitter, **cardGameGin**. After receiving this confirmation signal, **cardGameGin** becomes detected and disambiguates, by means of its expansion procedure, the cluster governing "**gin**". The detection of **cardGameGin** leads to the detection of **cardGame**, which, in turn, leads to the detection of the more abstract feature, **game**.

If **cardGameGin** were directly primed by **actionPlay**, no submissions would be necessary, as it would become immediately detected by being triggered by "**gin**" while being expected. Then if **actionPlay** primed **game** instead of **cardGame**, the chain of submissions would go from **cardGameGin** to **cardGame** to **game**, reflecting the cost of a more abstract (i.e., less specific) KB.

Let us consider the same sentence, but without any priming in the KB. Let us adopt, for example, the following KB assumptions:

1. The innate feature "**plays**" eventually triggers **actionPlay**.

2. The feature **cardGame** is an association of **cardGameGin**. The feature, **game**, is an association of **cardGame**.

3. Both **alcoholicBeverageGin** and **cardGameGin** are possible interpretations of "**gin**".

4. The features **actionPlayAGame** and **actionPlayAMusicalInstrument**, are possible interpretations of **actionPlay**.

5. The feature **actionPlayAGame** has a constraint that consists of the two triggers, **actionPlay** and **game**.

6. The feature **game** is a relay with, among others, **cardGame** as a supplier and **actionPlayAGame** as a customer.

The word "plays" eventually leads to the detection of **actionPlay**, which triggers the candidacy of **actionPlayAGame** and **actionPlayAMusicalInstrument**. It is assumed that the latter will not have enough evidence to become detected and eventually will have its candidacy expire. As for **actionPlayA-**

Game, it is still missing the trigger **game** after receiving the signal from **actionPlay**. From the input of the word "gin", **"gin"** is recognized, which eventually leads to the candidacies of **alcoholicBeverageGin** and of **cardGameGin**. It is also assumed that **alcoholicBeverageGin** will not have enough evidence to become detected and eventually will have its candidacy expire. Upon receiving the signal from **"gin"**, **cardGameGin** becomes a candidate and a submission signal is sent from **cardGameGin** to **cardGame** to **game** to the customers of **game**. These customers include **actionPlayAGame**, which is satisfied by this submission signal and sends a confirmation signal back to **game**, eventually leading to the detection of this chain of features.

I have used a relay for **game** to suggest that the "highest" (i.e., most general) feature of a particular generalization hierarchy of objects (implemented by the associations of the concerned features) can often be too general to require an expansion procedure and, therefore, can be specified as a relay. It is left to the user to avoid a deadlock where **game** would need **actionPlayAGame** to become detected and vice versa. Experimentation with the current prototype has shown that such deadlocks can be prevented through the judicious use of relays for such "abstract" features.

Such a strictly conceptual approach to disambiguation has its disadvantages. In the last hypothesized KB, **actionPlayAGame** becomes detected merely from the co-occurrence of **game** and **actionPlay** and, therefore, could erroneously specialize **actionPlay** to **actionPlayAMusicalInstrument** in the following example (Hirst, 1987, p. 78):

Example 9.3.2 *The baby played with the guitar.*

It could also specialize to **actionPlayAGame** as in this sentence:

Example 9.3.3 *John plays with his gin.*

(i.e., John makes noises while drinking his gin, or John toys with his glass)

A simple rule to prevent this would be to insist that the verb "play" have a direct object if it is to be specialized to **actionPlayAGame** or to **actionPlayAMusical-Instrument**. Such a syntactic check can be enforced by coding these features as buildable features with the following check at the start of their respective expansion procedure:

```
getCluster u1 governing actionPlay
testPresenceOf directObject in u1
```

In this case, the co-occurrence of the required triggers would not be sufficient, and the existing context would be checked by means of a **testPresenceOf** instruction. The disambiguation of **actionPlay** to one of its possible interpretations would then depend on this check.

However, this check is not sufficient for a sentence like the following:

Example 9.3.4 *John plays Hamlet with a gin in his hands.*

Here the co-occurrence of the required triggers and the presence of a direct object still lead to an erroneous interpretation.

A more demanding rule may insist that, for example, **actionPlay** be disambiguated to **actionPlayAGame** only if the game in question is the direct object of the verb "play". In other words, **actionPlayAGame**, for example, could require another check in its expansion procedure to verify that the cluster associated with the direct object, let's call it *DO*, denotes (i.e., has some features that denote) a game. Such an approach is problematic in that *DO* will not denote a game until "gin" has been disambiguated, but "gin" being disambiguated to **cardGameGin** necessitates a confirmation from feature **actionPlayAGame**, which has its syntactic check on the direct object fail because "gin" is not yet detected. In other words, the detection of **cardGameGin** would need a confirmation from **actionPlayAGame**, whose syntactic check would require that **cardGameGin** have been detected!

This chicken-and-egg problem is typical of lexical disambiguation, and syntactic rules are unhelpful, in this specific case, for they can only establish that the word "gin", not the concept **cardGameGin**, is the direct object of the word "play". Clearly, the specification of such a detection cycle must be avoided. The key to the problem is deciding which of the words "play" and "gin" is to be disambiguated first. I present, directly, a possible solution in which "play" is disambiguated only after "gin" has been specialized to the card game, and leave the reciprocal alternative as an exercise for the reader. The "trick" is to have the syntactic check(s) and the chain of features that will allow the detection of **cardGameGin** not involve **actionPlayAGame** (which will become detected only once **cardGameGin** has been disambiguated) but **actionPlay**. In other words, since it is assumed that "play" is disambiguated *after* "gin", the disambiguation process relies on the co-occurrence of the concept **actionPlay** with some "playable" direct object.

Here is a possible KB (which has been used with the current prototype of **IDIoT**) that summarizes this discussion and combines both syntactic and conceptual considerations:

1. Innate feature **"plays"** eventually triggers **actionPlay**.

2. Innate feature **"gin"** eventually leads to the detection of the relay, **noun**, and of a feature, **directObject**, which governs the cluster associated with **"gin"**.

3. Feature **cardGame** is an association of **cardGameGin; game** is an association of **cardGame**.

4. Features **alcoholicBeverageGin** and **cardGameGin**, are possible interpretations of **"gin"**.

5. Features **actionPlayAGame** and **actionPlayAMusicalInstrument**, are possible interpretations of **actionPlay**.

6. Feature **actionPlayAGame** has a constraint that consists of the two triggers **actionPlay** and **game**.

7. Feature **game** is a relay with, among others, **cardGame** as a supplier, and **actionPlay** as a customer. This modification circumvents the problematic cycle.

8. Feature **objectGin** has a constraint with the triggers **"gin"** and **directObject**, and has the following expansion procedure:

```
getCluster u1 governing directObject
testPresenceOf 'gin' in u1
```

9. Feature **cardGameGin** has a constraint with only the triggers **"gin"** and **objectGin**.

The word "plays" eventually leads to the detection of **actionPlay**, which triggers the candidacy of **actionPlayAGame** and **actionPlayAMusicalInstrument**. It is assumed that the latter will not have enough evidence to become detected, and eventually will have its candidacy expire. As for **actionPlayAGame**, it is still missing the trigger **game**, after receiving the signal from **actionPlay**. From the input of the word "gin", **"gin"** is recognized and notifies **objectGin**. Also, the constructed cluster of **gin** becomes the direct object of "play". The feature **directObject** becomes detected in this process of establishing the direct object and sends its presence signal to **objectGin**, which, in turn, becomes detected and notifies **cardGameGin**. Feature **alcoholicBeverageGin** becomes a candidate from the presence of **"gin"**, but again it is assumed that **alcoholicBeverageGin** will not have enough evidence to become detected and eventually will have its candidacy expire.

When **cardGameGin** receives the signal from **objectGin**, a submission signal is sent from **cardGameGin** to **cardGame** to **game** to the customers of **game**. These customers include **actionPlay**, which is satisfied by this submission and sends a confirmation signal back to **game**, eventually leading to the detection of this chain of features. Then, and only then, does the detection of **game** lead to the detection of **actionPlayAGame**.

I remark that the proposed solution illustrates a case- or role-based approach to the specification of knowledge, an approach that is often taken to be pervasive to human cognition (see Sowa, 1984): The specification of a particular "concept" involves the role of the concept. Finally, I claim that a strategy for disambiguation that would flag the word "gin", and *only* this word, as having multiple possible interpretations would miss the fact that the word "play" itself requires a lot of knowledge to interpret. For example, the following sentence is deemed to be nonsensical by some of my informants, whereas it is quite understandable to others:

Example 9.3.5 *The game plays well.*

If we admit the inchoative "play" ought to be disambiguated to **actionPlayA-Game**, then we realize that another constraint of **game** or of **actionPlay** must account for "game" being the subject (or agent) of the verb "play".

Let us now consider the case of an homonymous word such as "submarine" in the following sentence (Hirst, 1987, p. 88):

Example 9.3.6 *The sailor ate the submarine.*

This sentence can trigger a garden-path effect (i.e., a perceived awkwardness) if the idiosyncratic processing of a comprehender has the word "sailor" strongly prime the concept of the undersea ship rather than the concept of the sandwich. Hirst (personal communication) has tried similar sentences on informants and reports that most found the sentences "funny" and could not "see" the literal interpretation.

Let us momentarily ignore the figurative interpretations of the verb "eat" (e.g., "to eat one's words", "the sea eats ships and submarines", etc.). Paths supporting either of the candidate interpretations of "submarine" (e.g., sandwich or undersea ship) are buildable, at least in theory:

A sailor is a type of person. A person eats food. A sandwich is a type of food.

A sailor works on a ship. A submarine is an undersea ship.

Yet only the first of these two interpretations seems acceptable. If we assume equal retrievability of the candidates, then it is very possible that the path between "ate" and **submarineSandwich** (e.g., submarine–sandwich–food–eat) is the shortest to establish (with respect to processing time) and then inhibits the undersea ship candidacy. We could explain the potential awkwardness of the example by assuming that, typically, the sandwich interpretation is less familiar and thus longer to retrieve than the more frequent undersea ship interpretation. Consequently, the "acceptable" interpretation may take too much time to establish.

Why not simply postulate that the undersea ship interpretation is unacceptable because an undersea ship cannot be the direct object of the verb "eat"? To do so, we would need to

1. introduce the feature **objectSubmarine** to ensure that the submarine is the direct object of "to eat" and

2. make the inference that the direct object of "to eat" must be edible and that undersea ships are not. This inference could be captured by a path such as

submarineShip–metalConstruction–nonEdibleObject–actionEat.

In the end, however, such an inference would need to be somehow overridden in order to account for the disambiguation of "submarine" in the following passage:

Example 9.3.7 *Each Easter, it seems one can find more and more bizarre objects fashioned in chocolate. This year, the Pentagon released miniatures of its arsenal in milk chocolate. Yesterday, my son ate a submarine, but he still prefers an F-14.*

In this paragraph, the attribute of "submarine" that made it inedible must be replaced (in the corresponding cluster, through a series of complex inferences) by chocolate, a kind of food. In other words, disambiguation should always be contextual, an observation that suggests the systematic use of buildable features.

Writing knowledge units for disambiguation is further complicated by requiring that information that follows the ambiguous word also be taken into account, as in the following sentence:

Example 9.3.8 *John eats a submarine made out of chocolate.*

In this example, we should *not* immediately disqualify the undersea ship candidate once "submarine" has been established as the direct object of "to eat". Rather, it seems that a candidacy should use all of its allocated time in order to account for information later in the sentence.

Let us now turn to the problem of categorial ambiguity, as illustrated by the word "sink" in the following sentence:

Example 9.3.9 *John emptied the sink of its water.*

The word "sink" can be a noun or a verb. However, in the example, syntactic cues restrict the choice to the noun. Consequently, in **IDIoT**, I propose that the word "sink" trigger the candidates **sinkNoun** and **sinkVerb**, that would respectively submit the features **noun** and **verb**. A confirmation path would be obtained between **noun** and the existing syntactic context—the detection of the article "the" would either expect or confirm the feature **noun**—eventually leading to the detection of **sinkNoun**. The latter feature would, in turn, notify its possible interpretations, which could include **plumberSink, viceSink, heatSink**, and so forth. Similarly, if **sinkVerb** were detected, it would notify its possible interpretations.

It appears that if a rigid grammar, that is, one that systematically rejects ungrammatical sentences, is specified in the knowledge base, then the resolution of categorial ambiguity can rely mostly on syntactic cues (i.e., which sequences of parts-of-speech are allowed). However, as suggested in chapter 7, the mind typically possesses an enormous ability to cope with "ungrammaticalities" that can lead to more complex cases of categorial ambiguity, as with the word "bark" in the following sentence:

Example 9.3.10 *The dog's bark woke me up.*

Two other interesting examples handled by the current prototype of **IDIoT** follow:

Example 9.3.11 *The men man the submarine.*

Example 9.3.12 *The sailors man the submarine.*

In extreme cases, categorial ambiguity can create a genuine garden path effect as is typically the case with the following sentence:

Example 9.3.13 *The prime number few.*

Interestingly, this sentence often seems to present much less difficulty for a native French reader than for a native English reader. An explanation may reside in the historical development of these two languages: Like Latin, French is an analytic (as opposed to a synthetic) language where syntactic cues appear to be much more rigid and "verb-oriented" than the English ones, tending to prevent the French reader from making decisions until the verb has been found, and thus eliminating the "trap" of interpreting "prime number" as the mathematical idiom.

Let us now consider a sentence (Hirst, 1987, p. 126) in which several words are ambiguous:

Example 9.3.14 *Nadia's plane taxied to the terminal.*

The word "plane" has several possible interpretations (e.g., plane tree, tool for smoothing wood, geometric plane, aircraft) as a noun, and as a verb (e.g., to make smooth, to remove by planing). "Taxi" can be a noun or a verb. And the word "terminal" can, at least, be associated with **computerTerminal** and **airportTerminal**. Since "plane" has a categorial ambiguity, upon the recognition of **"plane"**, I suggest that the features **planeNoun** and **planeVerb** become candidates, eventually leading, through syntactic cues, to the detection of the former. Once **planeNoun** becomes detected, it notifies all its possible interpretations. A given knowledge base may cause the **aircraftPlane** to become detected as a result of a direct path between **actionTaxi** and **aircraftPlane**. In the case of a less fluent reader who ignores the fact that "to taxi" specifically applies to airplanes, the path between **actionTaxi** and **aircraftPlane** will simply be longer (e.g., actionTaxi–actionVehicleMovement–vehicle–aircraft-Plane).

The recognition of the preposition "to" causes its possible interpretations to become candidates. However, a path between "to" and **actionTaxi** is probably quickly built (e.g., actionTaxi–actionMove–movement–destination–destinationTo), leading to the disambiguation of **"to"** to **destinationTo** (see the next chapter).

The recognition of **"terminal"** leads to the candidacy of **computerTerminal** and **airportTerminal**. If "plane" has been disambiguated to **aircraftPlane** from "taxied", it is probable that either an expectation, or an inference in the form of a path between **airportTerminal** and **actionTaxi** or **aircraftPlane** will lead to the disambiguation of "terminal" to **airportTerminal**. However, if the knowledge of the reader has not allowed for the disambiguation of "plane", the disambiguation of "terminal" will probably fail, since both of its possible interpretations can act as destinations of a movement. Consider, for example, this sentence:

Example 9.3.15 *John walked to his terminal and compiled his software.*

Here the word "terminal" acts as the destination of a movement. In this particular example, "terminal" can be disambiguated to **computerTerminal** only by using an inferential path that would involve **software**.

The point to be grasped is that lexical disambiguation is not only contextual, but also often requires inferencing. This does not present a problem in **IDIoT**, given that inferences are path constructed by the grounded architecture. To further illustrate this point, consider the following (Hirst, 1987, p. 126):

Example 9.3.16 *The view from the window would be improved by a plant.*

An inference is assumed to be required in order to disambiguate the word "plant" to **vegetalPlant** instead of **industrialPlant**. Let me first briefly digress to stress that **vegetalPlant** is not *necessarily* the adequate interpretation. For example, a rich industrialist may prefer seeing a new factory he owns rather than some stupid vegetal that presents no interest whatsoever to his pragmatic sense of esthetics! A new building may also represent an improvement over some ugly sight. End of digression.

If we do assume that the sentence in vacuo favors the **vegetalPlant** interpretation, then the word "plant" will be disambiguated through features and paths that capture the complex hypothesized inference. Consider this example:

1. The words "the view from the window" lead to the detection of **windowView** and of its association, **roomLocation**, and of its association, **interiorLocation**.

2. The word "improved" leads to the detection of **actionImprove**.

3. The fact that **interiorLocation** is the object of **actionImprove** causes the detection of **interiorDecorationImprovement**.

4. The path (vegetalPlant, windowOrnamanent, ornament, additionOfRoomOrnament, interiorDecorationImprovement) is found leading to the confirmation and detection of **vegetalPlant**.

It is important to observe that this scenario is still simplistic, especially in that it does not account for the subtleties stemming from the use of the word "would".

Let us briefly turn to referential inferences for disambiguation, which were discussed earlier. Consider, for example, this sentence:

Example 9.3.17 *The astronomer married the star.*

Let us assume that some movie actress has been recently referenced. In this case, a cluster c denoting this specific actress has been constructed and includes the feature, **actorStar**. Upon the recognition of the word "star", **celestialBodyStar** and **actorStar** both become candidates. A reference is found for **actorStar** in the context if c is reachable. In this case, **actorStar** becomes detected.

To conclude, I want to emphasize that, in **IDIoT**, lexical disambiguation is non-deterministic, that is, disambiguation does not necessarily occur (see Corriveau, 1993b). More specifically, if there is not enough information to disambiguate a word, then the candidacies of the possible interpretations will simply expire, as in the following examples from Hirst, (1987, p. 126):

Example 9.3.18 *I want to eliminate some moles.*

Example 9.3.19 *Ross was escorted from the bar to the dock.*

9.4 ON IDIOMS AND FIGURATIVE LANGUAGE

The problem of "figurative" (i.e., non literal) language and of idioms has received a significant amount of attention in psycholinguistics (e.g., Cacciari, & Tabossi, 1988; Gibbs, Nayak, Bolton, & Keppel, 1989; Cacciari, & Glucksberg, 1994; Gibbs, 1994). Conversely, computational models for this problem are few in number (e.g., Martin, 1987, 1988 for metaphors; Miezitis, 1988 for idioms). Often, the understanding of metaphors has been incorrectly conflated with the problem of analogy (see Plantinga, 1986, 1987). Furthermore, existing models generally need some counterintuitive a priori warning in order to process figurative language. It is as though comprehension requires yet some more specialized algorithms to tackle this pervasive (Lakoff, & Johnson, 1980) aspect of language.

From my viewpoint, there can be no a priori distinction between a literal and a figurative interpretation, for this would imply some sort of improbable prescience: Each reader typically produces a private interpretation without knowing in advance what a text is about. In this section, I very briefly investigate how the problem of figurative language can be approached with **IDIoT**.

Let us first consider the simplest form of idioms. It is my opinion that lexical and structural ambiguities can often be eliminated through an efficient representation and processing of idioms, which, I believe, generally consist of a pattern whose global interpretation as a whole is faster than, and does not necessarily proceed from, the interpretation of its individual components. In other words, idioms are patterns to speed up processing, a standpoint that fits well a time-constrained cognitive architecture. For example, conventionalized <verb–preposition> patterns could be specified as idioms (e.g., "give up", "fall in love", etc.), de facto minimizing the number of possible interpretations for both verb and preposition. Clearly, this approach favors the word expert strategy (see Small, 1980, 1983) that was previously advocated, an exhaustive list of idioms being specified for each verb and preposition.

In **IDIoT**, an idiom may be specified as a feature **i** with the components of the idiom's pattern as a set of ordered triggers. Once triggered, **i** has its constraint(s) check for the semantic felicity of the idiom's interpretation in the existing context. More precisely, the key feature(s) of the interpretation are specified as inputs in these constraints. When an idiom has an interpretation that cannot be derived from the individual interpretation of its pattern's components, success or failure in being detected involves only the constraints of the idiom. Conversely, an idiom that can also be interpreted literally will typically be detected only if one of its constraints is satisfied *before* the literal interpretation can be assembled.

Idioms very often correspond to lexical patterns. The case where such a lexical idiom can also be interpreted literally (i.e., have an interpretation built from its components) is treated as a lexical ambiguity with the only difference that, if we assume equal retrievability of all relevant features, the idiom will be a candidate sooner, as it is directly triggered by a pattern of words that requires less time to detect than that required for assembling them into an interpretation. Let me clarify this discussion by considering the idiom "to kick the bucket", for which I propose the following definition:

KU kickTheBucket:
```
constraint 1:
  ordered triggers: rootKick, 'the', 'bucket'
  inputs:
      actionDie has a weight of 1
  exceptions:
      actionKick has a weight of 1
      bucket has a weight of 1
expansion:
      getCluster u1 governing rootKick
      renameFeature rootKick to actionDie in u1
      addFeature kickTheBucket to u1
      getCluster u1 governing 'the'
      removeCluster u1
      getCluster u1 governing 'bucket'
      removeCluster u1
```

This feature is essentially triggered by **rootKick** (i.e., the morphological stem of the verb "kick") followed by the words "the bucket". The input **actionDie** is submitted unless it has already been detected, in which case the constraint would be immediately satisfied. Once **actionDie** is confirmed by the context, the idiom becomes detected, provided neither of its exceptions has been detected. The expansion procedure simply takes note of the idiomatic form of **actionDie** and removes the clusters associated with the words "the bucket". Finally, the feature **kickTheBucket** must also be specified as an exception of **actionKick** and **bucket** in order to inhibit the literal interpretation. Consider, for example, these sentences:

Example 9.4.1 *John kicked the bucket; the milk spilled.*

Example 9.4.2 *John kicked the bucket. His widow celebrated.*

For both sentences, the features **actionKick, bucket,** and **kickTheBucket** will become candidates. In the first sentence, **actionDie** will not be confirmed, and thus the candidacy of the idiom will expire without success. In fact, an inference between "bucket" and "spilled" could probably be established, causing the detection of **bucket,** and thus the inhibition of **kickTheBucket**. In the second sentence, a confirmation path having been built between **actionDie** and "widow", **kickTheBucket** becomes detected.

Idioms can be viewed as conventionalized figurative language, their idiomatic interpretation not requiring any special treatment: In the process of becoming conventionalized by a reader or a culture, the initial inferences that are made to understand them are lost, and only the interpretation as a whole remains. In other words, idioms epitomize the diachronic nature of language: An idiom has a history that is generally unknown and irrelevant to the comprehender, who is taught an idiomatic interpretation as a single lexical item.

Plantinga (1986, 1987) suggested that if we think of figurative language usage as a spectrum, idioms are at one end: They have been conventionalized to the point where they constitute lexical items. In the middle of the spectrum we find the conventionalized metaphors (e.g., "argument is war", "instrument as companion", etc.; see Lakoff, & Johnson, 1980) that pervade our use of language. Finally, at the other end of the spectrum reside today's novel metaphors (which may become tomorrow's idioms). It is precisely the novelty of a usage, with respect to an individual's idiolect, that forces the comprehender to establish a new inference path (which may be missed or require more time to construct due to its complexity). Consider, for example, this passage (adapted from Hirst, 1987, p. 115):

Example 9.4.3 *As a writer, John had been humiliated; his pen breathed* *revenge.*

The context favors the disambiguation of "pen" as a "writing implement" rather than as a "female swan" (via a path between "writer" and "pen"). The comprehender must also

1. recognize the conventionalized metaphor "instrument as result" which takes a pen as meaning a writer's work.

2. set the interpretation of "to breathe" to "to mean", "to express".

3. make the link between revenge and humiliation and possibly infer a causal scenario such as "the humiliated seeks revenge".

Each of these three steps may seem quite straightforward (if not quite literal) for an experienced speaker of English. Yet they may be quite complex for a beginner who must either be taught the interpretation or must invest considerable time and effort in order to construct an interpretation by herself. The immediacy of an interpretation also varies with how well the words fit a comprehender's conventions, as illustrated in the following sentences:

Example 9.4.4 *His pen perspires revenge.*

Example 9.4.5 *His pen spits revenge.*

Example 9.4.6 *His pen produces revenge.*

Example 9.4.7 *His pen generates revenge.*

Example 9.4.8 *His pen inhales revenge.*

Example 9.4.9 *His pen exhales revenge.*

Example 9.4.10 *His pen smells revenge.*

Example 9.4.11 *His pen satisfies his revenge.*

This list epitomizes, in my opinion, the idiosyncratic nature of figurative language, and thus, of linguistic comprehension. As always, we should not forget that a reader may misunderstand or not understand. This possibility for misunderstanding or not understanding increases as we move on the axis of figurative usages. Consider the first few lines of Keats's "Ode on a Grecian Urn" (quoted from Bain, Beaty, and Hunter, 1977):

Thou still unravish'd bride of quietness,

Thou foster-child of silence and slow time,

Sylvan historian, who canst thus express

A flowery tale more sweetly than our rhyme.

The interpretation of these few lines will not only completely escape a "down-to-earth" kind of comprehender (e.g., how can an urn, which is inanimate object, be an unravish'd bride, a foster-child, a historian?), but will also remain somewhat "incomplete" in the case of a reader who is not familiar with the Rousseauist movement.

To conclude, the point is that figurative language can only be defined with respect to one's idiolect, one's experiences and knowledge, one's postulates and conventions: One man's evidence can be another man's mystery. In other words, figurative language ought not to be an a priori notion but an a posteriori classification of a usage with respect to a particular individual. From this standpoint, there is no need to hypothesize a separate interpretation mechanism: A novel usage merely requires more complex, possibly less immediate inferences. Moreover, in the end, the ascription of meaning may also depends on social factors such as the fear of losing face and the authority or power of the person proposing an interpretation (see Peckham, 1979), and so forth. For example, an individual may feel compelled to produce an interpretation for a surrealist poem, painting, or sculpture that he considers meaningless but that is regarded as a masterpiece by his teacher.

Chapter 10

Structural Disambiguation

10.1 INTRODUCTION TO STRUCTURAL DISAMBIGUATION

The problem of structural disambiguation stems from the fact that a sentence may have several parses. Hirst (1987, p. 135) suggested the following list to summarize attachment ambiguities in English:

PP attachment—to noun or verb?

  - Ross insisted on phoning the man with the limp.

  - Ross insisted on washing the dog with pet shampoo.

PP attachment—to which noun?

  - the door near the stairs with the "Members Only" sign

Relative clause attachment—to which noun?

  - the door near the stairs that had the "Members Only" sign

PP attachment—to which verb or adjectival phrase?

  - He seemed nice to her.

PP attachment—to which verb?

  - Ross said that Nadia had taken the cleaning out yesterday.

Adverb attachment—to verb or sentence?

  - Happily, Nadia cleaned up the mess Ross had left.

Participle attachment—to surface subject or sentence?

  - Considering his situation likely to go from bad to worse, he decided to offer his resignation.

- Considering the deficiencies of his education, his career has been extraordinary.

The following list summarizes (Hirst, 1987, p. 149) analytic ambiguities in English:

Relative clause or complement?

- The tourists objected to the guide that they couldn't hear.

- The tourists signaled to the guide that they couldn't hear.

Particle detection

- A good pharmacist dispenses with accuracy.

Prepositional phrase or adjectival phrase?

- I want the music box on the table.

Present participle or adjective?

- Ross and Nadia are singing madrigals.

- Pens and pencils are writing implements.

Present participle or noun?

- We discussed running.

Where does an NP end?

- Nadia gave the cat food.

- The prime number few.

Reduced relative clause or VP?

- The horse raced past the barn fell.

Determining noun group structure?

- airport long term car park courtesy vehicle pickup point

What is the subject of the supplementive?

- He drove the car home undismayed.

- He brought the car back undamaged.

Supplementive, restrictive relative, or verb complement?

- The manager approached the boy smoking a cigar.

- The manager caught the boy smoking a cigar.

Cleft or not?

- It frightened the child that Ross wanted to visit the lab.

Question or command?

- Have the crystals dissolved?

- Have the crystals dissolved.

How is the predicate formed?

- Ross is eager to please.

- Ross is ideal to please.

- Ross is easy to please.

- Ross is certain to please.

These categories are not claimed to be exhaustive, and structural disambiguation also involves other complex linguistic problems such as gap finding and filling (Hirst, 1987, section 6.2.2) as in these sentences:

Example 10.1.1 *Those are the boys that the police debated about fighting.*

Example 10.1.2 *Mary is the student whom the teacher wanted to talk to the principal.*

Also, structural ambiguities can involve categorial ambiguities and can lead to a garden-path phenomenon (Marcus, 1980), as one may have experienced while reading some of the previous examples.

Structural disambiguation, and in particular, the problem of PP attachment, have both been studied in psycholinguistics (e.g., see Mitchell, 1994 for a review) and in computational linguistics (e.g., see Hirst, 1987, chapter 6). In the rest of this chapter, I will essentially focus on the question of PP attachment, which exemplifies the difficulties of structural disambiguation.

To begin, I observe that, as with lexical disambiguation, the inherent non determinism of structural disambiguation is typically downplayed, if not ignored. Instead, it is generally assumed that a sentence that presents a structural ambiguity has a *preferred* (read correct) parse. Consequently, several researchers propose a strictly syntactic solution to structural disambiguation (e.g., Niv, 1992 for PP attachment). Most of such studies on attachment decisions originate in the principles of *Right Association* and of *Minimal Attachment*, which are purely syntactic (McRoy, 1988, p. 6):

> The principle of Right Association states that optimally, terminal symbols will be attached to the lowest non-terminal node that is on the right-most branch of the current structure; that is, they will be grouped with the terminal symbols immediately to their left. . . . Minimal Attachment, . . . requires that optimally a terminal symbol is to be attached into a parse tree with the fewest possible number of new non-terminal nodes linking it with the nodes already in the tree.

It is, however, generally accepted that syntax alone is not enough. Several researchers, therefore, also adopt the principle of *Lexical Preference*, which, in essence, states that verbs and other lexical items may prefer one pattern of complementation to another. The importance given to such preferences with respect to syntax differs considerably from one model to the next. Consider the following examples:

1. Hindle and Rooth (1993) presented a syntactic model that resolves PP attachment on the basis of the relative strength of association of the preposition with verbal and nominal heads, estimated on the basis of statistical preferences encoded in the lexicon and obtained from parsing a large corpus.

2. Against the syntactic trend, Wilks (1975) and Wilks, Huang, and Fass (1985) have argued for a very semantic version of lexical preferences, in which preferences correspond to selectional restrictions. Similarly, Whittemore, Ferrara, and Brunner (1990) argued that lexical preferences are the key to resolving attachment ambiguity.

Moreover, Schubert (1986) remarked that a discussion of preferences often degrades to a battle of "partisan informants", who often do not even agree on whether a sentence is "confusing" or not. Not surprisingly then, Hirst (1987, section 6.3) concluded:

> There is at present no agreement on any general principles that can be used for disambiguation. It seems clear, however, that knowledge from several different sources is used.

Thematic role expectations, for example, may play a significant role in attachment (e.g., Taraban, & McClelland, 1988). Closer to **IDIoT**, both McRoy (1988) and Gibson (1991) proposed single-sentence syntactic models (based on the theory of Government and Binding of Chomsky, 1982) in which attachments decisions may consider, among other factors:

1. the amount of work still remaining to be done, computed as a time estimate (McRoy).

2. the amount of work already performed (Gibson, 1991).

These symbolic models lack inferencing capabilities, but are interesting in that they not only emphasize the time-constrained nature of comprehension, but also consider the role of memory, especially capacity and processing limitations. For example, McRoy's (1988) work, which is based on the Sausage Machine Model (Frazier, & Fodor, 1978; Fodor, & Frazier, 1980), explicitly suggests viewing comprehension as a race process.

Both Hirst (1987) and Schubert (1986) offered more general symbolic models that attempt to synthesize syntactic and semantic factors involved in structural disambiguation. Let us very briefly overview each of these two models in order to use them as points of reference when discussing the approach taken in **IDIoT**.

Hirst suggested the use of a Semantic Enquiry Desk (SED), which is systematically consulted by his Paragram parser for assistance with prepositional phrase attachment and gap finding in relative clauses. The SED requires (Hirst, 1987, p. 167)

1. an annotation on each verb sense as to which of its cases are "expected" (COMPULSORY, PREFERRED, or UNPREFERRED).

2. a method for deciding on the relative plausibility of PP attachment.

3. a method for determining the presuppositions that would be engendered by a particular PP attachment, and for testing whether they are satisfied or not.

4. a method for resolving the issue when the strategies give contradictory recommendations.

For the second requirement, Hirst observed (1987, p. 168) the following:

> In the most general case, deciding whether something is plausible is extremely difficult. . . . However, there are two easy methods of testing plausibility that we can use that, though non-definitive, will suffice in many cases. The first of these[,] is the slot restriction predicates.... While satisfying the predicates does not guarantee plausibility, failing the predicates indicates almost certain implausibility. The second method is what we shall call the *EXEMPLAR PRINCIPLE*: an object or action should be considered plausible if the knowl-

edge base contains an instance of such an object or action, or an
instance of something similar.

For the third requirement, the SED relies on a referential heuristic that is very
close to the second method of plausibility testing. Hirst developed specific
decision algorithms for the fourth requirement (Hirst, pp. 173–174). These a
priori rules ignore inferences, context, and pragmatics. (A full discussion of
the SED and of its results can be found in Hirst, 1987, chapter 7.)

Schubert's approach to PP attachment is a lot more sketchy, involves
numerically weighted preferences, and also allows for trade-offs among syntactic and semantic/pragmatic preferences. The model relies on the following
six principles (1986, pp. 601–602):

1. **A graded distance effect**: Immediate constituents of a phrase prefer to be close to the *head lexeme* of the phrase. The effect is mediated
by an "expectation potential" that decreases with distance from the
head lexeme and increases with constituent size; As a result, larger
constituents admit larger displacements from the head lexeme.

2. **A rule of habituation effect**: There is an inhibitory potential or
"cost" associated with each phrase structure rule (including lexical
rules), leading to a preference for low-cost rules over high-cost rules.

3. **Inhibition by errors**: "Mild errors" such as concord errors contribute inhibitory potentials to the phrases in which they occur.

4. **Salience in context**: The potential of a word sense or phrase is high
to the extent that the denotation of that word sense or phrase is salient
in the current context.

5. **Familiarity of logical-form pattern**: The potential of a phrase is
high to the extent that its logical translation instantiates a familiar pattern of function-argument combination.

6. **Conformity with scripts/frames**: The potential of a phrase is high
to the extent that it describes a familiar kind of object or situation
(such as might be specified in a script or frame).

The first two principles are taken to capture syntactic preferences, and the others, semantic and pragmatic effects. In particular, the fourth principle "is
intended to allow for semantic priming by spreading activation" (Schubert,
1986, p. 602).

Most interestingly, Schubert's questionnaire asks an informant to read the
test sentence "at normal speed" and to "immediately" answer the question that

follows it "as *honestly* as one can" (my italics). The answers the informant has to choose from require that she decide whether she became self-conscious of an ambiguity, or of a need to reanalyze, or of a plausibility judgment, or unconsciously obtained the *correct* interpretation. Not surprisingly, several other researchers (e.g., Wilks, Huang, & Fass, 1985) severely criticize such a methodology, which depends not only on introspection, but also on the problematic notion of a norm (see chapter 2). Moreover, in the end, not only do we not know the relative importance of syntax and semantics for structural disambiguation (Britt, 1994), but also, none of the existing models are grounded.

10.2 PP ATTACHMENT WITH IDIoT

The fundamental hypothesis I make with respect to **IDIoT**'s treatment of structural disambiguation is that there is no need to postulate separate mechanisms and algorithms for structural disambiguation but, on the contrary, that disambiguation, *if it occurs*, will proceed from the *same* processes and strategies as those assumed for lexical disambiguation. More precisely, time-constrained memory seems well-suited for implementing a model of structural disambiguation that amalgamates some facets of the proposals of Hirst and Schubert while respecting the philosophy of Small's (1980, 1983) word experts. I sketch this model below for the problem of PP attachment.

Put in a simplistic way, the general problem of attachment reduces to having a word x that needs to be attached to some other element of the context, which will be called the "hook" for x. Prepositional phrase attachment consists in hooking the preposition that starts the PP; relative clause attachment, the relative pronoun that starts the clause; adverb attachment, an adverb by itself; and participle attachment, the participle that starts the subordinate proposition. From this perspective, the problem of attachment can be seen as consisting of the lexical disambiguation of the word x to be hooked.

Given that lexical disambiguation is non deterministic in **IDIoT**, it is possible for x to be left ambiguous at the end of its candidacy, an alternative seldom implemented in the existing models. Consider, this example (adapted from Hirst, 1987):

Example 10.2.1 *John insisted on drying the dog with a scarf.*

Since "drying with a scarf" and "dog with a scarf" (e.g., Scottish terriers are often depicted with scarfs) are both more or less plausible, the preposition "with" could be left ambiguous unless contextual evidence caused one of the two possible interpretations (namely **withInstrument** and **withAttribute**) to become detected. Similarly, consider this example (Hirst, 1987, p. 135):

Example 10.2.2 *He seemed nice to her.*

In my opinion, this sentence is ambiguous unless the context is taken into account. As suggested in chapter 9, in **IDIoT** "taking into account the context" typically entails the use of buildable features to verify certain contextual rules with respect to the current contents of STM.

Should we then ignore syntax altogether? Not surprisingly, I abandon the general principles of Right Association and Minimal Attachment, which always admit counter examples. Instead, I favor a multitude of word experts, each implementing syntactic, lexical, *and* contextual preferences. For syntactic preferences, I follow the first three principles of Schubert (1986):

> 1. In **IDIoT** the idea that the immediate constituents of a phrase prefer to be "close" to the head lexeme of this phrase can be correlated to the fact that features that will be attached to a cluster need to be detected "close" (*in time*) to the feature that causes the construction of the cluster. Otherwise, the latter will become unreachable, and the attachment will not be possible.

> 2. The notion of an "expectation potential" that decreases with distance from the head lexeme can be directly captured using **IDIoT**'s expectation mechanism, where the chances of detecting an expectation decrease with respect to time, and thus, as more inputs are processed (the number of processed inputs defining Schubert's notion of "distance").

> 3. The combination of **IDIoT**'s reachability and expectation mechanisms can capture Schubert's idea of a constituent's trade-off between wanting to be close to its head lexeme (in order to ensure the reachability of the latter), and becoming expected (due to the detection of the head lexeme), which allows this constituent (because of the possible greater time span of an expectation over a "normal candidacy") to be at a greater "distance" (in terms of the time between the two detections) of its head lexeme.

> 4. The retrievability coefficient of each KU, and thus of each user-specified rule and preference, handles Schubert's rule habituation effect: The less frequent (i.e., the more "expensive" to retrieve) a rule or preference is, the less chance it has of being considered.

> 5. "Mild errors" can be treated as syntactic conflicts (see chapter 7)

that may act as exceptions (see chapter 4) to knowledge units implementing rules of attachments.

Schubert's approach is still too sketchy to explain why the following examples (from Hirst, 1987, section 7.2.1), the first two of which are ungrammatical, are intelligible, implying the reader's ability to make the appropriate attachment(s):

1. Nadia for his birthday gave her secretary a gyroscope.

2. Nadia gave her secretary for his birthday a gyroscope.

3. The gyroscope for Nadia's secretary gave him great pleasure.

4. Nadia gave the secretary on the second floor a gyroscope.

Schubert's (1986) three remaining semantic principles of salience in context, familiarity, and conformity (with schemas) are also readily accounted for in **IDIoT**:

1. Confirmation paths can only be built from a candidate to the reachable context.

2. Familiarity is captured by the retrievability coefficients of the relevant features.

3. Conformity with schemas can be handled with expectations (Dyer, 1983).

In other words, it seems that the principles of Schubert can be grounded in **IDIoT**.

Schubert's model, being quite sketchy, does not address some of the semantic tasks that Hirst assumed to be necessary for attachment decisions, namely, plausibility judgments, presupposition identification and testing, and trade-off rules for when the strategies give contradictory recommendations. How do these tasks fit **IDIoT**'s approach to attachment?

Plausibility judgments are reduced in Hirst's work to two separate processes, namely, selectional restrictions and the examplar principle (see previous section). Selectional restrictions form an important facet of lexical disambiguation and have been discussed when considering the sentence, "The sailor ate the submarine", in the previous chapter. With respect to PP attachment, these restrictions would simply allow for the confirmation of one of the possible interpretations of the hook. Consider this example from (Hirst, 1987, section 7.2.4):

Example 10.2.3 *Ross loves the girl with a passion.*

For this example I propose the following scenario: From the co-occurrence of **actionLove** and **withPreposition** (respectively triggered from the words "love" and "with"), the feature **lovesWith** becomes a candidate. Its detection requires that the cluster corresponding to the noun phrase associated with the preposition (in this case, "a passion") include the feature **mannerQuality**. This tactic implements the selectional restriction that states that "with" can be attached to "love" "only as the MANNER case, but requires the filler to be a **manner-quality**" (Hirst, 1987). The detection of **withPreposition** also triggers the other possible semantic interpretations of "with", including **withAttribute**, whose detection attaches the PP to the preceding noun for which it constitutes an attribute. A cluster with feature, **mannerQuality**, is then constructed as a result from the processing of the words "a passion". At this point in time, the buildable feature **loveWith** has its restriction satisfied and becomes detected. The candidacies of the other interpretations of "with" could be inhibited or left to expire on their own.

Suppose the sentence (adapted from Hirst, 1987, section 7.2.4) were this:

Example 10.2.4 *Ross loves the girl with the brown eyes.*

Then **loveWith** would never become detected. Instead, "eyes" being inferred as an attribute of "girl", the feature **withAttribute** would eventually become detected, *without* any plausibility judgment based on the "referential felicity" of the string "the brown eyes" with respect to "the girl". Hirst instead suggested the examplar principle to make a plausibility judgment on the NP-PP attachment: If a reference to "girl with the brown eyes" (or something "similar") is found in the KB, then plausibility is granted and attachment can proceed. From my viewpoint, plausibility judgments are so problematic that attachment should not rely on them. In particular, implausibility is seldom perceived by the reader in the fictive worlds invented by authors (Graesser, & Clark, 1985, subsection 1.3.5). For example, suppose the sentence is this:

Example 10.2.5 *Ross loves the girl with purple polka dot eyes.*

Then the relative implausibility of such eyes (given that purple polka dot contact lenses are always possible) should not prevent attachment to "girl".

Similarly, I minimize the importance of testing for presupposition satisfaction for attachment decisions. Consider, this example (adapted from Hirst, 1987, section 7.2.5):

Example 10.2.6 *John loves the ocelot with the blue chipmunk.*

Let me quote at length Hirst's (1987) description of the relevant presuppositions:

> First, a definite NP presupposes that the thing it describes exists and that it is available in the focus or knowledge base for felicitous (unique) reference; an indefinite NP presupposes only the plausibility of what it describes. Thus, '*a* blue chipmunk,' presupposes only that the concept of a **blue chipmunk** is plausible; '*the* blue chipmunk further presupposes that there is exactly one blue chipmunk available for ready reference. Second, the attachment of a PP to an NP results in new presuppositions for the new NP thus created, but cancels the uniqueness aspect of the referential presuppositions of both constituent NPs. Thus, 'the ocelot with the blue chipmunk' presupposes that there is just one such ocelot available for reference (and that such a thing is plausible); the plausibility and existence of an **ocelot** and a **blue chipmunk** continue to be presupposed, but their uniqueness is no longer required. Third, the attachment of a PP to a VP creates no new presuppositions but rather always indicates new (unpresupposed) information.

Haddock's (1987) approach to such complex definite NPs has already been criticized in section 8.2. In **IDIoT**, I propose that the preposition "with" is attached to the NP "the ocelot" *without* any plausibility judgment or presupposition testing on "the blue chipmunk", "the ocelot", or "the ocelot with the blue chipmunk". I do, however, recognize the importance of "referential felicity" (as was discussed for lexical disambiguation). Let me elaborate by sketching a possible scenario for the last example. For clarity and simplicity, let us assume that the context "talks" of a nursery in a zoo where feline cubs are placed with smaller animals to play with, but that there is no explicit reference to either an ocelot or a chipmunk. Let us also postulate that attachment will result from the detection of the feature **withColocation** (which captures a colocation relation between its two arguments).

After reading the string "the ocelot", a cluster x is constructed for it and the buildable feature **referredNP** becomes a candidate (see chapter 8). Since it is assumed that there is no earlier reference to an ocelot, this candidacy will fail. Conversely, if such a reference existed and was reachable, then **referredNP** would immediately become detected and x would be replaced by this reference. And, if there were a reference to "an ocelot with a blue chipmunk", the matching process would succeed because **referredNP** uses a **findInclusiveReference** instruction. Again x would be replaced by this reference.

The recognition of the word "with" leads to the candidacy of all possible interpretations of "with" (including **withAttribute** and **withColocation**). A cluster y is then constructed for the NP "the blue chipmunk" and a new **referredNP** candidacy starts for "the blue chipmunk". Again, since it is assumed there is no earlier reference, this candidacy will fail. If a specific and reachable reference to a blue chipmunk existed, then y would be replaced by it. The context having suggested the co-location of animals, the feature **with-Colocation** is eventually detected, and other relevant candidacies expire or are inhibited. The execution of this feature's expansion procedure causes y to become a subcluster in x, governed by feature **colocation**. To reflect that the attachment of y to x forms a new noun phrase, a new candidacy of **referredNP** would be triggered as a result of the detection of **withColocation**. This third consecutive candidacy of **referredNP** would succeed if a reachable cluster describing an ocelot co-located with a blue chipmunk could be found. However, since it is assumed that no such reference exists, this candidacy will also eventually fail.

In summary, the attachment is realized through the disambiguation of "with", without considering plausibility or presuppositions. However, the referential felicity of each relevant presupposition is tested by means of the repeated candidacies of **referredNP**. This strategy, which restricts the search for a reference to reachable clusters during a short interval of time, seems psychologically more plausible than a search over a complete KB (as seems to be required by the exemplar principle of Hirst). Finally, in the case of indefinite noun phrases, there is no referential check, as **referredNP** is simply not triggered. This approach is still simplistic, and the user may wish to specify features that would account for the subtleties of de re versus de dicto readings.

Hirst also developed (1987, subsection 7.2.6) an algorithm that defines priorities for making attachment decisions when the results of verb expectation and presupposition and plausibility testing do not agree. This algorithm is limited to clauses with one VP and one NP, and does allow some counterexamples (Hirst, 1987, p. 191). Similar priorities could be implemented in **IDIoT** by either making less probable attachment rules less retrievable (an idea similar to Schubert's principles) and/or by specifying triggers for the less probable rules that would insure that more probable alternatives have been considered. However, because **IDIoT** favors an approach to attachment that does not rely on plausibility or presupposition, but rather on the lexical disambiguation of the hook, it seems that such a complex scheme is not necessary: The retrievability of the rules used to disambiguate the hook, and the expectations and context that affect such a disambiguation should generally suffice. In other words, in **IDIoT**, the complexity of attachment decisions is shifted from a priori procedures to user-specified word experts (e.g., feature **loveWith**). Furthermore, an attachment decision does not necessarily have to be made. Consider, for example, the following sentence, (from Hirst, 1987, p. 175), which is generally taken to be ambiguous:

Example 10.2.7 *Nadia saw the man in the park with the telescope.*

At least, "with the telescope" (if not also "in the park") should probably be left ambiguous, that is, either unattached or attached to "saw", "man", *and* "park". In other words, in the case of an ambiguity, no actual disambiguation should occur unless desired (and thus, set up by preferences) by the user.

To conclude, I observe that the relevance of word experts to other aspects of structural disambiguation should be obvious when one is considering the examples proposed at the beginning of this chapter. For example,

1. for relative clause attachment, the interpretation of the examples depends on the word experts associated with "objected" and "signaled".

2. for predicate formation, we need experts for "eager to", "easy to", and so forth.

10.3 EXAMPLES OF STRUCTURAL DISAMBIGUATION WITH IDIoT

Let us consider the following sentence (from Hirst, 1987, p. 175):

Example 10.3.1 *The women discussed the tigers on the beach.*

From my viewpoint this sentence *can* be ambiguous and the disambiguation of "on" will depend on the retrievability of the different possible interpretations and on the context. The same holds for this example from (Hirst, 1987, p.175):

Example 10.3.2 *The women discussed the dogs on the beach.*

Here Hirst preferred the NP-attachment ("dogs on the beach"). To illustrate these possible ambiguities and to demonstrate the importance of context and inference for attachment decisions, consider the following passages:

• **NP-attachment:** After supper, the two couples moved to the living room. The men talked about baseball. The women discussed the dogs (or the tigers) on the beach that were causing so much trouble with the tourists that summer.

- **VP-attachment**: The women discussed the dogs (or the tigers) on the beach, while sunbathing, and then went to the cottage to talk about the children.

In the first example, if this scene takes place in some exotic paradise or fictive world, the "tigers on the beach" is as likely and as much a problem for tourists as "dogs on the beach". In the second example, if these women are (or are close to) breeders, zoo keepers, and so forth, or love (or possess, etc.) exotic pets, then tigers are as likely a conversation topic as dogs: Context is unpredictable and ultimately controls the interpretation.

Let us develop a possible simplistic scenario for each of these examples. (A more complex attachment scheme, which recognizes forced attachment to an NP or to a verb, has been developed with the current prototype of **IDIoT**.) For both passages, the ambiguous preposition "on" is assumed to lead to the candidacy of its possible interpretations, including **onActionLocation** and **onObjectLocation**, which respectively capture the verb attachment (i.e., action performed in a specific location) and the noun attachment (i.e., object existing in specific location). Here are possible partial definitions for these two features.

For feature **onActionLocation**, consider this definition:

```
constraint 1:
    triggers: actionVerb, onPreposition
    exceptions: <all the other interpretations of 'on'>



expansion:
        getCluster u1 governing actionVerb
        testAbsenceOf location in u1
        getCluster u2 governing onPreposition
        getCluster u3 governedBy nounPhraseOfPP in u2
        testPresenceOf location in u3
        addFeature location in u1
        addSubCluster u3 to location in u1
        removeCluster u2
```

Unordered triggers are used so that attachment to the verb is not limited to the case where the PP follows the verb. The expansion procedure first checks that the verb does not have a specified location. If it does, the procedure fails. Oth-

STRUCTURAL DISAMBIGUATION

erwise, the noun phrase of the PP is checked for the feature **location**. If it has it, then attachment to the verb occurs. The cluster associated with the preposition in itself is eliminated because its semantic function has been captured by the feature under which the attachment is placed (in this case **location**). This strategy can be applied to any preposition.

For feature **onObjectLocation**, the definition is quite similar:

```
constraint 1:
   ordered triggers: NP, onPreposition
   exceptions: <all the other interpretations of 'on'>
expansion:
      getCluster u1 governing NP
      testPresenceOf object in u1
      getCluster u2 governing onPreposition
      getCluster u3 governedBy nounPhraseOfPP in u2
      testPresenceOf location in u3
      addFeature location to u1
      addSubCluster u3 to location in u1
      removeCluster u2
```

For this feature, triggers are ordered, because attachment requires that the PP follow the NP to which it is attached. Also, in the expansion procedure, u1 will be bound to the most reachable NP, that is, the NP that immediately precedes the PP.

A scenario for the first passage follows:

1. In the first sentence, the word expert for **actionMove** concludes that the subject (i.e., the two couples) of **actionMove** end up in the living room. More precisely, the detection of **actionMoveToLocation** causes the cluster associated with the subject to add the feature **location** that is set up to govern the cluster associated with the living room.

2. In the second sentence, an inference path is built between "the men" and the previously processed "the two couples" to recognize the implicit reference.

3. From the detection of this implicit reference, another rule deduces that the two arguments of this reference are still in the same "time

frame". (This inference involves the "tense rules" of English, which allow a reader to perceive a change or an absence of change in narrative time. The notion of "tense rules" and of "time frame", which are taken to be crucial to text interpretation, are discussed in chapter 11.)

4. Since the two arguments of the reference are in the same time frame, yet another rule infers that the action performed by the men (i.e., **actionTalk**) occurs in the current location of the men, that is, through the reference, the living room. The feature **location** is added to the cluster of **actionTalk** and is made to govern the cluster associated with the living room.

5. In the third sentence, the same rules lead the reader to infer that the action performed by the women (i.e., **actionDiscuss**) occurs in the current location of the women, that is, in the living room.

6. The words "the dogs" or "the tigers" lead to the construction of an NP cluster that becomes the direct object of **actionDiscuss**. The word expert associated with "discuss" then substitutes feature **topic** for feature **direct-Object**, in the **actionDiscuss** cluster. More specifically, the co-occurrence of **actionDiscuss** with a direct object leads to the detection of the feature **actionDiscussWhat**, which makes the direct object cluster associated with **actionDiscuss** its "topic" by making the direct object cluster become a subcluster of **actionDiscuss** governed by the feature **topic**. The processing of "the dogs" or "the tigers" also leads to the candidacy of **referredNP** through the detection of the **NP** feature. For simplicity, this candidacy is assumed here to fail.

7. The word "on" leads to the detection of **onPreposition**, which triggers the candidacy of all its possible interpretations. The feature **prepositionNP** becomes expected.

8. The words "the beach" lead to the construction of an NP cluster. Through this process, the feature **prepositionNP** is triggered and becomes detected because it was expected. As a consequence, feature **NP** is replaced by feature **nounPhraseOfPP** in the cluster constructed from the processing of "the beach", and this cluster is made a subcluster of the cluster constructed for "on" under feature **NP-PP**. In other words, the cluster resulting from the processing of the words "the beach" is attached to the preposition "on".

9. Since the cluster of **actionDiscuss** does have feature **location** the

testAbsenceOf instruction of its expansion procedure systematically fails. Consequently, the candidacy of **onActionLocation** never succeeds. All other possible interpretations of "on", except **onObjectLocation**, also fail from a lack of evidence.

10. The candidate, **onObjectLocation**, becomes detected if it finds the feature **location** in the NP cluster it governs. In the example, the processing of the word "beach" does lead to the construction of a cluster that includes feature **location** in order to capture the fact that a beach is a location. Thus, **onObjectLocation** has enough information to become detected but must wait, due to the exceptions of its triggered constraint, until the end of its candidacy, at which point it becomes detected. This detection results in the cluster denoting the beach to become a subcluster of the cluster associated with the "dogs" or "tigers", under feature **location**. In other words, the detection of **onObjectLocation** attaches "the beach" to the noun phrase which precedes it, under the feature **location**.

This scenario can be complicated if we assume a probable syntactic expectation resulting from a semantic observation: A path could be built between "talked about" and "discussed" detecting a similar action. Since the complement of "talked about" was a topic, it is possible that the reader may expect the complement of "discussed" to be treated, if possible, as a topic, and therefore, as an NP. In this case, the parsing of "the (dogs or tigers) on the beach" as an NP is favored through this expectation, and only those interpretations of "on" that correspond to an NP-attachment become candidates.

The features **onObjectLocation** and **onActionLocation**, are simplistic and somewhat inadequate for the more complex second passage. Let us assume instead that the word "on" triggers more general interpretations of the preposition, such as **onTime** and **onLocation**, reflecting the different possible semantic functions of the preposition. The detection of these features depends on the NP that follows the preposition. Another set of features is used for the attachment of the PP to other parts of the clause. For example, **onLocation** triggers the candidacy of **locationNPAttachment** and **locationVPAttachment**, which, respectively, attach any location PP to an immediately preceding NP, and any location PP to the verb of the clause. The definitions for these features are similar to those proposed above for **onObjectLocation** and **onActionLocation**. Also, it is possible that even more general features such as **attachPPToNP** and **attachPPToVP**, which would work for any type of PP, could be used (as is the case in the KB of the current prototype). This approach has the advantage of still respecting the "word expert" philosophy by using a first stratum of features that handle the different semantic functions of a preposition, while localizing attachment decisions in features not dependent on the particular prepositions but rather associated with general semantic categories (e.g., time, location, etc.).

A possible scenario that uses this more complex disambiguation scheme for "on" follows:

1. The processing of "dogs" or "tigers" leads to a cluster in which those animals are the topic of **actionDiscuss**.

2. The word "on" leads to the candidacy of the possible interpretations of its semantic function (e.g., **onLocation**, **onTime**, etc.).

3. The words "the beach" lead to the construction of a cluster that captures the fact that a beach is a location. This cluster is attached to the cluster constructed from the processing of "on". Feature **onLocation** becomes detected and triggers the candidacy of **locationNPAttachment** and **locationVPAttachment**. The feature **unattachedPP** is placed in the cluster corresponding to the PP in order to indicate the fact that the PP is not currently attached. This feature is deleted from the PP cluster when attachment features such as **locationVPAttachment** become detected.

4. Both of these features may have enough evidence to become detected, but must wait until the end of their candidacy, as other possible interpretations are specified as exceptions. This situation captures the structural ambiguity at that point of the processing.

5. The features corresponding to "while" become detected.

6. The features corresponding to "sunbathing" become detected. Through the use of "while", it is inferred that **actionDiscuss** and **actionSunbathe** occur in the same time frame and in the same location. A unique cluster with feature **unspecified** is constructed and made a subcluster of both verbs under feature **location**.

7. The co-occurrence of "beach" in an unattached location PP and of **actionSunbathe** triggers the inference that the subject of sunbathing performs this action on the beach (which belongs to the time frame of **actionDiscuss**). In order for this inference to become detected, it is required that the beach and the sunbathing be in the same time frame, which is the case. Thus, it is inferred that the sunbathing occurs on the beach. More precisely, the co-occurrence of "beach" and **actionSunbathe** triggers a buildable feature, **sunbatheOnBeach**, whose expan-

sion procedure checks that

> •the word "beach" belongs to an unattached loca-
> tion, PP. This check is performed by testing for the
> presence of **unattachedPP** and **location** in the clus-
> ter associated with the PP.

> •the unattached PP and **actionSunbathe** are in the
> same time frame (which can be thought of as a clus-
> ter whose subclusters under feature **cooccurrent-
> Facts** are the individual actions that occur in this
> time frame; see chapter 11).

Because these checks are satisfied, **sunbatheOnBeach** becomes detected. It
does not modify the context through its expansion procedure, but has **locationVPAttach** as an association. Thus, **locationVPAttach** becomes detected
upon receiving the signal from **sunbatheOnBeach**. The unattached PP is
attached to **actionSunbathe** under feature **location** and replaces the previous
"unspecified" cluster. Also, other possible interpretations of "on" are inhibited.

> 8. Since the **location** subcluster of the **actionDiscuss** cluster is bound
> to the **location** subcluster of **actionSunbathe**, the attachment to
> **actionSunbathe** de facto realizes the attachment to **actionDiscuss**. In
> other words, the structural ambiguity is resolved by an inference.

In fact, the inference that the sunbathing occurs on the beach can be erroneous:
The women could discuss "the dogs on the beach" while sunbathing in their
garden. If a reader does not make this inference, then the following scenario
could continue the previous one:

> 9. The words "and then" are processed leading the reader to infer a
> change of time frame.

> 10. The words "went to the cottage" are processed, leading the reader
> to perceive a change in location for the new time frame. I suggest that
> it is at this point that the verb attachment can occur. A change of loca-
> tion seems to imply that a previous location was specified. If this isn't
> the case, and there is an unattached location, PP, in the previous time
> frame, then **location-VPAttach** becomes detected.

In the example, the detection of a change of time and location would imply
that the actions of the previous time frame should have a **location** cluster. A
check to this effect, triggered by this change in location and time and per-

formed by (the expansion procedure of) feature **needVPLocationInPrevious-Frame,** reveals that they do not, leading to the candidacy of feature **findVPLocationInPreviousTimeFrame.** This feature becomes detected if an unattached location PP can be found in the previous time frame. The detection of this feature causes the detection of its association, **locationVPAttach.** In other words, in the example, the detection of **findVPLocationInPrevious-TimeFrame** leads to the resolution of the structural ambiguity.

The two proposed scenarios not only illustrate **IDIoT'**s treatment of attachment decisions as a lexical disambiguation problem, but also, and most importantly, suggest the omnipresent and complex role of context and inference for linguistic disambiguation. There are still some drawbacks with **IDIoT'**s strategy: For example, if no evidence favors either noun or verb attachment, then the user must specify either an order of preference or the detection of an ambiguity. Let us consider an example:

Example 10.3.3 *The women discussed the dogs at breakfast.*

Hirst (1987) stated that his system incorrectly attaches "at" to "the dogs" "because the subtle implausibility of the dogs at breakfast as a topic of conversation is not detected". In **IDIoT,** since plausibility judgments are not used per se, the NP-attachment must be prevented some other way. The user could specify KUs that detect this implausibility. In the current prototype of **IDIoT,** I have preferred having all the interpretations of "at" that allow NP-attachment to fail. In other words, "at breakfast" will not be attached to "dogs" because none of the interpretations of "at" correspond to this attachment.

As another example, consider this similar sentence:

Example 10.3.4 *The women discussed the bums at the train station.*

Out of context, this sentence is ambiguous: The women can be in their garden, talking about the bums of the train station, or they can be at the train station, discussing bums in general, or they can be at the train station discussing the bums of the train station. I leave it to the reader to invent passages in which each of these possibilities would be favored.

To conclude this chapter, here are some other examples handled by the current prototype of **IDIoT** that mix PP-attachment with reference resolution:

Example 10.3.5 *John watched the rabbit in the park.*

Here there is a double attachment of the PP, that is, to the VP and to the NP "the rabbit."

Example 10.3.6 *John watched the bench in the park.*

A lexical preference defined between "bench" and "park" leads to NP-attachment only.

Example 10.3.7 *R1 is a rabbit in a hat. John watched the rabbit in the hat.*

The reference found for "the rabbit in the hat" blocks VP-attachment.

Example 10.3.8 *John watched the rabbit with the telescope.*

A double attachment can be seen here also.

Example 10.3.9 *John watched the planet with the telescope.*

The lexical preference defined between "planet" and "telescope" leads to NP-attachment only.

Example 10.3.10 *R1 is a rabbit. R2 is a rabbit. John watched the rabbit with the hat.*

There is no reference resolution, but because "hat" is not an instrument for watching, the VP attachment will fail, leading the PP to be attached to the NP.

Example 10.3.11 *R1 is a rabbit with a telescope. John watched the rabbit with the telescope.*

The reference found for the NP prevents VP-attachment.

Example 10.3.12 *John watched the planet with the microscope.*

Note the double attachment unless an inference path between "watch" and "microscope" rules out "planet" as an candidate object to observe with a microscope.

Example 10.3.13 *R1 is a planet with a telescope. R2 is a planet. John watched the planet with the telescope.*

The reference found for "the planet with the telescope" prevents VP-attachment.

Example 10.3.14 *John eats in a park with a bench.*

The "in" PP is attached to "eats" and, by lexical preference, the "with" PP is attached to "park".

Chapter 11

Bridging Inferences

11.1 INTRODUCTION TO INFERENCE

It is a common view that forming inferences is an essential part of linguistic comprehension. Within the context of models for reading (see section 6.2), several psycholinguistic theories of inference have been proposed for text comprehension (e.g., see Flammer, & Kintsch, 1981; Rickheit, & Strohner, 1985; Garnham, 1989; Denhière, & Rossi, 1991; Singer, 1994). In general, these theories belong to the problematic "text linguistics" approach discussed in section 2.4. Recall that this approach is not grounded and relies on the existence of *macrostructures*. In this section, it is not my intent to revisit this conclusion, but rather to briefly comment on the plethora of models of inference in order to highlight a fundamental controversy still raging in text comprehension: the dichotomy between minimalist and constructionist accounts of inferencing.

Consider the following summary from Graesser and Kreuz (1993) regarding the status of research in text comprehension:

> [The] simple but controversial question in the field of discourse processing [is]: What classes of inferences are generated during comprehension of connected discourse? When an adult reads a novel, for example, the reader potentially generates inferences about the motives behind characters' actions, the traits of characters, the emotions of characters, the causes of anomalous events, spatial relationships among objects, expectations about future episodes in the plot, referents of pronouns, the attitudes of the writer, and so on. Some of these classes of inferences are normally generated 'on-line' (i.e., during the course of comprehension), whereas others are 'off-line' (i.e., generated during a later task but not during text comprehension). There have been substantial efforts in the fields of cognitive psychology and discourse processing to document and to explain which classes are generated on-line[.]

> Now that discourse processing researchers have investigated infer-
> ence generation for approximately 20 years, we should be ready to
> celebrate the fruits of our collective effort in the form of a mature the-
> ory. Surprisingly, a mature theory has not emerged. At best, there is a
> collection of minitheories, models, and hypotheses that apply to a
> very narrow sample of texts and pragmatic contexts. One possible
> explanation of this disappointing achievement is that we have not
> identified the experimental methodology that provides a perfect win-
> dow to those inferences that are truly on-line. . . . The current consen-
> sus is that there are trade-offs associated with each methodology, that
> there is no perfect methodology[.]

This assessment raises two important issues.

First, recall that beyond the pervasive inferencing underlying the different facets of comprehension addressed in the previous chapters, it is generally accepted that *bridging* inferences are required to perceive the coherence (whether local or global) of a text (e.g., see section 6.5). However, theories of bridging inferences often reduce to classification schemes (e.g., see Rickheit, Schnotz, & Strohner, 1985), leaving out several methodological and technical problems (e.g., see Singer, 1993, on the difficulty of building inferences between "distant" concepts). Furthermore, remember the claim of van der Meer (1987) that the types of bridging inferences used during comprehension are *not* the ones that researchers in text linguistics have been studying. In the same vein, Clark (1985) remarked that the social aspects of inferencing have generally been ignored in existing models. The point then, as stated by Graesser and Kreuz, is that we still lack a general theory of inference.

Second, taxonomies of inferences specifically suffer from not providing an answer to the question of *when* an inference is generated. More precisely, enumerating different categories of inferences does not say which of these categories of inferences are generated as the text is read, and which are produced subsequently. Two different viewpoints apparently confront each other in the literature.

On the one hand, the *constructionists* argue in favor of a multitude of on-line inferences. For example, Fletcher (1986), Trabasso and Suh (1993), and Suh and Trabasso (1993) contended that *goals* are a major source of local and global coherence because they organize sequences of states and actions over large surface distances in the text. Such a hypothesis is controversial. For example, Perfetti (1993) remarked that although those who argue for on-line goal-directed inferences may be correct, "the evidence in favor of such infer-ences is yet not substantial and is open to other interpretations".

To the goals of characters, some researchers (e.g., Ram, & Hunter, 1991;

Ram, & Leake, 1991; Graesser, & Kreuz, 1993) add the goals of the reader. Others propose yet different categories of inferences, and in the end, we obtain "very rich" models such as the one of Goldman and Varnhagen (1986), which, I repeat, relies on story categories, goal hierarchies, causal structures, and so forth. Long and Golding (1993) also assumed that "superordinate goal inferences are generated on-line", but quickly add the proviso, "when readers have sufficient time". Generally, however, the role of time in inferencing is downplayed. Instead, classes of inferences are categorized as on- or off-line, regardless of time. For example, contra Garnham (1993), Zwaan and Graesser (1993), and Zwaan and van Oostendorp (1993) argued that very few spatial inferences are generated on-line during "normal" reading.

The construction-integration model of Kintsch (1988, 1994), and the other models that proceed from it (e.g., Denhière, & Rossi, 1991) are of special interest here in that they indirectly grant some role to processing time by assuming that "reading a text leads, in addition to the activation of the *correct* representation, to the activation of non relevant, redundant, and even contradictory information, which will be, during a second phase, deactivated by a relaxation connectionist process". (Tapiero, & Denhière, 1993). Such a proposal, which relies on the existence of two phases, highlights the time course of inference, an aspect which is too often downplayed in existing theories of inference. Also, these models, which "don't use pre-stored schemata or "smart" rules for controlling the process of comprehension" (Tapiero, & Denhière, 1993) are strictly bottom-up: Expectations are not generated on-line. This hypothesis seems to be the dominant position in psycholinguistics (e.g., Magliano, Baggett, Johnson, & Graesser, 1993). Yet it has been rejected by Gernsbacher and Robertson (1992), who contended that expectations are automatic, and by Keefe and McDaniel (1993) and Murray, Klin and Myers (1993), who claimed that predictive inferences are drawn then deactivated.

On the other hand, McKoon and Ratcliff (1992) are often taken to epitomize a *minimalist* position, a standpoint rejected by constructionists (e.g., Glenberg, & Mathew, 1992; Glenberg, 1993). Garnham (1992) explained that, according to McKoon and Ratcliff, "only two kinds of inferences are made automatically during reading: those that establish local coherence and those based on readily available information. Other inferences can be made, but only if the reader engages in nonautomatic strategic processing". Garnham then argued that "the contrast between minimalism and constructionism is a false one since constructionist processes play an essential role in inferences that are made automatically". In his opinion, constructionism pertains to the use of both explicit and implicit knowledge, and thus, constructionist processes underlie even the perception of local coherence (which typically requires the use of implicit knowledge). Furthermore, Garnham highlighted the findings of Noordman and Vonk (1992) suggesting that subjects do not *necessarily* carry out inferential work as they read a sentence. It follows that not even the perception of local coherence entails automatic inferences. In the end, Garnham proposed a constructionist model that is "approximately minimalist": "Inferences are only made if they are both necessary to establish local coherence and based on readily available information. If the information is not readily available, the inference is not made". Clearly, this is in perfect agreement with the philosophy adopted in **IDIoT**. Interestingly, Garnham's proposal also emphasized the fact that "even 'simple'. . . inferences may depend on processes with complex *temporal* properties". (my emphasis).

It is clear that existing models of inference are generally oversimplified. For example, McKoon and Ratcliff (1992) and Garnham (1992) are among the few researchers that rejected the notion of "making" an inference at a given point in time. Instead, both proposed the idea of partially encoded inferences (which is close to **IDIoT**'s approach to reconstructable paths; see chapter 4). Other findings still need to be addressed. For example, Musseler, Rickheit, and Strohner (1985) claimed that a reader produces more elaborative inferences after listening, than after reading, for easy text, and that the reverse situation holds for difficult texts!

Yet beyond this oversimplicity, it is the study of inference altogether that must be questioned. We must consider that "we know virtually nothing about the neural mechanisms that underlie inference making" (Garnham, 1992). Also, van den Broek, Fletcher, and Risden (1993) warned us:

> The study of inferential processes constitutes a major focus of research on text comprehension. Recent research has resulted in interesting and important findings[.] Studies differ substantially, however, in the types of inferences that they consider and in the methodologies that they use. As a result, it is difficult to interpret and integrate the findings.

Such a warning ultimately explains this comment from Perfetti (1993):

> I am undecided at this point whether to think there is more to human inferencing talent than we have discovered or to conclude that inference making is not a good candidate for scientific study.

In light of this observation, in the rest of this chapter, I do not develop a grounded theory of inference, but rather investigate the mechanisms of inference in **IDIoT** without speculating on the existence, organization or "granularity" (i.e., specificity) of the knowledge that would be required to obtain "correct" inferences. For example, consider a passage such as this one:

Example 11.1.1 *John is hungry. He picks up the Michelin guide.*

It is ultimately, in my opinion, each user's responsibility to decide whether the co-occurrence of the features, "person x hungry" and "person x in possession on Michelin guide", should trigger a direct inference through the feature, "consult Michelin guide in order to satisfy hunger", or require a more elaborate chain of features (e.g., the goal-based explanation presented in subsection 2.2.2).

11.2 INFERENCES FOR TEXT COMPREHENSION

In this section, I want to briefly suggest that existing theories of inference can be at least partially modeled using **IDIoT**.

First, Garrod (1985) made a distinction between a "true inference", which proceeds from the application of an inferential schema, and a "pseudo inference", which arises from interpreting expressions against a mental model. In agreement with other researchers in text understanding (e.g., Graesser, & Clark, 1985; Garnham, 1992; Garnham, & Oakhill, 1992; Glenberg, & Mathew, 1992), he claimed that pseudo inferences are immediate, whereas true inferences are only established rarely during comprehension. In other words, most inference paths are constructed from the chaining of existing semantic features or from schema-matching, rather than by the application of formal reasoning rules. Thus, I do not focus here on formal inference but rather on these faster "pseudo inferences" typically involved in reading.

Second, recall that existing computational models in text linguistics (see subsection 2.2.2) can be separated into schema-matching models and inference-chaining ones. From my standpoint, inference for text comprehension requires both schema-matching *and* inference-chaining:

1. Schema-matching in **IDIoT** reduces to having the detection of a schema's "gate-keeper" feature cause the other features of the schema to become either immediately activated (through associations) or expected (through expectation signals). In other words, the activation of a schema reduces to the coretrieving of a group of features and the priming of another group of features, the two groups forming the schema proper.

2. Inference-chaining in **IDIoT** is implemented in terms of forward chaining using presence signals, and backward chaining using sub-

mission, confirmation, and reinforcement signals (see chapter 4).

To illustrate schema-matching in **IDIoT**, consider, for example, the "eat-at-a-restaurant" schema (Dyer, 1983; Norvig, 1987) for which I suggest the following possible partial definitions:

KU eatAtARestaurant:

```
% This feature corresponds to the schema of the same name.
 associations: contractualEvent
 constraint 1:
    triggers: actionEat, location, restaurant
    exceptions:
       eatAtFastFood has weight 1
    outputs:
       sends expectation signal to waiter
       sends expectation signal to beingSeated
       sends expectation signal to orderingAtRestaurant
       sends expectation signal to payFood
       ...
 expansion:
% I assume that actionEat would have replaced the subject feature
% with the feature eater, as was suggested earlier for the verb
% 'give'. The procedure checks that the eater is a person and that
% the location of actionEat is a restaurant.
       getCluster u1 governing eater
       getCluster u2 governedBy eater in u1
       testPresenceOf person in u2
       getCluster u3 governedBy actionEat in u1
       testPresenceOf location in u3
       getCluster u4 governedBy location in u3
       testPresenceOf restaurant in u4
       renameFeature actionEat to eatAtARestaurant in u1
```

KU beingSeatedAtRestaurant:

```
% This feature is a substep of the eat-at-a-restaurant schema.
 constraint 1:
   ordered triggers: eatAtRestaurant, actionSeat
 expansion:
% The procedure checks that the person being seated is the same as
```

```
% the eating. If so, the event of being seated is put under feature
% 'subSteps' in the cluster associated with 'eat-at-a-restaurant':
% by being governed, the substeps become less retrievable and more
% likely to be moved to LTM.
       getCluster u1 governing seated
       getCluster u2 governedBy seated in u1
       getCluster u3 governing eatAtARestaurant
       getCluster u4 governedBy eater in u3
       testEquivalenceOf u2 u4
       addFeature substeps to u3
       addSubCluster u1 to subSteps in u3
```

KU waiter:
```
% This feature is partly defined in terms of the schemata that may
% trigger it.
 constraint c1:
  ordered triggers: eatAtARestaurant, actionServe
 constraint c2:
  ordered triggers: drinkAtBar, actionServe

 ...

 expansion:
% Check that the person being served is also the actor of the
% triggered scenario.
       getCluster u1 governing actionServe
       getCluster u2 governedBy beingServed
    ifConstraint c1 then getCluster u3 governing eatAtARestaurant
     ifConstraint c1 then getCluster u4 governedBy eater in u3
     ifConstraint c2 then getCluster u3 governing drinkAtBar
     ifConstraint c2 then getCluster u4 governedBy drinker in u3
       testEquivalenceOf u2 u4
% If so, add the cluster corresponding to the service performed by
% the waiter to the substeps of the schema.
       addFeature substeps to u3
       addSubCluster u1 to substeps in u3
```

An example using these definitions is discussed later in this chapter. For now, let me briefly explain the use of feature **substeps** in schema matching. When a schema is detected, it typically sets up expectations. In turn, these are detected if they receive an input signal from all their triggers. The key point is that an expected feature can always be reconstructed from the feature that created the expectation, that is, the one that sent the expectation signal. Furthermore, it is commonly accepted that reconstructable items are less likely to be part of the final interpretation (e.g., Kintsch, & van Dijk, 1978, p. 365). Therefore, I suggest that all expected features of a schema that eventually become detected be governed by this schema, under the feature **subSteps**. In other words, the clusters corresponding to the substeps of a schema are subclusters, under the feature **subSteps** of the cluster associated with the schema. As subclusters, they are less reachable than the cluster of the schema itself, and thus, because of memory limitations, more likely to not be included in the final interpretation.

Let us now turn to inference chaining. Recall that Norvig's work (1987, p. 101) on inference-chaining hinges on the a priori definition of a small number of path shapes and inference classes: Only a path that matches one of the predefined shapes is considered for evaluation. If so desired, these notions can be readily duplicated in **IDIoT**. Consider, for example, Norvig's simplest inference class, namely reference resolution. In **FAUSTUS**, an inference class consists of a pair of path shapes that must be matched to the two halves of the total path of a marker collision. For the reference resolution inference, both halves must correspond to a reference path, which is defined as

$$\text{Reference: } origin \rightarrow I \rightarrow D^* \rightarrow collision,$$

in which I is an instance relationship, and D, a dominate one (where A dominates B if B is a subclass of A; see Norvig, 1987, pp. p. 60 and 105). Such relationships can be used in **IDIoT** instead of more direct links between KUs. Consider, for example, the following partial definitions:

KU johnPerson:
```
    associations: instanceOfMan, ...
    . . .
```
KU he:
```
    associations: instanceOfMan, ...
    . . .
```
relay KU instanceOfMan:
```
    suppliers: johnPerson, paulPerson, henryPerson, ...
    customers: man, instanceRelationship, ...
```
KU man:
```
    associations: subclassOfPerson, ...
```

KU subclassOfPerson:
```
suppliers: man, woman, child, ...
customers: person, subclassRelationship,...
```

relay KU instanceRelationship:
```
suppliers: instanceOfMan, ...
customers: refPathShape, ...
```

relay KU subclassRelationship:
```
suppliers: subclassOfPerson, ...
customers: refPathShape, ...
```

The feature **johnPerson** will lead, through **instanceOfMan**, to the detection of **instanceRelationship**, which notifies a feature, **refPathShape**, that would define Norvig's "reference" path shape. The feature **instanceOfMan** would also eventually lead to the detection of the **subclass** relationship that would also notify **refPathShape**. Recognizing a sequence of D shapes (i.e., a sequence of Dominate links) could be handled in the same way as for a sequence of adjectives (see section 7.3). A very similar approach can be used to capture the arc categories and composition rules suggested by Graesser and Clark (1985, p. 74).

Beyond the generation of inferences, a complete theory of inference must also address the convergence problem. That is, it must explain how to limit the actual number of inferences produced. Recall from chapter 2 that, in existing computational models, the problem is either ignored or, in the case of marker-passing systems, handled with magic numbers and anti-promiscuity rules (e.g., Hirst, 1987, section 5.2.3; Hendler, 1987, 1989). A few models emulate memory decay through attrition (e.g., Norvig, 1983b, 1987), but there is typically no attempt to model memory per se. Conversely, in neurolinguistics (Gigley, 1985a) and psycholinguistics, it is generally accepted, for example, that the constraints of the working memory (i.e., capacity and decay) do contribute towards convergence. Moreover, as suggested in section 11.1, it is often assumed that the construction of inference paths largely depends on the availability of the relevant features (e.g., Schnotz, 1985; Garnham, 1992; Long, & Golding, 1993). The point I want to make in conclusion is two-fold:

1. As suggested in section 4.7, the time-constrained nature of **IDIoT** inherently solves the convergence problem.

2. It follows that **IDIoT** does offer a grounded foundation for a com-

plete theory of inference during comprehension.

However, **IDIoT** still merely constitutes a first approximation of the complex memory processes involved in text comprehension. For example, I do not address some of the more sophisticated features of van Dijk and Kintsch's model of comprehension (1978, pp. 368–371; 1983):

1. I do not model the kind of processing cycles that they assume, whereby a group of propositions are processed together.

2. I do not tackle the tasks of recall and summarization and, therefore, I do not implement any sort of *reproduction probability*. Consequently, I oversimplify the passage of clusters from STM to LTM by not correlating it to frequency of reachability.

11.3 INFERENCE WITH IDIoT

In this section, I to suggest how the different facets of inference for text comprehension can be tackled with **IDIoT** on its own, that is, without attempting to accommodate the assumptions and ad hoc categories and processes put forth by existing models.

Let us start by discussing the functional relationships that exist between clauses, because, I argue, a proper treatment of inference, local coherence, and global coherence (see Sanford, & Garrod, 1994) ultimately depends on these relationships. It is commonly accepted that clauses must be related on the basis of their meaning, not just through reference, but this link can be complex to establish. For example, Kintsch and van Dijk (1978, pp. 390–393) saw this problem as the crucial missing component of their initial work:

> We do not have yet an adequate theory of such functional relations. The present model was not extended beyond the processes involved in referential coherence of texts because we do not feel that the problems involved are sufficiently well understood. However, by limiting the processing model to coherence in terms of argument repetition, we are neglecting the important role that fact relationships play in comprehension.

There are several possible classification schemes for "facts" (i.e., inter–clausal) relationships:

1. From the initial observation that a fact may be a possible, likely, or necessary consequence of another (through connectives such as "like", "because", "although", etc.) Kintsch and van Dijk (1978, pp.

390–393) suggested presuppositional relationships: compatibility, enablement, specification, correction, explanation, and generalization. A multitude of similar models have been proposed (see Graesser, & Clark, 1985).

2. Some (if not most) of the rules of story grammarians (see subsection 2.2.1) and some of Lehnert's plot units (1981) constitute fact relationships.

3. Norvig's (1987) inference classes, especially the "view" class, could also be taken as fact relationships.

In fact, as mentioned in section 11.1, a multitude of taxonomies for inferences have been proposed, most of them dealing with causal inter–clausal relationships.

From my standpoint, inter–clausal relationships constitute organizing principles for the construction of clusters. In other words, these relationships essentially specify how the clusters of the facts they relate are organized in STM. I propose distinguishing between local and global organizing principles. Local fact relations typically specify a government link between two clauses. For example, if A is a consequence of B, then there must be a government link between A and B. It is left to the user of **IDIoT** to choose a uniform strategy for each class of fact relation that is to be perceived. For example, if it is established that A is a consequence of B, then A could be systematically made a sub-cluster of B under the feature **consequence**. Similarly, a correction could always govern the fact that it corrects, and an explained fact, its explanation. More generally, given a taxonomy of inter–clausal relationships and the government strategy adopted by a specific reader for each such relationship, **IDIoT** can be used to implement, using expansion procedures, these strategies. Again, it is important to understand that, within the framework of a reader-based approach to comprehension, the onus of deciding on the realization of these relationships falls on the user of **IDIoT**. For example, the ordering of the clauses may be relevant to the specification of such strategies. Consider these sentences:

Example 11.3.1   *Because he is hungry, John eats.*

Example 11.3.2   *John eats because he is hungry.*

Here, it is up to the user of **IDIoT** to decide

1. whether in both sentences the reason clause ("because he is hungry") governs or is governed by the main clause ("John eats").

2. whether or not the temporal ordering of clauses affects the reproduction probability of each one (e.g., being the first processed, the
clause "because he is hungry" would have better chances of being
recalled in the first sentence than in the second).

Let us now turn to global coherence. Whereas local organizing principles
specify a government relation between the clusters of two clauses, I propose
that global organizing principles place each cluster on several orthogonal
"axes" of organization. This idea is close to Zavarin's (1983) notion of "stratification" of levels of representation during comprehension. More specifically,
I suggest that each cluster be, at the very least, placed on the time and location
axes. In a complete theory of inference, there could be an axis for each of the
different semantic roles that can be established within a clause (e.g., actors,
time, location, instrument, manner, etc.). Kintsch and van Dijk (1978, p. 391)
made essentially the same hypothesis when they developed the notion of *topic
change markers* (1983, p. 204).

Let me sketch the use and implementation of the time and location axes
in **IDIoT**. I hypothesize that each of these axes is organized in terms of
"frames". This word is, however, used in a totally different sense from its
usual one in AI: In **IDIoT**, a frame is merely a set of clusters and an axis of
organization, a set of frames. For example, two facts may be in the same time
frame but in different location frames:

Example 11.3.3 *Yesterday, John did the shopping and Mary played badmin-
ton.*

Each fact can be "placed" on one or more of these axes. Placing a fact on an
axis means making it a subcluster of the *current* frame of this axis. For each
axis, the user needs to specify features that detect a change of frame on this
axis (e.g., different times, different locations, etc.). For time, verb tenses and
explicit connectives such as the word "then" indicate such changes, which, if
implicit, must be inferred.

There is a relatively simple implementation of the notions of axes and current frames in the current prototype of **IDIoT**. An axis is, not surprisingly, a
cluster. One feature of an axis identifies the axis itself (e.g., **timeAxis** is a feature of the cluster denoting the time axis). Each of the other features of the
cluster governs a set of subclusters belonging to the same frame. In other
words, each other feature governs a frame. The current frame is identified by
a specific feature name. For example, to access the current frame on the time
axis, one could access the cluster governed by the feature **currentTime**, in the
cluster governing feature **timeAxis**. The user may set up the naming of fea-

tures so that the previous time frame could also be accessed using the name of its governing feature (e.g., **previousTimeFrame**). Assuming, for simplicity, that only the current time frame is directly accessible, a change of frame is still tricky: The set of clusters governed by **currentTime** should now be governed by some feature whose name is irrelevant (because we assume that only the current time frame is accessible), and the feature **currentTime**, should be made to govern a new empty set of clusters. To accommodate the idea of a feature whose name is irrelevant, that is, in essence, a run-time feature that cannot be referred to by the user, I introduce the "built-in" (i.e., system-supplied) feature **dummyFeature**. By renaming **currentTime** to **dummyFeature**, the user establishes a boundary between two distinct time frames and makes the current one the only accessible one. More precisely, in the current prototype, renaming a feature to **dummyFeature** in fact, renames the feature to a unique name generated by the system upon executing this instruction. This guarantees that no expansion procedure can refer to the renamed cluster.

Here are sketchy definitions for adding to the current time frame and switching time frames:

KU addToCurrentTimeFrame:

```
constraint 1:
 triggers: clauseFitsCurrentTime
expansion:
     getCluster u1 governing clauseFitsCurrentTime
     getCluster u2 governing timeAxis
     getCluster u3 governedBy currentTime in u2
     addSubCluster u1 to currentTime in u3
```

KU switchTimeFrame:

```
constraint 1:
 triggers: clauseFitsNewTime
expansion:
     getCluster u1 governing clauseFitsNewTime
     getCluster u2 governing timeAxis
     renameFeature currentTime to dummyFeature in u2
     addFeature currentTime to u2
     addSubCluster u1 to currentTime in u3
```

These definitions assume that when the ending boundary of a clause is detected, it is possible to infer whether the clause belongs to the current or to a new time frame, to the current or to a new location frame, and so forth. Beyond explicit connectives, rules for such inferences have already been proposed in the literature (e.g., Allen, 1982, for time relationships). In the context of a theory of comprehension that hypothesizes several axes, user-specified rules are required to classify each fact along each of these axes. In other words, I repeat, the user must specify rules that will decide, for each axis x, whether the current clause being processed belongs to the current frame of x or causes a new frame to be created for x. Because of the use of parallelism in **IDIoT**, a clause can be placed simultaneously on all the postulated axes.

To illustrate, for example, the use of a locational axis of organization, consider this sentence:

Example 11.3.4 *John eats in Ottawa. Mary sleeps in Toronto.*

For this sentence I suggest the following sketchy scenario:

> 1. The cluster associated with **actionEat** possesses a feature **location** that governs the cluster associated with "Ottawa".

> 2. The cluster associated with **actionSleep** possesses a feature **location** that governs the cluster associated with "Toronto".

> 3. The feature **checkLocation**, which is triggered each time the feature, **location**, is used (e.g., when a verb has its location specified), tests the difference between the new location and the current one. If these are not the same, the feature **checkLocation** becomes detected and triggers the candidacy of features **clauseFitsNewLocation** and **clauseFitsPreviousLocation**.

> 4. The feature **clauseFitsNewLocation** becomes detected only if the candidacy of **clauseFitsPreviousLocation** fails.

> 5. The feature **clauseFitsPreviousLocation** tries to match the new location with one of the clusters already on the locational axis. If it succeeds, the action (in this case, **actionSleep**) is made a subcluster of the relevant frame of the axis.

Evidently the suggested theory for these global axes is still quite simplistic, especially in view of the complexity of the retrieval process(es) that would have to access these axes in order to produce recalls, summaries, and answers to questions on the text read. Yet the importance of these axes should not be underestimated. Consider, for example, this passage:

Example 11.3.5 *John was hungry yesterday afternoon. [Other facts.] Next* *month, John will pick up a Michelin guide.*

The notation [*Other facts.*] denotes a series of zero or more facts. Any inference between "hungry" and "having a Michelin guide" must likely be blocked in this example, because such an inference involves concepts in different time frames. From this viewpoint, the axes implement semantic constraints for inference generation, in addition to the constraints already existing at the memory level, as illustrated in the following sentence:

Example 11.3.6 *John is hungry. [Other facts.] John picks up the Michelin guide.*

Assuming that all relevant knowledge is available

1. if [*Other facts.*] is empty, then the inference proceeds directly with both fact F1 ("John is hungry") and fact F2 ("John picks up the Michelin guide") in WM.

2. if [*Other facts.*] contains a few items, then the likelihood of the inference decreases slightly due to the fact that F1 will probably be less reachable (i.e., in STM, not in WM).

3. if [*Other facts.*] contains a large number of facts, then F1 will probably have been "moved" to LTM (or forgotten), in which case the inference between F1 and F2 will be missed.

Here is an example of such a semantic constraint involving, in this case, at least the location axis:

Example 11.3.7 *John is hungry in Ottawa, while Mary picks up a Michelin guide in Paris.*

Again, the different locations for the two facts should probably block the path between "hungry" and "Michelin guide". If, however, John and Mary were in the same location, then the link between "hungry" and "Michelin guide" could be made if John announced he was hungry, and Mary picked up the Michelin guide.

In summary, inter–clausal relationships directly correlate with a reader's perception of local and global coherence and, ultimately, with the perception of subject matter. It must be stressed that local and global coherence, and subject matter, are not taken to be perceived one after the other but, on the contrary, simultaneously and interdependently. In particular, local coherence is subject to global constraints, as explained by van Dijk and Kintsch (1983, p. 152). Similarly, both global coherence and subject matter depend on how clauses are interrelated (especially in terms of government) at the local level. Also, it is commonly accepted that differences between readers are more frequent at the level of global coherence than at the level of local coherence, which often involves *conventionalized* inter–clausal relationships. Thus, we would expect that different users of **IDIoT** may specify similar rules for handling the perception of local coherence, but would likely differ significantly on how global coherence and subject matter are established from the contents of the axes chosen by these users. In fact, it is possible that even the nature of these axes differ between users, if not, for a same user, between texts. In other words, ideally, which axes are used to process a text should not be necessarily prespecified, but rather determined dynamically.

To conclude, I remark that with respect to the notion of subject matter, we still lack a theory of topical inferences. More precisely, we have yet to understand how inter–clausal relationships correlate with topic changes (e.g., how do we delimit "episodes", etc.). This observation led Kintsch and van Dijk (1978) to acknowledge that in the general case where readers approach a text with no a priori goals or controlling schema, "the perception of subject matter can vastly differ from one reader to another".

11.4 MORE SEMANTIC RULES FOR INFERENCE

It is very probable that, during the processing of a text, erroneous and "premature" inferences will be drawn, eventually leading the reader to perceive a conflict between a previously established fact and one that has just been detected. I suggest handling such a semantic conflict in much the same way as what was proposed for syntactic conflicts in chapter 7. As an example of a semantic conflict, consider this passage:

Example 11.4.1 *John is dead. John eats.*

The sequence of facts "person x dead" followed by "person x does action" (detected from the action verb "eat") could cause the detection of the feature **deadPersonDoesNotAct** that captures this particular semantic conflict. (There is no conflict if John dies after eating. Thus, this conflict can only be detected if it has been somehow acknowledged that the death occurs before the action.) In turn, **deadPersonDoesNotAct** notifies its association, **semanticConflict**, which localizes, in one feature, the strategy for handling such conflicts.

There are several possible strategies to specify a feature like **deadPersonDoesNotAct**. For example, features could be specified so that a person can act only if alive. Otherwise, a conflict is perceived. Later, I suggest another approach, which uses a buildable feature to check that the action follows the death once both facts have been detected. The trick is to rely on the fact that if John is dead when he performs an action, then his associated cluster will already have (or govern) feature(s) reflecting this state. In this case, it is the dynamic co-occurrence of conflicting features within the cluster associated with John that will cause the detection of **deadPersonDoesNotAct**. Here is a possible definition:

KU deadPersonDoesNotAct:
```
associations: semanticConflict
constraint 1:
 triggers: personActs
% this trigger implies a present action (not a past action).
 expansion:
      getCluster u1 governing clause
      getCluster u2 governedBy subject in u1
% u2 is cluster of the subject.
      testPresenceOf person in u2
% subject must be a person.
      getCluster u3 governedBy personStateAttributes in u2
      testPresenceOf dead in u3
% subject of action is dead
 ...
```

This feature is triggered each time a person acts. It checks that the person who acts has the feature **dead** in the set of features corresponding to the **personStateAttributes** cluster associated with each person. A similar approach can be used to check more sophisticated conflicts, such as one where the same person is the subject of two actions taking place at the same time in different locations, as in the following example:

Example 11.4.2 *Today at 2 pm, John will meet Paul in Ottawa and Fred in Toronto.*

Here is a possible definition for a knowledge unit responsible for the detection of such a conflict:

KU ubiquitousPerson:
```
associations: semanticConflict
```

```
constraint 1:
  triggers: personActs
expansion:
      getCluster u1 governing clause
      getCluster u2 governing subject in u1
      testPresenceOf person in u2
      getCluster u10 governing previousClause
      getCluster u20 governing subject in u10
      testPresenceOf person in u20
% At this point u1 and u10 both govern actions performed by
% persons. Check it's the same person.
      getCluster u3 governedBy person in u2
      getCluster u30 governedBy person in u20
      testEquivalence u3 u30
% Check that the actions occur at the same time.
      getCluster u3 governedBy mainVerb in u1
      getCluster u4 governing time in u3
      getCluster u30 governedBy mainVerb in u10
      getCluster u40 governing time in u30
      testEquivalence u4 u40
% Check for actions occurring in the same location, in which case
% the conflict becomes detected.
% Alternatively, we could use the time and location axes.
      getCluster u5 governing location in u3
      getCluster u50 governing location in u30
      testEquivalence u5 u50
```

The features **deadPersonDoesNotAct** and **ubiquitousPerson** are extremely specialized (in the spirit of the word-expert philosophy I adopt, see Small, 1980, 1983). More general rules such as "an inanimate cannot act" and "an actor cannot be ubiquitous" could be defined in a similar way, the granularity of the knowledge being the choice of the user of **IDIoT**. Furthermore, as with other "types" of inferences, there is no single commonly accepted theory of semantic conflicts. What distinguishes such a conflict inference from another inference is that it may need to be "resolved". More precisely, Kintsch and van Dijk (1978) observed that, upon detecting a semantic conflict, it is typical to either ignore it or to invest more processing resources (e.g., time and memory capacity) in order to resolve it. In the latter case, they added, the increase of resources may increase the conflict's reproduction probability, that is, the likelihood of the conflict being recalled. Granger and Holbrook (1983) suggested a more complex theory: A conflict requires an *inference strategy* in order to be resolved. Given a preestablished and reachable fact x and a conflicting fact y that has just been detected, they propose three possible strategies:

1. **Perseverance**: Hold on to x and ignore y.

2. **Recency**: Choose y and forget x.

3. **Deferral**: Keep both facts and wait for a subsequent resolution.

A fourth strategy could be this:

4. **Reconciliation**: Invest more resources in order to find a path that could explain the conflict and reconcile the two facts.

More complex strategies, such as rereading or correcting (as opposed to eliminating) one or both conflicting facts, are also possible but generally not considered because they involve complex processes of attention and decision (if not self-awareness) that are currently beyond most computational models (including **IDIoT**).

In essence, these strategies are quite similar to the resolution strategies proposed (in chapter 8) for lexical disambiguation. Without going in detail, the first three strategies of Granger and Holbrook can be easily modeled in **IDIoT** through the expansion procedure of the **semanticConflict** feature. In the first two cases, the cluster corresponding to the fact to forget is simply deleted. In the third case, the clusters of the conflicting pair of facts could be marked with a special feature (e.g., **unsolvedConflict**), providing access once a resolution has been found within a short amount of time after the conflict has been detected. The fourth tactic, reconciliation, is the trickiest (and probably, the most infrequent) in that it involves requesting more time and memory capacity in order to find an explanatory inference between the two facts. Currently, neither the time–span of a candidacy nor the capacity of STM can be dynamically modified during a reading. In the future, however, a KU should be able to partially alter the time–span of its candidacy, and it should be possible for a KU to increase the STM capacity using a message to the memory manager. Finally, to reflect the possibility of using different strategies at different points in time, a future prototype of **IDIoT** could allow a KU to possess several expansion procedures and dynamically choose (i.e., during reading) which one to execute.

To conclude this chapter, let me briefly discuss two additional phenomena (not yet supported in **IDIoT**) relevant to inferencing and involving attentional processes. These phenomena will introduce some of the enhancements discussed in the next chapter.

First, Hidi and Baird (1986) reported that the perception of *interestingness* is partly idiosyncratic: "Interest occurs only in the interaction between stimulus and person so that one can never stipulate its origin in one to the exclusion of the other". They also remarked that "what is central to the response of interest is that a person is compelled to increase intellectual activity to cope with greater significance of incoming information". I suggest that "increasing intellectual activity" may correspond to the following actions in **IDIoT**:

> 1. **increasing STM capacity**: A KU requests from the memory manager that the membership to STM be momentarily extended to clusters that would otherwise be too long to retrieve.

> 2. **slowing down the rate of decay**: An individual KU could slow down its own rate of decay and/or notify the memory manager that all decay rates should be lowered for a short amount of time.

> 3. **increasing the time–span of candidacies**: A KU asks the memory manager to increase the time–span of candidacies for a short amount of time.

In essence, we want a KU to have the possibility to dynamically modify the processing environment for a limited period of time. At this point in my research, it seems this may best be accomplished by having the vocabulary for expansion procedures include two new instructions that would, respectively, increase and decrease intellectual activity as described previously. The major drawback of this approach is that special-purpose signals would have to be hypothesized to carry out complex operations. In turn, this points to the need to investigate the actual physiological reification of the currently very metaphorical memory manager, as discussed in the next chapter.

Second, as mentioned in section 11.1, several researchers (e.g., Ram, 1990b, 1991; Ram, & Hunter, 1991; Ram, & Leake, 1991; Graesser, & Kreuz, 1993) have suggested that the perception of subject matter often relies on the "knowledge" goals (or equivalently, *perspective*) of a reader. For example, Kintsch and van Dijk (1978) wrote:

> *Decameron* stories may be read not for the plot and the interesting events but because of concern with the role of women in fourteenth-century Italy or with the attitudes of the characters in the story toward morality and sin.

Thus, a reader has the ability to understand a text from different cognitive viewpoints, different perspectives. I emphasize that these perspectives are totally idiosyncratic and that each reading of a text may be initiated from a different one. Reading with a perspective corresponds to the frequent situation where a reader comes to a text already seeking a certain aboutness (Vipond, & Hunt, 1984). Within the framework of **IDIoT**, I suggest that a perspective consist of a set of features that are initially selected and detected at the beginning of a reading and that reside *permanently* in WM for this reading. The omnipresence of the perspective in WM guarantees its reachability, and thus its systematic consideration by all candidate inferences. (Such a strategy is, again, simplistic inasmuch as a reader may simultaneously possess several perspectives.)

Part IV
Conclusions

Chapter 12

Some last thoughts

12.1 ON EVALUATING IDIoT

Norvig (1987, chapter 7) started his conclusions by remarking that, "in a sense, **FAUSTUS** was an experiment in self-deprivation" in that it relied on only six basic inference classes, contrary to systems such as Dyer's (1983) **BORIS** where "one occasionally gets the suspicion that the system designer can just add one more rule to account for each new difficulty as it arises, as long as he or she is careful about interactions with previous rules" (Norvig, 1987). Yet, I have argued in chapter 2, that *all* existing symbolic approaches to text understanding are postulating a priori macrostructures that constitute rules of comprehension entrenched in these models. In other words, a debate between inference-chaining and schema-matching hides, from my viewpoint, the fact that neither of these approaches offers a grounded model for linguistic comprehension. Furthermore, in surveying existing work in psycholinguistics throughout Part III of this book, I have highlighted the absence of consensus on the nature and modus operandi of these hypothesized macrostructures. As Graesser and Kreuz (1993) remarked, we still lack a complete theory of text understanding.

    IDIoT does *not* constitute such a theory, merely a grounded architecture "on top of which" such a theory could be specified, as suggested throughout Part III. **IDIoT** is not a symbolic system per se. Instead, it adopts the processing model of local connectionist models and does allow, at least in theory, the use of distributed representations (whereby a single feature can be recognized through the activation of several knowledge units), but the use of distributed representations has not been discussed in this book and needs to be thoroughly investigated. Furthermore, **IDIoT** is not a PDP system: It does not possess a learning algorithm, and the processors forming its semantic network can build representations in memory, a key requirement for text comprehension. Conversely, existing PDP models do not build; they merely recognize what they were taught, an inadequate strategy for the understanding of large textual units. Moreover, it appears that PDP models do not scale up to the problems of text understanding without eventually resorting to a priori rules (Miikku-lainen, 1993b).

From this viewpoint, **IDIoT** offers a significantly different approach to text understanding, an approach ultimately concerned with an explanation of cognitive phenomena in terms of Minsky's (1986) "mindless stuff". Thus, the model is not readily comparable to existing research in computational linguistics inasmuch as it does not focus on knowledge per se, but rather on the processing of knowledge specified by an *individual* user. Such an idiosyncratic outlook on comprehension complicates an evaluation of **IDIoT**: We traditionally judge a system by the problems it solves or does not solve, and by the validity of the predictions it makes, but a reader-based model of text comprehension does not fit this mold:

1. Comprehension is diachronic and non–deterministic (Rastier, 1991). Therefore, for text understanding, we cannot refer to a single interpretation of a text, and even less to the *correct* interpretation of a text. Only through the problematic use of an improbable ideal (i.e., *competent*) reader can we decree normative rules of comprehension and macrostructures.

2. Comprehension depends on the knowledge of an individual. Certainly, some of this knowledge is conventionalized (e.g., syntactic rules, idioms, etc.), but such conventions seem to be largely limited to the sentential level (as emphasized throughout Part III of this book). The quest for a small eternal set of macrostructures that would explain all texts, a quest that entails the existence of a set of universal meanings, only proceeds, in the opinion of Rastier (1991), from a dogmatic approach to human cognition, an approach rooted in the self-blinded metaphor of an objective "expert" that discovers macrostructures (Barthes, 1977).

3. Beyond idiosyncratic knowledge, it is commonly accepted that comprehension also depends on the specific *"performance* parameters" of an individual. These parameters may vary considerably between readers and, for a same reader, at different points in time. For example, a student under the pressure of an exam may allow herself only a short amount of time to make inferences, a strategy that will likely lead to an interpretation that significantly differs from the one this student would obtain if she allowed herself more time to understand. Because performance parameters may vary with context, it is difficult to make decontextualized predictions regarding the nature of

an interpretation, and if every context is taken to be unique (Firth, 1957), then predictions pertaining to the contents of an interpretation are quite problematic.

IDIoT makes no predictions with respect to the knowledge used during comprehension: This is instead the object of a hermeneutic theory proper, a theory that I plan to develop and implement in **IDIoT**, starting from Rastier's interpretative semantics (1987, 1989, 1991). Such a theory will have to address the multitude of semantic questions left out of this book, as well as a posteriori tasks such as recall and summarization.

For now, however, the question remains how do we evaluate **IDIoT** on its own. First, we must understand that adopting the metaphor of time-constrained memory *does* entail predictions with respect to the processing of a text (as opposed to predictions regarding the contents of the interpretation): **IDIoT** is meant to model the processing taken to be common among readers during comprehension. For example, I assume that the decay rate, the capacity of STM and the time–span of candidacy races directly affect the number of inferences generated on-line. These assumptions and others of the model proceed from two sources:

1. The biological constraint (Feldman, 1984) that emphasizes the real-time nature of linguistic comprehension.

2. The psycholinguistic results pertaining to the role of memory during comprehension (e.g., for reference resolution, inferencing, etc.) as surveyed in Part III.

In other words, beyond my specific assumptions regarding the time-constrained nature of memory and comprehension, I have tried to adopt well-accepted hypotheses (e.g., memory possesses temporal partitions, STM has limited capacity, etc.) found in the psycholinguistic literature. Should a methodology successfully prevent a reader from allocating more resources to the comprehension process due to the "strain" of the experiment, we could then hope that such assumptions could be confirmed or proven incorrect. On this topic, however, the computer scientist is obviously dependent on the psycholinguist, and we must remember the warnings of Dillon (1980) and Spiro (1980), reasserted more recently by Perfetti (1993) and Graesser, and Kreuz (1993): An experiment always has a context, and this context may significantly affect the observed performance. The acknowledgment that performance is difficult to predict (due to the multitude of factors that affect it, including social and cultural ones) should not, however, lead us to postulate some self-validating notion of "readerly competence" (that abstracts away performance). Instead, we should pursue the characterization of an interpretation with respect to a performance context, and, from a pragmatic viewpoint, we should be ready to accept that, ultimately, it is the user of **IDIoT** that acts as the sole judge of the acceptability of an interpretation.

Second, we can evaluate **IDIoT** with respect to the goals put forth in chapter 1:

1. The primary goal of this work was to motivate and develop a grounded uniform architecture and illustrate its relevance to the interpretation of written text. In chapter 2, I have argued at length on the need for a grounded cognitive architecture. Then, in Part II, I have designed such an architecture while avoiding epistemological commitments. Finally, throughout Part III, I have emphasized the pervasive role of processing time during linguistic comprehension.

2. My second goal was to demonstrate that a grounded architecture standardizes both the processing and expression of knowledge. In order to achieve this goal, throughout Part III, I have provided examples of knowledge units that address the different facets of linguistic comprehension. My claim is that knowledge units do provide a grounded representation scheme for expressing the knowledge used during comprehension. I have also very briefly suggested how knowledge units could be used to "ground" existing representational schemes such as the one of Norvig (1987). Furthermore, I have promoted additional standardization for processing by having the model depend on user-specifiable performance parameters. In other words, **IDIoT** is meant to emulate a multitude of different processing strategies.

3. My third goal was to overview psycholinguistic evidence pertaining to a time-constrained model of memory for text comprehension. I have provided such a survey throughout the book, but this survey is still quite cursory in light of the breadth and depth of phenomena presented in Gernsbacher (1994).

4. My final goal was to demonstrate that the proposed model of memory is tractable with respect to both time and space complexity. The time-constrained nature of memory directly addresses time complexity. As for space complexity, I have suggested that the convergence mechanisms inherent to the model, and in particular, the fact that the STM capacity defines the maximum size of a cluster (in terms of number of elements), ensure space tractability. However, this argu-

ment still largely depends on the problematic issue of the size and hierarchical organization of a cluster.

In the end, **IDIoT** merely "grounds" a theory of text understanding into the more fundamental (representational and processing) level that memory constitutes. From this viewpoint, **IDIoT** is an experiment in *extreme* self-deprivation: The onus is on its user to develop a conceptual analyzer out of the proposed model of time-constrained memory, which has only six numeric signals and a small set of primitive cluster operations. The model, however, does offer several interesting characteristics:

1. Both forward and backward inference chaining, and expectations are available.

2. Both static and dynamic (contextual) constraints (using buildable features) are available.

3. Contrary to connectionist models, **IDIoT** can build cognitive structures during comprehension (using expansion procedures). The structures can be complex and hierarchical and are automatically managed by the memory model (in terms of temporal memberships to the partitions of memory).

4. The user does not need to prespecify a stopping criterion: Time acts as a default mechanism for convergence, the user being able to further restrict comprehension through the use of semantic constraints.

5. "Friendly" user interfaces (see chapter 5) simplify the task of specifying knowledge units.

6. As an experimentation tool, **IDIoT** allows the processing of a text using different knowledge bases and different processing strategies.

The fundamental drawback of the current prototype proceeds from its word-expert approach. Put simply, because knowledge cannot be expressed in a perfectly modular way, some rules need to know about others and getting the timing of such rules to work as expected can be quite tricky. In particular, the approach I propose for disambiguation rests on parallel candidacy races supervised by a resolution strategy. Clearly, the knowledge unit implementing this strategy must be aware of the different candidates and possibly define preferences among them, but keeping track of all possible candidates can become problematic in a large knowledge base. Instead, some sort of browser to display semantic dependencies between knowledge units is required. For now, without such a tool, the user of **IDIoT** must "tweak" (i.e., set by trial-and-error) the communication delay between two knowledge units to ensure that one rule is triggered before or after another one, or to leave enough time for a KU to force the detection or inhibition of another one. This task is as cumbersome as weight-tweaking in connectionist systems.

12.2 ENHANCEMENTS

Several enhancements will be implemented in the next prototype of **IDIoT**. They include

    1. **improvements to the processing model**:

• As previously suggested, upon its detection a KU will have the ability to increase or decrease the retrievability coefficient of its customers. This will make the detection of KUs far more dynamic in that, during comprehension, previous inputs will affect the likelihood of detection of a feature

• The distinction between knowledge units and clusters will be eliminated. More specifically, a KU will behave as a cluster retrievable through constraint satisfaction, whereas a constructed cluster will only be retrievable using the **getCluster** operation. (Thus, once out of STM, a constructed cluster becomes unretrievable, not a KU.) Consequently, the knowledge base will become totally integrated with the model of dynamic memory. KUs will start in LTM but, upon activation, will move to WM and eventually decay to STM and then to LTM. While in WM or STM, a KU will be "easier" to activate than if it were in LTM. This strategy will be implemented by setting the threshold of a KU according to its membership to one of the three temporal partitions of dynamic memory.

• As a consequence of the previous suggestion, the user of **IDIoT** will have to specify an initial activation level for each KU. The higher this level, the slower the decay rate of the KU once activated. This follows from the observation (e.g., Gernsbacher, 1985, 1990) that thematic information may take longer to become detected than syntactic information, but that the former is more permanent in memory than the latter.

• Through two new primitive memory operations, an expansion procedure will be able to increase or decrease, for a short amount of time, attentional resources (i.e., decay rate, length of races, capacity of memory). This will allow the user to simulate a fluctuation in interestingness (see chapter 11).

• For additional representational flexibility, a KU will be allowed to have several expansion procedures, each one associated with one or more constraints. At the time of its detection, the KU will execute the expansion procedure associated with its satisfied constraint. This will make it easy for the user to regroup several features in a same KU.

2. improvements of user support:

• Most importantly, an integration browser will be incorporated into **IDIoT**. Currently, the trace browser (see subsection 5.2.4) allows the user to view the clusters created for an interpretation, but it is the responsibility of the user to integrate these clusters with a knowledge base. The integration browser, instead assumes that each and every cluster corresponding to a fact (i.e., governed by the feature **newFact**) is a candidate to be put in a knowledge base. Consequently, for each such cluster x, the integration browser will automatically generate a KU. This KU will have all the features of x as equally weighted inputs of its sole constraint. Its expansion procedure will reconstruct x with the additional feature **knownFact**. Using the browser, the user will have the possibility to view all these generated KUs and to select which ones are to be put in a knowledge base. Clearly, once in a knowledge base, the definitions of these KUs will be modifiable by the user. This is important, as the user will want to define triggers and possibly adjust the weights of the constraint. The integration browser constitutes a simple and brute force approach to learning similar to the integration mechanism proposed by Bookman (1992, 1994).

• The knowledge browser will have a new menu item for obtaining a graphical layout of the knowledge base. A tool to navigate graphically in the knowledge base will be designed. In essence, from a KU, the user will be able to easily access the suppliers and customers of this KU. Thus, the semantic dependencies between KUs will be visible.

• Relays and innate features will be eliminated. Relays should be constructed automatically by the system (as an optimization option available to the user). Alternatively, the communication model could be changed to use a broadcast strategy (e.g., to the members of a same processing "group" or category). As for innate features, a morphological browser will be added to **IDIoT** in order to specify rules for morphological analysis. Then, as with the tools presented in section 5.7, knowledge units will be automatically generated from these rules.

• Following the strategy of Bookman (1992, 1994), a tool will be constructed to automatically produce KUs from a dictionary and a thesaurus. These KUs would then likely be edited by a user. In essence, the generated KUs would serve as the raw material for the word-experts of a user of **IDIoT**. Such an approach would present the advantage of readily capturing a lot of conventionalized meanings that most users will want to keep in their knowledge bases.

• The syntactic and semantic checking of expansion procedures will be improved.

• In order to implement the notion of a perspective (see previous chapter), before starting a reading, the user will be able to mark a set of KUs as being permanently detected for this reading and to construct clusters that reside in STM throughout a reading.

• Statistics on the level of parallelism achieved during an interpretation will be automatically accumulated and presented to the user at the end of a reading.

• There will be different levels of message logging during a reading in order to avoid having one large and very verbose log of all exchanges of signals and modifications of states during a reading.

12.3 FUTURE RESEARCH

The proposed model of time-constrained memory still has some important gaps that future research must address. These gaps are summarized in this section.

12.3.1 Memory Management

• An STM capacity limit defined in terms of maximal membership is simplistic (e.g., Schweickert, & Boruff, 1986; Schweickert, Guentert, & Hersberg, 1989). Several management schemes have been proposed in both psychology and artificial intelligence.

• The mechanisms of information loss (see Gernsbacher, 1985, 1990) need further investigation.

• The current retrieval mechanism of **IDIoT**, although relatively complex (e.g., for a **findInclusiveReference**) is oversimplified compared to theories proposed in psychology (e.g., the notion of synergy for engrams, see Tulving, 1983, 1984). Also, ideally, the model of retrieval should be parametrized in order for **IDIoT** to account for different retrieval strategies.

• In the long term, **IDIoT** may require some sort principle of self-organization. Such a principle (e.g., from category theory, see Peters, & Shapiro, 1987, and Peters, Shapiro, & Rapaport, 1989) would allow the user to specify a KU in isolation of others, leaving it to the tool to "link" the new KU to existing ones. This is readily achievable at the level of knowledge units (e.g., having the system automatically determine the ports of a KU). We also want a way, however, for the user to specify semantic categories to which to KUs would be *automatically* added. Rastier (1991) offered preliminary ideas on this topic.

• We should get rid of the memory manager, if possible, replacing it with a truly distributed process, at the risk of complicating KUs. More generally, **IDIoT** needs to be brought much closer to existing results in memory research (see section 4.2).

12.3.2 Learning

Psychologists have extensively studied the problem of learning (see Bower, & Hilgard, 1981). Yet, as previously mentioned, symbolic models of text comprehension seldom address learning. Those that do generally postulate complex algorithms and structures (e.g., Bhatta, & Ram, 1991; Cox, & Ram, 1991). An important exception is the work of Kintsch, Britton, Fletcher, Kintsch, Mannes, and Nathan (1993). These authors argued that text comprehension is central to the task of learning. Schmalhofer and Tschaitschian (1993) demonstrated this claim by proposing a *comprehension-based* model of learning, a model that has the virtue of fitting into Kintsch's (1988) construction-integration model of text comprehension. Such an achievement supports the position of Ling, Cherwenka, and Marinov (1993) that learning can be handled at least as adequately by symbolic approaches as by neural nets, but we are still far from the requirements put forth by Giraud-Carrier and Martinez (1994) for artificial learning systems (namely, incrementality of learning, non–monotonicity, inconsistency and conflicting defaults handling, abstraction, self-organization, generalization, computational tractability). Also, an algorithmic approach to learning must be reconciled with the position of Rich and Shepherd (1993) who claimed that learning is not innate but rather consists in a group of strategies that we are taught.

IDIoT severely lacks an approach to learning. In the short term, "learning from experience" should be added to **IDIoT**. More specifically, it should be possible for **IDIoT** to continuously monitor (e.g., through the memory manager) the contents of STM for new patterns of features that last long enough in STM to be suggested to the reader for addition to the knowledge base. In its simplest form, this would involve keeping a frequency/duration count of the co-occurrence, in STM, of "unrelated" features. Such a strategy would identify the most frequent "contexts" in order to possibly make them become retrievable KUs for future interpretations (using an approach similar to the one adopted by the integration browser). In the medium term, an automatic generalization mechanism would also be highly desirable. Ultimately, Kintsch's learning strategy needs to be studied in detail to see how a similar strategy could be realized using **IDIoT**.

12.3.3 Other Directions

• The role of culture, social context, emotions (e.g., Ledoux, 1994), and other factors that are computationally difficult to model should be researched. More specifically, we need to expand the notion of context to something more than just the contents of STM at a given point in time.

• The **SOAR** architecture (see Laird, Newell, & Rosenbloom, 1987; Newell, 1990; Lehman, Lewis, & Newell, 1991; Lewis, 1993; Rosenbloom, & Newell, 1993; Rosenbloom, Lehman, & Laird, 1993) is not cognitively grounded, but addresses several problems (e.g., chunking) that were left out of **IDIoT**. **SOAR** is also explicitly concerned with the real-time constraints of cognition. A detailed study of this work is required in order to understand which of its mechanisms are relevant to **IDIoT**.

• The claim that **IDIoT** can be used to ground existing models of text comprehension needs to be supported by several case studies (beyond the existing minimal work on the schemas of Dyer, 1983 and the inference classes of Norvig, 1987). More generally, the issue of reuse in a concurrent object-oriented framework for text comprehension must be further investigated. Similar studies should probe the use of metaknowledge in such a framework in order to simplify the expression of knowledge. In the same vein, "metacognition" (see Metcalfe, & Shimamura, 1994) and "metamemory" (see Cohen, 1988) could be researched. The importance of parallelism must also be thoroughly demonstrated.

• The notions of strategic reading (van Dijk, & Kintsch, 1983) and strategic inferences (Granger, & Holbrook, 1983) must be integrated in **IDIoT**. In particular, the user should be able to specify a strategy for the processing of conflicting inferences.

• The problems of recall, summarization, and question-answering must eventually be addressed. In particular, the notion of a central content selector (Graesser, & Clark, 1985) must be investigated for **IDIoT**. For question answering, a simple strategy could consist in constructing, from the processing of the question, a cluster to be matched in the representation built for the studied text.

12.4 AFTERMATH

IDIoT started out and remains nothing more than a tool to explore how much of linguistic comprehension depends on the time-constrained nature of human memory. By all means, the proposed model of memory is simplistic but already helpful in demonstrating the omnipresent and determinative role of time during comprehension.

Because all the complexities of the implementation of time-constrained memory are invisible to the user of **IDIoT**, it is tempting to believe that the trivial algorithm, that is, the modus operandi of time-constrained memory, is just that—trivial—and that the interpretation of a text results solely from the rules of the KB, IDIoT merely acting as an access system. This is a danger of any AI research where the focus of study is shifted away from conceptual rules, a I will not deny that the specification of rules and concepts for a knowledge base remains a crucial and enormous task. But we must not forget that we still lack a theory of common sense and generality (McCarthy, 1987), and that, unless we grant them the quality of being universal (if not innate), rules must keep a theoretical and thus provisional status. Hence the necessity to "ground" these rules, and the need for a tool that allows for experimenting with different sets of rules. Adopting the metaphor of human memory as the basis for a grounded cognitive architecture has the advantage of a) bypassing the mind–body problem and b) allowing the development of an architecture that can avoid epistemological commitments. As emphasized in section 4.2, however, memory has little that can be considered trivial, and thus, the memory processes that form the trivial algorithm of IDIoT can hardly be viewed as trivial.

We should not, however, ignore the metaphorical nature of memory. In its extreme form, acknowledging metaphors in scientific work leads to the radical criticism of the concerned disciplines (e.g., Searle, 1984; Arsac, 1987; and Dreyfus, 1992, for artificial intelligence), if not of science altogether (e.g., Jones, 1977). Such viewpoints remind me of the deconstructionist movement (Norris, 1982) in literary criticism: They threaten the establishment, the experts! As my friend Ed Plantinga would say, they profane the sacred texts. "Orthodox dogmatic cognitivism", as Rastier (1991) calls the dominant position in cognitive science, answers this threat by denying subjectivity, eliminating performance, and instead hiding behind the problematic notion of an innate competence. For some of the advocates of this approach to cognition, IDIoT is just that, an idiot. Having spared the reader from insipid quotes at the beginning of each chapter, let me summarize my standpoint with respect to the notion of a self-validating competence by quoting Jacob Brownowski (1973), a true scientist:

> It is said that science will dehumanise people and turn them into numbers. This is false, tragically false. Look for yourself. This is the concentration camp and crematorium at Auschwitz. This is where people were turned into numbers. . . And that was not done by gas. It was done by arrogance. It was done by dogma. . . When people believe that they have absolute knowledge, with no test in reality, this is how they behave. This is what men do when they aspire to the knowledge of gods.
>
> Science is a very human form of knowledge. We are always at the

brink of the known, we always feel forward for what is to be hoped. Every judgement in science stands on the edge of error, and is personal. Science is a tribute to what we can know although we are fallible. In the end the words were said by Oliver Cromwell: "I beseech you, in the bowels of Christ, think it possible you may be mistaken."

References

Adler, M. (1985). *Ten philosophical mistakes*. New York: Macmillan.

Ajjanagadde, V., & Shastri, L. (1989). Efficient inference with multi-place predicates and variables in a connectionist system. *Proceedings of the 11th Annual Conference of the Cognitive Science Society*.

Ajjanagadde, V., & Shastri, L. (1991). Rules and variables in neural nets. *Neural Computation*, 3, 121–134.

Akker, R. op den, Ablas, H., Nijholt, A., & Luttighuis P. oude (1992). *An annotated bibliography on parallel parsing: Updated version*. Memoranda Informatica INF 92-84, Department of Computer Science, University of Twente, The Netherlands. A compacted version of this bibliography appears in Ablas, H., & Akker, R. op den (1994). *ACM SIGPLAN Notices*, 29, 54–65.

Alba, J. W., & Hasher, L. (1983). Is memory schematic? *Psychological Bulletin*, 93, 203–231.

Ali, S. S. (1993). A structured representation for noun phrases and anaphora. *Proceedings of the 15th Annual Conference of the Cognitive Science Society*.

Allen, J. (1982). Modelling events, actions, and time. *Proceedings of the 4th Annual Conference of the Cognitive Science Society*.

Allen, J. (1987). *Natural language understanding*, New York: Benjamin Cummings.

Allen, P. A., McNeal, M., & Kvak, D. (1992). Perhaps the lexicon is coded as a function of word frequency. *Journal of Memory and Language*, 31, 826–844.

Alshawi, H. (1987). *Memory and context for language interpretation*, Cambridge, England: Cambridge University Press.

Alshawi, H. (1990). Resolving quasi logical forms. *Computational Linguistics*, 6(13), 133–144.

Alterman, R. (1985). A dictionary based on concept coherence. *Artificial Intelligence*, 25, 153–186.

Anandan, P., Letovsky, S., & Mjolsness, E. (1989). Connectionist variable-binding by optimization. *Proceedings of the 11th Annual Conference of the Cognitive Science Society*.

Anderson, J. R. (1980). *Cognitive psychology and its implications*, San Francisco, CA: W H Freeman and Company.

Anderson, J. R. (1983). *Architecture of cognition*, Cambridge, MA: Harvard University Press.

Appelt, D. E., Hobbs, J. R., Bear, J., Israel, D., & Tyson, M. (1993). FASTUS: A finite-state processor for information extraction from real-world text. *IJCAI*, 1172–1178.

Arbib, M., Conklin, J., & Hill, J. (1987). *From schema theory to language*, New York: Oxford University Press.

Ardissono, L., Lesmo, L., Pogliano, P., & Terenziani, P. (1991). Interpretation of definite noun phrases. *IJCAI*, 997–1002.

Arsac, J. (1987). *Les machines à penser*, Paris: Seuil.

Auroux, S. (1984). D'Alembert et les synonymistes. *Dix-huitième siècle*, 16, 93–108.

Bäckman, L. (1991). Recognition memory across the adult life span: The role of prior knowledge. *Memory and Cognition*, 19(1), 63–71.

Baddeley, A. (1976). *The psychology of memory*. New York: Basic Books.

Baddeley, A. (1986). *Working memory*, Oxford Psychology Series, No. 11, New York: Clarendon Press.

Baddeley, A., & Hitch, G. (1993). The recency effect: Implicit learning with explicit retrieval? *Memory and Cognition*, 21(2), 146–155.

Bain, C., Beaty, J., & Hunter, J.P. (Eds.) (1977). *The Norton Introduction to Literature*, Second edition, New York: W.W. Norton & Company.

Ballstaedt, S.-P., & Mandl, H. (1991). Knowledge modification during reading. In: G. Denhière, & J.-P., Rossi (Eds.), *Text and text processing: Advances in Psychology*, Amsterdam: North-Holland.

Balota, D. A. (1994). Visual word recognition. In: M. A., Gernsbacher (Ed.), *Handbook of psycholinguistics*, New York: Academic Press.

Balota, D. A., Flores d'Arcais, G. B., & Rayner, K. (1990). *Comprehension processes in reading*, Hillsdale, NJ: Lawrence Erlbaum Associates.

Bange, P. (1986). Towards a pragmatic analysis of narratives in literature. *Poetics*, 15, 73–87.

Barker, K., & Szpakowicz, S. (1994). Interactive semantic analysis of clause-level relationships, in press.

Barnden, J. A. (1983). On association techniques in neural representations schemes. *Proceedings of the 5th Annual Conference of the Cognitive Science Society*.

Barnden, J. A. (1990). Review of Kronfeld (1990). *Computational Linguistics*, 18(1), 98–103.

Barnden, J. A., & Pollack, J.B. (Eds.) (1991). *Advances in connectionist and neural computation theory 1: High level connectionist models*. Norwood, NJ: Ablex.

Barthes, R. (1977). *Roland Barthes by Roland Barthes*. (R. Howard, Trans.). London: Macmillan.

Barwise, J., & Cooper, R. (1981). Generalized Quantifiers and Natural Language. *Linguistics and Philosophy*, 4, 159–219.

Barwise, J., & Perry, J. (1983). *Situations and attitudes*, Cambridge, MA: MIT Press.

de Beaugrande, R. (1980). *Text, discourse, and process*, Norwood, NJ: Ablex.

Bechtel, W. (1994). Levels of description and explanation in cognitive science. *Minds and Machines*, 4, 1–25.

Berg, G. (1987). A parallel natural language processing architecture with distributed control. *Proceedings of the 9th Annual Conference of the Cognitive Science Society*, 487–495.

Berlin, B., & Kay, P. (1969). *Basic color terms: Their universality and evolution*, Berkeley, CA: University of California Press.

Bertelson, P. (1987). *The onset of literacy: Cognitive processes in reading acquisition*, Cambridge, MA: MIT Press.

Bhatta, S., & Ram, A. (1991). Learning indices for schema selection. *Proceedings of the fourth Florida AI Research Symposium*, 226–231.

Birnbaum, L. (1985). Lexical ambiguity as a touchstone for theories of language analysis. *IJCAI*, 815–820.

Birnbaum, L. (1989). A critical look at the foundations of autonomous syntactic analysis. *Proceedings of the 11th Annual Conference of the Cognitive Science Society*, 99–106.

Bookman, L. A. (1987). A microfeature based scheme for modelling semantics. *IJCAI*, 611–614.

Bookman, L. A. (1992). *A two-tier model of semantic memory for text comprehension*, (PhD thesis). Brandeis University.

Bookman, L. A. (1994). *A two-tier model of semantic memory for text comprehension*. Amsterdam: Kluwer.

Bookman, L. A., & Alterman, R. (1991). Schema recognition for text understanding: An analog semantic feature approach. In: J. A., Barnden, & J. B., Pollack (Eds.), *Advances in connectionist and neural computation theory 1: High level connectionist models*, Norwood, NJ: Ablex.

Bosch, P. (1983). *Agreement and anaphora: A study in the role of pronouns in syntax and discourse*, NY: Academic Press.

Bouma, G. (1992). Feature structures and nonmonotonicity.*Computational Linguistics*, 18(2),183–203.

Bower, G. H., & Hilgard, E. R. (1981). *Theories of learning*, Fifth Edition, Englewood Cliffs, NY: Prentice–Hall.

Bowers, J.S. (1994). Does implicit memory extend to legal and illegal nonwords. *Journal of Experimental Psychology*, 20(3), 534–549.

Brachman, R., & Levesque, H. J. (1985). *Readings in knowledge representation*. San Mateo, CA: Morgan Kaufman.

Braine, M. (1978). On the relation between the natural logic of reasoning and standard logic. *Psychological Review*, 85, 1–21.

Bransford, J., & Johnson, M. (1973). Considerations of some problems of comprehension, In: W., Chase (Ed.), *Visual Information Processing*, 383–435. NY: Academic Press.

Britt, A. (1994). The interaction of referential ambiguity and argument structure in the parsing of prepositional phrases. *Journal of Memory and Language*, 33, 251–283.

Britton, B. K., & Black, J. B. (Eds.) (1985). *Understanding expository text: A theoretical and practical handbook for analyzing explanatory text*, Hillsdale, NJ: Lawrence Erlbaum Associates.

Britton, B. K., & Glynn, S.M. (Eds.) (1987). *Executive control processes in reading*, Hillsdale, NJ: Lawrence Erlbaum Associates.

Brownowski, J. (1973). *The ascent of man*. Boston, MA: Little, Brown and Company.

Brown, G. D. (1989). A connectionist model of phonological short-term memory. *Proceedings of the 11th Annual Conference of the Cognitive Science Society*, 572–579.

Brown, J. C. (1993). Parallel natural-language parsing using multiple broadcasting. *Irish Journal of Psychology*, 14(3), 503–504.

Budd, T. (1991). *Object-oriented programming*. Reading, MA: Addison–Wesley,

Burns, A., & Davies, G. (1993). *Concurrent programming*. Reading, MA: Addison–Wesley.

Butler, K. (1994). Neural constraints in cognitive science. *Minds and Machines*, 4,129–162.

Cacciari, C., & Glucksberg, S. (1994). Understanding figurative language. In: M.A., Gernsbacher (Ed.), *Handbook of psycholinguistics*, NY: Academic Press.

Cacciari, C., & Tabossi, P. (1988). The comprehension of idioms. *Journal of Memory and Language*, 27, 668–683.

Chafe, W. (1990). Some things that narratives tell us about the mind. In: B., Britton, & A., Pelligrini (Eds.), *Narrative thought and narrative language*. Hillsdale, NJ: Lawrence Erlbaum Associates.

Chalmers, D. J. (1990). Why Fodor and Pylyshyn were wrong: The simplest refutation. *Proceedings of the 12th Annual Conference of the Cognitive Science Society*.

de Champeaux, D., Lea, D., & Faure, P. (1993). *Object-oriented system development.* Reading, MA: Addison–Wesley.

Charniak, E. (1983). Passing markers: A theory of contextual influence in language comprehension. *Cognitive Science,* 7,171–190.

Charniak, E. (1986a). A single-semantic-process theory of parsing.*Technical Report.* Providence, RI: Brown University, Department of Computer Science.

Charniak, E. (1986b). A neat theory of marker passing. *AAAI,* Philadelphia, PA: 584–588.

Charniak, E. (1994). *Statistical language learning.* Cambridge, MA: MIT Press.

Charniak, E., & Goldman, R. (1988). A logic for semantic interpretation. *ACL,* 87–94.

Chen, H.-C. (1990). Lexical processing in a non-native language: Effects of language proficiency and learning strategy. *Memory and Cognition,* 18(3), 279–288.

Chomsky, N. (1965). *Aspects of the theory of syntax.* Cambridge, MA: MIT Press.

Chomsky, N. (1980). *Rules and representations.* NY: Columbia University Press.

Chomsky, N. (1982). *Some concepts and consequences of the theory of government and binding.* Cambridge, MA: MIT Press.

Chomsky, N. (1984). La connaissance du langage. *Communications,* 40, 7–24.

Chun, H. W., & Mimo, A. (1987). A model of schema selection using marker passing and connectionist spreading activation. *Proceedings of the 9th Annual Conference of the Cognitive Science Society,* 887–896.

Chung, M, & Moldovan, D. (1994). Applying parallel-processing to natural-language processing. *IEEE Expert,* 9(1), 36–44.

Churchland, P. (1985). Eliminative materialism and the propositional attitudes. *Journal of Philosophy,* 73, 67–90.

Clancey, W. J. (1992). Model construction operators. *Artificial Intelligence,* 53, 1–115.

Clark, L. F. (1985). Social knowledge and inference processing in text comprehension. In: G., Rickheit & H., Strohner (Eds.), *Inferences in text processing.* Amsterdam: North–Holland: Advances in Psychology.

Clark, A. & Lutz, R. (1992). *Connectionism in context.* NY: Springer–Verlag.

Cohen, R. L. (1988). Metamemory for words and enacted instructions: Predicting which items will be recalled. *Memory and Cognition,* 16(5), 452–460.

Cole, M., John-Steiner, V., Scribner, S., & Souberman, E. (Eds.) (1978). *L.S. Vygotsky: Mind in society.* Cambridge, MA: Harvard University Press.

Colombo, L., & Williams, J. (1990). Effects of word-and sentence-level contexts upon word recognition. *Memory and Cognition,* 18(2), 153–163.

Conrad, M. (1985). On design principles for a molecular computer. *Communications of the ACM,* 28, 464–480.

Cooper, R. (1983). *Quantification and syntactic theory.* Dordrecht, Netherlands: D. Reidel.

Corriveau, J.-P. (1987). On the role of time in reader-based comprehension. *Proceedings of the 9th Annual Conference of the Cognitive Science Society*, 794–801.

Corriveau, J.-P. (1988). Review of Alshawi (1987). *Computational Linguistics*, 16(3).

Corriveau, J.-P. (1991a). *Time-constrained memory for reader-based text comprehension*, (PhD thesis). Department of Computer Science, (Technical Report no. 246), University of Toronto, Canada.

Corriveau, J.-P. (1991b). Interpretation of definite reference with a time-constrained memory. *Proceedings of the 13th Annual Conference of the Cognitive Society.*

Corriveau, J.-P. (1993a). Time and non-determinism in creativity. *Spring Symposium on Creativity*, Stanford, CA: *AAAI-93.*

Corriveau, J.-P. (1993b). Beyond deterministic lexical disambiguation. Vancouver, Canada: *PACLING.*

Corriveau, J.-P. (1993c). Non-deterministic prepositional phrase attachment. *Proceedings of the 15th Annual Conference of the Cognitive Society.*

Corriveau, J.-P. (1994a). On the design of a concurrent object-oriented spreading activation architecture. Maui, HA: *HICSS-27.*

Corriveau, J.-P. (1994b). Computational reader-based text comprehension. Florida: *FLAIRS.*

Corriveau, J.-P. (1994c). Modeling memory for convergence in text comprehension. *Cognitive Science and Natural Language Processing-3rd Workshop*, Dublin, Ireland.

Corriveau, J.-P. (1994d). *Interfaces for a time-constrained model of memory*, (Technical Report). Carleton University, Ottawa, Canada.

Corriveau, J.-P. (1995). A time-constrained architecture for cognition. Maui, HA:*HICSS-28.*

Corriveau, J.-P., & Saba, W. (1995). On the need for a cognitively plausible model for quantification. Submitted to *the 17th Annual Conference of the Cognitive Science Society*, Pittsburgh, PA.

Cottrell, G. (1984). A model of lexical access of ambiguous words. *AAAI*, Austin, Texas, 61–67.

Cottrell, G. (1989). *A connectionist approach to word sense disambiguation.* San Mateo, CA: Morgan Kaufmann.

Cowan, N. (1993). Activation, attention, and short-term memory. *Memory and Cognition*, 21(2), 162–167.

Cowan, N., Keller, T., Hulme, C., Roodenrys, S., McDougall, S., & Rack, J. (1994). Verbal memory span in children: Speech timing clues to the mechanisms underlying age and word length effects. *Journal of Memory and Language*, 33, 234–250.

Cox, M., & Ram A. (1991). Using introspective reasoning to select learning strategies. *Proceedings of the first international workshop on multistrategy learning*, 217–230.

Culler, J. (1975). *Structuralist poetics*. London: Routledge and Kegan Paul.

Cullingford, R. (1978). *Script applications: Computer understanding of newspaper stories*. (Ph.D. thesis), Department of Computer Science, New Haven, CT: Yale University.

Cunningham, P., & Veale, T. (1991). Organizational issues arising from the integration of the lexicon and concept network in a text understanding system. *IJCAI*, 986–991.

Daelemans, W., Smedt De, K., & Gazdar, G. (1992). Inheritance in natural language processing. *Computational Linguistics*, 18(2), 205–215.

Dagenbach, D., & Carr, T. H. (Eds.) (1994). *Inhibitory processes in attention, memory and language*, NY: Academic Press.

Daneman, M. (1987). Reading and working memory. In: J. R., Beech, & A. M. Colley (Eds.), *Cognitive approaches to reading*, 57–86, NY: Wiley and Sons Ltd.

Daneman, M., & Green, I. (1986). Individual differences in comprehending and producing words in context. *Journal of Memory and Language*, 25, 1–18.

Dark, V. J. (1988). Semantic priming, prime reportability, and retroactive priming are interdependent. *Memory and Cognition*, 16(4), 299–308.

Dascal, M. (1989). On the roles of context and literal meaning in understanding. *Cognitive Science*, 13, 253–258.

DeJong, G. (1982). An overview of the FRUMP system. In: W. Lehnert, & M. H. Ringle (Eds.), *Strategies for natural language processing*. Hillsdale, NJ: Lawrence Erlbaum Associates.

Delisle, S., (1993). *Text processing without a priori domain knowledge: Semi-automatic linguistic analysis for incremental knowledge acquisition*, (PhD thesis), University of Ottawa.

Delisle, S., Copeck, T., Szpakowicz, S., & Barker, K. (1993). Pattern matching for case analysis: A computational definition of closeness. *ICCI*, 310–315.

Denhière, G., & Rossi, J.-P. (Eds.) (1991). *Text and text processing*. Amsterdam: North–Holland: Advances in Psychology series.

Derthick, M., & Plaut, D. (1986). Is distributed connectionism compatible with the physical symbol system hypothesis? *Proceedings of the 8th Annual Conference of the Cognitive Science Society*, 639–644.

Devitt, M., & Sterelny, K. (1987). *Language and reality: An introduction to the philosophy of language*. Cambridge, MA: MIT Press.

Dillon, G. (1980). Discourse processing and the nature of literary narrative. *Poetics*, 9, 163–180.

Dolan, C.P. (1989). *Tensor manipulation networks: Connection and symbolic approaches to comprehension, planning and learning.* (PhD thesis), Computer Science Department, University of California at Berkeley, CA.

Dohsaka K. (1990). Identifying the references of zero-pronouns in Japanese based on pragmatic constraint interpretation. *Proceedings of the Ninth European Conference on AI.*

Dosher, B. A., & Rosedale, G. (1991). Judgment of semantic and episodic relatedness: Common time-course and failure of segregation. *Journal of Memory and Language,* 30, 125–160.

Dreyfus, H. L. (1992). *What computers still can't do: A critique of artificial reason.* Third Edition. Cambridge, MA: MIT Press.

Dyer, M. G. (1983). *In-depth understanding.* Cambridge, MA: MIT Press.

Ehrlich, M. F., Brebion, J., & Tardieu, H. (1994). Working-memory capacity and reading-comprehension in young and older adults. *Psychological Research-Psychologische Forschung,* 56(2), 110–115.

Eiselt, K., & Granger, R. (1987). A time-dependent distributed processing model of strategy-driven inference behavior. *Proceedings of the 9th Annual Conference of the Cognitive Science Society.*

Eizirik, L. M. R., Barbosa, V. C., & Mendes, S. B. T. (1993). A bayesian-network approach to lexical disambiguation. *Cognitive Science,* 257–283.

Elman, J. L. (1989). Structured representations and connectionist Models. *Proceedings of the 11th Annual Conference of the Cognitive Science Society,* 17–25.

Etherington, D., & Reiter, R. (1985). On inheritance hierarchies with exceptions. In: R., Brachman, & H. J., Levesque (Eds.), *Readings in knowledge representation.* San Mateo, CA: Morgan Kaufmann.

Fahlman, S. E. (1979). *NETL: A system for representing and using real-world knowledge.* Cambridge, MA: MIT Press.

Farah, M. (1994). Neuropsychological inference with an interactive brain: A critique of the 'locality' assumption. *Behavioral and Brain Science,* 17, 43–104.

Fauconnier, G. (1994). *Mental spaces — Aspects of meaning construction in natural language.* Cambridge, England: Cambridge University Press.

Feldman, J. (1984). Computational constraints from biology. *Proceedings of the 6th Annual Conference of the Cognitive Science Society,* 101.

Feldman, J. (1985a). Connectionist models and their applications: Introduction. *Cognitive Science,* 9, 1–2.

Feldman, J. (1985b). *Energy and the behavior of connectionist models.* (Technical Report No.155), Department of Computer Science, University of Rochester, NY.

Fetzer, J. H. (1992). Connectionism and cognition: Why Fodor and Pylyshyn are wrong. In: A., Clark, & R., Lutz (Eds.), *Connectionism in Context*. NY: Springer–Verlag.

Fillmore, C. (1968). The case for case. In: E., Bach, & R. Harms (Eds.), *Universals in linguistic theory*. NY: Holt, Rinehart and Winston.

Firth, J.R. (1957). A synopsis of linguistic theory: 1930–1950. In: J. R., Firth, (Ed.), *Studies in linguistic analysis*. Oxford, England: Basil Blackwell.

Flammer, A., & Kintsch, W. (Eds.) (1981). *Discourse processing*. Amsterdam: North–Holland: Advances in Psychology series.

Fletcher, C. R. (1986). Strategies for the allocation of short-term memory during comprehension. *Journal of Memory and Language*, 25, 43–58.

Fodor, J. (1975). *The language of thought*, Cambridge, MA: MIT Press.

Fodor, J., & Frazier, L. (1980). Is the human sentence parsing mechanism an ATN? *Cognition*, 8, 417–459.

Fodor, J., & Pylyshyn, Z. (1988). Connectionism and cognitive architecture: A critical analysis. *Cognition*, 28, 3–71.

Forbes, G. (1989). Indexicals. In: D., Gabby,& F., Guenthner, (Eds.), *Handbook of philosophical logic*. Volume IV, pp. 463–490, D. Reidel.

Forster, K. I. (1979). Levels of processing and the structure of the language processor. In: W. E., Cooper, & E., Walker (Eds.), *Sentence processing: Psychological studies presented to Merrill Garrett*, pp.27–85, Hillsdale, NJ: Lawrence Erlbaum and Associates.

Forster, K. I., & Stevenson, B. J. (1987). Sentence matching and well-formedness. *Cognition*, 26, 171–186.

Foss, D. J., & Hakes, D. T. (1978). *Psycholinguistics: An introduction to the psychology of language*. NY: Prentice–Hall.

Fox, B. (1989). *Discourse structure and anaphora: Written, conversational English*, Cambridge, England: Cambridge University Press.

Francini, M.-A. (1993). *The time course of activation and retrieval of multiplication facts in adults*. (Master thesis), Carleton University.

Fraser, N. M., & Hudson, R. A. (1992). Inheritance in word grammar. *Computational Linguistics*, 18(2), 133–153.

Frawley, W. (1992). *Linguistic semantics*. Hillsdale, NJ: Lawrence Erlbaum Associates.

Frazier, L., & Fodor, J. (1978). The sausage machine: A new two-stage parsing model. *Cognition*, 6,291–325.

Frazier, L., & Rayner, K. (1987). Resolution of syntactic category ambiguities: Eye movements in parsing lexically ambiguous sentences. *Journal of Memory and Language*, 26, 505–526.

Frazier, L., & Rayner, K. (1990). Taking on semantic commitments: Processing multiple meanings vs. multiple menses. *Journal of Memory and Language*, 29, 181–200.

Freeman, N. H., & Stedmon, A. J. (1986). How children deal with natural language quantification. In: I., Kurcz, I. et al. (Eds.), *Knowledge and language*. (pp.21–48), Amsterdam: North Holland.

Friederici, A. D., Weissenborn, J., & Kail, M. (1991). Pronoun comprehension in aphasia: A comparison of three languages. *Brain and Language*, 41, 289–310.

Gadamer, H.-G. (1976). *Philosophical hermeneutics*. (Translated by D. Linge). Berkeley, CA: University of California Press.

Galloway, P. (1983). Narrative theories as computational models: Reader-oriented theory and artificial intelligence. *Computers and the Humanities*, 17, 169–174.

Gardiner, J. M. (1988). Recognition failures and free-recall failures: Implications for the relation between recall and recognition. *Memory and Cognition*, 16(5), 446–451.

Gardiner, J. M, & Java, R. I. (1990). Recollective experience in word and nonword recognition. *Memory and Cognition*, 18(1), 23–30.

Gardner, H. (1983). *Frames of mind: The theory of multiple intelligences*. NY: Basic Books.

Gardner, H. (1985). *The mind's new science: A history of the cognitive revolution*. NY: Basic Books.

Garnham, A. (1983). What's wrong with story grammars. *Cognition*, 15,145–154.

Garnham, A. (1989). Inference in language understanding: What, when, why and how. In: R., Dietrich, & C. F., Graumann (Eds.), *Language processing in social context*. (pp.153–172). Amsterdam: North–Holland.

Garnham, A. (1992). Minimalism versus constructionism: A false dichotomy in theories of inference during reading. *Psycoloquy*, 3(63).

Garnham, A. (1993). Space: the final frontier? *Psycoloquy*, 4(17).

Garnham, A., & Oakhill, J. V. (1992). Discourse representation and text processing from a 'mental models' perspective. *Language and Cognitive Processes*, 7, 193–204.

Garrod, S. (1985). Incremental pragmatic interpretation versus occasional inferencing during fluent reading. In: G., Rickheit, & H., Strohner (Eds.), *Inferences in Text Processing*. Amsterdam: North Holland, Elsevier Science Publishers.

Garrod, S., Freudenthal, D., & Boyle, E. (1994). The role of different types of anaphor in the on-line resolution of sentences in a discourse. *Journal of Memory and Language*, 33, 39–68.

Garrod, S., & Sanford, A. (1990). Referential processes in reading: Focusing on roles and individual. In: D. A., Balota, *et al.* (Eds.), *Comprehension processes in reading*. Hillsdale, NJ: Lawrence Erlbaum Associates.

Gazdar, G., & Mellish, C. (1989). *Natural language processing in LISP*, Reading, MA: Addison–Wesley.

Gazdar, G., Klein, E., Pullum, G., & Sag, I. (1985). *Generalized phrase structure grammar*, Oxford: Blackwell.

Gentner, D., & Forbus, K. (1991). MAC/FAC: A model of similarity-based retrieval. *Proceedings of the 13th Annual Conference of the Cognitive Society.*

Gernsbacher, M. A. (1985). Surface information loss in comprehension. *Cognitive Psychology*, 17, 324–363.

Gernsbacher, M. A. (1990). Comprehension as structure building, Hillsdale, NJ: Lawrence Erlbaum and Associates.

Gernsbacher, M. A. (Ed.) (1994). *Handbook of psycholinguistics*. NY: Academic Press.

Gernsbacher, M. A., Hargreaves, D. J., & Beeman, M. (1989). Building and accessing clausal representations: The advantage of first mention versus the advantage of clause recency. *Journal of Memory and Language*, 28, 735–755.

Gernsbacher, M. A., & Robertson, R. R. W. (1992). Knowledge activation versus sentence mapping when representing fictional characters' emotional states. *Language and Cognitive Processes*, 7, 353–371.

Gerrig, R. J., & Littman, M. L. (1990). Disambiguation by community membership. *Memory and Cognition*, 18(4), 331–338.

Gibbs, R. (1984). Literal meaning and psychological theories. *Cognitive Science*, 8,275–304.

Gibbs, R. (1989). Understanding and literal meaning.*Cognitive Science*, 13, 243–252.

Gibbs, R. (1994). Figurative thought and figurative language. In: M. A., Gernsbacher, M.A. (Ed.), *Handbook of Psycholinguistics*. NY: Academic Press.

Gibbs, R., Nayak, N. P., Bolton, J. L., & Keppel, M. E. (1989). Speakers' assumptions about the lexical flexibility of idioms. *Memory and Cognition*, 17(1), 58–68.

Gibson, E. (1991). *A computational theory of human linguistic processing: Memory limitations and processing breakdown*, (PhD thesis). Carnegie Mellon (Technical Report CMU-CMT-91-125).

Gick, M. L., Craik, F. I. M., & Morris, R. G. (1988). Task complexity and age differences in working memory. *Memory and Cognition*, 16(4), 353–361.

Gigley, H. (1985a). Computational Neurolinguistics: What is it all about? *IJCAI*, 260–266.

Gigley, H. (1985b). Grammar Viewed as A Functional Part of a Cognitive System. *Proceedings of the 22nd Conference of the Association for Computational Linguistics*, 324–332.

Gigley, H. (1988). Process synchronization, lexical ambiguity resolution and aphasia. In: S., Small, G., Cottrell, & M., Tanenhaus, (Eds.), *Lexical ambiguity resolution: Perspectives from Psycholinguistics, Neuropsychology & Artificial Intelligence*. San

Mateo, CA: Morgan Kaufmann.

Giraud-Carrier, C., & Martinez, T. (1994). Seven desirable properties for artificial learning systems. *FLAIRS*, 16–20.

Givón, T. (1989). *Mind, code and context: Essays in pragmatics*. Hillsdale, NJ: Lawrence Erlbaum Associates.

Givón, T. (1991). Coherence: Toward a cognitive model. *Text and Discourse*: 1–12.

Givón, T. (1992). The grammar of referential coherence as mental processing instructions. *Linguistics*, 30, 5–55.

Givón, T. (1993b). Coherence in text, coherence in mind. *Pragmatics and Cognition*, 2, 171–227.

Givón, T. (1993a). *English grammar: A function-based introduction* (Vol.2), Philadelphia, PA: Benjamins.

Glenberg, A. M. (1993). Comprehension while missing the point: More on minimalism and models. *Psycoloquy* 4(31).

Glenberg, A. M., & Langston, W. E. (1992). Comprehension of illustrated text: Pictures help to build mental models. *Journal of Memory and Language* 31, 129–151.

Glenberg, A. M., & Mathew, S. (1992). When minimalism is not enough: Mental models in reading comprehension. *Psycoloquy* 3(64), reading-inference-2.1.

Godden, K. (1989). Computing pronoun antecedents in an English query system. *IJCAI*.

Goldberg, A. (1984). *SMALLTALK-80: The Interactive Programming Environment*, Reading, MA: Addison–Wesley.

Golden, R. M., & Rumelhart, D. E. (1993). A parallel distributed-processing model of story comprehension and recall. *Discourse Processes*, 16(3), 203–237.

Goldman, R. P., & Charniak, E. (1990). *A probabilistic approach to text understanding*, (Technical Report). Providence, RI: Department of Computer Science, Brown University.

Goldman, S. R. and Varnhagen, C. K. (1986). Memory for embedded and sequential structures. *Journal of Memory and Language* 25, 401–418.

Gordon, P. C., Grosz B. J., & Gilliom L. A. (1993). Pronouns, names, and the centering of attention in discourse. *Cognitive Science*, 17(3).

Gorfein, D. (1989). *Resolving semantic ambiguity*, NY: Springer–Verlag.

Graesser, A. C. (1993). Inference generation during text comprehension: Introduction. *Discourse Processing*, 16(1–2), 1.

Graesser, A. C., & Clark, L. (1985). *Structures and procedures of implicit knowledge*, Norwood, NJ: Ablex Publishing Corporation.

Graesser, A. C., & Kreuz, R. J. (1993). A theory of inference generation during text comprehension. *Discourse Processes*, 16(1–2), 145–160.

Grainger, J. (1990). Word frequency and neighborhood frequency effects in lexical decision and naming. *Journal of Memory and Language* 29, 228–244.

Granger, R., Eiselt, K., & Holbrook, J. (1986). Parsing with parallelism: A spreading activation model of inference processing during text comprehension. In: J., Kolodner, & C., Riesbeck (Eds.), *Experience, memory and reasoning*, Hillsdale, NJ: Lawrence Erlbaum Associates.

Granger, R., & Holbrook, J. (1983). Perseverers, recencies and deferrers: New experimental evidence for multiple inference strategies in understanding. *Proceedings of the 5th Annual Conference of the Cognitive Science Society.*

Granger, R., Holbrook, J., & Eiselt, K. (1983). STRATEGIST: A program that models strategy-driven and content-driven inference behavior. *Proceedings of the National Conference on Artificial Intelligence*, Washington, DC: American Association for Artificial Intelligence.

Greene, R. L. (1992). *Human Memory: Paradigms and Paradoxes.* Hillsdale, NJ: Lawrence Erlbaum Associates.

Greene, S. B., McKoon G., & Ratcliff, R. (1992). Pronoun resolution and discourse models. *Journal of Experimental Psychology: Learning, Memory and Cognition*, 18(2), 266–283.

Grosz, B. J. (1977). *The Representation and use of focus in dialogue understanding.* (PhD thesis). SRI Technical Note No.151, SRI International, Menlo Park, CA.

Grosz, B. J., & Sidner C. L. (1986). Attention, intentions, and the structure of discourse. *Computational Linguistics*, 12, 175–204.

Gupta, P., & Touretsky, D. S. (1994). Connectionist models and linguistic theory: Investigations of stress systems in language. *Cognitive Science*, 18, 1–50.

Habel, C. (1983). *Stories: An artificial intelligence perspective.* (Research Report No.19). Technische Universität Berlin, Berlin.

Haberlandt, K. (1980). Encoding of story constituents. *Poetics*, 9, 99–116.

Haberlandt, K. (1994). Methods in reading research. In: M. A., Gernsbacher (Ed.), *Handbook of Psycholinguistics.* NY: Academic Press.

Haberlandt, K., & Graesser, A. (1990). Integration and buffering of new information. In: A., Graesser, & G., Bower (Eds.), *Inferences and text comprehension.* NY: Academic Press.

Haddock, N. (1987). Incremental interpretation and combinatory categorial grammar. *IJCAI*, 661–663.

Hammond, K. J. (1986). *Case-based planning: An integrated theory of planning, learning, and memory.* (PhD thesis).Yale University, Department of Computer Science, New Haven, CT.

Hammond, K. J. (Ed.) (1989). *Proceedings of the case-based reasoning workshop.* San Mateo, CA: Morgan Kaufmann.

Harper, M. P. (1992). Ambiguous noun phrases in logical form. *Computational Linguistics*, 18(4), 419–465.

Harrap's New Shorter French and English Dictionary (1972). London, England: Billing and Sons Limited.

Hawkes, T. (1977). *Structuralism and semiotics.* University of California Press.

Hemforth, B., Koniecny, L., & Strube, G. (1993). Incremental syntax processing and parsing strategies. *Proceedings of the 15th Annual Conference of the Cognitive Society.*

Hendler, J. A. (1987). *Integrating marker-passing and problem-solving: A spreading-activation approach to improved choice in planning.* Norwood, NJ: Ablex.

Hendler, J. A. (1989). Marker-passing over microfeatures: Towards a hybrid symbolic/connectionist model. *Cognitive Science*, 13, 79–106.

Hendler, J. A. (1991). Developing hybrid symbolic/connectionist models. In: J. A., Barnden, & J. B., Pollack (Eds.), *High-level connectionist models.* Vol. 1. *Advances in connectionist and neural computation theory.* Norwood, NJ: Ablex Publishing Corporation.

Hendrix, G. (1979). Encoding knowledge in partitioned networks. In: N., Findler (Ed.), *Associative networks: Representation and use of knowledge by computers.* (pp. 51–92). NY: Academic Press.

Hidi, S., & Baird, W. (1986). Interestingness—A neglected variable in discourse processing. *Cognitive Science*, 10, 179–194.

Hindle, D., & Rooth, M. (1993). Structural ambiguity and lexical relations. *Computational Linguistics* 19(1), 103–120.

Hinton, G. (Ed.) (1991). *Connectionist symbol processing*, Cambridge, MA: MIT Press.

Hinton, G., & Plaut, D. (1987). Using fast weights to deblur old memories. *Proceedings of the 9th Annual Conference of the Cognitive Science Society.*

Hinton, G., & Sejnowski, T. (1984). Learning semantic features. *Proceedings of the 6th Annual Conference of the Cognitive Science Society*, 63–70.

Hintzman, D. (1988). Judgments of frequency and recognition memory in a multiple-trace memory model. *Psychological Review*, 95(4), 528–551.

Hirsch, E. D. Jr. (1967).*Validity in Interpretation.* New Haven, CT: Yale University Press.

Hirst, G. (1981). *Anaphora in natural language understanding.* NY: Springer–Verlag.

Hirst, G. (1984). Jumping to conclusions: Psychological reality and unreality in a word disambiguation program. *Proceedings of the 6th Annual Conference of the Cognitive Science Society*, 179–182.

Hirst, G. (1987). *Semantic interpretation and the resolution of ambiguity*, Cambridge, England: Cambridge University Press.

Hirst, G. (1988a). Resolving lexical ambiguity computationally with spreading activation and Polaroid Words. In: S., Small, G., Cottrell, & M., Tanenhaus (Eds.), *Lexical ambiguity resolution*. (pp.73–106). Los Altos, CA: Morgan Kaufmann.

Hirst, G. (1988b). Semantic interpretation and ambiguity. *Artificial Intelligence*, 34,131–177.

Hjelmslev, L. (1971). *Essais linguistiques*. Paris: Editions du Minuit.

Hjelmslev, L. (1985). *Nouveaux essais*. Paris: Presses Universitaires de France.

Hobbs, J. R. (1977). Resolving pronoun references. (Technical Report). Department of Computer Science, City College, CUNY, New York, 339–352.

Hobbs, J. R., Stickel, M., Appelt, D., & Martin, P. (1993). Interpretation as abduction. *Artificial Intelligence*, 63, 69–142.

Hobbs, J. R., Stickel, M., Martin, P., & Edwards, D. (1988). Interpretation as abduction. Buffalo: *ACL*.

Hockley, W. E., & Lewandowsky, S. (1991). *Relating Theory and Data: Essays on Human Memory in Honor of Bennet B. Murdock*. Hillsdale, NJ: Lawrence Erlbaum Associates.

Hofmann, T. R. (1989). Paragraphs, and anaphora. *Journal of Pragmatics*, 13, 239–250.

Hofstadter, D. (1985). *Metamagical Themas*. NY: Basic Book.

Holligan, C., & Johnston, R. S. (1988). The use of phonological information by good and poor readers in memory and reading tasks. *Memory and Cognition* 16(6), 522–532.

Holub, R. (1984). *Reception theory—A critical introduction*. NY: Methuen.

Horn, G. (1985). *Memory, imprinting, and the brain: An inquiry into mechanisms*. Oxford Psychology Series, No. 10, Clarendon Press.

Hwang, C. H., & Schubert, L. K. (1993). Episodic logic: A comprehensive, natural representation for language understanding. *Minds and Machines*, 3(4), 381–419.

Ide, N. (1986). A computational approach to meaning in literary texts. *Proceedings of the Conference on Computing and the Humanities: Today's Research, Tomorrow's Teaching*, 222–228.

Ingria, R. J. P., & Stallard, D. (1989). A computational mechanism for pronominal reference. *ACL*, pp.262–271.

Iser, W. (1974). *The implied reader*. Baltimore: The John Hopkins University Press.

Jackendoff, R. (1983). *Semantics and Cognition*. Cambridge, MA: MIT Press.

Jackendoff, R. (1987). *Consciousness and Computational Mind*. Cambridge, MA: MIT Press.

Jacobs, P. S. (1987). Knowledge-intensive natural language generation. *Artificial Intelligence* 33, 325–378.

Jacobs, P. S., & Rau, L. F. (1993). Innovations in text interpretation. *Artificial Intelligence* 63(1–2), 143–191.

Jacobson, I., Christerson, M., Jonsson, P., & Overgaar, G. (1992). *Object-oriented software engineering: A use-case driven approach*, Reading, MA: Addison–Wesley.

Jain, A. N. (1991). *PARSEC: A connectionist learning architecture for parsing spoken language.* (PhD thesis). Pittsburgh, PA: Computer Science Department, Carnegie Mellon University.

Johnson, M. (1987). *The body in the mind: The bodily basis of meaning, imagination, and reason.* Chicago, IL: University of Chicago Press.

Johnson, N., & Mandler, J. (1980). A tale of two structures: Underlying and surface forms in stories. *Poetics*, 9, 51–86.

Johnson, R. E. (1986). Remembering of prose: Holistic or piecemeal losses? *Journal of Memory and Language* 25, 525–538.

Johnson-Laird, P. (1982). Thinking as a skill. *Quarterly Journal of Experimental Psychology*, 34A, 1–29.

Johnson-Laird, P. (1994). Mental models and probabilistic thinking. *Cognition*, 50, 198–209.

Johnston, R. S., Rugg, M. D., & Scott, T. (1987). The influence of phonology on good and poor readers when reading for meaning. *Journal of Memory and Language*, 26, 57–68.

Jones, G. V. (1993). A protoconnectionist theory of memory. *Memory and Cognition* 21(3), 375–378.

Jones, R. (1977). *Physics as metaphor.* Minneapolis: University of Minnesota Press.

Just, M. A., & Carpenter, P. A. (1987). *The Psychology of Reading and Language Comprehension.* Newton, MA: Allyn and Bacon Inc.

Just, M. A., & Carpenter, P. A. (1992). A capacity theory of comprehension: Individual differences in working memory. *Psychological Review*, 99,122–149.

Kanerva, P. (1984). *Self–propagating search: a unified theory of memory.* (PhD thesis). Stanford, CA: CSLI.

Kaplan, D. (1979). On the logic of demonstratives. *The Journal of Philosophical Logic*, 8, 81–98.

Kass, A. (1986). Modifying explanations to understand stories. *Proceedings of the 8th Annual Conference of the Cognitive Science Society*, 691–696.

Katz, B. (1989). EBL and SBL: A neural network synthesis. *Cognitive Science,* 89, 683–689.

Katz, J. J., & Fodor, J. A. (1963). The structure of a semantic theory. *Language*, 39, 170–210.

Kawamoto, A. H. (1993). Nonlinear dynamics in the resolution of lexical ambiguity: A parallel distributed processing account. *Journal of Memory and Language*, 32, 474–516.

Keefe, D. E., & McDaniel, M. A. (1993). The time course and durability of predictive inferences. *Journal of Memory and Language*, 32, 446–463.

Khan, H. U., Ahmad, J., Mahmood, A., & Fatmi, H. A. (1993). Text compression as rule-base pattern-recognition. *Electronics letters*, 29(20), 1752–1753.

Kibler, D. F., & Conery, J. (1985). Parallelism in AI Programs. *IJCAI*, 53–56.

Kim, Y. H., & Goetz, E. T. (1994). Context effects on word recognition and reading-comprehension of poor and good readers: A test of interactive-compensatory hypothesis. *Reading Research Quarterly*, 29(2), 178–188.

Kintsch, W. (1980). Learning from text, levels of representation, or: Why anyone would read a story anyway. *Poetics*, 9, 87–98.

Kintsch, W. (1988). The use of knowledge in discourse processing: A construction-integration model. *Psychological Review*, 95, 163–182.

Kintsch, W. (1991). The role of knowledge in discourse comprehension: A construction-integration model. In: G., Dehnière, & J.-P., Rossi (Eds.), *Text and Text Processing*. Amsterdam: North Holland.

Kintsch, W. (1994). Text comprehension, memory, and learning. *American Psychologist*, 49(4), 294–303.

Kintsch, W., Britton, B. K., Fletcher, C. R., Kintsch, E., Mannes, S. M., & Nathan, M. J. (1993). A comprehension-based approach to learning and understanding. *Advances in research and Theory: Psychology of learning and Motivation*, 30, 165–214.

Kintsch, W., & Dijk van, T. (1978). Towards a model of text comprehension and production. *Psychological Review*, 85, 363–394.

Kintsch, W., & Dijk van, T. (1983). *Towards a model of strategic discourse processing*. NY: Academic Press Inc.

Kintsch, W., & Mannes S. M. (1987). Generating scripts from memory. In: E., van der Meer, & J., Hoffmann (Eds.), *Knowledge aided information processing*. Amsterdam: North–Holland.

Kitano, H. (1991). Massively parallel natural language processing. *IJCAI Workshop on Parallel Processing for AI*, 99–105.

Kitano, H. (1993). A comprehensive and practical model of memory-based machine translation. *IJCAI*.

Kitano, H., & Hendler, J. (1994). *Massively parallel artificial intelligence*, Cambridge, MA: MIT Press.

Kitano, H., & Higuchi, T. (1991a). Massively parallel memory-based parsing. *IJCAI*, 918–924.

Kitano, H., & Higuchi, T. (1991b). High performance memory-based translation on IXM2 massively parallel associative memory processor. *AAAI*: 149–154.

Kitano, H., Moldovan, D. and Cha, S. (1991). High performance natural language processing on semantic network array processor, *IJCAI*, 911–917.

Kitano, H. Moldovan, D., Higuchi, T., Waltz, D., & Hendler, J. (1991). Massively parallel artificial intelligence. *IJCAI*, 557–562.

Kleiber, G. (1981). *Problèmes de référence: Descriptions définies et noms propres.* Université de Metz, France: Centre d'analyse syntaxique.

Koestler, A. (1978). *Janus: A Summing Up.* NY: Vintage Books.

Kolodner, J. (Ed.) (1988). *Proceedings of the case-based reasoning workshop.* San Mateo, CA: Morgan Kaufmann.

Kristensen, B., & Østerbye, K. (1994). Conceptual modeling and programming languages. *ACM SIGPLAN Notices*, 29, 81–90.

Kronfeld, A. (1990). *Reference and computation: An essay in applied philosophy of language.* Cambridge, England: Cambridge University Press Book.

Lachter, J., & Bever, T. G. (1988). The relation between linguistic structure and associative theories of language learning: A constructive critique of some connectionist learning models. *Cognition*, 28, 195–247.

Laird, J. E., Newell, A., & Rosenbloom, P. S. (1987). SOAR: An architecture for general intelligence. *Artificial Intelligence*, 33(1), 1–64.

Lakoff, G. (1987). *Women, fire, and dangerous things: What categories reveal about the mind.* Chicago, IL: University of Chicago Press.

Lakoff, G., & Johnson, M. (1980). *Metaphors we live by.* Chicago, IL: University of Chicago Press.

Langacker, R. W. (1987). *Foundations of cognitive grammar* (Vol. 1). Stanford, CA: Stanford University Press.

Lange, T. E. (1993). Massively-parallel inferencing for natural language understanding and memory retrieval in structured spreading-activation networks. *AAAI*, 144–149.

Lange, T. E., & Dyer, M. (1989). Frame selection in a connectionist model of high-level inferencing. *Proceedings of the Eleventh Conference of the Cognitive Science Society.*

Lange, T. E., Hodges, J., Fuenmayor, M., & Belyaev, L. (1989). DESCARTES: Development environment for simulating hybrid connectionist architectures. *Proceedings of the 11th Annual Conference of the Cognitive Science Society*, 698–705.

Lange, T. E., & Wharton, C. (1993). Dynamic memories: Analysis of an integrated comprehension and episodic memory retrieval model. *IJCAI.*

Lappin, S., & McCord, M. (1990). Anaphora resolution in slot grammar. *Computational Linguistics*, 16(4), 197–212.

Le Ny, J.-F. (1991). Coherence in Semantic Representations: Text Comprehension and Acquisition of Concepts. In: G., Dehnière, & J.-P., Rossi, *Text and Text Processing*. Amsterdam: North Holland.

Leake, D. (1989). Anomaly detection strategies for schema-based story understanding. *Proceedings of the 11th Annual Conference of the Cognitive Science Society.*

Leake, D. (1993). Focusing construction and selection of abductive hypotheses. *IJCAI.*

Leake, D., & Owens, C. (1986). Organizing memory for explanation. *Proceedings of the 8th Annual Conference of the Cognitive Science Society*, 710–715.

Lebowitz, M. (1980). Generalization and memory in an integrated understanding system. (Technical Report No.186). Department of Computer Science, Yale University, New Haven, CT.

Lebowitz, M. (1988). The use of memory in text processing. *Communications of the ACM*, 31,1483–1501.

Ledoux, J. E. (1994). Emotion, memory and the brain. *Scientific American*, 270(6), 50–57.

Lee, G. (1991). *Distributed semantic representations for goal/plan analysis of narratives in a connectionist architecture.* (PhD thesis). Computer Science Department, University of California at Berkeley, CA.

Lee, G., Flowers, M., & Dyer, M. (1989). A symbolic/connectionist script applier mechanism. *Proceedings of the 11th Annual Conference of the Cognitive Science Society.*

Lee, W., & Moldovan, D. (1991). The design of a marker passing architecture for knowledge processing. *AAAI*, 59–64.

Lehman, J. F., Lewis, R. L., & Newell, A. (1991). Integrating knowledge sources in language comprehension. *Proceedings of the 13th Annual Conference of the Cognitive Science Society.*

Lehnert, W. (1981). Plot units and narrative summarization. *Cognitive Science*, 5, 293–332.

Lehnert, W. (1983). Narrative complexity based on summarization algorithms. *IJCAI*, 713–716.

Le Pore, E., & Garson, J. (1983). Pronouns and quantifier-scope in English. *Journal of Philosophical Logic*, 12, 327–358.

Levesque, H. J. (1984). A fundamental trade-off in knowledge representation and reasoning. *CSCSI*, 141–152.

Levin, B., & Pinker, S. (Eds.) (1992). *Lexical and conceptual semantics.* Blackwell Publishers.

Levine, D. S. (1991). *Introduction to neural and cognitive modeling*, Hillsdale, NJ: Lawrence Erlbaum Associates.

Levine, D. S., & Aparicio, M. (1994). *Neural networks for knowledge representation and inference*, Hillsdale, NJ: Lawrence Erlbaum Associates.

Lewandowsky, S., Dunn, J. C., & Kirsner, K. (1989). *Implicit memory: Theoretical issues*, Hillsdale, NJ: Lawrence Erlbaum Associates.

Lewis, R. L. (1993). An architecturally-based theory of human sentence comprehension. *Cognitive Science*, 108–113.

Lin, D., & Goebel, R. (1993). Context-free grammar parsing by message passing. *PACLING*, 203–211.

Lindsay, R., & Manaster-Ramer, A. (1987). Teuchistic natural language processes. *Proceedings of the 9th Annual Conference of the Cognitive Science Society*, 96–105.

Ling, C. X. F., Cherwenka, S., & Marinov, M. (1993). A symbolic model for learning the past-tenses of English verbs. *IJCAI*.

Lively, S., Pisoni, D., & Goldfinger, S. (1994). Spoken word recognition. In: M. A., Gernsbacher (Ed.), *Handbook of Psycholinguistics*. NY: Academic Press.

Long, D. L., & Golding, J. (1993). Superordinate goal inferences: Are they automatically generating during comprehension? *Discourse Processes*, 16(1–2), 55–73.

Longoni, A. M., Richardson, J. T. E., & Aiello, A. (1993). Articulatory rehearsal and phonological storage in working memory. *Memory and Language,* 21(1), 11–22.

Lucas M. M., Tanenhaus M. K., & Carlson G. N. (1990). Levels of representation in the interpretation of anaphoric reference and instrument inference. *Memory and Cognition*, 18(6), 611–631.

Lytinen, S. (1984). *The organization of knowledge in a multi-lingual integrated parser.* (PhD thesis). Yale University, Department of Computer Science, New Haven, CT.

Mac Cormac, E. (1985). *A Cognitive Theory of Metaphor*. Cambridge, MA: MIT Press.

MacDonald, M. C., & MacWhinney B. (1990). Measuring inhibition and facilitation from pronouns. *Journal of Memory and Language*, 29, 469–492.

MacLeod, C., & Cohen, I. L. (1993). Anxiety and the interpretation of ambiguity: A text comprehension study. *Journal of Abnormal Psychology,* 102(2), 238–247.

Maes, P. (1987). *Computational Reflection*. (PhD thesis). Laboratory for Artificial Intelligence, Vrije Universiteit Brussel. Brussel, Belgium.

Magliano, J. P., Baggett, W. B., Johnson, B. K., & Graesser, A. C. (1993). The time course of generating causal antecedent and causal consequence inferences. *Discourse Processes,* 16(1–2), 35–53.

Malcolm, N. (1977). *Memory and mind*. NY: Cornell University Press.

Manaster-Ramer, A. (1992). Review of Partee *et al.* (1990), *Computational Linguistics*, 18(1), 104–107.

Mandler, G. (1987). Determinants of recognition. In: E., van der Meer, & J., Hoffman (Eds.), *Knowledge aided information processing*. Amsterdam: North Holland.

Marcus, M. P. (1980). *A theory of syntactic recognition for natural language.* Cambridge, MA: MIT Press.

Marcus, M. P. (1984). Some inadequate theories of human language processing. In: T., Bever, J., Carroll, & L., Miller (Eds.), *Talking minds.* Cambridge, MA: MIT Press.

Mark, M. A., & Greer, J. E. (1991). The VCR tutor: Evaluating instructional effectiveness. *Proceedings of the 13th Annual Conference of the Cognitive Society.*

Márkus, A. (1983). Shifting the focus of attention. *IJCAI*, 66–68.

Marslen-Wilson, W. (Ed.) (1989). *Lexical representation and process.* Cambridge, MA: MIT Press.

Martin, C. (1989). Pragmatic interpretation and ambiguity. *Proceedings of the 11th Annual Conference of the Cognitive Science Society.*

Martin, J. H. (1987). Understanding New Metaphors. *IJCAI*, 137–139.

Martin, J. H. (1988). *A computational theory of metaphor.* (PhD thesis). University of California at Berkeley, CA.

Martin, R. C. (1993). Short-term memory and sentence processing: Evidence from neuropsychology. *Memory and Cognition,* 21(2), 176–183.

Martin, R. C., & Jensen, C. R. (1988). Phonological priming in the lexical decision task: A failure to replicate. *Memory and Cognition,* 16(6), 505–521.

Martin, R. C., Shelton, J. R., & Yaffee, L. S. (1994). Language processing and working-memory-neuropsychological evidence for separate phonological and semantic capacities. *Journal of Memory and Language,* 33(1), 83–111.

Masson, M. E. J. (1986). Comprehension of rapidly presented sentences: The mind is quicker than the eye. *Journal of Memory and Language,* 25, 588–604.

Masson, M. E. J. (1988). The interaction of sentence context and perceptual analysis in word identification. *Memory and Cognition,* 16(6), 489–496.

Masson, M. E. J. (1989). Lexical ambiguity resolution in a constraint satisfaction network. *Cognitive Science,* 89, 757–764.

Matsumi, N. (1994). Processes of words memory in 2nd-language acquisition: A test of bilingual dual coding theory. *Japanese Journal of Psycholinguistics,* 64(6), 460–468.

Matsuoka, S., Watanabe, T., & Yonezawa, A. (1991). Hybrid group reflective architecture for object-oriented concurrent reflective programming. *Proceedings of the European Conference on Object-Oriented Programming, Lecture Notes in Computer Science,* No. 512, (pp. 231–250). NY: Springer–Verlag.

Matthews A., & Chodorow M. S. (1988). Pronoun resolution in two-clause sentences: Effects of ambiguity, antecedent location, and depth of embedding. *Journal of Memory and Language,* 27, 245–260.

Mayberry, M., & Miikkulainen, R. (1994). Lexical disambiguation based on distributed representations of context frequency. (Technical Report). University of California at Los Angeles, Los Angeles, CA.

McCarthy, J. (1987). Generality in Artificial Intelligence. *Communications of the ACM*, 30(12), 1030–1035.

McClelland, J. L., & Kawamoto, A. H. (1986). Mechanisms of sentence processing: Assigning roles to constituents. In: J. L., McClelland, & D., Rumelhart (Eds.), *Parallel distributed processing*, Vol. 2, Cambridge, MA: MIT Press.

McClelland, J. L., & Rumelhart, D. (1986). *Parallel distributed processing*. Vol. 2, Cambridge, MA: MIT Press.

McElree, B. (1993). The Locus of lexical preference effects in sentence comprehension: A time-course analysis. *Journal of Memory and Language*, 32, 536–571.

McKoon, G., & Ratcliff, R. (1992). Inference during reading. *Psychological Review*, 99, 440–466.

McKoon, G., Ratcliff, R., & Seifert, C. (1989). Making the connection: Generalized knowledge structure in story understanding. *Journal of Memory, and Language*, 28, 711–734.

McRoy, S. (1988). *The influence of time and memory constraints on the resolution of structural ambiguity*. (Technical Report CSRI-209). University of Toronto, Department of Computer Science, Toronto, Canada.

McRoy, S. (1992). Using multiple knowledge sources for word sense discrimination. *Computational Linguistics*, 18(1), 1–30.

Merlo, P. (1993). For an incremental computation of intrasentential coreference. *IJCAI*.

Metcalfe, J., & Shimamura, P. (1994). *Metacognition*. Cambridge, MA: MIT Press.

Meutsh, D. (1986). Mental models in literary discourse: Towards the integration of linguistic and psychological levels of description. *Poetics*, 15, 307–331.

Meyer, D. E., & Kornblum, S. (1993). *Attention and Performance XIV: Synergies in Experimental Psychology, Artificial Intelligence, and Cognitive Neuroscience*, Cambridge, MA: MIT Press, Cambridge, MA.

Miezitis, M. (1988). *Generating lexical options by matching in a knowledge base*. (Technical Report CSRI–217). University of Toronto, Department of Computer Science, Toronto, Canada.

Miikkulainen, R. (1993a). *Subsymbolic case-role analysis of sentence with embedded clauses*. (Technical Report). University of California at Los Angeles, Los Angeles, CA.

Miikkulainen, R. (1993b). *Subsymbolic natural language processing: An integrated model of scripts, lexicon and memory*. Cambridge, MA: MIT Press.

Miller, G. (1985). Dictionaries of the mind. *Proceedings of the 22nd Conference of the Association for Computational Linguistics*, 305–314.

Millikan, R. (1987). *Language, thought, and other biological categories.* Cambridge, MA: MIT Press.

Millikan, R. (1993). *White queen psychology and other essays for Alice.* Cambridge, MA: MIT Press.

Millis, K. K., & Just, M. A. (1994). The influence of connectives on sentence comprehension. *Journal of Memory and Language,* 33(1), 128–147.

Millis, M. L., & Button, S. B. (1989). The effect of polysemy on lexical decision time: Now you see it, now you don't. *Memory and Cognition,* 17(2), 141–147.

Minsky, M. (1975). A framework for representing knowledge. In: P., Winston (Ed.), *The Psychology of Computer Vision.* NY: McGraw–Hill.

Minsky, M. (1980). K-lines: A theory of memory. *Cognitive Science,* 4 (2).

Minsky, M. (1986). *The Society of Mind.* NY: Simon and Schuster.

Minsky, M., & Papert, S. (1988). *Perceptrons,* Cambridge, MA: MIT Press.

Mitchell, D. C. (1982). *The process of reading: A cognitive analysis of fluent reading and learning to read.* NY: John Wiley & Sons.

Mitchell, D. C. (1994). Sentence parsing. In: M. A., Gernsbacher (Ed.), *Handbook of Psycholinguistics,* NY: Academic Press.

Miyake, A., Just, M., & Carpenter, P. (1994). Working memory constraints on the resolution of lexical ambiguity: Maintaining multiple interpretations in neutral contexts. *Journal of Memory and Language,* 33, 175–202.

Moldovan, D. I., Lee, W., & Lin, C. (1993). Parallel Knowledge Processing on SNAP. *IEEE Transactions on Knowledge and Data Engineering.* 5 (1), 65–75.

Montague, R. (1974). *Formal Philosophy.* New Haven, CO: Yale University Press.

Mooney, R., & DeJong, G. (1985). Learning schemata for natural language processing. *IJCAI,* 681–687.

Moran, D. B. (1988). Quantifier scoping in the SRI core language. *ACL,* 33–40.

Morton, J. (1969). The interaction of information in word recognition. *Psychological Review,* 76, 165–178.

Morton, J., Hammersley, R. H., & Bekerian, D. A. (1985). Headed records: A model for memory and its failures. *Cognition,* 20, 1–23.

Muller, C. (1977). *Principes et méthodes de statistique lexicale,* Paris: Hachette.

Murray, J. D., Klin, C. M., & Myers, J. L. (1993). Forward inferences in narrative text. *Journal of Memory and Language,* 32, 464–473.

Musseler, J., Rickheit, G., & Strohner, H. (1985). Influences of modality, text difficulty, and processing control on inferences in text processing. In: Rickheit, G., & Strohner, H. (Eds.), *Inferences in Text Processing.*

Nairne, J. S. (1988). A framework for interpreting recency effects in immediate serial recall. *Memory and Cognition,* 16(4), 343–352.

Nelson, T. J. (1983). A neural network model for cognitive activity. *Biological Cybernetics,* 49, 79–88.

Nenov, V. I. (1991). *Perceptually grounded language acquisition: A neural/procedural hybrid model.* (PhD thesis). Computer Science Department, University of California at Berkeley, CA.

Newell, A. (1990). *Unified theories of cognition.* Cambridge, MA: Harvard University Press.

Niv, M. (1992). Right association revisited. *ACL.*

Nolan, R. (1994). *Cognitive Practices: Human language and human knowledge,* Cambridge, MA: Blackwell Publishers.

Noordman, L. G. M., & Vonk, W. (1992). Reader's knowledge and the control of inference in reading. *Language and Cognitive Processes,* 7, 373–391.

Norris, C. (1982). *Deconstruction—Theory and practice.* NY: Methuen.

Norris, D. (1986). Word recognition: Context effects without priming. *Cognition,* 22,93–136.

Norvig, P. (1983a). Six problems for story understanders. *Proceedings of the National Conference on Artificial Intelligence.* (pp.284–287). American Association for Artificial Intelligence, Washington, D.C.

Norvig, P. (1983b). Frame activated inferences in a story understanding program. *IJCAI,* 624–626.

Norvig, P. (1987). *Unified theory of inferences for text understanding.* (PhD thesis). University of California at Berkeley, Department of Computer Science, Berkeley, CA.

Norvig, P. (1989). Marker passing as a weak method for text inferencing. *Cognitive Science,* 13, 569–620.

Oakhill, J. V. (1994). Individual differences in children's text comprehension. In: M. A., Gernsbacher (Ed.), *Handbook of Psycholinguistics.* NY: Academic Press.

Odell, J. (1984). On the possibility of natural language processing: Some philosophical objections. *Theoretical Linguistics,* 11, 127–146.

Ogden, C. K., & Richards, I. A. (1923). *The meaning of meaning.* London: Routledge and Kegan Paul.

Osterhou, L., & Swinney, D. A. (1993). On the temporal course of gap-filling during comprehension of verbal passives. *Journal of Psycholinguistic Research,* 22(2), 273–286.

Palmer, M. S., Passonne, R. J., & Weir, C. (1993). The Kernel text understanding system. *Artificial Intelligence,* 63(1–2), 17–68.

Parkin, A. J. (1993). *Memory: phenomena, experiment and theory.* Blackwell Publishers.

Parkin, A. J., Reid, T. K., & Russo, R. (1990). On the differential nature of implicit and explicit memory. *Memory and Cognition,* 18(5), 507–514.

Partee, B. (1984). Quantification, pronouns, and VP-anaphora. In: J., Groenedijk, et al. (Eds.), *Truth, Interpretation and Information.* Dordrecht: Foris.

Partee, B., Meulen ter, A., & Wall, R. E. (1990). *Mathematical methods in linguistics.* Dordrecht, Netherlands: Kluwer Academic.

Peckham, M. (1979). *Explanation and power—The control of human behavior,* NY: Seabury.

Penney, C. G. (1989). Modality effects and the structure of short-term verbal memory. *Memory and Cognition,* 17(4), 398–422.

Pereira, F. C. N. (1990). Categorial semantics and scoping. *Computational Linguistics,* 16(1), 1–10.

Pereira, F. C. N., Gazdar, G., Pulman, S., Joshi, A., & Kay, M. (1987). Unification and the new grammatism. (panel), *Proceedings of Theoretical Issues in Natural Language Processing,* TINLAP–3, 32–55.

Pereira, F. C. N., & Grosz, B. (1993). Introduction. Special Issue on: Natural Language Processing, *Artificial Intelligence,* 63, 1–15.

Pereira, F. C.N., & Grosz, B. (1994). *Natural language processing.* Cambridge, MA: MIT Press.

Perfetti, C. (1993). Why inferences might be restricted. *Discourse Processes,* 16, 181–192.

Perrig, W. J., & Perrig, P. (1988). Mood and memory: Mood-congruity effects in absence of mood. *Memory and Cognition,* 16(2), 102–109.

Peters, S. L., & Shapiro, S. C. (1987). A representation for natural category systems. *Proceedings of the 9th Annual Conference of the Cognitive Science Society,* 379–390.

Peters, S. L., Shapiro, S. C., & Rapaport, W. (1988). Flexible natural language processing and Roschian category theory. *Proceedings of the 10th Annual Conference of the Cognitive Science Society,* 125–131.

Phillips, M. (1985). *Aspects of text structure.* Amsterdam: North Holland.

Piaget, J. (1970). *Genetic epistemology.* NY: Columbia University Press.

Piatelli-Palmarini, M. (Ed.) (1980). *Language and learning.* Cambridge, MA: Harvard University Press.

Pinker, S., & Prince, A. (1988). On language and connectionism: Analysis of a parallel distributed processing model of language acquisition. *Cognition,* 28, 73–193.

Plantinga, E. (1986). Who decides what metaphors mean? *Proceedings of the Conference on Computing and the Humanities: Today's Research, Tomorrow's Teaching*, 194–204.

Plantinga, E. (1987). Mental models and metaphor. *Proceedings of Theoretical Issues in Natural Language Processing*, TINLAP-3, 164–172.

Pollack, M. E., & Pereira, F. C. N. (1988). An integrated framework for semantic and pragmatic interpretation. *ACL.*

Pollard, C., & Sag, I. (1988). *An Information–Based Approach to Syntax and Semantics: Volume I Fundamentals*, CSLI Lecture Notes no.13, Chicago University Press.

Posner, M. I. (1989). *Foundations of Cognitive Science*. Cambridge, MA: MIT Press.

Propp, V. (1968). *Morphology of the folktale*. University of Texas Press, Austin.

Prust, H., & Scha, R. (1990). A Discourse Approach to Verb Phrase Anaphora. *Proceedings of the 9th European Conference on Artificial Intelligence.*

Pustejovsky, J., & Bergler, S. (Eds.) (1991). *Lexical semantics and knowledge representation*. Lecture Notes in Artificial Intelligence 627, Amsterdam: Springer–Verlag.

Pylyshyn, Z. (1984a). *Computation and cognition: Toward a foundation of cognitive science*. Cambridge, MA: MIT Press.

Pylyshyn, Z. (1984b). Why computing requires symbols. *Proceedings of the 6th Annual Conference of the Cognitive Science Society*, 71–73.

Quillian, R. (1967). Word concepts: A theory and simulation of some basic semantic capabilities. *Behavioral Science*, 12, 403–417.

Radeau, M., Morais, J., & Dewier, A. (1989). Phonological priming in spoken word recognition: Task effects. *Memory and Cognition*, 17(5), 525–535.

Ram, A. (1990a). Incremental learning of explanation patterns and their indices.*Machine Learning: Proceedings of the 7th International Conference*, 313–320.

Ram, A. (1990b). Knowledge goals: A theory on interestingness. *Proceedings of the 12th Annual Conference of the Cognitive Science Society*, 206–214.

Ram, A. (1991). Interest-based information filtering and extraction in natural language understanding systems. *Bellcore Workshop on High-Performance Information Filtering: Foundations, Architectures and Applications*, 1–11.

Ram, A., & Hunter, L. (1991). A goal-based approach to intelligent information retrieval. *Machine Learning: Proceedings of the 8th International Conference*, 265–269.

Ram, A., & Leake, D. (1991). Evaluation of explanatory hypotheses. *Proceedings of the 13th Annual Conference of the Cognitive Science Society*, 867–871.

Rastier, F. (1987). *Sémantique Interprétative*. Paris: Presses Universitaires de France.

Rastier, F. (1989). *Sens et Textualité*. Paris: Hachette.

Rastier, F. (1991). *Sémantique et recherches cognitives*. Paris: Presses Universitaires de France.

Ratcliff, J. E. (1987). The plausibility effect: Lexical priming or sentential processing? *Memory and Cognition*, 15(6), 482–496.

Raymond, J. E., Shapiro, K. L., & Arnell, K. M. (1992). Temporary suppression of visual processing in RSVP task: An attentional blink? *Journal of Experimental Psychology: Human Perception and Performance*, 18, 849–860.

Reddy, M. (1979). The conduit metaphor—A case of frame conflict in our language about language. In: A., Ortony (Ed.), *Metaphor and thought*. Cambridge, England: Cambridge University Press.

Regier, T. (1992). *The acquisition of lexical semantics for spatial terms: A connectionist model of perceptual categorization*. (PhD thesis). Computer Science Department, University of California at Berkeley. (Technical Report TR-92-64).

Reilly, R., & Sharkey, N. (1992). *Connectionist Approaches to Natural Language Processing*. Hillsdale, NJ: Lawrence Erlbaum Associates.

Reyna, V. F., & Kiernan, B. (1994). Development of gist versus verbatim memory in sentence recognition: Effects of lexical familiarity, semantic content, encoding instructions, and retention interval. *Developmental Psychology*, 30(2), 178–191.

Rich, R., & Shepherd, M. J. (1993). Teaching text comprehension strategies to adult poor readers. *Reading and Writing*, 5(4), 387–402.

Rickheit, G., Schnotz, W., & Strohner, H. (1985). The concept of inference in discourse comprehension. In: G., Rickheit, & H., Strohner (Eds.), *Inferences in Text Processing*. Amsterdam, North Holland.

Rickheit, G., & Strohner, H. (Eds.). (1985). *Inferences in text processing in advances in psychology*. Amsterdam: North–Holland.

Rieger, C. (1975). Conceptual memory and inference, In: Schank, R. (Ed.), *Conceptual information processing*. Amsterdam: North–Holland.

Riesbeck, C., & Martin, C. (1985). *Direct memory access parsing*. (Technical Report No.354). Department of Computer Science, Yale University, New Haven, CT.

Riley, G. L. (1993). A story structure approach to narrative text comprehension. *Modern Language Journal*, 77(4), 417–432.

Roderick, W. (1986). Word recognition in early reading: A review of the direct and indirect access hypotheses. *Cognition*, 24, 93–119.

Roget's Thesaurus (1962). Third Edition, Toronto, Canada: Fitzhenry & Whiteside.

Rosch, E. (1974). Linguistic Relativity. In: A., Silverstein (Ed.), *Human Communication*. NY: Hasted Press.

Rosenbloom, P. S., Laird, J. E., & Newell, A. (1993). *The SOAR papers: Research on integrated intelligence*. Cambridge, MA: MIT Press.

Rosenbloom, P. S., Lehman, J. F., & Laird, J. E. (1993). Overview of SOAR as a unified theory of cognition: Spring 1993. *Proceedings of the 15th Annual Conference of the Cognitive Society.*

Rosenfield, I. (1988). *The invention of memory: A new view of the brain.* NY: Basic Books.

Rossi, J.-P. (1991). Input-output: Processing and representation., In: G., Dehnière, & J.-P., Rossi (Eds.), *Text and Text Processing.* Amsterdam: North Holland.

Rumelhart, D. E. (1975). Notes on a schema for stories. In: D. G., Bobrow, & A., Collins (Eds.), *Representation and Understanding: Studies in Cognitive Science.* NY: Academic Press.

Rumelhart, D. E. (1984). The emergence of cognitive phenomena from sub-symbolic processes. *Proceedings of the 6th Annual Conference of the Cognitive Science Society,* 59–62.

Sandberg, J., & Wielinga, B. (1991). How situated is cognition? *IJCAI,* 314–346.

Sanford, A. J., & Garrod, S. C. (1994). Selective processing in text understanding. In: M. A., Gernsbacher (Ed.), *Handbook of Psycholinguistics.* NY: Academic Press.

Sato, S., & Nagao, M. (1990). Toward memory-based translation. *COLING,* 247–252.

de Saussure, F. (1916). *Cours de Linguistique.* (Translated by W., Baskin). NY: Philosophical Library, 1959.

Schacter, D. (1989). Memory. In: M., Posner (Ed.), *Foundations of Cognitive Science.* Cambridge, MA: MIT Press.

Schacter, D., & Tulving, E. (1994). *Memory systems.* Cambridge, MA: MIT Press.

Schank, R. (1972). Conceptual dependency: A theory of natural language understanding. *Cognitive Psychology,* 552–631.

Schank, R. (1982). *Dynamic memory.* NY: Cambridge University Press.

Schank, R., & Abelson, R. (1977). *Scripts, plans, goals, and understanding.* Hillsdale, NJ: Lawrence Erlbaum Associates.

Schank, R., & Birnbaum, L. (1984). Memory, meaning, and syntax. In: T., Bever, J., Carroll, & L., Miller (Eds.), *Talking minds.* Cambridge, MA: MIT Press.

Schank, R., Collins, C. G., Davis, E., Johnson, P. N., Lytinen, S., & Reiser B.J. (1982). What's the point? *Cognitive Science,* 6, 255–276.

Schmalhofer, F., & Tschaitschian, B. (1993). The acquisition of a procedure schema from text and experience. *Proceedings of the 15th Annual Conference of the Cognitive Society.*

Schneider, W. (1993). Varieties of working memory as seen in biology and in connectionist/control architectures. *Memory and Cognition,* 21(2), 184–192.

Schnotz, W. (1985). Selectivity in drawing inferences. In: G., Rickheit, & H., Strohner

(Eds.), *Inferences in text processing*. Amsterdam: North Holland.

Schogt, H. (1976). *Sémantique synchronique*. Toronto, Canada: University of Toronto Press.

Scholes, R. (1974). *Structuralism in literature: An introduction*. Yale University Press.

Schubert, L. (1986). Are there preference trade-offs in attachment decisions? *Proceedings of the National Conference on Artificial Intelligence*, American Association for Artificial Intelligence, 601–605.

Schweickert, R., & Boruff, B. (1986). Short-term memory capacity: Magic number or magic spell? *Journal of experimental Psychology: Learning, Memory, and Cognition*, 3, 419–425.

Schweickert, R., Guentert, L., & Hersberg, L. (1989). Neural network models of memory span. *Proceedings of the 11th Annual Conference of the Cognitive Science Society*, 852–859.

Searle, J. (1979). Literal meaning. In: *Expression and meaning*. NY: Cambridge University Press.

Searle, J. (1984). *Minds, brains, and science*, Cambridge, MA: Harvard University Press.

Sebrechts, M. M., Marsh, R. L., & Seamon, J. G. (1989). Secondary memory and very rapid forgetting. *Memory and Cognition,* 17(6), 693–700.

Selman, B. (1985). *Rule-based processing in a connectionist system for natural language understanding*. (Technical Report CSRI–168). Department of Computer Science, University of Toronto, Toronto. A summary of this work can be found in: B., Selman, & G., Hirst (Eds.), A Rule-Based Connectionist Parsing System. *Proceedings of the 7th Annual Conference of the Cognitive Science Society*, 212–219.

Selman, B., & Hirst, G. (1987). Parsing as an energy minimization problem. In: D., Davis (Ed.), *Genetic algorithms and simulated annealing*. Pitman Research Notes in Artificial Intelligence.

Shanks, D. (1993). Breaking Chomsky's rules. *New Scientist*, 30 January 1993, 23–30.

Shapiro, L. P., & Nagel, H. N. (1993). Preferences for a verb's complements and their use in sentence processing. *Journal of Memory and Language*, 32, 96–114.

Sharkey, A. J. C., & Sharkey, N. E. (1989). Lexical processing and the mechanism of context effects in text comprehension. *Proceedings of the 11th Annual Conference of the Cognitive Science Society.*

Sharkey, N. E. (1990). A connectionist model of text comprehension. In: D. A., Balota, G. B., Flores d'Arcais, & K., Rayner (Eds.), *Comprehension Processes in Reading*. Hillsdale, NJ: Lawrence Erlbaum Associates.

Shastri, L. (1993). Harnessing massive parallelism for tractable reasoning: A cognitively motivated approach. *AAAI Spring-Symposium* on "Innovative Applications of Massive Parallelism," 200–205 (also printed as A computational model of tractable reasoning: taking inspiration from cognition.*IJCAI*-93).

Shastri, L., & Ajjanagadde, V. (1993). From simple associations to systematic reasoning: A connectionist representation of rules, variables and dynamic bindings using temporal synchrony. *Behavioral and Brain Sciences*, 16, 417–494.

Shiffrin, R. M. (1993). Short-term memory: A brief commentary. *Memory and Cognition:*, 21(2), 193–197.

Simon, H. A., (1993). Artificial intelligence: An experimental science. *AAAI* Keynote Address.

Simmons, R. F., & Yu, Y.-H. (1990). Training a neural network to be a context sensitive grammar. *Proceedings of the Fifth Rocky Mountain Conference on Artificial Intelligence*, 251–256.

Simpson, G. B. (1994). Context and the processing of ambiguous words, In: M. A., Gernsbacher (Ed.), *Handbook of Psycholinguistics*. NY: Academic Press.

Simpson, G. B., & Krueger, M. A. (1991). Selective access of homograph meanings in sentence context. *Journal of Memory and Language, 30*, 627–643.

Singer, M. (1993). Global inferences of text situations. *Discourse Processes,* 16(1–2), 161–168.

Singer, M. (1994). Discourse inference processes. In: M. A., Gernsbacher (Ed.), *Handbook of Psycholinguistics*. NY: Academic Press.

Singer, M., Graesser, A., & Trabasso, T. (1994). Minimal or global inference during reading. *Journal of Memory and Language, 33*(4) 421–441.

Skousen, R. (1985). *Analogical modeling of language,* Kluwer Academic Publishers.

Small, S. L. (1980). *Word expert parsing: A theory of distributed word-based natural language understanding.* (PhD thesis). (Technical Report No 954). Department of Computer Science, University of Maryland.

Small, S. L. (1983). Parsing as cooperative distributed inference: Understanding through memory interactions. In: M., King (Ed.), *Parsing Natural Language*. London, England: Academic Press.

Small, S., & Rieger, C. (1982). Parsing and comprehending with word experts. *Proceedings of the National Conference on Artificial Intelligence*. American Association for Artificial Intelligence, 247–250.

Smolensky, P. (1988). The proper treatment of connectionism. *Behavioral and Brain Sciences*, 11(1), 1–74.

Somers, H. L. (1987). *Valency and case in computational linguistics.* England: Edinburgh University Press.

Sommerville, I. (1992). *Software engineering.* Fifth edition, NY: Addison–Wesley.

Sowa, J. F. (1984). *Conceptual structures: information processing in mind and machine.* Reading, MA: Addison–Wesley Publishing Company.

Sowa, J. F. (1991). *Principles of semantic networks: Explorations in the representation of knowledge.* San Mateo, CA: Morgan Kaufmann Publishers.

Speer, S. R. Crowder, R. G., & Thomas, L. M. (1993). Prosodic structure and sentence recognition. *Journal of Memory and Language, 32,* 336–358.

Sperber, D., & Wilson, D. (1986). *Relevance: communication and cognition.* Cambridge, MA: Harvard University Press.

Spiro, R. (1980). Prior knowledge and story processing. *Poetics, 9,* 313–327.

Squire, L. (1987). *Memory and brain.* NY: Oxford University Press.

St. John, M. F. (1990). *The story gestalt: text comprehension by cue-based constraint satisfaction.* (PhD thesis). Department of Psychology, Carnegie-Mellon University, Pittsburgh, PA.

St. John, M. F. (1992). The story gestalt: A model of knowledge intensive processes in text comprehension. *Cognitive Science, 16,* 271–306.

Stabler, E. (1993). Parsing as non-horn deduction. *Artificial Intelligence, 63,* 225–264.

Stallard, D. (1987). The logical analysis of lexical ambiguity. *ACL,* 179–185.

Stanfill, C., & Waltz, D. L., (1986). Towards memory-based reasoning. *Communications of the ACM, 29,* 1213–1228.

Sternberg, R. J. (1990). *Metaphors of mind: Conceptions of the nature of intelligence,* Cambridge, England: Cambridge University Press.

Stevenson, R. J. (1986). The time course of pronoun comprehension. *Proceedings of the 8th Annual Conference of the Cognitive Science Society,* 102–109.

Stevenson, R. J., Crawley, R. A., Wilson, G., & Kleinman, D. (1990). Thematic roles and pronoun comprehension. *Proceedings of the 12th Annual Conference of the Cognitive Science Society.*

Stevenson, R. J, Nelson, A. W. R., & Stenning, K. (1993). Strategies in pronoun comprehension. *Proceedings of the 15th Annual Conference of the Cognitive Science Society.*

Suh, S., & Trabasso, T. (1993). Inferences during reading: Converging evidence from discourse analysis, task-aloud protocols, and recognition priming. *Journal of Memory and Language, 32,* 279–300.

Sumida, R. A. (1991). Dynamic inferencing in parallel distributed semantic networks. *Proceedings of the 13th Annual Conference of the Cognitive Science Society.*

Sumida, R. A., & Dyer, M. G. (1992). Propagation filters in PDS networks for sequencing and ambiguity resolution. In: J. E., Moody, S. J., Hanson, & R. P., Lippman (Eds.), *Advances in Neural Information Processing Systems 4.* San Mateo, CA: Morgan Kaufman.

Sun, R. (1989). A discrete neural network model for conceptual representation and reasoning.*Proceedings of the 11th Annual Conference of the Cognitive Science Society.*

Sun, R. (1993). An efficient feature based connectionist inheritance scheme. *IEEE Transactions on Systems, Man, and Cybernetics*, 23 (11).

Tabossi, P., & Zardon, F. (1993). Processing ambiguous words in context. *Journal of Memory and Language*, 32, 359–372.

Taft, M. (1990). Lexical processing of functionally constrained words. *Journal of Memory and Language*, 29, 245–257.

Tapiero, I., & Denhière, G. (1993). Simulation of cued-recall and recognition of expository texts by using the construction-integration model. *Proceedings of the 11th Annual Conference of the Cognitive Science Society*.

Taraban, R., & McClelland, J. L. (1988). Constituent attachment and thematic role assignment in sentence processing: Influences of content-based expectations. *Journal of Memory and Language*, 27, 597–632.

Tello, E. R. (1989). *Object-oriented programming for artificial intelligence*. Reading, MA: Addison–Wesley.

Thagard, P., Holyoak, K., Nelson, G., & Gochfeld, D. (1990). Analog retrieval by constraint satisfaction. *Artificial Intelligence*, 46, 259–310.

Thagard, P. (1986). Parallel computation and the mind–body problem. *Cognitive Science*, 10, 301–318.

Thorndike, P., & Yekovich, F. (1980). A critique of schema-based theories of human story memory. *Poetics*, 9, 23–49.

Till, R. E., Mross, E. F., & Kintsch, W. (1988). Time course of priming for associate and inference words in a discourse context. *Memory and Cognition*, 16(4), 283–298.

Tomabechi, H., & Levin, L. (1989). Head-driven massively-parallel constraint propagation: Head-feature and subcategorization as interacting constraints in associative memory. *Proceedings of the 11th Annual Conference of the Cognitive Science Society*, 372–379.

Trabasso, T. (1991). The development of coherence in narratives by understanding intentional action. In: G., Denhière, & J.-P., Rossi (Eds.), *Text and Text Processing*. Amsterdam: North Holland.

Trabasso, T., & Suh, S. (1993). Understanding text: Achieving explanatory coherence through on-line inferences and mental operations in working-memory. *Discourse Processes*, 16(1–2), 3–34.

Tulving, E. (1983). *Elements of episodic memory*. NY: Oxford University Press.

Tulving, E. (1984). Précis of elements of episodic memory, *The Behavioral and Brain Sciences*, 7:223–268.

Underwood, G., & Batt, V. (1995). *Reading and understanding: An introduction to the psychology of reading*. Blackwell Publishers.

Uramoto, N. (1994). Example-based word–sense disambiguation. *IEICE Transactions on Informations and Systems*, 240–246.

van den Broek, P. (1994). Comprehension and memory of narrative texts: inferences and coherence. In: M.A., Gernsbacher, (Ed.), *Handbook of psycholinguistics*, NY: Academic Press.

van den Broek, P., Fletcher, C., & Risden, K. (1993). Investigations of inferential processes in reading: A theoretical and methodological integration. *Discourse Processes*, 16,169–180.

van den Broek, P., & Lorch, R. (1993). Network representations of causal relations in memory for narrative texts. *Discourse Processes*, 16,75–98.

van der Linden, E.-J. (1992). Incremental Processing and the Hierarchical Lexicon. *Computational Linguistics*, 18(2), 219–223.

van der Meer, E. (1987). Mental representation of events. In: E., van der Meer, & J., Hoffman (Eds.), *Knowledge-Aided Information Processing*. Amsterdam: North–Holland.

van der Meer, E., & Hoffmann, J. (1987). *Knowledge aided information processing*. Amsterdam: North–Holland.

van Dijk, T.A. (1980). Story comprehension: An introduction. *Poetics*, 9:1–21.

van Dijk, T.A., & Kintsch W. (1983). *Strategies of discourse comprehension*, NY: Academic Press.

van Gelder, T. (1989). Compositionality and the explanation of cognitive processes. *Proceedings of the 11th Annual Conference of the Cognitive Science Society*, 34–41.

von der Malsburg, C. (1985). Algorithms, brain, and organization. In: J., Demongeot, E., Golès, & M., Tchuente (Eds.), *Dynamical systems and cellular automata*. London: Academic Press.

von Eckardt, B. (1992). *What is cognitive science?* Cambridge, MA: MIT Press.

Vernon, P. A. (Ed.) (1994). *The neuropsychology of individual differences*. NY: Academic Press.

Vipond, D., & Hunt, R. (1984). Point-driven understanding: Pragmatic and cognitive dimensions of literary reading. *Poetics*, 13, 261–277.

Wagenaar, W. (1988). Calibration and the effects of knowledge and reconstruction in retrieval from memory. *Cognition*, 28, 277–296.

Wagener, M., & Wender, K. F. (1985). Spatial representations and inference processes in memory for text. In: G., Dehnière, & J.-P., Rossi (Eds.), *Inferences in Text Processing*.

Waltz, D. L. (1990). Massively parallel ai. *AAAI*, 1117–1122.

Waltz, D. L., & Pollack, J. B. (1985). Massively parallel parsing: A strongly interactive model of natural language interpretation. *Cognitive Science*, 9, 51–74.

Ward, N. (1988). Issues in word choice. *Proceedings of the 12th International Conference on Computational Linguistics*, 726–731.

Warner, J., & Glass, A. L. (1987). Context and distance-to-disambiguation effects in ambiguity resolution: Evidence from grammaticality judgments of garden path sentence. *Journal of Memory and Language*, 26, 714–736

Webster's Ninth New Collegiate Dictionary (1981). MA: Merriam–Webster Inc.

Wharton, C. M., Holyoak, K. J., Downing, P. E., Lange, T. E., & Wickens, T. D. (1991). Retrieval competition in memory for analogies. *Proceedings of the 13th Annual Conference of the Cognitive Society.*

Whittemore, G., Ferrara, K., & Brunner, H. (1990). Empirical study of predictive powers of simple attachment schemes for post-modifier prepositional phrases. *ACL*, 23–30.

Whittlesea, B. W., & Brooks, L. R. (1988). Critical influence of particular experiences in the perception of letters, words, and phrases. *Memory and Cognition*, 16(5), 387–399.

Wilks, Y. (1989). *Theoretical issues in natural language processing*, TINLAP–3, Hillsdale, NJ: Lawrence Erlbaum Associates.

Whorf, B. (1956). *Language, thought, and reality*, Cambridge, MA: MIT Press.

Wilensky, R. (1978). *Understanding goal-based stories.* (Research Report). Department of Computer Science, Yale University, New Haven, CT.

Wilensky, R. (1982). Points: A theory of the structure of stories in memory. In: W., Lehnert, & M. H., Ringle (Eds.), *Strategies for Natural Language Processing.* Hillsdale, NJ: Lawrence Erlbaum Associates.

Wilensky, R. (1983a). Story grammars versus story points. *The Behavioral and Brain Sciences*, 6, 579–623.

Wilensky, R. (1983b). *Planning and understanding.* Reading, MA: Addison–Wesley.

Wilensky, R. (1986). Some problems and proposals for knowledge representation. (Report No. UCB/Computer Science Dept.86/294). Computer Science Division, University of California at Berkeley.

Wilks, Y. A. (1975). A preferential pattern-seeking semantics for natural language inference. *Artificial Intelligence*, 6, 53–74.

Wilks, Y. A. (Ed.) (1989). *Theoretical Issues in NLP*, Hillsdale, NJ: Lawrence Erlbaum Associates.

Wilks, Y. A., Huang, X., & Fass, D. (1985). Syntax, preference, and right attachment. *IJCAI*, 779–784.

Williams, L. D., (1993). *Organizing lexical representations: A study of orthographic and phonological neighborhoods.* (Master thesis). Carleton University.

Wilson, S., Rink, M., McNamara, T., Bower, G., & Morrow, D. (1993). Mental models and narrative comprehension: Some qualifications. *Journal of Memory and Lan-*

guage, 32, 141–154.

Winograd, T. (1983). *Language as a cognitive process: Syntax*. Reading, MA: Addison–Wesley.

Winograd, T., & Flores, C. (1986). *Understanding computers and cognition: A new foundation for design*. Norwood, NJ: Ablex Publishing Corporation.

Wittgenstein, L. (1953). *Philosophical investigations*. Oxford: Basil Blackwell.

Woods, W. (1981). Procedural semantics as a theory of meaning. In: B., Webber, A., Joshi, & I., Sag (Eds.), *Elements of Discourse Understanding*. (pp. 301-334). Cambridge, MA: Cambridge University Press.

Wu, D. (1993a). Approximating maximum-entropy ratings for evidential parsing and semantic interpretation. *IJCAI*, 1290–1296.

Wu, D. (1993b). Estimating probability distribution over hypotheses with variable unification. *AAAI*, Washington, D.C.

Wu, D. (1993c). An image-schematic system of thematic roles. *PACLING*, Vancouver, Canada.

Yu, T.-H., & Simmons, R. F. (1989). Truly parallel understanding of text.*AAAI*, 996–1001.

Zajac, R. (1992). Inheritance and constraint-based grammar formalisms. *Computational Linguistics*, 18(2),161–171.

Zavarin, V. (1983). Stratification in story. *Proceedings of the 5th Annual Conference of the Cognitive Science Society*.

Zeevat, H. (1989). A compositional approach to discourse representation theory. *Linguistics and Philosophy*, 12, 95–131.

Zola-Morgan, S., & Squire, L.R. (1990).The primate hippocampal formation: Evidence for a time-limited role in memory storage. *Science*, 250, 288–290.

Zwaan, R. A., & Graesser, A. C. (1993). Reading goals and situation models. *Psycoloquy* 4(3).

Zwaan, R. A., & van Oostendorp, H. (1993). Do readers construct spatial representations in naturalistic story comprehension? *Discourse Processes*, 16(1–2),125–143.

Author Index

396

AUTHOR INDEX

Britton, B.K., 22, 210, 353
Brooks, L.R., 115
Brown, G.D., 113
Brown, J.C., 102
Brownowski, J., 356
Brunner, H., 302
Budd, T., 101, 103–105, 132
Burns, A., 104
Butler, K., 59
Button, S.B., 277

C

Cacciari, C., 294
Carlson, G.N., 252
Carpenter, P., 114, 210, 277
Carr, T.H., 122
Cha, S., 101
Chafe, W., 34, 210, 227
Chalmers, D.J., 58
Charniak, E., 27, 28, 30, 31, 218
Chen , H.-C., 64
Cherwenka, S.A., 354
Chodorow, M.S., 252
Chomsky, N., 20, 34, 47, 59, 66, 68, 72,
        73, 227, 250, 302
Christerson, M., 95, 101, 103
Chun, H.W., 53
Chung, M., 101
Churchland, P., 59
Clancey, W., 102
Clark, A., 46
Clark, L.F., 5, 22, 24, 34, 36, 37, 46, 119,
        211, 219–224, 252, 308, 322,
        325, 329, 331, 355
Cohen, R.L., 277, 355
Cole, M., 44
Collins, C.G., 23
Colombo, L., 274
Conery, J., 100
Conrad, M., 59, 116
Cooper, R., 264, 265
Copeck, T., 32, 227
Corriveau, J.-P., 5, 53, 81, 93, 150, 198,
        200, 251, 264, 270, 294
Cottrell, G., 46, 278

Cowan, N., 112–114, 118
Cox, M., 26, 353
Craik, F.I.M., 113
Crawley, R.A., 252
Crowder, R.G., 113
Culler, J., 61, 66
Cullingford, R., 3, 25
Cunningham, P., 102

D

D'Alembert, 74, 75
Daelemans, W., 102, 104
Dagenbach, D., 122
Daneman, M., 11, 114
Dark, V.J., 211
Dascal, M., 38
Davies, G., 104
Davis, E., 23
de Beaugrande, R., 21
de Champeaux, D., 13, 101, 103
de Saussure, F., 19, 33, 77, 230
DeJong, G., 25
Delisle, S., 32, 227
Denhière, G., 321, 323
Derthick, M., 47
Devitt, M., 12
Dewier, A., 274
Dillon, G., 36, 347
Dohsaka, K., 250
Dolan, C.P., 53, 54
Dosher, B.A., 113
Downing, P.E., 114
Dreyfus, H.L., 35, 356
Dunn, J.C., 113
Dyer, M.G., 4, 23–25, 36, 40, 52–54, 61,
        62, 105, 213, 214, 216, 224, 227,
        252, 278, 307, 326, 345, 355

E

Edwards, D., 28
Ehrlich, M.F., 113
Eiselt, K., 27, 46
Eizirik, L.M.R., 228, 277
Elman, J.L., 58
Etherington, D., 33

Subject Index

For Product Safety Concerns and Information please contact our EU
representative GPSR@taylorandfrancis.com
Taylor & Francis Verlag GmbH, Kaufingerstraße 24, 80331 München, Germany